D1124513

Assessing
the Criminal

Assessing the Criminal

Restitution, Retribution, and the Legal Process

Edited by
Randy E. Barnett
John Hagel III
Harvard University

Ballinger Publishing Company • Cambridge, Massachusetts
A Subsidiary of J.B. Lippincott Company

International Standard Book Number: 0-88410-785-X

Library of Congress Catalog Card Number: 77-21388

Printed in the United States of America

Library of Congress Cataloguing in Publication Data

Main entry under title:

Assessing the criminal.

"Ten of the papers included in this collection were originally presented at a Symposium on 'Crime and Punishment' held at Harvard Law School on March 4-6, 1977."
  1. Punishment—Congresses. 2. Criminal liability—Congresses.
3. Crime and criminals—Congresses. I. Barnett, Randy E.
II. Hagel, John.
HV8675.A74   364   77-21388
ISBN 0-88410-785-X

Contents

Acknowledgments

Ten of the papers included in this collection were originally presented at a symposium on "Crime and Punishment" held at Harvard Law School on March 4–6, 1977. We are deeply indebted to the Liberty Fund in Indianapolis for its decision to sponsor this symposium as part of its program and we are especially grateful to the executive director of the Liberty Fund, Dr. A. Neil McLeod, for his patience and kind encouragement during the planning stages of the symposium.

We also wish to thank the Center for Libertarian Studies in New York which directed the project under contract for the Liberty Fund. Both Walter Grinder and Leonard Liggio at the Center for Libertarian Studies participated in the initial planning of the symposium, and we relied heavily on them for ideas and suggestions. Our intellectual debt to the individuals affiliated with the Center for Libertarian Studies extends far beyond this individual project and we would like to take this opportunity to acknowledge that debt.

Many other people assisted us during the course of the symposium and the preparation of this edited collection of papers but we owe special thanks to Marjorie Cooke for her willingness to spend many hours reviewing the manuscript and for offering suggestions for its improvement.

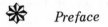

Thinking Practically About Crime

James Q. Wilson

The debate over the proper rationale for a system of criminal justice, and especially the debate over the proper rationale for punishment, once had substantial practical implications. So long as the theory of criminal rehabilitation was seriously defended, as it was for over a century and a half, the specific policies one might support depended crucially on the persuasiveness of the rehabilitation position. If rehabilitation is both feasible and desirable, then its defenders are led—I would say, irresistibly driven—to support the indeterminate sentence, administrative rather than judicial control over sentence length, and a shift of power within the correctional system toward occupations claiming to provide therapy and away from occupations supplying only custody and punishment.

Today, the rehabilitative ideal is everywhere in retreat, though the institutional forms and burdens of pseudo-rehabilitation are very much with us. In its place have arisen retributivist and utilitarian theories of punishment, each with a long and honorable intellectual history, but now suddenly recalled from the disfavor in which they were so long held. If prisoners have not been rehabilitated, punishment has, in part out of frustration over rising rates of predatory crime and in part out of a growing concern over the injustices committed in the name of therapy.

Now that the shallow orthodoxy of rehabilitation has begun to dissipate, the intellectual discussion of crime and punishment has become livelier and more interesting. In particular, the debate between the retributivists and the utilitarians has become especially intense, perhaps because so little is at stake. To be sure, much seems to be at stake, and in theory much is. We are all familiar with the classic rebuttals that advocates of each position have devised to show the absurdity of the other's view. A strict retributivist winces, no doubt, at being reminded of Kant's dictum that if the world will end tomorrow, the last condemned murderer must hang tonight. But of course he takes delight in the discomfort of the strict utilitarian who frets over the possibility that Bentham's use of penalties simply to deter people from committing crimes would allow him to tolerate punishing an innocent man so long as the citizenry believed him guilty.

But in practical terms, and especially within the context of the debate between the more moderate advocates of each position, there are only modest changes that would occur in the criminal justice system if one view or the other holds sway. The reason is that each theory requires the swift, certain, and fair apprehension and conviction of the criminal. Once a conviction has been obtained, a retributivist and a utilitarian might well disagree on the magnitude of the penalty or on whether restitution is preferable to punishment. And both within as well as between these positions, there may be considerable controversy over what kind of behavior ought to be made the object of criminal proceedings. But with respect to predatory street crime—robbery, burglary, larceny, assaults on strangers, auto theft—there surely is little dispute that these are criminal offenses and that the perpetrators ought to be brought into account. A retributivist will be desirous that equivalent offenses receive equivalent penalties (just deserts are not just if not proportional), though he will not be indifferent to the swiftness of their imposition; a utilitarian might be particularly eager to see the penalties swiftly imposed (delayed costs will be heavily discounted and thereby lose some deterrent effect), but he will also wish to see penalties scaled to the social costs of the crime.

But how is the swift, certain, and equal imposition of penalties or costs to be achieved? No amount of philosophical discourse will answer that question or even provide much guidance as to how to approach it. The reasons are obvious. The criminal justice system is not a system—is not, that is, a set of consciously coordinated activities—nor is it the responsibility of a single political authority or jurisdiction. Though the various parts of the enterprise are related in that the outputs of one organization (say, the police) become the inputs of another organization (say, the courts), the relationships are characterized by mutual suspicion and an effort to maintain the autonomy of each participant, with every subunit primarily responsive to peer group values and workload problems. Furthermore, at almost every step, the operation of the "system" depends on the voluntary cooperation of victims, witnesses, and other citizens, many of whom have strong incentives to withhold that cooperation or to offer it only for self-serving purposes.

This state of affairs is, in general terms, well known. I should like to dwell on it, however, because only by a detailed appreciation of the intricacies of these institutions are we likely to reach a reasonable judgment as to how much effort, for policy purposes, should be devoted to understanding such intellectually interesting questions as the causes of crime or the philosophy of punishment. Any new approach to reducing crime or enlarging fairness must devise ways of inducing the various members, citizen and official, of the criminal system to act toward those goals. Let me sketch some of the problems.

THE CITIZEN

Only about half the FBI Index crimes are reported to the police, but happily the probability of reporting increases with the gravity of the offense and the magnitude of the loss. Unhappily, there are costs attached to citizen cooperation with the authorities: the fear of reprisal from criminals, especially those known to the victim; the loss in time and wages from appearing before prosecutors and judges; the embarrassment or confusion of court testimony. There are few offsetting benefits save a sense of justice or a desire for revenge: often the stolen property is not recovered, the money loss is not restored, and the injury, if any, is not compensated.

Victim-witness information and testimony are vital to arrests as well as to prosecutions. Most arrests are made by patrol officers acting on information supplied by a victim or witness; subsequent investigation by detectives, especially investigation based on a scientific search for physical evidence, accounts for only a tiny portion of arrests.[1] If it is reasonable to suppose that would-be criminals act rationally, it is just as reasonable to suppose that would-be witnesses act that way as well. The effect of citizen nonreporting that is attributable to the perceived costs of cooperation can be substantial. In Newark, for example, about half (50.4 percent) of the robberies in 1972 were not reported to the police. Of these, about a third went unreported because the victim thought them unimportant offenses. But 58 percent went unreported because, according to the victim,

1. Peter W. Greenwood and Joan Petersilia, *The Criminal Investigation Process: Volume I, Summary and Policy Implications* (Santa Monica, California: RAND, 1975), ch. 3.

the police would not want to be bothered, it was inconvenient, he or she feared reprisals, or other private reasons operated.[2] People in other cities have somewhat different distributions of reasons, suggesting that in some places police indifference or the prospects of reprisal are greater than in other places. No one knows what the optimal level of nonreporting might be, but it is quite likely that it is lower than at present.

Everyone knows that most assaults occur among friends and relatives and that these relationships explain why such crimes, even if reported, are rarely prosecuted. I call these "communal," as opposed to predatory, crimes. Two aspects of these offenses may be less well known. First, there is a distinct possibility that the failure to prosecute or otherwise take seriously communal assaults may increase materially the chances of a murder occurring. In Kansas City, a study by the police department revealed that the police had previously responded at least once to disturbance calls at the addresses of about 90 percent of the homicides in that city and had responded to five or more such disturbance calls at the addresses of about 50 percent of the homicide victims. In short, homicide is the final episode in a series of disturbances, almost all of which produce at least one police intervention and about half of which produce five or more.[3] The failure to deal adequately with these assaultive episodes before they become fatal—by treatment programs (which I confess I find implausible), by the imposition of sanctions, by confiscating guns, or by levying peace bonds—may contribute materially to the total homicide rate.

The second aspect of communal crime is that it is not limited to fights and assaults. A study by the Vera Institute in New York City found that one-third of the robberies, one-third of the burglaries, and one-fifth of the auto thefts that resulted in arrest were communal.[4] (This is not to say that these proportions of *all* such crimes were communal, only that these proportions were found in the arrests for these crimes.) Routinely, cases were dismissed or convicted offenders were let off with no penalty when the offense was communal. The criminal justice system in New York, and probably in most places, treats these offenses as private rather than public matters. In some sense, they may well be just that: perhaps poor persons use direct

2. Calculated from data supplied to the author by the Law Enforcement Assistance Administration, U.S. Department of Justice, from the 1972 Newark victimization survey.

3. Kansas City Police Department, "Domestic Violence and the Police," a report prepared for the Police Foundation (mimeographed).

4. Vera Institute of Justice, *Felony Arrests: Their Prosecution and Disposition in New York City's Courts* (New York: Vera Institute, 1977).

action and police intervention to handle disputes that among middle
class persons are managed by negotiation and the intervention of
lawyers. But it is also possible that serious criminals steal from
friends as readily as they steal from strangers, that only the friends
are able to identify them in ways that make an arrest possible, but
such friends then drop the charges out of fear or because they themselves are offenders. To the extent this is the case, the inclination of
citizens and prosecutors alike to leave in private hands offenses that,
if committed by strangers, would be dealt with severely may be to
place a large fraction of the population outside the protection of the
law and to encourage the resort to vengeance. Such a practice was
rightly condemned when Southern sheriffs ignored what they dis-
gustingly called "nigger crime"; now that a rough analogue of that
practice is found in the North, we praise the "flexibility" and "sensitivity" of the system.

THE POLICE

A mounting body of data suggests that police behavior does make a
difference in the crime rate. My own research comes to conclusions
similar to that of others: the higher the probability of an arrest for a
crime, the lower the rate at which that crime is committed, other
things being equal.[5] Unfortunately, there is scarcely any systematic
evidence that explains differences in police arrest rates. We know
that in some cities, the average officer will arrest five or six times as
many serious criminals as the average officer in another city. We
know also that in Washington, D.C., fewer than 10 percent of the
police officers accounted for over half of all the arrests brought
before the superior court in 1974.[6]
   Some of the factors associated with high arrest rates for serious
crimes are suggested by various studies. When the police have an
"aggressive" patrol strategy, making many "street stops" and issuing
large numbers of traffic tickets, they are likely to make more felony
arrests. When police officers patrol in plain clothes they seem to
make more arrests than when they patrol in uniform. Police units
with a fast response time make more arrests than units with a slow
response time. But other explanations are entirely a matter of conjecture. Some officers, for reasons we do not understand, make more
arrests than other officers—by a large margin.

   5. James Q. Wilson and Barbara Boland, "The Effects of Police on Crime
Rates" (Washington, D.C.: The Urban Institute, forthcoming).
   6. Institute for Law and Social Research, PROMIS Research Project no. 1,
"Highlights of Interim Findings," p. 29 (mimeographed).

The problem may be analogous to that encountered in World War II when military observers discovered that only a small fraction of all combat infantrymen were doing all the shooting. Since the rate of fire was closely related to the chances of success, it became important to get more soldiers to do what an outsider would have supposed they all would have done instinctively—shoot their guns at the enemy.

Though most police officers find making a felony arrest to be rewarding, there are many other things they find rewarding as well, and the result is often low productivity. High arrest rates require being alert, stopping and questioning suspicious persons, persuading citizens to name names, developing information about the location and activities of known offenders, waiting long hours on stakeouts during cold weather, spending time filling out arrest forms, and testifying in court. In short, high arrest rates result from costly, frustrating, and conflict-laden activities that, understandably, some officers would just as soon avoid.

PROSECUTORS

About half the arrests made by police do not result in prosecution. The reason usually given is "insufficient evidence." In most cases, this refers to the difference between "probable cause" (which is necessary to justify an arrest) and "beyond a reasonable doubt" (a standard that must be met to justify a conviction). But it is also possible that prosecutors have other reasons, unrelated to the quality of the evidence, for declining prosecution: heavy workloads, a disinterest in certain kinds of offenses, or other factors. One study, for example, found that whereas 60 percent of the arrests on serious robbery charges in Dade County (Miami) resulted in a felony prosecution, only 46 percent of a similar set of robbery arrests in Multnomah County (Portland) led to felony prosecutions. Interestingly, this difference cannot be explained by workload: the felony caseload per prosecutor, and the size of the backlog, is much greater in Dade than in Multnomah.[7]

Even stronger evidence of prosecutorial discretion can be found in a study in Los Angeles. The robbery arrests made by the Los Angeles Sheriff's office led to very different outcomes depending on which branch office of the Los Angeles District Attorney screened the case: in Santa Monica, only 17 percent of the arrests were rejected, where-

---

7. Sorrel Wildhorn et al., *Indicators of Justice: Measuring The Performance of Prosecution, Defense, and Court Agencies Involved in Felony Proceedings* (Santa Monica, California: RAND, 1976), chs. 6, 7.

as in Pasadena, 63 percent were.[8] It is unlikely that these differences result from different police practices, since the same police agency was involved in each case.

One factor contributing to the dismissal of an arrest has already been mentioned: a prior relationship between victim and offender. But there are other factors operating that are less easy to rationalize. A study in Washington, D.C., suggested that the amount of effort a prosecutor will devote to a case will depend (as expected) on the seriousness of the offense but will *not* depend on the prior criminal history of the defendant. Since repeat offenders contribute disproportionately to the crime rate, it is disturbing that a prosecutor's decision to carry a case forward is unaffected by the extensiveness or recency of the defendant's arrest record. The other factors affecting prosecutorial discretion involve the weight of evidence: stronger cases get more resources.[9] In short, the prosecutor seems to behave as if he were primarily interested in winning a large proportion of his cases and in convicting very serious offenders, but not in reducing crime by convicting repeat offenders.

Moreover, prosecutors—like most of us—tend to attach great significance to the difference between felonies and misdemeanors. But these legal categories do not correspond to the actual behavior of career criminals. Offenders with long arrest records are about as likely, at any given time, to be arrested for a misdemeanor as for a felony. By assigning prosecutorial resources disproportionately to serious felonies, we fail to take seriously the continued criminality of the most serious offenders whenever they have the good fortune to be arrested for a misdemeanor.

To obtain a conviction, the prosecutor can offer the defendant a reduced charge in exchange for a guilty plea. Plea bargaining accounts, as is well known, for most convictions. Using the prospect of a lesser penalty to induce a guilty plea means that, as research has shown, persons committing similar offenses and with similar criminal histories will receive different penalties depending on whether they plead or go to trial. This outcome raises obvious questions of fairness and effectiveness: should similar offenses lead to different sentences, and should more serious offenders who plead guilty receive smaller penalties than less serious ones who stand trial?

The problems of the prosecutive stage of the criminal justice system should not all be laid at the feet of the district attorney. One major, but often overlooked, constraint on producing swift and cer-

8. Peter W. Greenwood et al., *Prosecution of Adult Felony Defendants* (Lexington, Massachusetts: Lexington Books, 1976), p. 88.
9. Institute for Law and Social Research, "Highlights," pp. 34–38.

tain justice is the availability of the defendant. When William Landes studied the bail system in New York City in 1971, he found that nearly one-third of all the criminal defendants in New York City simply disappeared. Some eventually were recaptured, but many were not. Indeed, the problem is even worse: of those who disappeared, 29 percent had not been released on bail. This means that over a fourth of all those who disappeared *did so while in custody.* The Corrections Department "lost" them.[10]

COURTS

Because the sentence imposed (or not imposed) by the judge can be viewed as an explicit statement in a particular case of whatever general theory of punishment may inform the judicial process as a whole, great attention has been paid to sentencing practices, the disparities among them, and the implications of these sentences for concepts of deterrence, incapacitation, and retribution. And because the sentence is a visible, discrete, and important decision, efforts have been made to constrain that exercise of discretion by various legislative measures such as presumptive sentencing laws, determinate sentencing laws, and mandatory minimum sentences.

The evidence, so far as we have it, on judicial discretion can be quickly summarized. There is no question that two judges faced with identical factual issues and defendants will respond with very different sentences. On the other hand, it is also the case that given a set of cases differing in the severity of the offense, judges will scale the penalties imposed roughly in accordance with the gravity of the behavior. The differences between judges in the penalties they impose cannot generally be explained, it may surprise some to learn, by the obvious racial or socioeconomic characteristics of the offender. Though there are important exceptions to this, in the great majority of studies of sentencing practices, the race (and where measured, the class as well) of the offender does not explain much of the variance in sentences.[11] What does explain the differences is a matter of dispute. To some, it is the personal idiosyncracies of judges—their personality, mood, ideology, or social background. To others, it is the

10. William M. Landes, "Legality and Reality: Some Evidence on Criminal Procedure," *Journal of Legal Studies* (June 1974), p. 289.

11. John Hagan, "Extra-Legal Attributes and Criminal Sentencing: An Assessment of a Sociological Viewpoint," *Law and Society Review* (Spring 1974), pp. 357–83, reviews twenty empirical studies of this issue. See also Carl E. Pope, "Sentencing of California Felony Offenders," Analytic Report No. 6, National Criminal Justice Information and Statistics Service, U.S. Department of Justice (1975).

institutional and peer group processes at work in the court, and especially the interactions between prosecutors, judges, and the defense bar. Whatever the explanations, the amount of variation in sentences that exists and that is not related to the apparent facts of the case or the nature of the defendant is substantial. A recent study of felony courts in three large cities found that whereas the average sentence (adjusted for parole) for robbery was 56.5 months in Baltimore, it was only 25.1 months in Chicago.[12]

PRISONS

A major constraint on any sentencing practice is the real or perceived shortage of adequate space in a correctional program. After a decade or more during which the prison population declined despite the increase in crime, the prison population is now rising rapidly, and in the opinion of all concerned, exceeds any reasonable definition of capacity in most states. (Even so, the proportion of the population in prison is still lower today than it was in 1955, when the crime rate was less than half of what it is now.[13]) We allowed, during the 1960s, our prison population and perhaps even our prison capacity to lag far behind the increase in crime, and now we are paying the price of deferred construction and deferred sentences. William Shaffer has shown that, at least for Massachusetts, the shortage of prison capacity is the major constraint on the criminal justice system and contributes more than police or judicial conduct to the system's inability to increase the deterrent or incapacitative effect of the criminal sanction.[14] The governor and others have begun to act, with predictable results: every community proposed as the location for a new correctional facility is vociferous in its opposition. Everyone, it seems, wants more criminals put in prison, but not in prisons near him.

One could go on at length, but by now the point should be evident: though most persons managing the criminal justice system no doubt want to produce lower crime rates and see that justice is done, the component parts of that system do not act as if crime reduction were the objective. Each part—victim, witness, police officer, prosecutor, judge, prison warden, probation officer—behaves, in the aggregate, as if each sought chiefly to minimize its costs. Victims and

12. James Eisenstein and Herbert Jacob, *Felony Justice* (Boston: Little, Brown & Company, 1977), p. 281.

13. *Statistical Abstract of the United States (1975)*, p. 168.

14. William Andrew Shaffer, "Court Management and the Massachusetts Criminal Justice System" (Ph.D. dissertation, Sloan School of Management, Massachusetts Institute of Technology, 1976).

witnesses wish to minimize the burdens of identifying, of testifying, and sometimes even of reporting. Police officers welcome the chance to make a good arrest but not the arduous efforts that might increase the probability of an arrest. Prosecutors must manage a heavy workload and want a high conviction rate, but achieving these goals is not always the same as taking the most dangerous offender off the street as promptly as possible. Judges seek to move a caseload along and to minimize the chances of appellate reversal or collegial criticism. Prison wardens might wish to think about rehabilitation or other objectives, but the realities of their situation require them to worry chiefly about maintaining order under difficult conditions of population pressure and external criticism. Communities want more criminals imprisoned, but not in their neighborhoods.

The renewed interest in swift and certain penalties, for reasons of deterrence or retribution, has affected the participants in this system, but the effect has primarily been, I suspect, on the *attitudes* of persons working in the system. These attitudes have always been favorably disposed toward reducing crime and doing justice, and if deterrence or retribution are more defensible theories than rehabilitation, they will be given widespread verbal support. And in some places, new laws will be enacted based on these newer views, such as the Maine determinate sentencing statute or the California presumptive sentencing statute. In general, I share these theories and support the statutes that give them practical expression. But I am keenly aware that, by themselves, neither these theories nor these laws will in themselves make much difference in how much crime is committed or even, perhaps, in how evenly justice is administered.

What is required is to increase the incentives of persons managing the criminal justice system to act as if crime control or just deserts or (ideally) both were the goals. I suspect that inducing them to act justly is easier than inducing them to act so as to minimize crime, for a sense of justice animates all of us in varying degrees, and in the case of victims, police officers, or judges it probably operates with some intensity. Indeed, were it not for a sense of justice, or at least a sense of duty that derives in part from shared standards of right conduct, far fewer arrests would be made, and far lighter and more capricious penalties would be imposed.

There is no single grand strategy that will induce the participants in the criminal justice process to act in ways more consistent with the goal of crime reduction. If by the "bureaucracy problem" we mean the difficulty in getting large organizations to serve public purposes at reasonable cost, then that problem exists in an especially acute form in criminal justice. Let me suggest, briefly and inadequately, some of the changes that could be adopted—that in fact are being adopted in certain jurisdictions—which might provide greater incentives for system participants to act as we (and for that matter, as they themselves) wish.

Victims and Witnesses. Programs of victim compensation and victim restitution might be designed that would require, for the benefits to be available, the cooperation of the victim in the reporting of a crime and the identification and conviction of the accused. Along with efforts to increase the benefits of being a victim should go programs to decrease the costs of being a witness, such as ways of minimizing the time and burdens associated with giving testimony, and policies that would return promptly, rather than after the final appeal is exhausted, any stolen property that is recovered. At one time, the burden of prosecution and even of apprehension fell entirely on the victim; now, the accused is prosecuted in the name of the state, and such representation as the victim might have in the proceedings is entirely vicarious. Furthermore, the mobilization of communities to assist in law enforcement, with such programs as "Neighborhood Watch," may be necessary if we wish to see any increase in arrest rates. That mobilization cannot occur when citizens feel that law enforcement could be fully delegated to police officers.

Police. Some police departments, and some officers within a single department, make many more arrests than others. Obviously, skills will vary in this occupation as in any, but it is remarkable that in this occupation, and not in most others, we have absolutely no idea why arrest rates are higher in some places, or for some men, than others. I suspect that departmental policies that minimize the costs of arrest, by reducing the time and energy required to complete it, make a difference. There have been some experiments directed at measuring the extent to which various deployment strategies affect arrest rates and crime rates, but so far the results are only suggestive. Merely having more officers on the street does not seem to make a difference, though having them patrol aggressively (stopping and questioning suspicious persons) or unobtrusively (in plain clothes) or provocatively (disguised as typical victims) does appear to increase arrests. We know very little about how, and to what degree, and at what costs, these strategies work, and I regret there are so few police agencies willing to find out in a systematic and objective manner. Of course, if maintaining the organization and criticizing "outsiders" are your dominant objectives, then the behavior becomes quite understandable.

Prosecutors. A few prosecutors, but more every year, have shown that a reorganization of their staffs and working rules can increase the speed and certainty with which the most serious offenders are convicted. Such efforts are usually called "major offender bureaus" or "career criminal programs" and they now operate in several cities and counties. They require not only leadership, but also additional resources (unless other cases are to be ignored) and information systems that will quickly and accurately identify for prompt action those cases and suspects most deserving of rapid attention. Properly done, such programs result in major offenders being indicted within seventy-two hours of arrest and tried within sixty days, with higher rates of conviction and less opportunity for jumping bail or fleeing the jurisdiction.[15]

Judges. The indeterminate sentencing law encourages both inequitable and socially inappropriate penalties. Determinate or presumptive sentencing laws are sufficiently new so that the problems with them—and no doubt there will be many—have not yet been fully identified. It may be that we shall need an extended period of experimentation before we can agree on reasonable sentencing guidelines. Whatever the case, a narrowing of the range of permissible judicial discretion is necessary if we are to avoid excessive leniency, severity, or inequity. There is, in my view, little chance that any voluntary system or educational process will produce greater rationality in sentencing. If you doubt it, recall that most judges have tenure, and then reflect on the ability and willingness to engage in cooperative behavior exhibited by another tenured group, the professoriat. And in many jurisdictions, such as Massachusetts, a significant increase in the number of judges will be required to reduce the pressures for excessive plea-bargaining concessions.

Prisons. We face, and will continue to face for some time even under the most optimistic assumptions, a severe shortage of correctional facilities, especially of the small, medium security variety. One can predict—and with a determinate sentencing law, one can predict with even greater accuracy—the size of the future prison population. If the growing population cannot be housed in decent, safe, and small facilities, then several things will happen: judges, offended by what they take to be undesirable prison conditions, will refuse to send prisoners to them and will discover ways of closing the facilities

15. Office of Technology Transfer, Law Enforcement Assistance Administration, U.S. Department of Justice, "The Major Offense Bureau: An Exemplary Project" (1976).

down; and wardens, faced with large and overcrowded facilities, will find it impossible to maintain order and to avoid riots and prison breaks. The response to these events will include demands for the enlargement of "prisoners rights" and a decrease in the number and security of prisons, thus leading to more crime and more prison disorders.

I remarked at the outset that the outcome of the debate over the proper philosophical basis for punishment was not likely to influence significantly the working of the criminal justice system. Let me now qualify that position a bit. To the extent that judges come to accept deterrence or retribution over rehabilitation, their behavior will probably change to some degree. It is possible—we have no data—that we are even now witnessing the effects on our prison population of a new, "get tough" attitude among judges and a diminished confidence in the rehabilitative idea. The significance of this change, if in fact it has occurred, may not be great, however, unless other parts of the system function more effectively to identify and convict offenders.

It is also possible that the change in inducements that I have suggested will lead to a greater emphasis on the crime control rather than the justice-administering functions of the system. A career criminal program in a prosecutor's office, for example, may lead to selective prosecution such that a person's prior record will make a substantial difference in his chances for conviction, for a speedy hearing, and for receiving a sentence, even though he has committed an act identical in all respects to that of a person with a different prior record and, in consequence, with a different set of probable outcomes. These are not trivial issues. At the margin, equality of treatment and reduction in crime may be incompatible and thus trade-offs will have to be made. This should be unsettling only to those, if any, who suppose that human values are not always in conflict and thus that single principles should govern and simple choices are possible.

Introduction

✳ *Chapter 1*

Assessing the Criminal: Restitution, Retribution, and the Legal Process*

Randy E. Barnett
John Hagel III

COMPETING GOALS AND THE QUEST FOR CRIMINAL JUSTICE

Perhaps the single most important characteristic of the contemporary criminal justice system in the U.S. is the profound sense of malaise, if not crisis, that pervades the entire field. Thomas Kuhn, in his path-breaking work on *The Structure of Scientific Revolutions*, has noted that a growing awareness of the breakdown of the capacity for problem solving within an existing paradigm has typically preceded a major transition to a new paradigm. It is precisely this type of breakdown that has generated so much concern both among professionals within the criminal justice system and among concerned citizens who are exposed to the consequences of this breakdown.

In an important sense, however, this analogy is not entirely appropriate, since it is not clear that there is an existing paradigm of criminal justice, at least in the sense of an explicitly and systematically articulated framework for dealing with the problem of criminal behavior. Certainly at the intellectual level the most remarkable feature of the criminal justice system is the almost complete lack of consensus regarding the most appropriate policies for responding to criminal behavior.

Furthermore, at the institutional level the situation becomes even more confused. As James Q. Wilson notes in the preface of this col-

*We would like to express our appreciation to the Liberty Fund for the financial support that enabled us to devote the time necessary to prepare this study.

lection, it may be misleading even to describe the criminal justice system as a "system." Partly this is a result of the fact that the administration of criminal justice in the United States is largely undertaken at the local or state level and thus considerable variations in procedures and institutions may be encountered from one jurisdiction to the next. Probably more important, however, is the fact that our institutions reflect the confusion of our intellectual efforts to confront the problem of criminal justice. Moreover, since institutions change only slowly over time, they tend to represent a complex amalgam of existing policies and residues of earlier policies, some of which may have long since been discarded at the intellectual level.

In examining the prevailing conceptual approaches to the problem of criminal justice, it is possible, despite the conflicting goals that differentiate these approaches, to identify two characteristics that they all share. The first is the assumption that there is a fundamental distinction to be made between tort law and criminal law. While the reasons for this distinction sometimes vary, the effective result is to define criminal behavior primarily in terms of the relationship between the criminal and society or, more specifically, between the criminal and various governmental institutions that presumably reflect the interests of society. While the individual victim of criminal behavior may be seen as triggering this relationship, there is considerable ambiguity regarding the role of the victim after the criminal act has occurred and has been reported to the appropriate government authorities. In fact, the broad category of so-called "victimless crimes" raises the question as to whether current concepts of crime even require the existence of a victim.

A second characteristic shared by prevailing intellectual approaches to the problem of criminal justice is that they seek to define the relationship between the criminal and society in terms of future-oriented goals. While the precise content of these goals may vary considerably, they all seek, in the words of John Hospers, "to make the future better." From this perspective, society's response to crime is measured by its effectiveness in reducing the incidence of criminal behavior. Since there is a scarcity of resources, it becomes necessary to choose among conflicting goals and to establish some schedule of priorities in which some goals acquire precedence over others. It is generally thought that the selection process should be governed by some form of utilitarian calculus that weighs the costs and benefits associated with each goal.

It is at this point that the various approaches begin to diverge and the resulting confusion becomes apparent. For, while there may be general agreement over the need for some type of utilitarian selection process, no single process has yet been able to achieve widespread acceptance, and some observers have begun to suggest that this failure may be the result of certain fundamental flaws in the underlying utilitarian assumptions. Thus, the formulation of criminal justice policies has been hampered by an inability to choose among numerous conflicting goals, and this has resulted in policies marked by contradictory goals and shifting, ad hoc institutional compromises.

The malaise within the criminal justice system stems not so much from the existence of contradictory goals but from the apparent inability of the criminal justice system to meet *any* of the goals that have been proposed. It is illuminating, if somewhat depressing, to review some of this evidence.

The three most widely accepted goals within the criminal justice system are: (1) *deterrence*—maximizing the perceived costs to potential criminals and thereby reducing their willingness to engage in criminal behavior; (2) *rehabilitation*—developing treatment programs for those who have already committed criminal acts in an effort to ensure that these individuals will not repeat their acts in the future; and (3) *incapacitation*—isolating in prisons those who have committed criminal acts so that they will be prevented, at least for specified periods of time, from engaging in further criminal conduct.

In evaluating the deterrent impact of current criminal justice policies, a brief examination of the FBI's crime statistics for 1975 provides a revealing introduction to the extent of the crime problem in the U.S. today. For example, an average of twenty-one serious crimes are reported every minute in the U.S., while one violent crime is reported every thirty-one seconds. Not only is the problem serious, but there is evidence that it is getting worse, suggesting that, whatever deterrent effect the criminal justice system does have, its effectiveness in deterring crime may be decreasing over time. According to these statistics, the crime rate increased by almost 9 percent in 1974—1975 alone and, over the period 1960—1975, the crime rate has increased by almost 180 percent.

As Roger Meiners indicates in Chapter 14, recent surveys of criminal victimization rates by the Law Enforcement Assistance Administration (LEAA) suggest that much of this increase in reported crimes may actually be a result of more effective reporting of criminal behavior rather than the result of actual increases in criminal activity. While this is somewhat reassuring, the LEAA surveys also indicate that the rate of *actual* victimization is considerably higher than the reported crime statistics of *reported* crime suggest. Growing concern over the reliability and interpretation of crime statistics has further complicated the utilitarian approach to the criminal justice problem by underscoring the fact that any evaluation of goals on the basis of statistical evidence alone can never be conclusive.

Attaining the goals of rehabilitation, incapacitation, and perhaps to a lesser extent, deterrence critically depends on the ability of the criminal justice system to accurately identify and successfully prosecute the criminal. Unfortunately, there are strong reasons to question its abilities in performing these functions. The FBI's statistics for 1975 reveal that only 21 percent of all serious crimes were "cleared"[1] in that year. Moreover, only 80 percent of the adults arrested for serious crimes were prosecuted in the courts, and of these, only 66 percent were found guilty as charged. While allowing for the fact that a single offender may have committed a number of serious crimes, such statistics indicate that roughly 11 percent of all reported crimes result in the conviction of an offender for the specific crime committed. When the vast number of unreported crimes are considered, these figures become an even greater cause for concern.

With regard to the goal of incapacitation, James Q. Wilson has observed that fewer people, as a proportion of the total population, are in prison today than were in prison in 1955, despite the fact that the crime rate has more than doubled in the same time period. Thus, the existence of more criminals and fewer prisoners suggests that even the relatively limited goal of incapacitation has been increasingly difficult to achieve.

While recidivism is notoriously difficult to measure statistically, the limited available evidence casts considerable doubt on the rehabilitative effect of imprisonment. One important study of California correctional programs concluded that variations in recidivism rates could not be explained in terms of the correctional programs to which the criminal had been assigned, but rather that these variations were largely attributable to initial differences among the offenders processed. In other words, none of the correctional programs examined had any measurable effect on the likelihood that a particular offender would commit another criminal act in the future.

Actual estimates of recidivism rates, which vary depending on the nature of the crime and the particular methodological assumptions employed, range from a low of approximately 35 percent to 80—90 percent. One study of FBI data on offenders who were released in

1. "Clearance" is defined as the identification of an offender and the accumulation of sufficient evidence to charge the offender and to bring the offender into custody. The threshold standard is one of "probable cause" to believe the offender is guilty. This figure does not, therefore, reveal the percentage of cases which were "provable," i.e., where the evidence of guilt is beyond a reasonable doubt.

1972 indicated that, depending on the particular category of crime involved, between 64 and 81 percent had been rearrested by 1975.

In view of the doubtful effectiveness of existing policies, the magnitude of their monetary costs becomes particularly disturbing. In 1973, public expenditures at all levels of government on correctional programs alone totaled $2.74 billion, while expenditures on the criminal justice system as a whole reached nearly $13 billion in the same period.

Thus, even if one were to accept the utilitarian assumptions underlying most contemporary discussions of the criminal justice system, it seems clear that serious problems have emerged, and the ability of the system to confront these problems effectively appears increasingly open to question. Measured then by their own standards and their own goals, the prevailing approaches to criminal justice are found wanting.

REDISCOVERING RIGHTS AS A FOUNDATION FOR JUSTICE

The growing dissatisfaction with this performance has given rise to an increasing receptivity to new perspectives and has made people more willing to question the fundamental assumptions that have guided policy formation for so long. In particular, there has been renewed interest in two theories of criminal justice that have a rather long tradition but have generally been in disfavor among more "social science"—oriented policymakers. These two theories—retribution and restitution—by requiring a reconsideration of the question of individual rights and of the extent to which policy formulation must be constrained by a prior conception of rights, demand a fundamentally different conception of criminal justice. As a consequence, there has been considerable resistance to this revival by defenders of contemporary utilitarian orthodoxy.

This development in the theory of criminal justice has been reinforced by recent developments in contemporary political and legal philosophy for, in these fields, the question of individual rights has once again become a hotly debated issue. This new concern is not with *legal* rights, but with the existence and content of individual *moral* rights that are independent of the state and the will of the majority.

John Rawls, in his monumental study of *A Theory of Justice*, has done more perhaps than any other philosopher in precipitating this debate. His theory challenged the dominant positivist and utilitarian traditions in philosophy and eloquently developed an alternative framework within which philosophical discussion might proceed. Most significantly, this new framework prepared the way for a new examination of the concept of justice from the perspective of individual rights. Robert Nozick, Professor Rawls' colleague in the philosophy department at Harvard University, expanded upon the concept of individual rights in his book *Anarchy, State and Utopia* and explored some of its implications for moral and political philosophy.

Nozick begins by asserting that "individuals have rights, and there are things no person or group may do to them (without violating their rights)."[2] In describing his conception of rights, Nozick makes an intriguing distinction between moral goals that are to be judged by utilitarian considerations and rights that no goal may override and that are therefore termed "moral side-constraints." "A specific side-constraint upon action toward others expresses the fact that others may not be used in the specific way the side constraint excludes. Side constraints express the inviolability of others in the way they specify."[3]

Although Nozick specifically declined to lay out a theory of rights, this task was undertaken shortly afterward by Ronald Dworkin, professor of jurisprudence at Oxford University. His book, *Taking Rights Seriously*, outlines a theory of rights that is both far-reaching and a sharp break with the positivist theory that has dominated political and legal philosophy for so long. Dworkin draws an almost identical distinction between rights and moral goals. "I shall say that an individual has a *right* to a particular political act, within a political theory, if the failure to provide that act, when he calls for it, would be unjustified within that theory even if the goals of the theory would, on balance, be disserviced by the act."[4] And: "Rights based theories are . . . concerned with the independence rather than the conformity of individual action. They presuppose and protect the value of individual action and choice."[5] The assumption of a rights-based theory is "that individual rights must be served even at some cost to the general welfare."[6] His final formulation of the concept of rights is strikingly similar to Nozick's: " . . . if someone has a right

2. Robert Nozick, *Anarchy, State and Utopia* (New York: Basic Books, 1974), p. ix.

3. Ibid., p. 32.

4. Ronald Dworkin, *Taking Rights Seriously* (Cambridge: Harvard University Press, 1977), p. 169.

5. Ibid., p. 173.

6. Ibid.

to something, then it is wrong for the government to deny it to him even though it would be in the general interest to do so."[7]

Discussions of criminal justice frequently refer to "rights," but in this context the word has traditionally been accorded a different meaning. What are usually at issue are "constitutional rights," rights granted the individual by the state, and even these rights are usually procedural in nature, e.g., the right to counsel or the right to a speedy trial, etc. These discussions have another marked characteristic: they are almost exclusively concerned with the constitutional rights of criminal defendants and the so-called rights of society. Contemporary attitudes leave little room for the possibility that other participants in the criminal justice process may have rights as well.

What makes the approaches of Nozick and of Dworkin so important is that they force us to contemplate the rights of *all* persons in all contexts including, *a fortiori*, the rights of all participants in the criminal justice system, and to do so outside the narrow context of constitutional construction and reasoning. A framework of individual rights enables us to analyze each problem from a new perspective. Such a methodology offers us an opportunity to confront the inadequacies of existing institutions by critically challenging each assumption underlying the establishment of these institutions. This approach offers a promise of new solutions that could scarcely even be conceived within the existing paradigm.

To perceive the significance of this new approach, it is necessary to examine more carefully the traditional formulation of the rights of the parties in the criminal justice system. We should begin by identifying the individuals considered to be parties to the criminal action. Crime has, since the Norman conquest, been viewed as an offense committed against the king and later the state. The person against whom the crime was actually committed—the "victim"—was (and still is) considered to be only a witness to the crime. Given this vision, it is not difficult to predict how rights in such a system will be allocated. Since the function of the criminal justice system was, until recently, primarily to inflict suffering on "bad" criminals for their evil acts in the name of society, it was necessary to balance the rights of society against the rights of the accused. In this regard, procedural safeguards can be seen as performing a vital role; they serve to assuage the consciences of the community when it is confronted with the sight of criminals suffering "for their sins."

In Chapter 10, "Crime and Tort: Old Wine in Old Bottles," Richard Epstein shows that the traditional distinction between the criminal

7. Ibid., p. 269.

and civil legal processes can only be explained (and he believes justified) by the moralistic posture of the criminal law, which gives rise to the need to judge the mental state of the accused and to punish accordingly. This, in turn, contributes to the need for procedural safeguards against wrongful punishments. The brutalities that such a system can produce and the lack of any resemblance to rationality in proportioning punishments has led some, like Walter Kaufmann in Chapter 9 to reject punishment and justice altogether.

Another consequence of a theory of justice that focuses on the moral attributes of those accused of crimes is the need to probe the psyche to determine the extent of "badness" present. This often leads to the paradoxical result that those persons who commit the most heinous crimes may escape punishment entirely. Such a result arises when the criminal act is so inhumane as to raise a question about the offender's "sanity."

In this context, sanity is defined by the psychiatric establishment with reference to "some gross deviation from normal human behavior" and thus a savage, shocking crime may in itself be interpreted as strong evidence of psychiatric abnormality. As a result, psychiatric examinations are routinely ordered in any particularly severe crime (provided no monetary motive is present). The offender who is found "insane" is "not responsible for his acts," a conclusion that can only be understood in the context of moral responsibility. Since this approach is exclusively concerned with judging the moral attributes of offenders (as opposed to judging the morality of their acts), when an offender is incapable of "understanding right and wrong," he is not to be punished even if he perfectly well understands how to use a car, gun, knife, or axe.

What then happens to those acquitted by reason of insanity? Consistent with the assumptions underlying this approach to criminal conduct, an effort is made to instill in the offender a sense of moral responsibility. In Chapter 3, Dr. Thomas Szasz examines the uses and inevitable abuses of so-called "psychiatric diversion" programs that may result in imprisonment for much longer periods than the statutory penalty for the crime or, alternatively, in the quick release of criminals who, regardless of the severity of their offense, have been deemed "rehabilitated." As a result, Szasz condemns the entire category of criminal defenses involving insanity, incompetence, and reduced capacity.

Far from being isolated examples of the misapplication of current philosophies of punishment, the lack of proportionality between punishment and criminal conduct is a natural result of "intent theories of punishment" which require the court to investigate and pass judgment upon the mental processes of those accused of criminal conduct. By shifting our attention from the criminal's mental state to the nature of the criminal's acts, and the consequences of these acts, we can begin to extricate ourselves from these theoretical and practical difficulties. Once we shift our inquiry to the nature of the criminal act as opposed to the criminal's mental state, we are immediately confronted with the other party to crime—the victim. Only by examining the relationship between the criminal and the victim that is created by a criminal act are we able to judge the moral status of the act.

In an unpublished manuscript, Murray N. Rothbard has illustrated this point with the example of a person who is observed to be forcibly taking a watch from another person. He correctly points out that this observation alone is not sufficient to allow the attachment of criminal liability, for the man taking the watch might be stealing it, or he might be trying to retrieve the watch from a thief. It is not the intent of the parties that determines the outcome; it is the respective rights of the parties, in this case to the watch in dispute. Only when this is determined—when the rights question is resolved—can we attach liability.

It should be apparent, then, that the contemporary exclusion of the victim described in Chapter 13 is no institutional accident. The intent theories of punishment simply provide no place for a victim except as a witness to the manifestation of evil intent. Although the traditional theoretical approach as formulated, for example, by John Hospers in Chapter 8, "Retribution: The Ethics of Punishment," with its focus on the criminal's moral "desert," contains no comfortable "slot" for the victim, Randy Barnett, in Chapter 16, "Restitution: A New Paradigm of Criminal Justice," cites historical evidence that this has not always been the case. In fact, until the rise of European nation states and the consolidation of the institution of the monarchy, the victim of aggression had occupied the central focus in traditional legal systems in Europe. Under these earlier systems, which prevailed for centuries, aggression by one individual against another had been dealt with by requiring the aggressor to make payment of money or personal services to the victim or the victim's kin to compensate for any losses.

As Barnett's account demonstrates, the current view that contemporary forms of state monopoly justice arose to protect individuals from the uncontrollable violence of blood feuds is a serious distortion of history. Blood feuds had in fact largely been replaced by institutional forms of restitution long before the rise of feudal monarchies and the forcible imposition of a new system for dealing with criminal behavior. Such commonly accepted myths determine in many respects our prevailing responses to the criminal justice problem. Only by challenging them will we be able to explore the dimensions of a new paradigm based on a systematic examination of the rights of each individual involved in the criminal act. We should be forewarned that any new paradigm may raise more questions than it answers, but what really matters is the promise of solutions.

We may begin to explore the dimensions of this new paradigm by considering the rights of the victim. Perhaps the most important insight of this new paradigm is that a crime exists because the rights of an individual, rights that each of us possess, have been violated in some way. Once this is acknowledged, the victim must be considered a party to the criminal prosecution.

In contrast with a positivist conception of crime, this conception defines crime in terms of the actions of one or more individuals that violate, or threaten to violate, the rights of one or more other individuals. One implication of this is that a criminal action necessarily involves a minimum of two individuals: an aggressor and a victim. It will be readily seen that this formulation diverges fundamentally from the positivist approach, which defines crime as any action that has been prohibited by statute. Our view of criminal conduct, on the other hand, would encompass any action that violates individual rights regardless of whether that action has been statutorily prohibited. Similarly, our conception would regard "victimless" crimes as a contradiction in terms: there can be no crimes without victims.

Any discussion of criminal justice presupposes a definition of what constitutes criminal behavior. Ronald Hamowy's paper (Chapter 2) represents an important contribution to our understanding of the process by which many sexual activities that do not violate the rights of other individuals came to be declared illegal. Contrary to popular conception, many of these activities had not been legally prohibited prior to the first few decades of the twentieth century, and the expansion of American criminal law into these areas was not precipitated by a revival of religious zeal. Rather, the nineteenth century may generally be characterized as a period of relatively limited statutory intrusions into private sexual activity. The dramatic growth in statutory law in this field was actively promoted by the medical and psychiatric professions which had come to view certain forms of sexual behavior as immoral conduct to be suppressed through criminal law. The medical and psychiatric theories that served to justify such a significant inflation of statutory law have long since been discredited, but their legacy lives on in the statute books. Until the entire concept of victimless crimes has been abandoned, it will continue to obscure the true nature of crime, thereby frustrating efforts to confront the problem of criminal justice.

Our definition of crime focuses on the violation of rights and, in particular, the fundamental right of all individuals to be free in their person and property from the initiated use of force by others. If this right is violated, an imbalance is created between the offending party and the victim. We are accustomed to speaking of a criminal paying his "debt to society," but we would suggest that this is a remnant of our feudal past. Within the framework presented here, it is more appropriate to speak of paying one's "debt to the victim." Only when the imbalance created by the criminal act has been rectified can it be said that justice has been done. Although such a concept of crime has only recently become academically respectable, it has never been beyond the common sense of the nonphilosopher. Nor is this attitude foreign to traditional American concepts of justice. In Chapter 13, William F. McDonald points out that the American system of justice abandoned this view in favor of the societal view of crime only gradually and reluctantly.

While the new paradigm focuses on the right of a victim to demand rectification of the imbalance created by the criminal act, the precise nature of this rectification continues to be a controversial issue. In Chapter 11, "Punishment and Proportionality," Murray N. Rothbard stresses the important insight that the rights of the victim to seek rectification are necessarily limited by the nature and consequences of the offense against which rectification is sought. In other words, the concept of rectification implies a rigorous standard of proportionality relating the sanction imposed upon the offender to the nature of the offense.

The controversy, however, arises over the precise nature of the sanctions that may be employed for a particular crime. Rothbard would argue that, if the criminal act had involved the infliction of pain, the victim would be entitled to inflict a proportional degree of pain on the offender. However, the victim would have discretion to decide to impose a lesser sanction or even no sanction at all.

An alternative approach would be to limit the range of sanctions available to the victim by declaring that the deliberate infliction of pain or suffering upon an offender will not be permitted as an end in itself and that only if the pain or suffering results from an attempt to enforce some other form of sanction will it be permitted. Under this alternative approach, only sanctions that were designed to provide constructive reparation to the victim, either in the form of money or services, would be permitted. Since this debate has just begun, the contours of these alternative approaches can only be tentatively and somewhat sketchily outlined. What is important, however, is the very existence of the debate.

As already suggested, this new paradigm of criminal justice would allocate to the victim a central decisionmaking role in determining the nature of the sanction to be imposed upon the convicted offender. Within the limits established by the principle of proportionality, the victim may specify the form of sanction to be imposed, or he may delegate this responsibility to another (perhaps the court) or he may partially or completely forgive the criminal. This discretion may be exercised by the victim for any reason whatsoever. In this respect, a rights approach to crime does not foreclose the pursuit of various goals within the criminal justice system; it merely stipulates the party (the victim) that will have the discretion, always within the limits imposed by the nature of the original criminal act, to choose among a wide variety of possible goals.

It should be noted that, while a restitutive theory recognizes important rights in the victim and seeks to redress the long-standing neglect of the victim in the criminal justice system, this does not imply an endorsement of *any* measure that purports to assist victims. Roger Meiners (Chapter 14) demonstrates convincingly the profound economic and practical problems that would be encountered in the implementation of any of the programs for government-financed victim compensation that have been presented in Congress in recent years. The restitutive theory would also reject such programs on moral grounds since, rather than providing for compensation of the victim by convicted offenders, these programs would place an additional tax burden on the rest of the population to compensate the victim for his misfortune. In effect, such programs are not very different from conventional welfare programs, and they would entail a violation of the rights of innocent third parties in order to achieve the goal of compensating victims.

In a significant sense, a restitutionary theory of justice shifts the focus of decisionmaking to the victim, but at the same time, it reserves certain important rights to the criminal, rights that are more specific and meaningful than the rights of the criminal that are recognized by the present system. Currently, as long as the sanction is determined according to law, in adherence to the procedural due process rights of the accused, and as long as the sanction is not so extreme as to be considered "cruel and unusual" (a very narrowly defined standard), the criminal does not have a right to any limiting standards of proportionality.

Partly in response to this situation, there has, in recent years, been a growing movement on behalf of so-called "prisoner's rights." In fact, this movement does not reflect a proper understanding of the meaning of "rights," at least in the sense in which the word has been used here. Rather, in an effort to shield individuals from the extreme vagaries of a penal system generally acknowledged to be irrational and unjust, this movement argues that the "interests" of the criminal must be balanced with a variety of other factors in an effort to achieve a "fair" system.

In contrast to this balancing approach, the restitutionary theory of justice suggests that the criminal has certain rights that need not be "balanced" at all. In his famous pronouncement, Hegel asserted that "punishment is regarded as containing the criminal's right and hence by being punished he is honored as a rational being." While the restitutionary approach shares little with Hegelian philosophy, this statement, cut loose from its underlying theory, is suggestive of an important insight.

The criminal does have a right to punishment or, rather, a right to limited punishment measured by the extent of his transgression. This right stems from the underlying assumption that all persons have rights and that the criminal has only abrogated his to the extent that he has violated the rights of others. Therefore, "the criminal's right as a rational being" is the right to be protected from a sanction that goes beyond the nature and consequences of his acts. In short, the criminal's rights pick up at the exact point that the victim's rights leave off. Furthermore, since we are advocating a relatively specific approach to sanction formation, the criminal has as much right to insist upon adherence to that approach as does the victim. Moreover, as a party to the action (with considerable knowledge about the crime committed), he has a right to participate in the determination of the sentence. This is in sharp contrast to the current arguments in mitigation, which are usually heard at the discretion of the court and which usually serve merely as a device to provoke sympathy for the accused.

It would be misleading to characterize the present system as excessively harsh or excessively permissive since, by restitutionary standards, it may sometimes be one or the other. The point is precisely that, as a consequence of the reliance on faulty conceptions of justice, the present system will almost certainly be one or the other. Some criminals may be punished too harshly, while others are punished too leniently. Advocates of "law and order" will tend to focus on one aspect, while civil libertarians will be more concerned with the other. As may be expected in such a long-standing dispute, the two sides are focusing on two dimensions of the same problem, and yet neither side has been able to identify the underlying problem.

The convicted offender, then, has a right to a just sanction, which is ultimately based on the nature and consequences of his acts and which, within this limit, may be specified by the victim. This does not, however, tell us about the rights of the *accused*. The right to impose sanctions on the criminal can only be derived from the fact that he did indeed trespass on the rights of others. What about those who are accused of a crime but who either did not commit the crime or against whom the evidence is weak?

The assumption underlying the rights approach is, to repeat, that all individuals have certain rights that can only be alienated by their own free choice. The accused who is in fact innocent has, therefore, all the rights of the nonaccused, for he has done nothing to alienate those rights. *Any* forceful imposition is, therefore, an unjustifiable violation of that individual's rights. It is not sufficient to define certain procedural requirements and then to permit an infringement upon an individual's substantive rights as long as those procedural requirements are satisfied. Even if undertaken in good faith, the prosecution of an innocent person that results in the infringement of that person's substantive rights in any way is itself a crime. The authority responsible for such a prosecution would be liable, provided, of course, that the falsity of the prosecution can be established. The standards of proof necessary to implement this approach are discussed below.

Of course, the inherent uncertainties of human knowledge must be acknowledged. The rights we posit are ontologically grounded, that is, grounded and derived from the facts of human existence and the facts of specific actions. In order to identify the rights of each individual in a particular situation, it is first necessary to ascertain the factual context and it is inevitable that humans will occasionally err in pursuing this factual inquiry. The possibility of such error must be recognized, and procedures must be devised that will remedy any injustice caused by such errors.

The American adversary system has often been criticized as an inadequate process for "truth seeking." However, even more broadly, it might be suggested that any system that structures judicial decision-making on the basis of presumptions and procedural devices rather than on the basis of an explicit and overriding concern for the facts of the specific case must, to some extent, compromise its "truth seeking" function. It is a tribute to our common sense rejection of the positivist imperative that the current system seeks the truth to the extent that it does. As a consequence of its affirmation of the primacy of the truth-seeking function, the restitutionary theory of justice provides philosophical support for our deeply ingrained intuitive beliefs.

Since this chapter is primarily concerned with outlining a substantive theory of criminal justice, the many problems of crafting a legal process consistent with that theory must unfortunately remain largely beyond its scope. However, Lloyd Weinreb, a professor at Harvard Law School, has recently published a study entitled *Denial of Justice* that moves beyond a critique of the adversary system and presents a proposal for an alternative system.[8] While Weinreb's proposal ignores the role of the victim, his suggestions are not incompatible with the theory of criminal justice developed in this study and they provide significant insights regarding the viability of one potential alternative process.

One additional aspect of a restitutionary rights approach is perhaps the most difficult to accept as a result of our somewhat schizophrenic attitude toward crime. On the one hand we recognize that crime is perpetrated against specific, identifiable victims, but at the same time a certain holist conception of society leads us to believe that, in some sense, society is the real victim. By focusing on crime in terms of individual rights, the preceding analysis has at least implicitly been highly critical of the latter conception of crime. However, it is still necessary to consider what rights, if any, third parties would possess once a crime has been committed. This question must be strictly distinguished from the important, but far different, question of what *interests* third parties might have when a crime is committed. Members of the community are interested in crime in a number of ways: there may be fear that similar acts will be committed against them in the future; there may be economic consequences to the community of criminal activity; and the rest of the community may share a common moral outrage at the criminal act itself.

Do these and other potential interests give third parties *rights* in the same sense that victims and accused or convicted offenders have rights? Under the restitutionary theory outlined above, a criminal act does not vest any rights in third parties. A specific action is defined as criminal within the context of this theory only if it violates the right of one or more identifiable individuals to person and property. These individuals are the victims of the criminal act, and only the victims, by virtue of the past infringement of their rights, acquire the right to demand restitution from the criminal.

This is not to deny that criminal acts frequently have harmful effects upon other individuals beside the actual victims. All that is denied is that a harmful "effect," absent a specific infringement of rights, may vest rights in a third party. While an elaboration of this

8. Lloyd Weinreb, *Denial of Justice* (New York: The Free Press, 1977).

principle, which would require a detailed analysis of the concept of rights, is beyond the scope of this study, we contend that a violation of rights cannot occur unless one individual has used force, the threat of force, or fraud against another individual.

ENFORCING RIGHTS
AND PURSUING GOALS

As indicated at the outset of this discussion on individual rights, a fundamental distinction must be made between moral rights and moral goals. While the two concepts are analytically distinct, they are also integrally related to each other in that moral rights provide a framework within which one may properly pursue a variety of moral goals. To recall Nozick's illuminating phrase, rights constitute "moral side-constraints" that define the limits of permissible action in striving to attain moral goals.

Another useful way of developing the distinction between moral rights and moral goals would be to indicate its similarity with the distinction that Lon Fuller has made in his *The Morality of Law* between the morality of duty and the morality of aspiration.[9] In Fuller's view, the morality of aspiration concerns the never-ending quest for excellence and perfection within human society, while the morality of duty involves the defining of basic rules that are necessary for the very existence of an ordered society. Fuller argues that the only proper function of law within society is to enforce the morality of duty and, while he does not equate the morality of duty with a concept of rights, the two are very compatible. In effect, Fuller contends that the morality of aspiration operates within boundaries established by the morality of duty.

Thus far, our discussion has focused on an elaboration of the concept of moral rights, and it is now appropriate to shift our attention back to the question of moral goals. It should now be clear that any evaluation of the various goals that have been proposed for the criminal justice system must begin with an analysis of their compatibility with the moral rights framework that has been elaborated above. If we accept the existence of moral rights, we must reject any goals that would require us to violate the constraints implied by such rights. Much of the confusion characterizing the current debate over proper goals for the criminal justice system stems from the failure to recognize that such a debate cannot occur in a moral vacuum. Without a moral rights framework that provides an objective standard for eval-

9. Lon Fuller, *The Morality of Law* (New Haven: Yale University Press, 1964), pp. 3–32.

uating each goal, we are left to wander aimlessly from one goal to another. A moral rights framework provides the necessary context within which a utilitarian calculus may properly be employed to select among competing goals.[10] Freed from a prior commitment to a concept of rights, the utilitarian calculus may result in the adoption of policies that, although advancing certain goals, entail a massive infringement upon individual rights.

In discussing the various goals that have been proposed for the criminal justice system, it soon becomes apparent that virtually every one of these goals may be subsumed under the broad rubric of crime prevention. Thus, such diverse goals as deterrence, rehabilitation, and incapacitation in fact represent subsidiary ends that are all directed toward the larger goal of preventing crime. While the goal of crime prevention is certainly a legitimate and important one for any social system, it is not, strictly speaking, an appropriate goal for the criminal justice system.

Once a certain action has occurred, it should be the function of the criminal justice system to determine whether that action has violated the rights of individuals and, if it has, to take the steps necessary to rectify the imbalance created by the criminal act. The criminal justice system, then, is designed to address only one dimension of the crime problem: justice. In performing this function, the criminal justice system necessarily adopts an exclusively past-oriented approach, focusing on past criminal actions.

This is not to say that crime prevention is unimportant or even that an efficient administration of criminal justice will not contribute to the attainment of this goal. However, it does imply that the prevention of crime or any such goal should constitute merely a by-product of the primary function of the system: the administration of justice. As Professor Weinreb has noted in his book *Denial of Justice:*

> The function of criminal process is to determine criminal guilt with a view toward imposing a penalty. If it provides a civic education for some people (which is doubtful) or a public entertainment, so much the better; but these are not its functions, any more than it is the function of the judicial system to provide comfortable berths for the friends of successful politicians, as it does. Nor is it the function of the criminal process itself to punish or rehabilitate criminals or deter the commission of crime, although

---

10. Throughout this paper we shall describe judgments about moral goals as "utilitarian" in nature. This should not be interpreted as an endorsement of conventional utilitarian methodology. Rather, we mean that within this area our concern is properly with what "works." *How* one determines this is another matter. Although we would suggest a "legal naturalist" methodology—one in which the form of a given process is crafted to follow its intended purpose or function—the articulation of such a theory cannot be undertaken here.

there too, it may be, so much the better if it does. Criminal process is not
a means to redistribute income, or encourage patriotism, or promote individual expression, except incidentally.[11]

To the extent that this primary function of the administration of
justice is performed effectively, it is reasonable to assume that this
in itself will contribute in several ways to the broader goal of crime
prevention. For example, as Randy Barnett points out, to the extent
that the certainty of a sanction for criminal behavior will deter such
behavior, the administration of an effective criminal justice system
will have a deterrent effect on criminal behavior. In Chapter 15,
"Restitution as an Integrative Punishment," Burt Galaway has also
cited a growing body of evidence suggesting that a restitutionary
approach to criminal behavior has at least a potentially significant
reconciliative effect on the offender.

However, these positive effects arise as a consequence of the administration of criminal justice, and they are not properly goals to
which the administration of justice may be subordinated. To do so
would be to suggest that certain violations of individual rights should
remain unrectified in the interest of some goal, but the only person
who may properly make such a choice is the victim of the criminal
action. If the victim insists upon the rectification of the previous
rights violation, then it is the responsibility of a criminal justice system to assure that such a rectification occurs. In such a situation,
justice requires the rectification of the past rights violation, and the
subordination of this task to any other goal, would itself constitute
an injustice and would contradict the very definition of a criminal
justice system. It should be repeated, however, that this insistence on
the proper role of a criminal justice system *qua* criminal justice system is not meant to deny or minimize the desirability of pursuing
outside the framework of criminal justice certain goals designed to
prevent crime.

This point is especially relevant to a consideration of widely
quoted criticisms of the administration of the criminal justice system
by Alan Dershowitz, a professor at Harvard Law School. Dershowitz
argues that prevention has always been an implicit goal of the criminal justice system and that the failure to acknowledge this fact has
long obscured a major dimension of the system. According to Dershowitz, a systematic and explicit analysis of the goal of crime prevention would enable us to structure the institutions and procedures
of the criminal justice system more effectively.

However, this perspective neglects the crucial distinction between

11. Weinreb, pp. 1–2.

rights and goals. It is true that crime prevention has traditionally been a goal but, as a goal, it is completely irrelevant to the question of criminal justice. The point has already been made that, in its focus on prior rights violations, justice is uniquely and exclusively backward-looking and, as such, it is not properly concerned with such forward-looking goals as prevention of future crime. There is a broad spectrum of activities that may contribute to a goal of crime prevention, ranging from installing a burglar alarm to the hiring of private guards, but that are entirely outside the scope of criminal justice.

To the extent that Dershowitz suggests that it may be proper to infringe individual rights if such infringements would contribute to the goal of crime prevention, he is ignoring the fact that rights, by their very nature, may never be "properly" infringed upon in pursuit of any goal. They are constraints upon goal-oriented policies and are not simply additional goals that may be balanced and subordinated in a utilitarian calculus. In Chapter 16, Randy Barnett has demonstrated that this strict distinction between rights and goals in the area of criminal justice would in fact entail a fundamental reevaluation of the law of criminal attempt. Thus, unless it could be demonstrated that a so-called "attempt" was in fact a past action that had violated another individual's rights, it would be impermissible for the criminal justice system to impose any sanctions against the accused individual. This would be true even if it could be demonstrated that the accused individual had the intent of committing an aggressive act and that such an intention made it probable that the individual would seek to commit the act again.

While sanctions could not be imposed by the criminal justice system upon the accused individual, this does not mean that other individuals in the community could not take certain actions against the accused individual, provided that these actions do not infringe upon that individual's rights. For example, individuals in the community might seek to isolate the accused individual by refusing to associate or trade with him. Such forms of voluntary action can often prove very effective in enforcing the norms of a community and in discouraging the accused individual from pursuing his attempted course of action.

A similar form of analysis would be necessary at any other point in the criminal justice system where it might be demonstrated that sanctions have been applied, not on the basis of past actions, but on the basis of anticipated actions. The purpose of a criminal justice system is to rectify the imbalance created by past violations of individual rights; it should not, and it cannot, seek to do more and still remain true to its fundamental purpose.

In discussing the broad goal of crime prevention, it becomes particularly important to seek a better understanding of the origins of criminal behavior. Perhaps more than any other area of the crime problem, this subject has been one of enormous controversy in which passion and prejudice have often prevailed over reasoned analysis. This is especially troubling since it is very difficult to conceive of the formulation of policy goals in this area without a prior agreement as to the major factors responsible for the behavior that these policy goals will seek to prevent.

In this regard, the path-breaking research by Dr. Stanton Samenow and the late Dr. Samuel Yochelson at St. Elizabeth's Hospital in Washington, D.C., deserves special attention. In Chapter 4, Samenow summarizes the results of their fourteen year project. In the course of their research, they eventually found themselves unable to accept many of the conventional assumptions regarding the origins of criminal behavior, assumptions that they also shared when they began the project. For example, they came to the unexpected conclusion that psychological disorders did not adequately account for criminal behavior, thus confirming many of the theoretical insights of Thomas Szasz. They also could not identify any environmental factors, such as lack of educational opportunities or poverty, that would explain why certain individuals became habitual criminals.

After intensive interviewing of "habitual" or "career" criminals, Samenow and Yochelson concluded that these individuals all shared certain distinctive thinking patterns and that these thinking patterns were not inherited but, instead, represented a series of conscious choices made by each individual, usually at a relatively early stage in life. One immediate implication of their observation is that the conventional goal of "rehabilitation" has been fundamentally misguided. As Samenow indicates, the very term "rehabilitation" suggests restoration to a previously existing condition, whereas his research questions whether the "career" criminal has ever developed the thinking patterns necessary to live responsibly. Based on their initial research, Samenow and Yochelson sought to develop a treatment program that would systematically change the distinctive thinking patterns of the career criminal and, through a process of "habilitation," instill new thinking patterns that would enable the individual to live and act responsibly in society.

Samenow demonstrates considerable sensitivity to the moral and policy implications of his research, and his study explores some of these issues. In particular, he questions the traditional goals of rehabilitation and deterrence and he suggests that criminal sanctions may have the least deterrent effect on precisely those extreme criminals that he has studied. Based on his research, Samenow also questions whether a restitutionary approach to criminal justice would have any significant rehabilitative effect on the career criminal.

Samenow's work is extremely important for anyone concerned with developing appropriate goals for dealing with the problems of crime. The challenge will be to articulate goals consistent with his analysis that can be pursued without violating the constraints imposed by a framework of moral rights. For example, Samenow's research suggests the need to develop new forms of testing and counseling to identify and treat individuals who appear to exhibit the thinking patterns characteristic of criminal behavior. However, unless such programs are formulated and administered in a manner that is entirely consistent with individual rights, it is not difficult to imagine the enormous potential for abuse that such programs might have. Such programs could not be tolerated unless they relied exclusively on the voluntary and informed participation of the subjects. Potential models do exist for such programs—Alcoholics Anonymous and Synanon are two particularly prominent examples.

Edward Banfield's insights on the relevance of time horizon to criminal behavior, a subject that he discusses in Chapter 5, "Present-Orientedness and Crime," appear to correspond closely with the results of Samenow's empirical research. Banfield argues that an individual's psychological orientation toward the future underlies distinctive patternings of attitudes and that certain individuals exhibit a significantly greater degree of present-orientedness than others. While cautioning that a high degree of present-orientedness in certain individuals will not necessarily result in criminal behavior, Banfield does suggest that such individuals are more likely to commit crime and that they will be less deterred by the threat of punishment.

Gerald O'Driscoll's paper (Chapter 6) on Banfield's concept of time horizon underscores the extent to which this concept is compatible with the theory of time preference developed by the economist Ludwig von Mises. O'Driscoll also contends that Banfield's theories are difficult to reconcile with the assumptions underlying much of the existing literature on the economics of crime. A common characteristic of this literature is to assume that every individual's orientation toward the future is identical and therefore that each will be equally affected by a given structure of incentives and penalties. On the other hand, if Banfield is correct that individuals differ in their orientation toward the future, then one would anticipate that the same structure of incentives and penalties would have a differential effect on each person. Such a conclusion would be particularly disturbing for anyone favoring a utilitarian approach to criminal sanctions, since it suggests the impossibility of measuring the differential deterrent effect of a particular sanction. O'Driscoll observes that this may be one reason for the enormous difficulties already encountered in the statistical measurement of the impact of various approaches to punishment. The final portion of O'Driscoll's study argues that a strictly utilitarian approach to policy formation would be inadequate.

While Banfield concentrates almost exclusively on the role of various cultures in reinforcing or weakening the natural disposition of the individual to prefer present to future rewards, his analysis tends to overlook the extent to which social institutions may also influence "present-orientedness." Since institutions are far more susceptible to modification than cultures, more systematic research into the relationship between social institutions and individual "time horizons" might suggest institutional reforms that could indirectly contribute to the goal of crime prevention.

Mario Rizzo's paper on "Time Preference, Situational Determinism and Crime" (Chapter 7) critically evaluates the entire concept of present-orientedness as a hypothesis for explaining why some individuals commit crime while others do not. Rizzo also questions whether, in certain contexts, present-orientedness might be considered a rational, rather than defective, attitude. In pursuing this analysis, he focuses attention on the role of political institutions as a source of present-oriented behavior within a social system.

As already mentioned, Samenow's study questions whether a restitutionary approach to criminal justice would have any positive habilitative impact on the hardcore criminal. While there is still insufficient evidence to resolve this question conclusively, the research cited in Burt Galaway's paper on "Restitution as an Integrative Punishment" (Chapter 15) provides reason to believe that a restitutionary system may perform a positive habilitative role for individuals who are not hard core criminals. By requiring the offender to undertake positive actions designed to rectify the imbalance that has been created between the offender and the victim, restitutionary sanctions may help to instill a sense of responsibility and to reduce the offender's sense of alienation from the rest of society. Since restitutionary sanctions have thus far only been applied on a very limited scale within the criminal justice system, the likelihood of such positive effects must remain largely speculative at this point. However, the experimental evidence that is available suggests that, far from requiring the abandonment of habilitation of criminal offenders, a restitutionary system of criminal justice may actually contribute to the attainment of this elusive goal.

Leonard Liggio's paper on "The Transportation of Criminals" (Chapter 12) provides an illuminating historical analysis of one criminal sanction—the transportation of criminal offenders to distant penal colonies—that was primarily designed to incapacitate the criminal offender by isolating him or her from the rest of society. As Liggio notes, the widespread use of prisons in England to achieve the same goal occurred at a much later date as a result of the influence of Bentham's utilitarian political and economic theories. Liggio is critical of the shift from penal colonies to prisons, noting that it imposed a significant additional tax burden upon the population and that it was prompted by a futile desire to rehabilitate the criminal rather than simply to isolate the criminal from the rest of society. In his conclusion, Liggio proposes that we return to the original goal of isolating the criminal.

As with any other goal, the isolation of criminal offenders is a legitimate approach to crime prevention provided that it is undertaken in a manner that does not violate individual rights. In this regard, Liggio indicates that, under Anglo-Saxon common law in England, neighbors formed voluntary, personal associations at the local level and expelled from their association anyone found guilty of a felony crime. Thus, through individual private action involving their right to trade and associate with whomever they chose, neighbors developed highly effective procedures for isolating habitual offenders from their midst.

The papers by John Hospers and Walter Kaufmann in this collection serve to focus attention on certain issues raised by some retributionist theories of justice. One of the great difficulties in discussing a retributionist theory of justice is that there are in fact many variants of the theory, and it becomes essential to identify specifically which one is being discussed. Many traditional formulations of this theory, such as the one expounded by Immanuel Kant, appear to justify the deliberate infliction of pain on criminal offenders, not so much because of the specific criminal action that the offender committed but instead because the offender, by his or her demonstration of reprehensible character, deserved such punishment. Under the influence of this theory the focus of attention shifts subtly from the *action* that deserves punishment to the *individual* who deserves punishment. The criminal act tends to be considered only as an overt indication of the lack of moral worth of the individual committing the act. This approach to criminal legal theory is exemplified by Richard Epstein's attempt to rationalize the distinction between tort and criminal law. As he correctly indicates, the historical distinction is based on just such a moral judgment.

Kaufmann's paper is critical of all variants of retributionist theories, but he appears especially critical of the variant outlined above. In contrast, John Hospers' effort to defend retributionist theories of justice involves the presentation of a "deserts theory" of justice that shares many similarities with the "Kantian" view. For this reason, it is essential to distinguish this variant of retributionist theory from the theory of criminal justice developed earlier in this paper.

The fundamental weakness of this type of retributionist theory is that it does not rest on an explicitly developed theory of rights. This, in turn, has a number of unfortunate consequences. By focusing attention too heavily on the moral worth of the criminal offender, the theory is led to reject the imposition of sanctions upon individuals who had violated the rights of others but who, for a variety of reasons, might not be considered deserving of sanctions. Such a retributive approach is inconsistent with the concept of justice that requires the rectification of all past violations of rights. Moreover, by departing from a theory of criminal justice that is based upon a relationship between two parties, such an approach ignores the rights of the victim entirely and the victim is reduced to the relatively marginal role of witness. For the same reason, by viewing punishment as essentially related only to the moral worth of a given defendant, this approach would encourage the uninvited participation of third parties. By denying the victim's legitimate role in the criminal justice process, there remains no reason why the evaluation of an individual's moral worth and the levying of punishments could not be performed by anyone.

The problems arising from this failure to ground a retributionist theory of criminal justice firmly on a prior explicit theory of individual rights confirms the importance of the rights-goals framework that this paper has described. To summarize the argument this far, we have identified two analytically distinct questions that arise in any systematic consideration of the problem of crime: the justice question and the utilitarian question. We have contended that the general failure to distinguish between the issues raised by each question has been responsible for much of the confusion that characterizes most contemporary discussions of crime.

The first question is the one with which the institutions of the criminal justice system should be exclusively concerned. The issues raised by the justice question are: the definition of individual rights, the identification of categories of acts that constitute violations of those rights, and the rectification of imbalances created by actions that have violated the rights of others. To analyze each of these issues in the detail that they deserve would require a separate book;

our purpose at this point is merely to emphasize that this type of analysis constitutes the foundation of a restitutive theory of justice.

In contrast, the utilitarian question has a much broader focus and concerns the issue of how we can maximize various goals (such as deterrence, habilitation, and incapacitation) that seek to prevent crime or to achieve other socially desirable objectives while remaining within the constraints imposed by a framework of moral rights. Properly understood, the latter question can only be answered by first addressing the justice question. The current confusion plaguing the criminal justice system arises typically in one of two ways: either one assumes that the second question can be answered without explicitly addressing the first question or one assumes that the two questions are in fact indistinguishable. The search for a new paradigm must begin with the realization that these two questions are in fact distinct and that, without a firm grounding in a theory of rights, the search for goals in dealing with crime will ultimately prove fruitless.

SUMMARIZING THE RESTITUTIONARY THEORY OF JUSTICE

The preceding discussion seeks to provide a very brief introduction to the elements of a new theory of criminal justice, one combining the strengths of varying traditional theories while, hopefully, resolving many of the contemporary dilemmas. Such a theory might be called a "restitutionary theory of justice." There are two main aspects of this theory: first, it attempts to define the proper scope of any criminal justice system *qua* justice system, and second, it identifies the principles by which a just system should operate. In other words, this theory focuses on the questions that have traditionally occupied the attention of philosophers: it defines the boundaries of justice and it specifies within those boundaries wherein justice resides.

Under a restitutionary theory of justice, the dominant concern of any criminal proceeding should be the fact that some person or persons have violated the rights, properly defined, of another. The settlement of this dispute using principles of justice may not achieve any independent social goals, but it will vindicate the rights of the aggrieved party and thereby vindicate the rights of all persons. For too long we have lost sight of this ultimate purpose of criminal law, and we are now beginning to recognize the consequences. If the rights of one of us is not respected, if the rectification of any one of our rights is ignored for the sake of any "larger" purpose, then the very notion óf individual rights itself has been demeaned and all of our rights diminished. In short, there can be no larger or more important goal than the rectification of each individual wrong. This goal has been entrusted exclusively to the criminal justice system, and it must therefore take precedence over any other competing goal.

One corollary of this analysis is that the traditional objectives of our present institutions have far exceeded the proper function of any criminal justice system. Because of this, not only have additional goals not been attained, but their pursuit has impeded the attainment of the only proper concern of a criminal justice system: justice.

Having stipulated what to some must seem obvious—that a criminal justice system should confine its activities to discovering and enforcing justice—it is necessary to determine with greater precision what constitutes restitutionary justice. While a detailed analysis of this concept would take us far beyond the confines of this work, certain basic principles have been identified in the preceding discussion and should be briefly noted here. These principles of justice are universal and apply with equal force to an infinite variety of specific fact situations.

The Parties to a Criminal Action

A restitutionary theory of justice begins with the principle that there are two parties to any criminal action. They are not, as traditionally conceived, the state and the defendant(s), but are, rather, the victim and the defendant. The state, if it is to play any role, would be restricted to mediating the dispute and enforcing the judgement.

This statement of the principle should not minimize the profound difficulties that may be encountered in defining with greater precision whether someone may be considered a "victim" of certain actions. These difficulties will only be surmounted if we are first able to elaborate a theory of rights that defines the specific rights possessed by all individuals and the circumstances under which these rights would be considered violated. Such a theory would be indispensable, for example, in evaluating the claim that certain so-called "victimless crimes" do in fact involve victims and therefore are an appropriate concern of the criminal justice system.

The Principle of Rectification

The criminal act creates an imbalance between the parties that requires rectification. This imbalance results from the fact that the criminal has infringed upon, and thereby denied, the rights of the victim. The nature of this imbalance is most clearly revealed in the example of stolen property that must be returned to the original owner. In that case, what has been violated is the victim's right to his property. This circumstance differs only in visibility, and not in principle, from any violation of the victim's rights. Because this imbalance arises from a wrongful imposition on the victim, one variant of the theory of restitutionary justice would hold that this wrongful imposition cannot be rectified by simply inflicting unpleasantness—punishment—on the offender. Rather, the criminal act creates a nexus between the offender and his victim that will be removed only when the offender has performed some constructive act of reparation (either a monetary payment or performance of services) for the victim or the victim's heirs.

This act of reparation should be designed to put the victim or the victim's heirs in the position that they would have been in if the original criminal act had never occurred. While it is a truism that nothing can ever fully compensate for the suffering, or even death, of the victim, this unfortunate fact should not be used as a justification for passivity: there is still an obligation to try as best we can to rectify the imbalance that the criminal act has created.

While we feel more comfortable with a theory of constructive, reparative sanctions, as indicated earlier, others, most notably Murray N. Rothbard in Chapter 11, favor another variant of restitutive justice that more nearly approximates the traditional concept of *lex talionis*. The differences between these two variants of restitutive justice cannot be ignored, but we believe that there are far greater similarities which justify their classification as variants of a single paradigm.

Both variants of restitutionary theory hold that an objective, if occasionally somewhat imprecise, proportioning of a sanction can be achieved through an examination of the nature and extent of the criminal act. Perhaps the most difficult challenge confronting the restitutive approach is, as Walter Kaufmann points out, the determination of what constitutes a "just" sanction. The difficulties of such an undertaking cannot be denied, but the promise of a restitutive paradigm is that, unlike current approaches or even a Kantian form of retribution theory, it provides principles to aid the determination.

Once a determination is made, it is the responsibility of the enforcing agency to protect the rights of the criminal as well as the victim by setting an upper limit on the severity of the sanction that may be imposed. This upper limit would be determined on the basis of the severity of the offense. Extraneous factors should not influence this finding, since what is being judged is not the moral worth or depravity of either the victim or the defendant but the extent to which the defendant's actions created an imbalance between the defendant and the victim.

The Role of the Victim in Sentencing

Since it is the victim whose rights have been violated, it is up to the victim to insist upon the punishment of the criminal or to pardon. The only person who may forgive an offense is the person who suffered the offense. Possible motives influencing the victim's decision may include preventive considerations, prospects for rehabilitation, blind hatred, or compassion and charity. We may seek to educate victims as to goals that any of us feel are appropriate for him to consider, but we cannot remove from the victim's hands the ultimate decision and responsibility for the sanction.

Since third parties lack any standing in a restitutionary theory of justice, the decision to punish the convicted offender cannot be affected by any broader societal concerns except to the extent that these concerns are shared by the victim and influence his or her decision. More broadly, however, an important societal concern is enforced by a restitutionary system of justice since, in handling each instance of criminal behavior, such a system not only reaffirms the victim's rights but assures everyone else in society that their rights will be similarly vindicated if ever transgressed.

While some have expressed the concern that a criminal proceeding could place an undue burden on the victim by assigning him or her such a prominent role in sentencing, early pilot programs suggest that this role could be structured in a manner that will increase, rather than diminish, the victim's security and well-being. Nevertheless, this concern is a real one and the form of a restitutive system will have to be crafted with great care to avoid any unnecessary burden on the victim. Such a consideration may lead to basic reforms in the adversary system.

The Rights of the Accused

The theory of restitutionary justice is based on the recognition that all individuals possess rights by virtue of their humanity. For this reason, the rights of the victim must be rigorously enforced, but we should not lose sight of the fact that those accused of crime are individuals as well and similarly possess certain rights that may not be violated. If the defendant is, in fact, innocent, then that individual possesses the same rights as any other person. Even if the defendant is in fact guilty, then the individual loses his or her rights only to the extent that his or her actions transgressed against the rights of others and the individual retains all other rights.

Any attempt to structure a criminal proceeding must cope with the fact that our knowledge of the true circumstances of any past criminal act will necessarily be imperfect and yet realize that our ability to do justice in each case will depend on our success in discovering the truth. While we must be prepared to act on the basis of occasionally erroneous information, we should always recall that the rights of each party are determined by the facts themselves and not by the fact that certain procedures were observed in reaching a particular outcome. Thus, a particular criminal proceeding may result in the injustice of convicting an innocent person on the basis of imperfect information, and the fact that certain procedures were observed cannot eliminate the fact that an injustice has occurred. To hold otherwise would seriously undermine our quest for the procedures and institutions that will be most effective in performing the truth-seeking function. This once again underscores the fact that the questions of criminal process are intimately related to the substantive concept of justice and that it is necessary to consider this latter question before one can begin to craft the procedures and institutions of a criminal justice system.

Standards of Proof

It is incumbent on any neutral third party mediating a dispute to establish a standard of proof before it acts to enforce the claim of a victim against a particular accused individual. Only in this way will the third party be able to minimize its potential liability should the accused individual later charge that the third party wrongfully infringed his or her rights on the basis of imperfect information. By explicitly adopting a standard of proof, the third party provides an objective standard by which any outsider may independently judge the correctness of the decision.

A restitutionary theory of justice would require a fundamental reevaluation of the standard of proof presently employed in criminal proceedings by the state. Two alternatives are consistent with a restitutionary theory of justice that recognizes two parties to a criminal action who each possess certain rights:

Preponderance of the Evidence Standard. If the prosecution can prove by a preponderance of the evidence that the defendant is guilty, then the defendant would be judged to have committed the crime and he would be required to attempt to restore the victim. If, however, the prosecution fails to meet its burden, then the defendant would be judged to be innocent and would therefore be entitled to compensation by the charging authority for the injustice of being forced to participate in the criminal process. The injury may have included physical confinement, loss of income, assorted expenses, and other less tangible injury as well. In this procedure it would be easier to prove a person guilty than in the current system, but this would be offset by the more serious consequences to the charging authorities in the event that they fail to prove their case.

Reasonable Doubt Standard. An alternative method would raise the requisite standard of proof for both sides. In order to be found guilty of the crime, the defendant would have to be proved guilty beyond a reasonable doubt. By the same token, before the defendant could be compensated for being forced to participate in the criminal process, his or her innocence would have to be established beyond a reasonable doubt as well. If neither party could prove its case, then the resultant losses would remain with the parties originally sustaining them.

CONCLUSION

Any theory that involves a set of clear, concise principles will inevitably be accused of "oversimplification." Although this essay has only attempted to outline the restitutionary view in a highly schematic fashion, even a more detailed elaboration of this position would not escape such a criticism. It is an unfortunate fact that any statement of absolute moral principles today is regarded as inherently suspect. The irony is that the dominant utilitarian and empiricist attitudes in our society have produced a legal system that glorifies complexity and is captivated by the verbal sleight of hand. In fact, it is the present criminal process that "overcomplicates" the crime problem by being theoretically unable to choose among conflicting goals and rationales to arrive at a swift, predictable, and just result. While some may still wish to defend the current system by arguing that justice requires careful and slow deliberation, there is a growing awareness that, rather than serving the ends of justice, the delay and confusion pervading the system only result in the classic case of justice denied. We all pay the price for the unprincipled (or, in some cases, false-principled) nature of the current system.

To defend a principled approach to justice, however, is not to minimize the difficulties involved in its application. The tenets of restitutionary justice may be articulated, understood, and inernalized, but still present major problems as one seeks to translate these principles into a viable system of criminal justice. Examples of these problems include the attempt to proportion punishment to fit the crime and the obstacles that will be encountered in seeking to administer efficiently a system of restitutionary payments.

Hard cases cannot be eliminated, but the recognition of this fact is not a condemnation of restitution. The proper function of any theory of justice is to discern the complexities inherent in any legal process and to provide the criteria for solving them. A restitutionary paradigm of justice performs this function by confronting the realities of the criminal act, recognizing the respective rights of the parties, and, thereby, pointing the way to a settlement of the dispute that may be ameliorative and constructive, but that is, above all else, just.

Part I

The Concept of the Criminal: An Analysis

Since the primary focus of this collection is on the nature of criminal justice, it is necessary to begin by assessing the very meaning of the concept of criminality and, therefore, to identify those categories of action that would properly fall within the scope of criminal justice. In this regard, Ronald Hamowy's account of the emergence of a broad spectrum of "victimless crimes" underscores the point that many activities that would be considered crimes according to a strict legal definition do not involve the infringement of individual rights. Thomas Szasz, in his forceful critique of "psychiatric diversion" programs, demonstrates the injustices that arise when courts go beyond the specific acts that an individual allegedly committed and begin to probe the mental state of that individual.

Stanton Samenow summarizes extensive research that indicates that the "career criminal" engages in criminal activity not as a result of psychological illness or environmental factors but rather as a result of a conscious choice to adopt certain patterns of thought at a relatively young age. By focusing on crime as a series of voluntary choices, Samenow rejects determinist theories of criminal behavior and provides support for the view that every individual must be held morally responsible for his or her actions.

Edward Banfield investigates the role of "present-orientedness" as a trait increasing the proclivity of individuals to engage in criminal behavior, and he suggests that contemporary cultural trends may encourage this trait. Both Gerald O'Driscoll and Mario Rizzo explore Banfield's concept of present-orientedness, and O'Driscoll, in partic-

ular, indicates its relevance to the growing body of economic literature on crime. Rizzo questions whether present-orientedness provides
a useful hypothesis for explaining propensity to commit crime and
cautions against theories tending toward "situational determinism."

✳ *Chapter 2*

Preventive Medicine and the Criminalization of Sexual Immorality in Nineteenth Century America*

Ronald Hamowy

What this chapter will attempt to show is that while, during the nineteenth century, the prohibition of sexual immorality played a comparatively unimportant role in American criminal law, the medical profession arrogated to itself the task of dealing with moral questions. Psychological medicine in particular, by substituting "treatment" of disease for legal punishment of moral transgression, placed itself in the position of enforcer of virtuous conduct. Medicine was so successful in assuming this function that, by the end of the century, it had enlisted the great mass of the literate public in support of its findings respecting the connection between sexual behavior and mental disease. At that point it became possible to alter the direction of American law to encompass the conclusions reached by the psychiatric and medical professions and to criminalize sexual immorality under the guise of legislating in the area of preventive medicine.

The expansion of the medical discipline into the area of private moral conduct is as old as the history of psychiatry—the branch of clinical medicine purporting to deal with the arcana of psychic life. In the United States, however, it was only in the last third of the nineteenth century that its influence reached significant proportions. By that time, the profession was successful not only in maintaining social sanctions against immoral behavior with which the criminal law was not concerned but of enlarging, without theoretical limit, the area of private behavior within its purview.

*I am indebted to Mr. W.M. Bartley of the University of Alberta for his assistance in researching much of the data presented in this paper.

The thesis of this chapter assumes that legal rules are distinct from moral rules and holds that while the American legal system found it inconvenient to enforce the latter, the task was taken on by medicine, and particularly by psychiatry. It is, therefore, essential to fix the area in which law, in the sense in which I mean it, can be differentiated from morality.[1] A contemporary legal theorist writing on the subject points to three cardinal features that permit the one to be distinguished from the other.[2] First, the concern of law, at least in the Western tradition, is far narrower in scope than is that of morality. Law ideally attends only to those aspects of conduct indispensable to the maintenance of the basic fabric of society. Morality has no such limitation; rather, it calls for conformity with an ideal in both thought and behavior. Second, the law is primarily concerned not with interior attitudes but with external conduct. Responsibility in the law is assumed solely on the basis of criminal intention established by external evidence. Morality's concern rests primarily with the nature of the motive of the actor, with his interior attitudes, states of mind, and the long-run condition of his soul. Finally, the most salient difference between law and morality revolves around the nature of sanctions imposed and who imposes them. With respect to legal rules, sanctions take the form of deprivation of property or liberty—possibly even of life—and are imposed by some formalized governmental apparatus; moral sanctions, on the other hand, when not self-imposed by conscience, are generally nonviolent, such as social ostracism, and are imposed by individuals acting on their own behalf or voluntarily with others.

The Protestant Reformation and a capitalist economic system that culminated in nineteenth century liberal doctrine both worked toward a more pronounced distinction between legal rules and moral rules. The earlier ideal, based on the Platonic tradition of a system where the law was as comprehensive as the moral code and where its primary function was to promote virtue, gave way to emphasizing individual activity wherein one's behavior, freely chosen, privately determined one's salvation or damnation, either in this world or the next.[3]

1. The argument that law and morality are, in most significant respects, coextensive impresses me as the result more of a confusion in terminology than of analytic insight. In any case, the sense in which I mean to distinguish the two is, I trust, made clear by Mr. St. John—Stevas.

2. Norman St. John—Stevas, *Life, Death and the Law* (London: Eyre & Spottiswoode, 1961), pp. 14—15.

3. Ibid., pp. 18—25. Historical discussions are also contained in H.L.A. Hart, *Law, Liberty and Morality* (Stanford, California: Stanford University Press, 1963), passim; id., *The Morality of the Criminal Law* (Jerusalem: The Magnes

The growing distinction between law and morality is intimately connected with the history of freedom and the theory of inalienable private rights,[4] enshrined in the American legal framework, in the Declaration of Independence, and the first ten amendments to the Constitution.[5] The movement to secure individual rights in the United States, making all government intrusion into the peaceful daily lives of citizens suspect, undermined the rationale by which the state could be regarded as having authority over private moral decisions. That the government should take onto itself the task of offering a positive function in moral affairs contravened the political philosophy inherent in a structure of law consistent with limited government.[6]

It is true that the criminal law in colonial America was active in the enforcement of public morality. In seventeenth century New England especially, the penal codes of the colonies were heavily oriented toward the punishment of sin.[7] However, after the Revolu-

---

Press, Hebrew University, 1964), pp. 31—54; and, Patrick Devlin, *The Enforcement of Morals* (London: Oxford University Press, 1965), passim.

4. See, for example, F.A. Hayek, *The Constitution of Liberty* (Chicago: University of Chicago Press, 1960), pp. 145—47.

5. In discussing the relation between government and the legal enforcement of virtue in the United States, Walter Berns remarks that:

> in a real sense it is against the American tradition to suggest that political conflicts do not always lie between government and the citizen, and more specifically, that the basic political conflict is not one of man versus the state—or freedom versus authority, as it is frequently referred to. Both the Declaration of Independence and the Bill of Rights share this view. The very notion that the citizen possesses rights against the government, rights that he enjoys from some non-governmental source, is not only a modern idea, but is one that makes no sense unless government is viewed as some hostile force, or at least some necessary evil, which constantly threatens to prey on its subjects.

Walter Berns, *Freedom, Virtue, and the First Amendment* (Baton Rouge: Louisiana State University Press, 1957), p. 67.

6. The shift in emphasis from "enforcer and guardian of Christian society" to "preserver of individual liberty" that occurred in Massachusetts law after the Revolution is ably discussed by William E. Nelson in *Americanization of the Common Law: The Impact of Legal Change on Massachusetts Society, 1760—1830* (Cambridge, Massachusetts: Harvard University Press, 1975), passim, esp. pp. 89—110.

7. Lawrence M. Friedman, *A History of American Law* (New York: Simon & Shuster, 1973), pp. 62—63. Also, Nelson, p. 37.

Nelson notes that of the 2,784 prosecutions in the superior and general sessions courts of Massachusetts between 1770 and 1774, 38 percent of these prosecutions were for sexual crimes. Yet the punishment of immoral conduct during these few years immediately prior to the Revolution cannot have been the sole, perhaps not even the primary, motive behind the enforcement of statutes concerned with sexual behavior since, as Nelson points out, 95 percent of

tion, American law significantly altered its direction. The law then, and throughout most of the nineteenth century, was strongly biased toward individual autonomy and the free market as against public power. This was true not only of the law of contract, as would be expected in a system based on economic individualism, but of tort and criminal law as well.[8] The singular importance of placing strict limits on governmental power led to a reduction in the importance of criminal law generally[9] and, with it, crimes that were regarded as transgressing sexual morality.[10] With respect to sexual behavior, the

---

these sexual offenses were for fornication and, with but one exception, only mothers of illegitimate children were prosecuted.

Figures offered by Michael S. Hindus confirm Nelson's findings. Of all criminal prosecutions in Middlesex County, Massachusetts, between 1760 and 1774, those relating to bastardy and fornication accounted for 63 percent and all but 10 of the 210 fornication prosecutions during this period involved illegitimate births. (Michael S. Hindus, "The Contours of Crime and Justice in Massachusetts and South Carolina, 1767–1878," *American Journal of Legal History* [July 1977] pp. 9, 14, forthcoming).

See also Daniel Scott and Michael S. Hindus, "Premarital Pregnancy in America, 1640–1971: An Overview and Interpretation," *Journal of Interdisciplinary History* 5 (1975):537–570.

8. James Willard Hurst, *Law and the Conditions of Freedom in the Nineteenth-Century United States* (Madison: University of Wisconsin Press, 1956), p. 18.

9. Friedman, pp. 256–57.

10. Nelson, pp. 110, 118. This was true even of Massachusetts, consistently the state most repressive in its laws governing sexual behavior. Nelson notes that, beginning in the 1780s, there was a "virtual cessation of criminal prosecutions for various sorts of immorality." By 1800, only 7 percent of all prosecutions were for conduct offensive to morality as compared with 38 percent thirty years earlier.

Hindus, although agreeing in the main with Nelson's conclusions, argues that the shift from "crime as sin" to "crime as theft" in Massachusetts took not several decades but 200 years! Hindus maintains that "crimes against morality" never ceased to be a major concern of Massachusetts law; rather, the nineteenth century witnessed a shift in emphasis in what constituted immoral behavior away from sexual offenses to liquor-related crimes such as drunkenness and violations of the licensing laws. His inclusion of violations of the liquor license laws under the broader category of "crimes against morality, order and chastity," however, serves only to obscure a highly significant downward trend in prosecutions and correctional commitments for sexual offenses and, indeed, for all real offenses against morality that took place throughout the first seventy years of the nineteenth century. Figures that Hindus presents elsewhere in this monograph indicate that during the period 1833–1858 no less than 35 percent of *all* criminal prosecutions in Massachusetts were for license law violations, and that of the category "drunkenness and license law violations," prosecutions for drunkenness accounted for only 4.37 percent of the total during this period, violations of the licensing laws accounting for the remaining 95.63 percent. During this same period, prosecutions for sexual offenses represented only 5.7 percent of the total of all prosecutions.

With respect specifically to sexual offenses, Hindus' data clearly confirm a secular decline in correctional commitments for sexual crimes as a proportion of

common law heritage was almost invariably the guide in determining which acts were indictable. The canon of criminal law that developed throughout most of the nineteenth century was an amalgam of judicial extensions based on common law analogies and statutory enactments that themselves codified preexisting common law.[11]

In the area of sexuality, indictable offenses were—in the main—limited to the common law felonies of rape and sodomy and to lesser wrongs such as adultery, notorious lewdness, and frequenting or keeping a bawdy house.[12] Because of the common law bias in the interpretation of criminal law, the determination of criminal liability in the area of sexual conduct—in the absence of an explicit statutory provision to the contrary—was customarily interpreted to rest on proof of the "open," "notorious," "public," and "scandalous" nature of the act. For example, at common law an indictment on a charge of haunting a house of ill fame had expressly to charge the open and notorious nature in which the bawdy house was frequented by the defendant.[13] Lewd and indecent conduct was indictable only when "habitual, open, and notorious."[14] "Mere private lewdness or in-

---

commitments for all crimes throughout the period he covers. In Suffolk County (the cities of Boston and Chelsea), where the commitment rate was significantly higher for sexual offenses than was the rate for Massachusetts as a whole, commitments for sexual offenses accounted for 6.96 percent of all commitments during the period 1839–1841; 3.98 percent during the period 1848–1851; 2.39 percent during the period 1859–1861; and 2.31 percent during the period 1869–1870.

Additionally, Hindus' graphic summary of the commitment rate for "crimes against morality, order and chastity," showing a peak in 1855, is deceptive. This category—consisting of drunkenness and breaches of the licensing laws as well as sexual offenses—does not speak to the particular question of commitments for specifically sexual crimes nor, because of the inclusion of license law violations, can it offer much insight into the trend with respect to commitments for true moral offenses. Employing the tabulated data for Suffolk County, however, specifically sexual offenses represent a decreasing proportion of the larger category: 18.46 percent in the period 1839–1841; 11.73 percent in the period 1849–1851; 5.31 percent in the period 1859–1861; and 4.48 percent in the period 1869–1870. Moreover, the *absolute rate* decreased markedly between 1851 and 1859 by these same data, from 137.5 to 39.3 commitments per 100,000 population. (Hindus, passim.)

11. Francis Wharton, *A Treatise on the Criminal Law of the United States* (Philadelphia: James Kay, Jr. and Brother, 1846), p. 3.

12. Ibid., pp. 1, 5.

13. Ibid., p. 507. See also *Wharton's Criminal Law*, 12th ed., 3 vols. (Rochester, New York: Lawyers Co-operative Publishing Co., 1932), II:2004 (Section 1719).

14. *Wharton's Criminal Law*, II:1988 (Section 1703); Joel Prentiss Bishop, *Commentaries on the Law of Statutory Crimes*, 2nd ed. (Boston: Little, Brown, and Company, 1883), p. 438 (Section 714); Sir William Blackstone, *Commentaries on the Laws of England*, 4 vols., ed. William G. Hammond (San Francisco: Bancroft-Whitney Company, 1890), IV:85.

decency," in itself, was not an offense.[15] With respect to this requirement, a recent commentator writing on indecent exposure notes:

> To be indictable at early common law this act not only had to be public,
> but had to actually be seen by more than one nonconsenting person. The
> "more than one person" rule was soon relaxed to the extent that acts were
> held indictable if they were committed in a place "so situated that what
> passes there can be seen by a considerable number of people if they hap-
> pen to look." [Van Houten v. State, 5 N.J.L. 311 (Essex Quarter Sess.,
> 1882), *aff'd*, 46 N.J.L. 16 (Sup. Ct., 1884).] However courts retaining this
> modified requirement have still refused to indict the act when committed
> in private before a single nonconsenting person. [E.g., Lockhart v. State,
> 116 Ga. 557, 42 S.E. 787 (1902); State v. Wolf, 211 Mo.App. 429, 244
> S.W. 962 (1922).][16]

The provision that a sexual act, to be regarded as criminal, required an open and public flaunting of social norms found its way
into a number of statutes prohibiting adultery and fornication. Of
the states that eventually enacted statutes prohibiting adultery,[17]
fifteen[18] required that proof of a single act was not in itself sufficient to substantiate a charge of adultery. To be criminal, the adul-
terous relationship had to be "open and habitual." The same was

15. *Wharton's Criminal Law*, II:1990 (Section 1703).

16. "Note: Private Consensual Homosexual Behavior: The Crime and its Enforcement," *Yale Law Journal* 70 (1961):624n.

Prior to 1786, Massachusetts had a strict fornication statute forcefully administered. As William E. Nelson points out in his excellent survey of Massachusetts
law,

> in 1786 the General Court enacted a new statute for the punishment of
> fornication, permitting a woman guilty of the crime to confess her guilt
> before a justice of the peace, pay an appropriate fine, and thereby avoid
> prosecution by way of indictment in the court of sessions. The number of
> prosecutions for sexual offenses immediately declined to an average of
> eleven per year during 1786–1790 and to less than five per year during the
> four decades thereafter. It appears that after 1790 women simply stopped
> confessing their guilt of fornication, apparently aware that even though
> they did not confess it was most unlikely that they would be indicted. In-
> deed, only four indictments for fornication were returned in the entire
> Commonwealth after 1790.

Nelson, p. 110.

17. By 1920, forty-three states had legislated against adultery, the exceptions
being Arkansas, Louisiana, Nevada, New Mexico, and Tennessee. Although most
adultery statutes date back to the earliest criminal codes enacted by the state,
several state legislatures waited quite some time before prohibiting the act. For
example, Florida did not proscribe adultery until 1874. South Carolina enacted
its first adultery statute in 1880; California, in 1901; and New York, in 1907.

18. Alabama, California, Colorado, Florida, Illinois, Indiana, Kansas, Mississippi, Missouri, Montana, Ohio, South Carolina, North Carolina, Texas, and Wyoming.

true of the fornication statutes. By 1920, thirty-two states had prohibited fornication; of these only fifteen[19] made a single act a crime. In the other seventeen states the offense was not, properly speaking, fornication but "lewd and vicious cohabitation."[20]

With respect to rape—"carnal knowledge of a woman without her consent"—it is notable that, during the nineteenth century, the age below which a female was presumed by law to be unable to consent was, in most jurisdictions, ten years.[21] Thus, the current crime of statutory rape—which is not really rape at all—effectively did not exist throughout most of the century since the penal codes defining rape either stipulated ten or twelve years as the age of consent or were silent on an age of consent, in which case the common law age of ten years would apply.

Sodomy, at common law, consisted solely in "sexual connection, per anum, by a man, with a man or woman."[22] Although almost every state prohibited the act by statute, prosecutions throughout the nineteenth century were exceedingly rare inasmuch as both parties to the act were regarded as accomplices, equally guilty of the crime.[23] As a result, the courts held that a conviction could not be sustained on the basis of the unsupported testimony of a party to the commission of the offense. Vern Bullough, in his history of sexuality, points out that the effect of this provision "was to exclude sexual activities between consenting adults in private from prosecution, whether homosexual or heterosexual," especially "since solicitation to commit a sex act was not an offense."[24]

The intrusion of the law into sexual behavior throughout most of the nineteenth century was far less extensive than the comprehensive system of legal restrictions that obtains today. Indeed, except for a few offenses such as adultery and sodomy, the criminal law was concerned more with proscribing the public flaunting of sexual activities than with prohibiting the sexual acts themselves. Morris Ploscowe

19. Connecticut, Florida, Georgia, Kentucky, Massachusetts, Maine, Minnesota, New Hampshire, New Jersey, North Dakota, Pennsylvania, Rhode Island, Utah, Virginia, and West Virginia.

20. Alabama, Arkansas, Colorado, Idaho, Illinois, Indiana, Iowa, Michigan, Mississippi, Montana, Nebraska, Nevada, New Mexico, Oregon, South Carolina, Washington, and Wyoming.

21. *Wharton's Criminal Law*, I:910 (Section 682); Bishop, pp. 357–58 (Section 482); Blackstone, IV:270.

22. Francis Wharton, *A Treatise on Criminal Law*, 8th ed., 2 vols. (Philadelphia: Kay and Brother, 1880), I:512 (Section 579).

23. Ibid., Section 580.

24. Vern L. Bullough, *Sexual Variance in Society and History* (New York: John Wiley & Sons, 1976), p. 578.

has pointed out that since the ecclesiastical courts of the Church of England, traditionally responsible for a large area of sexual behavior, were not received in the United States, American law initially provided no institutionalized means for dealing with sexual conduct that had been ignored by the common law. Lacunae had, therefore, to be filled by statute.[25] Although the statutory law underwent a general inflation over the course of the nineteenth century, laws relating primarily to sexual conduct began to be enacted in great numbers only in the last two decades of the century. Even as late as 1916, in the midst of a period that saw a great many statutes respecting sexual morality enacted by the various legislatures, one prominent member of the New York bar could still complain that:

> All communities and people find themselves quite in accord as to the seriousness of the crimes of murder and theft, but until recently, there was no law in the United States that made pandering a more serious crime than disorderly conduct, and in a few States pandering is still so little defined as to make the crime "merely a breach of manners and to put it in the same class of offenses as selling a street-car transfer." The treatment of commercialized prostitution not only differs in each city, but changes in the same city under each different administration. The prohibition in the Decalogue against adultery is no less definite than that against murder, and yet, while the law against murder is uniform and constant, that against adultery has been diverse and unstable. In some States adultery is a felony, in others a misdemeanor; . . . In New York, adultery did not become a criminal offense until 1907, and since then it has been practically impossible to obtain a conviction in the absence of unusually aggravating circumstances. Illicit sexual intercourse is a crime in only a very few States, and in other States only becomes such when it is attended by notorious lewdness and indecency, resulting in public scandal and nuisance. In rape, the age of consent ranges throughout the United States from the common-law age of ten years to that fixed in New York at eighteen years.[26]

With nineteenth century America governed by criminal laws incorporating comparatively few restrictions on private sexual conduct and with a general laxity in enforcement of those laws that did exist, the medical profession found circumstances particularly favorable for assuming the role of arbiter of the moral behavior of the nation left vacant by the law. The rise of the science of psychiatry as a specialized branch of medicine, armed with the prestige accorded to all

25. Morris Ploscowe, "Sex Offenses: The American Legal Context," *Law and Contemporary Problems* 25(1960):218.

26. Arthur B. Spingarn, *Laws Relating to Sex Morality in New York City* (New York: The Century Co., 1916), pp. x-xi.

scientific disciplines together with the power to compel treatment, provided physicians the opportunity to employ sanctions to enforce moral rules. Asserting that they had uncovered the fundamental laws governing mental health and disease, physicians and psychiatrists were able to offer their moral pronouncements as objective truths and, ultimately, to force compliance with their conclusions through liberal commitment laws.[27]

Psychiatry from its inception as a distinct area of medicine at the end of the eighteenth century had underscored the singular importance of sexual life in the etiology of psychic disease. Although the psychiatric and medical professions—up until the last decades of the nineteenth century—suffered from some of the same reticence regarding uninhibited discussion of sexual matters as did the general public, doctors felt comparatively free to speak of sexual issues that they considered of immediate and common concern. This was especially true of masturbation, to which they devoted particular attention. There are several reasons for this: first, although viewed as having serious consequences, it was a common practice among the young and the mentally disturbed, groups less able to hide their activity than were prudent adults; second, if it could be shown that masturbation were harmful and linked to psychic disorders, so would it be true of excessive fornication. Thus, masturbation and "excessive venery" were commonly linked in medical discussions of sexuality. Finally, if it were scientifically demonstrated that masturbation and incontinence led to neuropathic conditions, *a fortiori* this would be true of the more recherche forms of sexual expression, such as homosexuality. Indeed, it has been argued by Vern Bullough and Martha Voght that many physicians, fearful of offending the sensibilities of

27. In addition to the traditional bases of commitment—danger to one's self, or to others—a new consideration was added in 1845. In that year, the Massachusetts Supreme Judicial Court denied a habeas corpus petition of Josiah Oakes, who sought his discharge from the McLean Asylum on the grounds that he had been illegally committed by his family. Affirming a lower court denial of Oakes' petition, the court ruled the standard of commitment to be "whether a patient's own safety, or that of others, requires that he should be restrained for a certain time, and *whether restraint is necessary for his restoration, or will be conducive thereto.*" To this the court added that "the restraint can continue as long as the necessity continues." (Italics added.) (Matter of Oakes, 8 Law Rep. 122, at 125 [Massachusetts 1845]).

An extensive discussion of the history of American commitment laws is contained in Albert Deutsch, *The Mentally Ill in America: A History of Their Care and Treatment from Colonial Times* (Garden City, New York: Doubleday, Doran & Company, Inc., 1937), pp. 417–39. For an account of the public controversy that erupted in the 1870s over abuses of the commitment procedure and the professional reaction to the criticism, see Ruth B. Caplan, *Psychiatry and the Community in Nineteenth-Century America* (New York: Basic Books, Inc., 1969), pp. 190–98.

the more squeamish, employed words such as "masturbation" and "onanism" as generic terms under which they meant to include all sexual aberrations, including homosexuality.[28] Although the Bullough-Voght thesis is somewhat problematic, it is certainly true that it was within the context of their disquisitions on masturbation that physicians and psychiatrists developed a general theory of sexuality covering all sexual conduct.

By the end of the nineteenth century, medical science had elaborated a comprehensive doctrine relating sexual indulgence and mental disease. As a result, when, largely at the urging of physicians and moral reformers, a flood of legislation restricting sexual conduct was introduced in the period from 1880 to 1920, the theoretical foundation, scope, and direction of these new laws were provided primarily by the scientific conclusions earlier reached by physicians and psychiatrists. This chapter proceeds to discuss both these movements. The next section of this essay traces the development of the theory of sexuality that emerged in nineteenth century medical discussions of the interrelationship between masturbation, incontinence, and mental disease. It is followed by a discussion of the efforts made by physicians to translate these findings into law through an intensive lobbying campaign aimed at the passage of legislation prohibiting a wide range of sexual behavior.

I

During the formative period of the psychoanalytic movement in the United States, from 1910 to 1918, when Freud's theories gained prominence on this side of the Atlantic, much hostility was aroused among portions of the public because of the heavy emphasis psychoanalysis placed on sexual matters.[29] What many lay readers were unaware of was that medical men, particularly those concerned with diseases of the mind, had early investigated the effects of sexual behavior on the psyche. Masturbation was of particular concern and was commonly regarded as the root of a host of medical and physical disorders. By the beginning of the nineteenth century, the emerging field of psychiatry had concluded that sexual self-stimulation, when

28. Vern L. Bullough and Martha Voght, "Homosexuality and Its Confusion with the 'Secret Sin' in Pre-Freudian America," *Journal of the History of Medicine* 28 (1973):143–55.

29. For an account of the American public's reception of Freud's psychoanalytic system, see Nathan G. Hale, Jr., *Freud and the Americans: The Beginnings of Psychoanalysis in the United States, 1876–1917* (New York: Oxford University Press, 1971), passim, especially pp. 417–21.

chronic, invariably brought insanity in its wake.[30] The earliest definitive statement of this thesis is that which appears in the work of the father of American psychiatry, Dr. Benjamin Rush.[31]

Rush, whom Thomas Szasz describes as "the first American physician to urge the medicalization of social problems and their coercive control by means of 'therapeutic' rather than 'punitive' sanctions,"[32] held that even occasional masturbation "produces seminal weakness, impotence, dysury, tabes dorsalis, pulmonary consumption, dyspepsia, dimness of sight, vertigo, epilepsy, hypochondriasis, loss of memory, manalgia, fatuity, and death."[33] Indeed, as Rush points out, "the morbid effects of intemperance in a sexual intercourse with women are feeble, and of a transient nature, compared with the train of physical and moral evils which this solitary vice fixes upon the body and mind."[34]

The hypothesis that masturbation was a significant cause of insanity became a prominent tenet in international psychiatric thinking between the publication of Rush's work in 1812 and midcentury and was echoed in the most advanced medical literature of Britain and Europe. In France the pioneer psychiatrist J.E.D. Esquirol joined Rush in claiming that masturbation was symptomatic of mania and that it reduced those who practiced it "to a state of stupidity, to phthisis, marasmus, and death."[35] He was joined by, among numerous others, Guislain of Belgium, who observed that the habit gave

---

30. The following accounts of the history of masturbation in nineteenth century medicine and psychiatry have proved most helpful: E.H. Hare, "Masturbatory Insanity: The History of an Idea," *Journal of Mental Science* 108 (1962): 1–25; René A. Spitz, "Authority and Masturbation: Some Remarks on a Bibliographical Investigation," *The Yearbook of Psychoanalysis* 9 (1953):113–45; John Duffy, "Masturbation and Clitoridectomy: A Nineteenth-Century View," *Journal of the American Medical Association* 186(1963):166–68; John S. Haller, Jr., and Robin M. Haller, *The Physician and Sexuality in Victorian America* (Urbana: University of Illinois Press, 1974), pp. 191–234; Alex Comfort, *The Anxiety Makers: Some Curious Preoccupations of the Medical Profession* (London: Thomas Nelson and Son, Ltd., 1967), pp. 69–113; Thomas S. Szasz, *The Manufacture of Madness* (London: Routledge & Kegan Paul, 1971), pp. 180–206. See also Robert H. MacDonald, "The Frightful Consequences of Onanism: Notes on the History of a Delusion," *Journal of the History of Ideas* 28 (1967):423–31; and, R.P. Neuman, "Masturbation, Madness, and the Modern Concepts of Childhood and Adolescence," *Journal of Social History* 8 (1975): 1–27.

31. Hare, p. 4.

32. Szasz, p. 139.

33. Benjamin Rush, *Medical Inquiries and Observations upon the Diseases of the Mind* 1812; rprt ed., New York: Hafner Publishing Co., 1962), p. 347.

34. Ibid., p. 33.

35. Hare.

rise to hysterical attacks, asthma, epilepsy, melancholia, mania, suicide, and dementia—often dementia with paralysis.[36]

In the meanwhile, preoccupied with the same problem, British students of insanity had also uncovered the pernicious consequences of the vice. For example, in 1838 Sir William Ellis, then superintendent of Harwell Asylum, concluded that "by far the most frequent cause of fatuity is debility of the brain and nervous system . . . in consequence of the pernicious habit of masturbation." Ellis provided a physiological explanation for this; the act of masturbation, he contended, diverted needed blood from the brain to other portions of the body, thus damaging the cerebellum and bringing on dementia.[37]

An actual case of masturbation eventuating in death is reported by Dr. Alfred Hitchcock in 1842. A young man of twenty-three was noticed to have become timid, dilatory, languid, and lacking in perception. After the onset of jaundice, dyspepsia, and epileptic fits, Dr. Hitchcock was sent for and gained from the man the admission that he had, for the previous six years, been regularly masturbating. "In view of the imbecile and delirious state of his mind," the physician recounts, "I expressed to his father my opinion of the cause of his sickness, and advised his immediate removal to the lunatic hospital. This opinion and advice was rejected by the father, although corroborated by several medical gentlemen who saw the patient, and more positively confirmed by confessions from his ruined son." The patient is reported to have died some five months after this interview, "the body wasted to the most extreme degree of atrophy."[38]

36. Ibid., p. 6.

37. Sir William Ellis, *A Treatise on the Nature, Symptoms, Causes and Treatment of Insanity* (London: Samuel Holdsworth, 1838), p. 336.
   The commonly accepted physiological theory by which masturbation was linked to insanity up to the time that Ellis put forward his hypothesis was that supplied by the Swiss physician Samuel Tissot. In 1758, Tissot published a Latin version of a work translated into French two years later under the title *l'Onanisme, ou Dissertation physique sur les malades produites par la masturbation*; German, English, and Italian translations quickly followed. In it, Tissot argues that the pernicious effects of masturbation on the nervous system are attributable to the discharge of semen—"la liqueur séminale"—causing an *increased* flow of blood to the brain. "This increase of blood explains how these excesses produce insanity. The quantity of blood distending the nerves weakens them; and they are less able to resist impressions, whereby they are enfeebled." (Samuel Tissot, *Onanism: or a Treatise upon the Disorders produced by Masturbation: or the Dangerous Effects of Secret and Excessive Venery*, A. Hume, trans. [London: 1766], p. 61; quoted by Hare, p. 3.)
   R.P. Neuman quotes Tissot as claiming that semen was so essential to the human physiology that the loss of so much as an ounce of it would weaken the body more than the loss of forty ounces of blood. (Neuman, p. 2.)

38. Alfred Hitchcock, "Insanity and Death from Masturbation," *Boston Medical and Surgical Journal* 26 (June 8, 1842):285.

That the result of sexual impurity was such an insidious disease, under which the body and mind tottered and decayed into insanity and death, was an established principle of psychiatry at midcentury. What was lacking, however, was a theory of mental disease within which masturbation could be shown to result in a discrete, identifiable symptomology.

A significant analytic breakthrough in this regard occurred in 1863 when David Skae, a Scottish psychopathologist and physician superintendent of the Royal Edinburgh Asylum, maintained that masturbation brought on a particular and specific variety of insanity, producing characteristic, clearly identifiable symptoms.[39] Skae's classification of the forms of mental disease, first postulated in his book on the subject,[40] was based solely on the assumed causes of insanity, of which there were three specific types: idiocy, epilepsy, and masturbation.[41] In the Morisonian Lectures of 1873,[42] Skae's nosological system was expanded to thirty-four distinct forms of insanity; masturbation remained, but satyriasis and nymphomania, previously classified under masturbational insanity, were made separate entities.[43] Skae's symptomology of masturbation is extensive: nervous debility, mental and physical depression, palpitation of the heart, noises in the head and ears, indecision, impaired sight and memory, indigestion, loss of energy and appetite, pains in the back, timidity, self-distrust, groundless fears, muscular relaxation, a dislike of female society, "the inability to look you straight in the face," suicidal, and sometimes homicidal, impulses, and, occasionally, religious delusions.[44] With respect to a prognosis, much depended on how early in the development of the disease the masturbator came under the care of an alienist. "If these cases are put under proper care and treatment before the mind has become too impaired to exert self-control when reasoned with," Skae notes, "they gener-

---

The belief that masturbation resulted in premature death persisted throughout the whole of the nineteenth century. As late as 1893, one physician writing on the subject recounted several instances of masturbators descending into slow and hideous deaths brought on by the vice. See Nicholas Francis Cooke, *Satan in Society: A Plea for Social Purity* (Chicago: N.C. Smith, 1893), pp. 96—97.

39. Hare, p. 6.

40. David Skae, *The Classification of the Various Forms of Insanity on a Rational and Practical Basis*, Address delivered at the Royal College of Physicians, London, 9th July 1863 (London: 1863).

41. Gregory Zilboorg, *A History of Medical Psychology* (New York: W.W. Norton & Company, Inc., 1941), pp. 420—21.

42. David Skae and T.S. Clouston, "The Morisonian Lectures on Insanity for 1873," *Journal of Mental Science*, Lecture I:19 (October 1873):340—55; Lecture II:19 (January 1874):491—507.

43. Ibid., p. 348.

44. Ibid., pp. 498—99.

ally recover. But when dementia has begun to show itself in impaired memory, and energy, silly vanity, and self-satisfaction, the cases assume a very hopeless aspect, with a tendency to gradually increasing dementia if the vice is persevered in."[45]

Skae's analysis of masturbational insanity as a specific variety of mental disorder was taken up by the great British psychiatrist Henry Maudsley, who, in 1868, published an extensive paper on the "mental derangement brought on by self-abuse."[46] Maudsley distinguishes between the characteristic features of masturbatory insanity when the act is first engaged in by those still in their teens and in cases where the habit continues on into adult life. Among younger masturbators the psychic disorder is easily recognizable. "The miserable sinner whose mind suffers by reason of self-abuse becomes offensively egotistic. . . . His manner is shy, nervous, and suspicious, his dress often untidy or slovenly; there is a want of manliness of appearance as of manliness of feeling. The pupils are often dilated, the breath bad, the face sallow, and the body somewhat emaciated.[47] Maudsley is reluctant to assign the term insanity to this stage of the disease.[48] In the older masturbator, however, the symptoms of complete lunacy are unmistakable and consist in large measure of the symptomology that present-day psychiatry would diagnose as paranoid schizophrenia: violent outbursts of anger and abuse, delusions of persecution, hallucinations, deep gloom and depression, and wild frenzies of passion alternating with moody self-absorption.[49]

The early work of Skae and Maudsley on the relation between masturbation and mental disease had a profound impact on the

45. Ibid., p. 499.

46. Henry Maudsley, "Illustrations of a Variety of Insanity," *Journal of Mental Science* 14 (July 1868): 149–62.

47. Ibid., pp. 153–54.

48. Ibid., p. 154. Insanity due to masturbation at or soon after the age of puberty was, in the 1880s, subsumed under the broader category of *hebephrenia*, the mental derangement of adolescence. This classification originated with the German psychiatrist Ewald Hecker in 1871; its first systematic description in the United States was given by William A. Hammond, surgeon general of the Union Army during the Civil War and later president of the American Neurological Society, in his *Treatise on Insanity in Its Medical Relations* (New York: Appleton, 1883). In an article on the subject that appeared some years later, Hammond notes that: ". . . masturbation, when practiced to excess, may modify to a greater or lesser degree the symptoms of hebephrenia, but the product is not entitled to be considered a separate form of mental derangement. The *insanity of masturbation* is simply hebephrenia with the additional phenomena due to excessive onanism." ("Hebephrenia—Mental Derangement of Puberty," *Virginia Medical Monthly* 19 [April 1892]:6–7.)

49. Maudsley, pp. 156–61.

course of nineteenth century psychiatry in Britain and the United States.[50] Indeed, masturbation as a proximate cause of insanity was accepted by a significant percentage of the American medical profession into the early twentieth century, even while the thesis was losing currency among more observant psychological clinicians. Medical journals in the United States are filled with articles on the evils of the practice, despite the obvious absence of any scientific justification for these conclusions. A strikingly heterogeneous collection of symptoms were assigned to the disease, all of which were comprehended under one causal mechanism. That this was possible reflects on the nature of the category of mental disease however used. As an historian of medicine recently pointed out:

> Although vice and virtue are not equivalent to disease and health, they bear a direct relation to these concepts. Insofar as a vice is taken to be a deviation from an ideal of human perfection, or "well-being," it can be translated into disease language. In shifting to disease language, one no longer speaks in moralistic terms (e.g., "You are evil") but one speaks in terms of a deviation from a norm which implies a degree of imperfection (e.g., "You are a deviant"). The shift is from an explicitly ethical language to a language of natural teleology. To be ill is to fail to realize the perfection of an ideal type; to be sick is to be defective rather than to be evil.[51]

American psychiatry particularly seized on the ability to shift from the language of ethics to the language of science in dealing with sexual behavior. Once "the mind who would choose to act immorally" became, in the language of psychiatry, the diseased mind, it lay open to "treatment" and "cure" and, under the guise of enforcers of mental health, psychiatrists and physicians became the enforcers of sexual morality. The direction of psychological medicine in the United States was clearly to provide this scientific basis for the prevailing moral orthodoxy.

Toward this end, masturbation was a singularly appealing subject of study for American medicine because, once shown to be pathogenic, it laid open the possibility that all sexual behavior differing from orthodox morality was also disease-causing and strongly suggested that all deviations from acceptable sexual practice were psychic perversions of the natural sexual function.

In diagnosing the causes of mental and physical disorders, the same clinical acumen shown by Skae and Maudsley was displayed by

50. Hare, p. 7.

51. H. Tristram Engelhart, Jr., "The Disease of Masturbation: Values and the Concept of Disease," *Bulletin of the History of Medicine* 48 (1974):247–48.

American psychiatrists and doctors, the great bulk of whom, by the 1870s, accepted the theory that masturbation brought on dementia. In 1876 Dr. A. Jacobi, clinical professor of diseases of children at the College of Physicians and Surgeons in New York, observed that children who masturbated were given to headaches, convulsive attacks, trigeminal neuralgia, and, generally, to severe irritation of the whole nervous system.[52] Continued overexcitation of the genital nerve centers in the young, he concluded, could eventuate only in hysteria and dementia.

Three years after the appearance of Jacobi's article, Dr. Allen Hagenbach, one of the senior physicians at the Cook County Hospital for the Insane, wrote that of the 800 male inmates admitted to the hospital since its opening in 1860, the exciting cause of insanity in 49 was masturbation.[53] The author describes symptoms similar to those observed previously by Skae and Maudsley, with the disease passing through two stages, the first, or conscious, stage terminating in a second, or unconscious stage, "when owing to impaired mental and especially weakened volitional powers" reform is impossible and dementia and death result.[54]

More importantly, Dr. Hagenbach touches upon a theme that became of significant interest to other alienists over the succeeding thirty years, that part of the clinical character of masturbatory insanity in some cases included an increased morbidity of the sexual sense before the onset of complete dementia, which resulted in further perversion of the sexual instinct. He notes the case of a masturbator who began forming morbid attachments for another male, presumably because he was unable to control his passions and was driven to frenzy by habitual practice of the vice.[55] The theory that masturbation lay at the root of other sexual perversions was taken up by a number of subsequent medical writers and instilled new life into the notion that masturbation would cause severe harm to those who indulged in it, at the same time offering a causal mechanism for all sexual degeneracy.

It proved a simple matter for psychiatry to show a connection between masturbation among females and nymphomania. Since the normal nonaberrant sexual state of women was one in which no

52. A Jacobi, "On Masturbation and Hysteria in Young Children," *The American Journal of Obstetrics and Diseases of Women and Children* 8 (February 1876):595–606; 9 (June 1876):218–38.

53. Allen Hagenbach, "Masturbation as a Cause of Insanity," *Journal of Nervous and Mental Disease* 6 (October 1879):603.

54. Ibid., pp. 607–608.

55. Ibid., p. 606.

gratification was found, almost any indication of sexual pleasure exhibited by women could be taken as a perversion of their natural sexual condition. That women had no natural sexual drive was an accepted tenet of nineteenth century medicine. For example, this is what a professor of physiology and pathological histology of some eminence had to say on the subject of impotence in women:

> The ideal young woman is almost necessarily impotent. From time immemorial the prerequisites in her moral and social qualifications have been modesty and chastity. Those lapses from absolutely virtuous living that in the male are condoned as charming little irregularities, when indulged in on her part, invariably call down upon her luckless personality a damnation worse than death, at the same time often barring her from her highest mission—maternity. That a universal law, acting through the ages, calling for unquestioned chastity in the maid and mother, should have had its effect in a large proportion of the sex in modifying the sexual organs and desires is not surprising; that it has not absolutely extirpated sensuality is perhaps more surprising.[56]

Sexual norms have become scientific truths, and deviations from propriety, diseases. Nowhere is this translation from vice to disease more palpable than in the observed effects of masturbation on the two sexes. The consequences masturbation had for males and females were, clinicians found, significantly different; but what they had in common was the socially unacceptable—hence "diseased"—nature of the resultant behavior. "The boy masturbator," writes a prominent American psychiatrist,

> usually becomes shy, and above all when in presence of female company. The girl masturbator, while shy in general society, seeks out persons of the opposite sex, makes advances to boys, and may even seduce them. To

56. E.R. Palmer, "A Contribution to the Physiology of Sexual Impotence," *New York Medical Journal* 56 (July 2, 1892):5—6.
American physicians were heavily influenced by the work of Dr. William Acton, a respected British venereologist and author of one of the most influential texts on the proper functioning and disorders of the reproductive organs. First published in 1857, the book went through eight American editions by 1895. With respect to female sexuality Acton noted that "the majority of women (happily for society) are not very much troubled with sexual feeling of any kind." Scientific observation leads one to conclude, he continues, that "there are many females who never feel any sexual excitement whatever." (William Acton, *The Functions and Disorders of the Reproductive Organs*, 7th ed. [Philadelphia: P. Blakiston, Son & Co., 1888], pp. 208—10.) Acton's conclusions on this and a variety of other sexual subjects are extensively discussed in Steven Marcus, *The Other Victorians: A Study of Sexuality and Pornography in Mid-Nineteenth Century England* (New York: Basic Books, 1966); and in Comfort, pp. 38—60.

some extent this difference between the two sexes is maintained through-out later life. The adolescent and adult male masturbator, with a few exceptions,. . . . has in the earlier period of his vice a shyness before, and in later ones an aversion to women. The adolescent and adult female onanist usually entertains ideas of an erotic character, develops foolish marriage notions, and may throw away all reserve before males.[57]

A firm theoretical foundation supplying the causal link between masturbation, sexual excess, and the more spectacular sexual perversions such as nymphomania was offered by the American neurologist George M. Beard, who in 1869 published his first paper on a neurological disorder to which he supplied the term "neurasthenia."[58] Beard's first essay was supplemented by a more extensive one that appeared ten years later[59] and finally was expanded to book length in 1880.[60] Neurasthenia, or nervous exhaustion, Beard defined as being a chronic functional disease of the nervous system marked by abnormal susceptibility to internal and external irritants, liability to quick exhaustion, deficiency of reserve, and the lack of controlling powers, both physical and mental. The disorder he regards as increasingly frequent "among the in-door class of civilized countries," and particularly common to the United States.[61] The symptomology is extensive and includes headache, irritability, lack of concentration, morbid fears, insomnia, nervous chills, palpitations of the heart, sweating hands and feet, tremulous pulse, and heaviness of the loins and limbs.[62] Untreated, neurasthenia could result in, among other things, melancholic insanity.

The frailty of the reproductive systems of Americans, Beard felt, required sexual restraint lest the sexual sense be overexcited and the delicate balance of the nervous system be disturbed and debilitated. "One of the many evils of our time," he writes,

is, that the habit of self-abuse is on the increase, and that men are more indulgent than formerly. Hence the increase of nervous diseases that are

57. E.C. Spitzka, "Cases of Masturbation (Masturbatic Insanity)," *Journal of Mental Science* 33 (April 1887):61.

58. George M. Beard, "Neurasthenia, or Nervous Exhaustion," *Boston Medical and Surgical Journal* 80 (April 29, 1869):217–21.

59. George M. Beard, "American Nervousness: Its Philosophy and Treatment," *Virginia Medical Monthly* 6 (July 1879):253–76.

60. George M. Beard, *A Practical Treatise on Nervous Exhaustion (Neurasthenia)* (New York: William Wood, 1880). I have consulted a later edition, edited and with notes and additions by A.D. Rockwell (New York: E.B. Treat, 1892).

61. Ibid., p. 23.

62. Ibid., pp. 34–107.

connected with the genital functions; and hence the terrific results that sometimes follow early begun and long-continued masturbation. But so far as can be learned from all sources of information on these difficult themes, it would appear that among savages and the semi-civilized, sexual abuse, both in a natural and unnatural way, is carried to a far higher degree, on the average, than among the civilized; we cannot, indeed, bear these abuses as our fathers could. The observation . . . that it requires a strong constitution to be dissipated, is a just and sound one. The modern young man is not strong enough to abuse himself as perhaps he would be willing to do, or as his ancestor did. Both natural and unnatural methods of sexual indulgence react with fearful and almost immediate power on the nervous system, . . .[63]

Masturbation and sexual indulgence—both "natural" and "unnatural"—might have proved physiologically manageable for those who lived a hundred years earlier, but its results on the constitutions of nineteenth century Americans were nothing less than disastrous.

In 1884 Beard's work on sexual neurasthenia was posthumously published, and it is here that he presents a fuller version of his theory of nervous disease relating specifically to sexual behavior. Of masturbation he writes that "when long kept up it is the cause of insanity, usually of the form classed under melancholia, in quite a proportion of the cases that enter our asylums."[64] With respect to nymphomania, erotomania (lustful thoughts), and satyriasis, "these desires, though not necessarily, usually depend on sexual neurasthenia, although they may be in some degree and in some cases complicated with it."[65] Beard's causal theory of homosexuality is of particular interest because of its impact on contemporaneous American psychiatry. Homosexuality, he claimed, was occasioned by debilitation and irritation of the nervous system, either through masturbation or excessive venery, leading to a species of nervous disease in which the system seeks relief in the condition opposite to that which brings on the disorder. "Exhaustion of the sexual organs, through excess or masturbation," he theorizes,

brings on at first indifference to the opposite sex, then positive fear or dread of normal intercourse; confirmed, long-standing masturbators of

63. Beard, "American Nervousness," p. 256.
64. George M. Beard, *Sexual Neurasthenia (Nervous Exhaustion)*, ed. A.D. Rockwell (New York: E.B. Treat, 1891), p. 93. One of Beard's followers went so far as to link neurasthenia caused by masturbation with the general paresis of tertiary syphilis. See F.B. Bishop, "Sexual Neurasthenia as it Stands in Relation to the Border-Land of Insanity, and Insanity in General," *Virginia Medical Monthly* 18 (December 1891):754.
65. Beard, *Sexual Neurasthenia*, p. 98.

either sex care little or not at all for the opposite sex; are more likely to fear than to enjoy their presence, and are especially terrified by the thought of sexual connection; similarly, excess in a normal way tends to make us hate the partners in our excess; the unhappiest marriages are those where there is the greatest indulgence; irritability, aversion, positive hatred and disgust toward the object of our former love follow protracted debauches. The subjects of these excesses go through the stages of indifference and of fear, and complete the circle; the sex is perverted; they hate the opposite sex, and love their own; men become women, and women men, in their tastes, conduct, character, feelings, and behavior. Such, as appears to me, is the psychology of sexual perversion, whenever and wherever found.[66]

The notion of sexual excess and masturbation proliferating into a broader spectrum of perversions, morally less acceptable and hence more clearly pathological, was quickly adopted by Beard's contemporaries in the last two decades of the century.[67] At the same time, the earlier theory of masturbatory insanity as propounded by Skae and Maudsley was losing ground. The work of Edward Spitzka seems to indicate a turning point in the treatment of masturbation by American psychiatry. Although Spitzka, one of the founders of the New York Neurological Society and a highly respected neuropathologist, rejected Beard's concept of neurasthenia as nonsensical and contined to adhere to the Skae-Maudsley thesis, he too observed that masturbation could, in certain instances, eventuate in sexual perversion. Of the twenty-eight cases of masturbatory insanity he discusses in an extensive monograph on the subject,[68] two showed sexual perversion as part of their clinical character and two more manifested what he calls "moral perversion" with sexual overtones.[69] Indeed, as Spitzka elsewhere observes, "unlimited indulgence and absence of responsibility are competent to make sexual monsters out of mere voluptuaries."[70] Following the publication of Spitzka's paper in

66. Ibid., pp. 106–107.

67. "Within a decade of Beard's death in 1883," an historian of medicine observed: ". . . the diagnosis of nervous exhaustion had become part of the office furniture of most physicians. Few textbooks and systems of medicine failed to discuss it, and in 1893 neurasthenia received its ultimate legitimatization—the publication of a German *Handbuch der Neurasthenie*." (Charles E. Rosenberg, "The Place of George M. Beard in Nineteenth-Century Psychiatry," *Bulletin of the History of Medicine* 36 [1962]:258.)

68. Edward Spitzka, "Cases of Masturbation (Masturbatic Insanity)," *Journal of Mental Science* 33 (April 1887):57–73; (July 1887):238–54; (October 1887): 395–401; 34 (April 1888):52–61; (July 1888):216–25.

69. Ibid., 33 (April 1887): foldout between 62 and 63.

70. Quoted in James G. Kiernan, "Psychological Aspects of the Sexual Appetite," *Alienist and Neurologist* 12 (April 1891):199.

1887–1888, few psychiatrists continued to accept the older form of the doctrine of masturbatory insanity. Henceforth most psychiatrists in the United States adopted some variation of Beard's theory that masturbation was causally associated with severe aberrations of the sexual instinct through perturbations and overexcitations of the genital nerve center, leading to derangement of the sexual sense.

For example, one of the most prominent American clinicians of sexual perversion, J.G. Kiernan, superintendent of the Cook County Hospital for the Insane and professor of forensic medicine in Chicago, adopted Beard's hypothesis of sexual exhaustion as the link between masturbation, sexual excess, and perversion. In classifying the sexual aberrations, Kiernan held that there is a category of vices—such as pederasty, necrophilia, and oral-genital contacts—that sprang from "conditions in which sated libertines seek abnormal stimuli for exhausted sexual appetite."[71]

It is illustrative of the success of Beard's hypothesis that in 1889 G.F. Lydston, possibly the foremost American sexual pathologist, accommodated the neurasthenic theory in his etiological classification of perversion. Lydston's nosology was divided into two principal classes, "congenital, and perhaps hereditary, sexual perversion," and "acquired sexual perversion," of which one subgroup was clearly Beardian: "sexual perversion from over-stimulation of the nerves of sexual sensibility and the receptive sexual centres, incidental to sexual excesses and masturbation."[72] To this category could be charged instances of homosexuality, bestiality, the desire for "abnormal methods of gratification," satyriasis, and nymphomania.[73]

A significant proportion of the American medical profession were strong adherents of the theory linking masturbation and sexual deviance after the work of specialists in the area confirmed Beard's thesis. It is therefore not surprising that "over-stimulation of the sexual centers brought on by masturbation" was observed to be the cause of a case of lesbianism reported in an editorial in a prominent medical journal in 1892;[74] it was found to be responsible for the sadism,

71. Kiernan, letter to the editor, *Detroit Lancet* 8 (September 1884):121. Kiernan further explains: "It should be remembered that repeated stimulation tends to exhaust the power of nerves to respond to the normal stimulation; for this reason the sated voluptuary seeks to arouse his flagging sexual system by unwonted stimuli." Kiernan offers a lengthier analysis of this view in two subsequent essays. See his "Psychological Aspects of the Sexual Appetite," pp. 188–219; and "Psychical Treatment of Congenital Sexual Inversion," *Review of Insanity and Nervous Disease* 4 (June 1894):293–95.

72. G. Frank Lydston, "Sexual Perversion, Satyriasis and Nymphomania," *Medical and Surgical Reporter* 61 (September 7, 1889):254.

73. Ibid., 253–58; (September 14, 1889):281–85.

74. Editorial, *Medical Standard* 11 (March 1892):79–80.

pederasty, and bestiality that physicians claimed were common
among Southern Negroes;[75] and in 1896, it was offered as one of the
contributing causes of the rampant pederasty practiced among inmates at the New York State Reformatory at Elmira, in an article
penned by its chief physician.[76]

In 1905 the noted psychiatrist William Lee Howard offered a further example of "the insidious and baneful effects of masturbation"
on a girl who, in later life, became bisexual. When fourteen years old,
Howard recounts, the girl was sent to a boarding school some distance from her home. While on the journey, the train became snow-
bound and the passengers took shelter in a nearby town. There a
woman passenger "took a motherly interest in the child." "The rest
of the story is soon told," notes Howard. "That night, the weak,
undeveloped sexual cells of the cortex were awakened—directed in
the wrong channel, and a child masturbator with psychic imaginings
and fancies of women constantly arising, was the result. These in-
verted pictures kept up until the woman reached the age of about
thirty, when the condition gradually made its appearance. . . . In this
case," the psychiatrist concludes, "we have an undoubted case of
inversion through acquirement."[77]

It should be noted that Howard is not suggesting anything untoward in the behavior of the older woman toward his patient; the
proximity of her interest in the young girl to the child's masturbatory act alone seems to have been sufficient to direct her desires into
a perverse channel. Clearly, awakening the weak, undeveloped sexual
cells of the cortex was fraught with danger.

Howard's conclusions were by no means atypical of psychiatric
opinion in the first decade of the new century. Almost one hundred
years after the birth of the profession in the United States, masturbation was as firmly condemned by medical opinion as it had been
when Rush penned his immortal words in 1812. Sexual behavior
differing from the Protestant orthodoxy, narrowly conceived, was
entrenched in the medical and psychiatric schema as products of
diseased minds desperately in need of the physical and mental therapy that the medical profession alone could offer.

Since masturbation was conceived of as seriously harmful to the

75. Elliott T. Brady, "Perversion of Sexual Instinct—Sadism in Southern
Negroes—Its Remedy, Castration," *Virginia Medical Monthly* 20 (June 1893):
277–82.

76. Hamilton D. Wey, "Morbid Sensuality in a Reformatory," *Chicago Medical Recorder* 10 (February 1896):143–45.

77. William Lee Howard, "Masturbation in the Young Girl the Cause of
Acquired Sexual Perversion," *Buffalo Medical Journal* 61 (December 1905):
291–92.

body and mind and as the exciting cause of a series of far more severe psychological disorders, it is understandable that psychological and medical practitioners were prepared to employ radical methods of treatment if they were found necessary to avoid such dire consequences. The history of the treatment of masturbation is testament to the atrocities that men, otherwise of good will, are prepared to perpetrate in the name of saving damned souls. Those who are familiar with Alex Comfort's account of the methods employed to deal with masturbators[78] will have already been apprised of how commonly surgical interventions and physical restraints were resorted to during the nineteenth century. It is in their treatment of sexual offenders that the professions whose putative purpose was to heal the sick most clearly showed the punitive aspect of their role. Under the guise of therapy, psychiatrists and physicians—convinced of the necessity of stamping out sexual deviance in general and masturbation in particular and faced with habitual offenders for whom moral exhortation did no good—turned to forcible restraint and, if need be, to genital mutilation to prevent the further degeneration of their patients.

Advocacy of these extreme measures was not confined to only a few of the particularly zealous. Throughout a good part of the nineteenth century, a substantial number of physicians supported radical therapeutic techniques in dealing with masturbation. Indeed, there seems to have been an escalation in the severity of treatment over time. While up to 1850 it was still common to prescribe bland diets, vigorous exercise, and a host of drugs, many of which were patented as "cures" for chronic onanism, by midcentury surgical interventions and the use of physical restraints were supported by fully three-quarters of the medical profession in the United States.[79]

Surgery as a repressive measure for masturbation is apparently the invention of the British physician Isaac Baker Brown who, in 1858, introduced the operation of clitoridectomy.[80] His overenthusiastic support for this procedure led to his being expelled from the Obstetrical Society in 1867, after a series of contentious debates. The operation subsequently fell into some disrepute in England as a standard method of treating female masturbators except in the more "severe" cases. Even after the operation lost favor with the British medical profession, however, it seems to have remained a viable therapeutic tool in America. Thus, in 1877 one American physician notes that he would not hesitate to resort to clitoridectomy to save a patient from

---

78. Comfort, pp. 95–110.
79. Spitz, p. 122.
80. Ibid.; and Comfort, p. 101.

the pernicious consequences of the habit "should all else prove unavailing," although the preferred method of treatment involved the administration of camphor, chloral, the bromides, belladonna, and digitalis.[81] Six years later, in 1883, Dr. Joseph Howe recommended the operation in instances of chronic masturbation complicated by symptoms of nymphomania.[82]

A renewed interest in clitoridectomy seems to have been sparked by the connection made between masturbation and the more serious sexual perversions in the 1880s and 1890s. In 1894, for example, Dr. A.J. Bloch, visiting surgeon at the Charity Hospital in New Orleans, published a paper on sexual perversion in women in which he characterized masturbation as a "moral leprosy" of late reaching epidemic proportions. "Its taint," he remarks, "is entering into the homes of our most elegant and refined; this contagion exists in our schools, seminaries and asylums; its handiwork is shown by our many obscure and unrecognized nervous disorders. It is not only necessary that we pursue a curative course, but prophylactic measures should be used, and to us belongs this responsibility."[83]

Clitoridectomy had the advantage, we assume, of serving both curatively and prophylactically, for Bloch clearly admired the operation. He describes an instance of masturbation in a girl of two and a half years that he successfully treated by excision of the clitoris.[84]

A somewhat similar case is reported several months later by Dr. Alvin Eyer, surgeon at St. John's Hospital in Cleveland. A girl of seven was found engaged in habitual masturbation despite "thorough and complete" medical treatment which included blistering and severe cauterization of the clitoris and vagina. The physician decided that a clitoridectomy was indicated, whereupon "the operation was performed, care being taken that the entire organ, with a considerable portion of its two crura, was removed." Both mother and doctor were delighted with the results.[85]

Physicians who were loathe to surgically intervene had at their disposal a host of other methods by which they could cope with female masturbators. These ran the gamut from simply tying the hands at night to more medieval contraptions such as the "girdle of chastity,"

81. C.B. Miller, "Masturbation," *American Practitioner* 15 (May 1877): 285–86.

82. Joseph W. Howe, *Excessive Venery, Masturbation, and Continence* (New York: Bermingham & Company, 1883), pp. 110–11.

83. A.J. Bloch, "Sexual Perversion in the Female," *New Orleans Medical and Surgical Journal* 22 (July 1894):1.

84. Ibid., p. 4.

85. Alvin Eyer, "Clitoridectomy for the Cure of Certain Cases of Masturbation in Young Girls," *International Medical Magazine* 3 (November 1894):261.

originally developed by Dr. John Moodie of Edinburgh in 1848. In the United States, such girdles were easily available from medical supply houses into the twentieth century and, for a time, could be found for sale in the Sears-Roebuck catalogues.

Given nineteenth century attitudes toward women, it should be noted, the problem of paramount concern to the medical profession in the United States was not that of masturbation in the female—who, after all, was only in the most unusual instances capable of any but the barest sexuality—but of the vice when practiced among males. Here a variety of measures were applied to discourage the habitual offender.

Infibulation seems to have been one of the more popular methods of treatment in the United States and Britain in the 1870s. It was a leading topic of discussion at one of the quarterly meetings of the British Medico-Psychological Association in 1876, where the superintendent of the Glasgow Royal Asylum reported satisfactory results in a dozen instances where the operation was performed.[86] The operation was suggested by the fact that the prepuce was anatomically necessary for erection of the penis. Infibulation, as described by the superintendent, consisted of piercing the prepuce at the root of the glans with a silver needle, the ends of which were then tied together. The result, we are informed, was erections to painful as to be practically impossible, and an almost certain end to masturbation among the patients upon whom he had operated.[87]

In 1878, Dr. James Hyde of Chicago joined Dr. Yellowlees of the Glasgow Asylum in championing the procedure. He reported a case of chronic masturbation treated in a similar manner and its successful issue.[88] Despite its success, however, Dr. Hyde was not wedded to infibulation as the only therapeutic technique worthy of consideration. In the same article he makes mention of an instance of habitual onanism in a young man that was effectively treated by leeching. As each attack of masturbation was about to recur, he recounts, leeches, about fifteen in number, were applied to the nape of the patient's neck. Repetition of this therapy over the course of two months proved successful and the patient is reported to have quit his habit.[89]

86. D. Yellowlees, "Masturbation," *Journal of Mental Science* 22 (July 1876):336–37.

87. Ibid., p. 337.

88. James Hyde, "Precocious and Other Phenomena of Sexual Orgasm," *Chicago Medical Journal and Examiner* 36 (June 1878):582. Professor Jacobi of the College of Physicians and Surgeons and a contemporary of Dr. Hyde's held that infibulation could well "be replaced by an artificial sore on the surface of the penis," with equal success. (Jacobi, p. 606.)

89. Hyde, p. 585.

For physicians who found it difficult to acquire silver wire or who did not have a ready access to leeches, a large number of mechanical devices were employed to restrain patients from continued self-abuse. One of the more notorious authors of the cautionary literature that flooded the United States during the second half of the century mentions a few, by way of warning to the chronic onanist of what can be expected should he persist in his habit; these include being placed in a strait jacket, having the hands fastened behind one's back, tying the hands to the posts of the bed, or fastening them by ropes or chains to rings in the wall.[90]

One of the leading psychiatrists of the period, Dr. Charles Dana, professor of nervous and mental diseases at the New York Post-Graduate School, reported success using a variety of different measures, including a splint of his own contrivance "by which the legs were kept apart and immovable."[91] In a more intractable case of a young man suffering from adolescent neurasthenia brought on by nocturnal masturbation, several methods were tried with negative results, including first tying the hands behind him at bedtime and, when this failed, tying the hands to the bedposts above his head; in both instances the patient managed to untie the knots and free himself. "Finally," Professor Dana continues, "I put him in the masturbation drawers, devised by my colleague, Professor Graeme M. Hammond. These consist of strong canvas drawers, fastened about the waist with steel bands, the sides of which are padlocked. The patient locked himself in the drawers every night, hid the key, and his pollutions ceased."[92]

Each physician seems to have had his own favorite method of dealing with the practice. Dr. Joseph Howe, professor of medicine at New York University and author of a widely read work on masturbation, regarded the use of electricity as the most efficacious remedial agent for combatting the vice. "I have used it invariably in every case which has come under my care," he writes, "and have rarely found it to fail in accomplishing all that is claimed for it." A typical treatment is described:

> The applications of electricity are best made when the patient is in a recumbent posture, though they can readily be given while the patient is sitting or standing. When the battery is ready for use and the patient's hips, back and genitals exposed, the *urethral electrode* insulated to within

90. Sylvanus Stall, *What a Young Boy Ought to Know* (Philadelphia: Vir Publishing Company, 1887), p. 117.

91. Charles L. Dana, "On Certain Sexual Neuroses," *Medical and Surgical Reporter* 65 (August 15, 1891):244.

92. Ibid.

an inch of its point is attached to the negative pole of the battery. The other electrode with a moistened sponge on its extremity is attached to the positive pole. The urethral electrode well oiled and warmed is slowly introduced through the urethral canal to the neck of the bladder, while the sponge covered electrode is placed over the genito-spinal center at the junction of the dorsal with the lumbar vertebrae, and moved up and down over the vertebral column as far as the tip of the coccyx. While the sponge is being moved over these parts the urethral electrode is slowly withdrawn until its point reaches the bulbous portion of the urethra. There it is allowed to remain until the termination of the *séance*.[93]

"Séances" were to last some seven or eight minutes, enough time to totally desensitize the urethral passage. The reader is assured that these treatments, when applied regularly for about two months, invariably produce the desired results. Masturbation ceases, virile power is increased, and the patient's health restored.

Not all physicians were as confident as was Dr. Howe in the efficacy of electrical devices in halting the habit. Silver wires through the foreskin, ropes, splints, plaster casts, canvas drawers, even egg-shaped pessaries inserted into the rectum which pressed on the ejaculatory ducts—all had the overwhelming disadvantage that they could be removed and the habit renewed. There was only one certain road to a masturbation-free, sexually pure life and that was through direct genital mutilation that physiologically prevented emission. Toward this end, several different approaches were employed, including sectioning the dorsal nerves of the penis,[94] cauterizing the genitalia,[95] and tying the spermatic ducts.[96]

93. Howe, p. 254.

94. See, for example, Edgar J. Spratling, "Masturbation in the Adult," *Medical Record* 48 (September 28, 1895):442–43. Spratling contends that, although sectioning the dorsal nerves is a rational procedure in the treatment of masturbation, it is somewhat too radical for constant, routine practice.
      The same operation was also employed as a therapeutic technique for homosexuality. See "The Gentleman Degenerate: A Homosexualist's Self Description and Self-Applied Title," *Alienist and Neurologist* 25 (February 1904):68.

95. The favored method of cauterizing the genitalia apparently involved catheterization of the urethra with silver nitrate, the effect of which would be to burn it and thus make it insensible. It is highly recommended by certain physicians who observed that even chronic masturbators halted the habit once treatments began. See L.L. Hale, and others, letters to the editor under the title "Involuntary Seminal Emissions," *Medical World* 4 (August 1886):274–76; and Dana, pp. 244–45. Bernard Sachs, onetime president of the American Neurological Association and professor of mental and nervous diseases at the New York Polyclinic, writes that "actual cautery to the spine and even to the genitals are the only possible means of effecting a cure" for masturbation. (Sachs, *A Treatise on the Nervous Diseases of Children* [New York: William Wood and Company, 1905], p. 540.)

96. The technique was used successfully in a case dating back to 1869. Some two decades later the method had been perfected and involved sectioning the

Even these mutilations were not sufficiently severe for some members of the medical profession. In 1894, Dr. F. Hoyt Pilcher, superintendent of the Kansas State Institution for Feeble-Minded Children at Winfield, instituted the ultimate treatment for the vice by castrating eleven boys consigned to his charge on the ground that they were confirmed masturbators. A howl was raised in several of the Kansas newspapers at the barbarity of the treatment; one unfriendly newspaper account went so far as to carry the story under the banner, "Diabolism at the Imbecile Asylum," and claimed that Dr. Pilcher had treated his patients no better than "the farmer treats his hogs in the Spring of the year."[97]

The medical and psychiatric professions, however, were quick to rush to the superintendent's defense. The *Kansas Medical Journal* immediately launched an attack on the lay press for making far too much of the incident. "The political wail," it editorialized, "is amusing when the facts in the case are seen through plain glasses."

> Viewed from a humanitarian standpoint, what do these newspaper accounts tell us? That a number of imbecile youth were castrated. They were confirmed masturbators—unless the attendant was with them, and even if his back was turned to them while in his presence they would commit the act. This abuse weakened the already imbecile mind, and destroyed the body. The practice is loathsome, disgusting, humiliating and destructive of all self-respect and decency, and had a bad moral effect on the whole school.[98]

To the objection raised by another newspaper that Dr. Pilcher's predecessor as superintendent had employed nothing harsher than moral suasion and the strait jacket in similar cases,[99] the *Journal* replied:

> Dr. Pilcher, like a brave and capable man, sought something better. There could be much saved from such wrecks. He could give back a restored mind and robust health, a bestial function destroyed, and he did it. He called around him a council of competent medical men; they determined on the operations, for here was cure, and the operations were performed, and for which he should have the profound respect and acknowledgement of the State, humanity, and kindred.[100]

---

ducts midway between the external inguinal ring and the testes. See Robert J. Preston, "Sexual Vices—There Relation to Insanity—Causative or Consequent," *Virginia Medical Monthly* 19 (June 1892):201.

97. *Topeka Capital*, Sunday, 26 August 1894. See, also, the *Winfield* (Kansas) *Courier*, Friday, 24 August 1894.

98. Editorial, *Kansas Medical Journal* 6 (September 1, 1894):455–56.

99. *Topeka Lance*, Saturday, 1 September 1894.

100. Editorial, *Kansas Medical Journal* 6 (September 8, 1894):471.

The prestigious *American Journal of Insanity* added its influential voice and editorially commented that "from a medical point of view the achievements of [Dr. Pilcher] are highly interesting." It added: "We shall hope to hear further from Doctor Pilcher, and we trust the benefits observed in nine of the eleven boys may be permanent. . . . We believe these are appropriate cases for study and operation, and are in sympathy with every effort in which science and humanity combine for discovery of new ways of benefit to the race."[101]

Even physicians writing in the lay press rushed to support the actions of the superintendent. Dr. Henry Roby of Topeka, who edited a department titled "The Family Doctor" for the *Kansas Farmer* held that

> the presumption of both law and science is in favor of the doctor. . . . Emasculation is not a crime when done to save a life, or to cure an insanity or an imbecility, as it often is. It is no crime when it is done to restrain a diseased boy from an otherwise incurable tendency to self-destruction, either of suicide or the sure damnation of an unchecked vice.[102]

So vocal and so overwhelming was the support tendered Pilcher by his brethren that by the spring of the following year, an article in the *Pacific Medical Journal* could report that "as was expected the political press raised a great howl . . . but the medical profession sustained him and he has been further supported by his board of trustees."[103]

Dr. Pilcher's was not the first such surgical intervention employed as a cure for masturbation, but its sensational nature occasioned much professional interest in the operation. The *Texas Medical Journal*, for example, noted that the publicity attending the events at Winfield clearly indicated that there was a growing sentiment among physicians and psychiatrists in favor of castration, "not only for disease, but as a prophylactic against a long train of evils, and particularly against the hereditary transmission of vice, disease, and the propensity to crime." Unfortunately, the *Journal* pointed out, the public was not yet in full agreement with the profession and would have to be educated in this respect.[104]

Therapeutic castration for masturbation had been employed previ-

101. Editorial, *American Journal of Insanity* 51 (April 1895):581. In July 1921, the *American Journal of Insanity* was renamed the *American Journal of Psychiatry*.

102. Quoted in the *Texas Medical Journal* 10 (November 1894):239.

103. A.E. Osborne, "Castrating to Cure Masturbation," *Pacific Medical Journal* 38 (March 1895):151.

104. "Emasculation of Masturbators—Is It Justifiable?" *Texas Medical Journal* 10 (November 1894):239.

ously, but with indifferent results.[105] An instance is reported by Dr. Robert Preston, superintendent of the Southwestern Virginia Asylum, where "a young man, at his earnest request, had been castrated in 1885 by his physicians in Bland county, Va., for the cure of masturbation." The patient subsequently came under Dr. Preston's observation at the Southwestern Asylum. At that time, the doctor reports, "he experienced no relief and no diminution in sexual power or desire."[106] This finding was sustained by Dr. A.E. Osborne, superintendent of the California Home for Feeble-Minded Children, who recounts a similar instance where a chronic masturbator was castrated. "The operation as a cure," concludes Dr. Osborne, "had been a total failure."[107]

Why, then, this renewed interest in the procedure in the 1890s? The answer, or a significant part of it, can, I think, be found in a paper delivered before the International Medico-Legal Congress in August 1893, by Dr. F.E. Daniel. The paper received enormous publicity; it was offered before the American Medico-Legal Society in New York in October of that year, and in December was published in no fewer than three medical journals—the *Medico-Legal Journal*, the *Psychological Bulletin*, and the *Texas Medical Journal*, of which Dr. Daniel was editor.[108] In it Dr. Daniel was injudicious enough to drop the pretense of employing castration as a therapeutic measure for masturbation. Rather, he suggested the procedure be used primarily as a *punishment* for *all* sexual perverts, including habitual masturbators. "It is not alone in asylums," he holds, "that castration should be done. . . . Rape, sodomy, bestiality, pederasty and habitual masturbation should be made crimes or misdemeanors, punishable by forfeiture of all rights, including that of procreation; in short by castration, or castration *plus* other penalties, according to the gravity of the offense."[109]

When Daniel's paper appeared in 1893, American psychiatry was

---

105. This, despite the *Kansas Medical Journal*'s insistence that "these operations are old as the profession, are the remedy, and only remedy for extreme and reprobate cases [of onanism], recognized as legitimate in the profession, and constantly practiced by men eminent in standing and learning." (Editorial *Kansas Medical Journal* 6 [September 8, 1894]:471.)

106. Robert Preston, "Sexual Vices—Their Relation to Insanity—Causative or Consequent," p. 200.

107. Osborne, p. 152.

108. F.E. Daniel, "Castration of Sexual Perverts," *Texas Medical Journal* 9 (December 1893):255–68. In April 1894, a two page précis of the article was carried in the *Medical Record*. Daniel's sentiments were of such long-standing interest to the profession that the *Texas Medical Journal* reprinted the article twenty years later (27 [April 1912]:369–85).

109. Ibid., p. 267.

in the midst of undergoing a shift in emphasis away from the view that sexual disorders were occasioned by environmentally determined perversions of the will that were open to successful treatment. The inability of the profession to actually cure masturbators and other sexual deviants, together with the growing proportion of seemingly hopeless cases filling the asylums, encouraged the conviction that mental diseases, especially those manifested in the form of crime and sexual vice, were, in fact, hereditary and inherently incurable.[110] Daniel's paper captured this change in emphasis by suggesting that individual therapeutic procedures and efforts to cure were, for the most part, fruitless, and that what was needed for the eradication of sexually pathological behavior was an extensive eugenics program. In ringing testimony to the glory of eugenics and the role of medicine in bringing about a world made free of un-Calvinist sexual longings, Dr. Daniel writes:

> While we can not hope ever to institute a Sanitary Utopia in our day and generation, it would seem within the legitimate scope and sphere of Preventive Medicine, aided by the enactment and enforcement of suitable laws, to eliminate much that is defective in human genesis, and to improve our race mentally, morally and physically; to bring to bear in the breeding of peoples the principles recognized and utilized by every intelligent stock-raiser in the improvement of his cattle; . . . I predict that in twenty years the beneficial results of castration for crimes committed in obedience to a perverted (diseased) sexual impulse will be established and appreciated.[111]

Although not all physicians and psychiatrists shared the growing scepticism regarding individual treatment in dealing with sexual deviants, most were prepared to support the sentiments put forward by Dr. Daniel. Even before the publication of his essay, Dr. William Hammond had read a paper before the New York Society for Medi-

110. See Norman Dain, *Concepts of Insanity in the United States, 1789–1865* (New Brunswick, New Jersey: Rutgers University Press, 1964), pp. 205–206; and David J. Rothman, *The Discovery of the Asylum* (Boston: Little, Brown and Company, 1971), pp. 265–69.
  Pessimism regarding the curability of mental disorders, particularly those occasioned by or manifested in sexual aberrations, was early given impetus by several investigations into the conditions of the insane in American asylums. For example, Edward Jarvis noted, in 1855, that although the curability rate at the Worcester Hospital was as high as 72 percent for those patients whose insanity sprang from "religious excitement and emotions" or ill health, it dropped to 11 percent of those whose mental disorders were caused by "the lowest sensuality." (Edward Jarvis, *Report on Insanity and Idiocy in Massachusetts by the Commission on Lunacy* [1855; rprt ed., with an introduction by Gerald N. Grob, Cambridge, Massachusetts: Harvard University Press, 1971], p. 75).

111. Ibid., p. 267.

cal Jurisprudence supporting the substitution of castration for capital punishment;[112] and, in May 1893, Dr. G. Frank Lydston had called for the castration of sexual perverts—particularly of Negro rapists—"if the operation be supplemented by penile mutilation according to the Oriental method."[113] The proposal to castrate those guilty of sexual sin caught the imagination of the medical profession. Within two years of the publication of Daniel's article, no fewer than four major papers appeared in the more prominent medical periodicals supporting and enlarging Daniel's recommendations.[114] By 1900, the eugenics movement had raised asexualization to the first rank among the solutions to mental disorder espoused by the medical profession.[115]

One of the noblest moments in the history of psychiatry is captured by the painter Robert Fleury, in which he shows Dr. Philippe Pinel ordering the chains removed from the patients at the Salpêtière in 1795. The Enlightenment spirit from which issued the great humanitarian principle that moved Dr. Pinel and the few other early physicians of the mind to liberate the insane from their fetters is tribute to the highest ideals of the profession—to soothe the perturbations of tortured souls and to resolve the conflicts that made of the lives of the mentally ill an unceasing torment. Yet so perverted had this original ideal become when in the hands of lesser men that a century later the profession in the United States was calling for violent physical mutilation of the unfit in the name of ending defect and degeneracy in society.

By the twentieth century, American psychiatry had so altered its nature that it no longer defined its primary role as servitor to the patient in need of help. Instead, it saw itself in the basically anti-indi-

---

112. William A. Hammond, "Castration as a Substitute for Capital Punishment," *Medical News* 60 (April 2, 1892):390—91.

113. Hunter McGuire and G. Frank Lydston, "Sexual Crimes Among the Southern Negroes—Scientifically Considered—An Open Correspondence," *Virginia Medical Monthly* 20 (May 1893): 122.

114. F.L. Sim, "Asexualization for the Prevention of Crime and the Curtailment of the Propagation of Criminals," *Journal of the American Medical Association* 22 (May 19, 1894):753; Robert Boal, "Emasculation and Ovariotomy as a Penalty for Crime and the Reformation of Criminals," *Journal of the American Medical Association* 23 (September 15, 1894):429—32; B.A. Arbogast, "Castration the Remedy for Crime," *Denver Medical Times* 15 (August 1895): 55—58; and, J.W. Frazier, "Castration for Crime as Preventive and Curative Treatment," *Texas Medical Journal* 11 (March 1896):498—503. Dr. James Weir of Owensboro, Kentucky, published an article in 1895 taking the somewhat unusual position of supporting the lynching of rapists as an effective deterrent against sexual crimes. ("The Sexual Criminal," *Medical Record* 47 [May 11, 1895]:581—85.)

115. See Deutsch, pp. 353—85.

vidualistic role of protector of a reified social body, to which it was prepared to sacrifice its sick and ailing members. One eminent psychiatrist, calling for the castration of the morally, mentally, and physically unfit, invoked this new alliance between psychiatry and the repressive arm of the state when he wrote:

> Is it asking too much, is it requiring more than is due, when the state . . . seeks to protect itself against the degrading influences of the continually flowing stress of transmitted pollution, which saps the mental, moral and physical vitality of its citizens, by asking the parents and guardians of the irresponsible defectives to yield their consent to the performance of an operation which in some instances may prove to be curative and in many to be palliative, by abrogating sexual perversions and thus establishing conditions favorable to mental and moral cultivation, and in all, through its far-reaching result, is able to render them impotent to do harm? Failing to obtain this consent, has not the state the right to adopt such measures in the interest and in the protection of its citizens?
>
> The members of our noble profession are not only the conservators of the public health, but are, or should be, in every sense the promoters of the public good. Equipped through training for the effective performance of their professional duties, with cultured mentality, with courageous convictions, to do the right, they stand at the gateway of civilized conditions, ever able, ever ready, to lend a helping hand in promoting that which is for the public weal. May we not ask that the study and investigation of this subject [the castration of the unfit] shall be approached with the "open mind," with the judgment unwarped by an emotional sentimentality. May we not feel assured that, when so studied, there can be but one verdict— that of enlightened approval.[116]

116. J. Ewing Mears, "Asexualization as a Remedial Measure in the Relief of Certain Forms of Mental, Moral and Physical Degeneration," *Boston Medical and Surgical Journal* 161 ((October 21, 1909):585–86.

Professor Lydston went even further. He writes that:

> . . . consumptives, epileptics, insane, incurable inebriates, and criminals at least should not be allowed to marry unless they consent to sterilization. This would prevent the crime of permitting a degenerate child to be born.
>
> The State would stand in a parental relation to the children of the poor and orphans. It should see that all children are physically and morally trained. Australia has proved the practicality of this system.
>
> I would make every school a military school and gymnasium in modified form. Manual training of children should replace some of our modern educational fads and fancies. The brain is developed and trained through manual training as well as through special senses.
>
> All criminals and insane, epileptics, prostitutes, and confirmed inebriates should be regarded as culls until they have established their right to be considered "cured" and worthy of replacement as social integers. If incurable, they are social excreta, and should be placed beyond the possibility of contaminating the body social.

G. Frank Lydston, "Sex Mutilations in Social Therapeutics," *New York Medical Journal* 95 (April 6, 1912):684.

Sex had, throughout the whole of the nineteenth and on into the twentieth centuries, been the great blind spot of psychiatry. In this area of psychic life, the profession had refused to accept its original therapeutic role of helping the sick, and instead had taken upon itself the theological task of punishing those guilty of moral wrongs. It had, in fact, armed itself with the theological tools of damnation. But, cloaked in the mantle of science, its method was not excommunication from God but rather the use of the strait jacket, the lunatic asylum, and the scalpel.

Nineteenth century American psychiatry seems to have blinded itself to one of the more usual aspects of mental disease; that it is within its nature that when an etiologic factor is once accepted by the great mass of people, this alone may make it a cause of mental imbalance irrespective of the original justification for its place in the lexicon of mental ailments. The very fact that masturbation, nymphomania, homosexuality, and so on, as specific forms of psychoneuroses, were given ontological existence in the medical vocabulary and accepted as such by the public, led to their becoming the cause of the disease—for the nature of mental disturbances is that the imaginary, as easily as the real, may bring about mental disorders.

The hypothesis that masturbation as a cause of insanity was ultimately iatrogenic was not examined with any thoroughness until 1932, when a paper by Drs. William Malamud and G. Palmer of the Iowa State Psychopathic Hospital appeared in the *Journal of Nervous and Mental Disease*.[117] After examining fifty cases of insanity where masturbation was singled out as a significant causative factor, Drs. Malamud and Palmer concluded that

> the mental deviations in these cases were due not to the effects of masturbation as such, nor to an organic injury brought about by it, but to a conflict introduced by the erroneous belief of the effects of the practice and its ethical and moral implications. . . . The characteristic feelings expressed by most of these patients [are] that they have "wasted away" their lives.[118]

There is little doubt that these "wasted lives" would have been saved were it not for the psychiatric and medical professions whose putative functions were to tender such people aid and solace.

Although belief in the notion that masturbation would eventuate

117. William Malamud and G. Palmer, "The Role Played by Masturbation in the Causation of Mental Disturbance," *Journal of Nervous and Mental Disease* 76 (September 1932):220–33; 76 (October 1932):366–79.

118. Ibid., p. 377.

in severe psychological disorder was still espoused by a few medical authorities on into the 1930s and after, it had, for all practical purposes, been abandoned by most of the medical profession. True, it lingered in the cautionary literature published for the laity by religionists and moral purifiers, but among the psychiatric profession the theory that masturbation was psychologically harmful continued on only in the much adulterated form that its excessive practice contributed to or was symptomatic of certain sexual neuroses. Yet, as the historian Ronald Walters points out, old myths die hard; a survey taken in 1959 of future doctors graduating from medical schools in the Philadelphia area revealed that almost half of those questioned still held that masturbation was a common cause of insanity.[119]

A far more significant and enduring legacy left by the medical profession's theory of sexuality was its effect on the content of American criminal law respecting sexual conduct. Beginning in the 1880s, psychiatrists and physicians in ever increasing numbers seized upon the criminal prohibitions of the law as one method of circumscribing vice and immorality. In their campaign against unrestrained licentiousness, doctors increasingly viewed individual treatment as only secondary in importance to "that wholesome and definite dread of legal punishment which is at present the chief protection of society."[120] Even where the causes of crime and immorality were discovered to be the product of hereditary predisposition, the fear of criminal sanctions was thought to be an effective deterrent. Thus Dr. Frank Lydston, writing on the hereditary aspects of vice, and particularly of prostitution, notes that even in such cases punishment could still prove efficacious in deterring open manifestations of these morbid physical conditions, "for even insane persons . . . may restrain their morbid impulses where they have such a powerful incentive as the dread of commitment to an asylum."[121] By the end of the nineteenth century, these sentiments were shared by the bulk of the medical profession; and by 1920, in part instigated by the propagandizing efforts of physicians and psychiatrists, American criminal law had become an active force in determining the limits of permissible sexual behavior.

---

119. Ronald Walters, "Introduction," *Primers for Prudery: Sexual Advice to Victorian America*, ed. Ronald Walters (Englewood Cliffs, New Jersey: Prentice-Hall, Inc., 1974), p. 15.

120. G. Frank Lydston, "A Contribution to the Hereditary and Pathological Aspects of Vice," *Chicago Medical Journal and Examiner* 46 (February 1883): 147.

121. Ibid.

II

The contributions of the medical profession to the crimination of sin, particularly in the areas of sexual perversion, prostitution, and sexual contacts with adolescents, is attested to by the prominent role psychiatrists and physicians played in the social hygiene movement that emerged in the Progressive Era.[122] Medical opinion, taking, as it had, the view that the eradication of vice was an essential ingredient to a healthy society, had quickly championed the reforms espoused by the moral education societies—themselves dominated by female physicians[123]—which had come into existence in the 1880s and 1890s. Calling for the suppression of prostitution and other untoward forms of sexual expression, the banning of obscene and pornographic materials, and the punishment of sexual offenders with castration—positions either implicitly or explicitly suggested by the scientific findings of preventive medicine—these reformist elements developed a close working relationship with physicians. So closely associated did preventive medicine and purity reform become that the reformist elements began to employ the very language of medicine in their campaigns, frequently employing the metaphors of moral contagion in their literature and looking upon themselves as "physicians to society."[124]

With respect to prostitution, the medical profession had openly allied itself with the suppressive aims of the reform movement as early as 1882, as its journals reflected.[125] Physicians, noting the grave danger of venereal disease, argued that this could best be brought under control by first eliminating prostitution and, eventually, by eradicating all promiscuity. In the same vein, it was observed that obscene literature was an important factor in encouraging licentiousness and commercialized vice. The medical profession, influenced by, among others, the work of Dr. William Sanger on prostitution, held that an intimate connection existed between pornography and

122. See David J. Pivar, *Purity Crusade: Sexual Morality and Social Control, 1868–1900* (Westport, Connecticut: Greenwood Press, Inc., 1973), passim; John C. Burnham, "Psychiatry, Psychology and the Progressive Movement," *American Quarterly* 12 (1960):457–65; id., "The Medical Inspection of Prostitutes in America in the Nineteenth Century: The St. Louis Experiment and its Sequel," *Bulletin of the History of Medicine* 45 (1971):203–18; id., "Medical Specialists and Movements Towards Social Control in the Progressive Era: Three Examples," in, Jerry Israel, ed., *Building the Organizational Society* (New York: Free Press, 1971), pp. 19–30.

123. Pivar, p. 80.

124. Ibid., p. 150.

125. Ibid., p. 92.

sexual lust; the result of reading books and seeing pictures suggestive of sexuality drove the victim to seek sexual thrills either through frequenting brothels or in some more violent and perverted manner.[126]

The social purity movement, which physicians had enthusiastically endorsed, quickly became a mass movement with a national organization. In 1895, at the National Purity Congress in Baltimore, the American Purity Alliance was formed. It listed a number of prominent reformers from the major national reform groups on its executive board, including representatives of temperance unions, societies for the suppression of impure literature, antivice organizations, law and order societies, and women's suffrage groups.[127] Its New York congress, held soon after, won the unreserved support of the New York medical profession. As David Pivar reports, signatures were there collected for a Medical Declaration of Chastity. "This 1895 Declaration was a milestone for purity reformers in social medicine. They had convinced the medical profession of New York that regulation was inadequate for combatting social diseases and conserving morality, and had further proved to the satisfaction of physicians the efficacy of purity reform for social medicine."[128] Indeed, the physicians in New York did not need much convincing. So firmly were they wedded to the aims of the reform movement as a result of their own investigations that in 1905 they formed their own organization, the American Society for Sanitary and Moral Prophylaxis.

The object of the society, as announced by its first president, Dr. Prince A. Morrow, comprised "the study of the means of every order —sanitary, moral, and legislative—(the legalization of prostitution excepted)—which promise to be the most effective in preventing or diminishing the spread of diseases which have their origin in the Social Evil."[129] Dr. Morrow recognized the broader implications of this mandate and its relation to social reform generally. "In their essential nature," he remarks of venereal diseases, "they are not merely diseases of the human body, but diseases of the social organism. The problem of their prevention or control involves not only questions of hygiene, but questions of morality—questions affecting

126. Paul S. Boyer touches on the role the medical profession and the social hygiene movement played in the antipornography campaign at the end of the nineteenth century. See his *Purity in Print: The Vice-Society Movement and Censorship in America* (New York: Charles Scribner's Sons, 1968), pp. 23–30.

127. Pivar, pp. 187, 283–84.

128. Ibid., p. 189.

129. Prince A. Morrow, "A Plea for the Organization of a 'Society of Sanitary and Moral Prophylaxis'," (Read before the Medical Society of the County of New York, May 23, 1904), *Transactions of the American Society of Sanitary and Moral Prophylaxis*, 1 (1906):17.

the most intimate relations of our social life. . . . To correct these evil conditions there should be a union of all the social forces which work for the good in the community."[130] The intimate connection between preventive medicine as dictated by science and advances in sexual morality—enforced advances, if need be—are spelled out in a paper Dr. Morrow delivered before the society two years after its founding.

> Recognizing that the irregular exercise of the sex function, whether it is termed "incontinence" or "immorality," is the most prolific cause of venereal diseases, we recommend premarital continence as the safest and only sure preservative against infection. Recognizing that the most powerful predisposing cause of licentiousness in men is the physiological fallacy of the "sexual necessity," we repudiate this counterfeit presentment of physiological truth. . . . The teaching of continence does not imply a Pharasaical assumption of superior virtue, but is simply an impersonal interpretation of the physiological laws of man's nature as developed by science and confirmed by human experience. If the hygienic precepts formulated by this Society conduce to moral living, if the moral grows out of the scientific, so much the better for the interests of morality.[131]

In keeping with the position outlined by Dr. Morrow, the society joined its sister organizations in the reform movement in calling for an extensive system of sexual instruction for the young and for legislation making all aspects of sexuality outside the marriage bond illegal. In addition, it supported the suppression of obscene materials and the raising of the female age of consent, i.e., the age below which consent by a female is not a defense to a prosecution for rape.[132]

So successful was the society in expanding its membership beyond the New York area that by 1910 it had established branches and sister societies among physicians in Philadelphia, Milwaukee, Baltimore, Chicago, Indiana, St. Louis, Denver, Portland, Spokane, California, West Virginia, Jacksonville, and Mexico City; in addition, locals were in the process of formation in Georgia, Connecticut, Texas, and New Jersey.[133] The Chicago society—established by the

---

130. Ibid.

131. Prince A. Morrow, "Results of the Work Accomplished by the Society of Sanitary and Moral Prophylaxis," *Transactions of the American Society of Sanitary and Moral Prophylaxis*, 2 (1908):117.

132. Reference to these reforms are scattered throughout the *Transactions*. On changes in legislation, see especially Mrs. William H. Baldwin, Jr., "The Social Evil in New York City, with Reference to Law Enforcement," *Transactions of the American Society of Sanitary and Moral Prophylaxis*, 3 (1910): 186–211.

133. Prince A. Morrow, "Results Achieved by the Movement for Sanitary and Moral Prophylaxis—Outlook for the Future," *Transactions of the American Society of Sanitary and Moral Prophylaxis* 3 (1910):94.

respected urologist Dr. William T. Belfield in October 1906—brought forth the terms "social hygiene" and "sex hygiene" to describe their work.[134] These terms served the dual purpose of relieving the more timid from having to employ words like "venereal" or "prostitution," while at the same time underscoring the medical orientation of the organization's interests. So popular did the terms become that both old and new societies commonly adopted them in their titles. In June 1910, the central organization changed its name from the cumbersome American Society for Sanitary and Moral Prophylaxis to the American Federation for Sex Hygiene.[135]

Finally, in December 1913, the physicians' groups organized into the American Federation for Sex Hygiene, and the National Vigilance Association, successor to the American Purity Alliance and comprised mainly of social workers and clergymen, joined into one massive association for the promotion of their common ends. At a meeting in Buffalo attended by the leaders of the two federations, the American Social Hygiene Association was founded, with Charles Eliot, president of Harvard University, as its first president, and Dr. William Snow of the California Board of Health as its first general secretary.[136]

The merger originally led to some internal bickering. Charles W. Clarke, at one time medical director of the newly formed association, recounts the mutual suspicion that early emerged between, on the one hand, those primarily interested in the medical aspects of sex and, on the other, those who were particularly concerned with its moral implications.

> The clergy and social workers in the abolitionist organizations suspected that the medical men were "materialists" who cared nothing for spiritual values and social justice. The physicians and sanitarians were often impatient at the preoccupation of the abolitionists with the protection of the civil rights of prostitutes. As one doctor remarked, "They don't give a damn how many babies die of syphilis so long as streetwalkers are not molested by policemen."[137]

In this struggle, the more repressive policy prevailed when the membership was convinced that "there is no fundamental conflict between the highest moral and social concepts of what sex conduct

134. Charles Walter Clarke, *Taboo: The Story of the Pioneers of Social Hygiene* (Washington, D.C.: Public Affairs Press, 1961), p. 58.

135. Ibid., p. 61.

136. Ibid., p. 62; Pivar, pp. 243–44; and "The American Social Hygiene Association," *Vigilance* 26 (December 1913):1.

137. Clarke, p. 75.

ought to be and the most scientific medical and sanitary plans for eradicating the venereal diseases."[138] Thus, in the controversies over whether to support medical inspection of prostitutes and whether to make chemical prophylaxis available to the public, the association ultimately agreed that both policies were of questionable medical benefit and would only encourage illicit sexual relations.[139]

Perhaps the best statement of the goals of the new organization is that put forward by its first president, Charles W. Eliot, in an address to the first annual meeting of the association.

An . . . important object of the Association is to devise and advocate effective police procedure and effective legislation with regard to vice. In some American communities improved laws, courts, or police administration have already been secured. The Association should try to make the best experience of any state, city, or town available, as lesson or example, to all other cities or towns. . . .

Part of the work of the Association should be contributory to the work of other organizations—such as those that advocate the suppression of disorderly houses and disreputable hotels, . . . the substitution of weak alcoholic drinks for strong, the promotion of total abstinence, and the provision of wholesome pleasures, both out-of-doors and indoors. The Association should always be ready to take part in the prosecution of men or women who make a profit out of obscene publications, indecent shows, immoral plays, and prostitution.

The Association ought to advocate actively the common use of the recognized safeguards against sexual perversions—such as bodily exercises, moderation in eating, abstinence in youth from alcohol, tobacco, hot spices, and all other drugs which impair self-control, even momentarily. Social hygiene would be effectively promoted by reduction or rejection of the drinking and smoking habits in American communities. In the white race the connection between drinking alcohol and prostitution is intimate.[140]

The reforms advocated by the American Social Hygiene Association and by its predecessor organizations in the social purity movement had as their aim nothing short of a fundamental transformation in the value system manifested by American law. The comparatively limited intrusions into private sexual matters that had characterized the criminal law throughout most of the nineteenth century were, between 1880 and 1920, augmented by statutes regulating every aspect of sexual conduct, both public and private, and the inflation

138. Ibid., p. 76.
139. Ibid., p. 75.
140. Charles W. Eliot, "The American Social Hygiene Association," *Social Hygiene*, 1 (December 1914):3-4.

of the statutory law in this area came about largely through the propagandizing efforts of the sex hygiene societies. The theoretical foundation for the attacks leveled by these groups on vice, sexual perversion, and obscene literature were laid by the medical profession's conclusions respecting the pernicious effects of masturbation, incontinence, and the other perversions that stemmed from them. Not one reform in the area of sexuality advocated by these groups was at odds with accepted medical canon; no piece of legislation regulating sexual conduct could not be supported by substantial medical and psychiatric evidence.

Backed by the weight of scientific testimony, reformist elements in the United States were successful in convincing the state legislatures that stamping out vice was a primary desideratum of law. Criminal codes in each of the states, already in the process of undergoing a marked expansion,[141] were further swollen to encompass a host of new laws dealing with sexual behavior. As an example, in 1915 alone —not an atypical year with respect to this kind of legislation—over eighty bills concerning the regulation of sexual behavior were introduced into the state legislatures, of which over half were passed into law.[142] These included statutes dealing with the age of consent, indecent exposure, obscene publications, sexual perversion, adultery,

141. Friedman, pp. 508–12.

142. "Social Hygiene Legislation in 1915," *Social Hygiene*, 2 (April 1916): 245–56.
The following are among the bills introduced in the California legislature during its 1915 session: (1) A. B. 287, increasing the penalty for rape to from twenty to fifty years; (2) A. B. 288, raising the age of consent to twenty years; (3) A. B. 78, making single acts of adultery or fornication misdemeanors; (4) A. B. 1, prohibiting intercourse between Caucasians and Japanese and Chinese; (5) A, B. 496, prohibiting advertisements purporting to cure venereal diseases; (6) S. B. 1018, providing for mandatory asexualization of sex perverts; (7) A. B. 274, increasing the penalty for seduction to from five to ten years; (8) S. B. 76, making illegal the use of a tenement house for purposes of prostitution [enacted as Ch. 572]; (9) A. B. 1262, allowing the courts to commit sex perverts to a state hospital for treatment [enacted as Ch. 519]; (10) A. B. 219, making "sexual perversion" a felony [enacted as Ch. 586]; (11) S. B. 983, prohibiting employment agencies from sending women to places of known immorality [enacted as Ch. 551].
The Wisconsin legislature was no less zealous in caring for the sexual morals of its citizens. A dozen bills were brought forward in 1915, of which four were passed and signed into law: (1) A. B. 410, holding it a felony if a man commits fornication that results in a pregnancy with a single female and subsequently leaves the state; (2) A. B. 436 and S. B. 286, prohibiting single acts of fornication; (3) S. B. 29, prohibiting taxi drivers and others from transporting a person to a place of prostitution; (4) S. B. 156, making illegal soliciting in restaurants and saloons; (5) S. B. 147 and H. B. 543, prohibiting sexual relations between persons afflicted with venereal diseases; (6) A. B. 562, prohibiting the marriage of epileptics; (7) A. B. 599, prohibiting women from being in dance halls where liquor is sold; (8) S. B. 30, prohibiting indecent exhibitions; (9) S. B. 26, pro-

fornication, and various aspects of prostitution—including pandering, pimping, keeping a house of prostitution, soliciting, and transporting for the purposes of prostitution. The rationale, eagerly adopted by the state legislatures, that excused such wholesale incursions into the private lives of citizens was that provided by medical science— namely, that these new laws did not issue from any attempt to enforce a particular value system but were scientifically grounded in the conclusions reached by preventive medicine and sexual hygiene. Their aim was not to make Americans moral, but to prevent them from becoming sick.

It is beyond the scope of this essay to attempt anything like a complete catalogue of the successes that the sex hygiene associations had in their lobbying efforts. Between 1880 and 1920 many hundreds of statutes were either passed into law or amended to bring the states' penal codes into line with the reforms advocated by physicians and other moral reformers. The following categories are, however, indicative of the scope and direction of statutory enactments during the period and are briefly discussed: (1) changes in age of consent legislation; (2) expansion of the sodomy statues to include perversions other than coitus per anum; and (3) legislation aimed at stamping out prostitution.

Age of Consent Legislation

"Age of consent" in the sense in which I here employ the term refers to that age below which a female is held by law to be incapable of agreeing to sexual intercourse, so that any male who has sexual relations with a girl below the stipulated age is indictable on a charge of rape. It might also be taken to refer to the maximum age at which a female may be seduced or abducted, since in most jurisdictions a male is deemed innocent of these offenses unless the female was under a certain age. Although the age of consent in both these instances was often the same, it is specifically to the former that the reformist groups turned their attention.

At the beginning of 1886, the age of consent to sexual intercourse remained at ten years throughout most of the country. Several states had statutorily increased the age to twelve years, but the great majority continued to adhere to the traditional age of ten—either via stat-

---

hibiting hotel clerks, livery men, bell boys, etc., from sending or taking a person to a prostitute [enacted as Ch. 161]; (10) S. B. 150, raising the age of consent to eighteen years, and if the female were previously chaste, twenty-one years [enacted as Ch. 611]; (11) S. B. 154, prohibiting employment agencies from sending females to places of known immorality [enacted as Ch. 115]; (12) A. B. 476, making illegal "improper" liberties with a child [enacted as Ch. 199].

ute or by relying on the common law. Under intense pressure from the social hygiene movement, this situation was substantially altered over the succeeding three decades. By the time of America's entry into World War I, only Georgia remained with an age of consent of ten, and it raised the age to fourteen in the following year. All the other jurisdictions, by 1917, had statutorily raised the age to fourteen or above. Twenty-two states had set sixteen as the age of consent; seventeen states had raised the age to eighteen; and two states, Tennessee and Wisconsin, had raised the age to twenty-one.[143]

Sexual Perversion

Throughout most of the nineteenth century, the law against sodomy stood alone as the only legal prohibition against sexual deviance. The common law had limited the crime of sodomy solely to sexual intercourse per anum by a man with a man or woman, and when the states initially enacted sodomy statutes no other sexual behavior was interpreted as being proscribed—excepting bestiality or necrophilia in those states explicitly including such conduct in their statutes. However beginning in 1879, the various state legislatures were encouraged to expand their statutory prohibitions to cover fellatio, cunnilingus, and other "unnatural" acts that medical science had shown to be the product of diseased and perverted minds. The intervention of the law was necessary, it was argued, both to discourage the spread of these vices and to bring to the attention of the legal authorities sexual perverts in need of psychiatric treatment. In addition, in 1907 Indiana became the first of a number of states to pass a compulsory sterilization law.[144] It thus became legally possible to include sex perverts in the far-reaching asexualization plans that physicians so strongly supported.[145] A comprehensive eugenics program,

143. See Appendix I, pp. 86–88.

144. Between 1907 and 1937, thirty-three states had enacted sterilization laws of one sort or another. They are, in order of passage: Indiana (1907); California, Connecticut, Washington (1909); Iowa, Nevada, New Jersey (1911); New York (1912); Kansas, Michigan, North Dakota, Wisconsin (1913); Nebraska (1915); New Hampshire, Oregon, South Dakota (1917); Alabama, North Carolina (1919); Colorado (1920); Delaware, Montana, Virginia (1924); Idaho, Maine, Minnesota, Utah (1925); Mississippi (1928); Arizona, West Virginia (1929); Oklahoma, Vermont (1931); South Carolina (1935); and, Georgia (1937).

For a discussion of these laws, see Harry L. Laughlin, "Eugenical Sterilization in the United States," *Social Hygiene* 6 (October 1920): 499–532; and St. John–Stevas, pp. 160–97, 291–309.

145. Most states drafted their sterilization statutes in such a way that sex perverts could fall under the provisions of the act although they were not specifically included as subject to sterilization. Several states, however, explicitly included sexual perverts as subject to asexualization. These were California, Idaho,

however, would first require that sex perverts be identified and committed to state institutions. As a result, a number of states that expanded their criminal codes to include perversions other than coitus per anum also made statutory provision for the hospitalization, treatment and—in some cases—castration of perverts.

Not all the states found it necessary to amend their sodomy laws in order to prohibit acts not covered by the common law. The original statutes—all of which prohibited "sodomy," "buggery," "the crime against nature," or a combination of these terms—did not explicitly specify which acts were included within the meaning of the law. Traditionally, the common law interpretation prevailed, thus limiting the prohibition to anal intercourse. However, because of the vagueness of the language, when a particular "unnatural" act was charged as being in violation of the statute, the courts had the option of extending the sense of the statute by construing it as covering the particular act before it. Between 1904 and 1925 the courts in eleven states adopted this approach and broadened the area covered by the sodomy laws sufficiently to make legislative action unnecessary.

From 1879, when Pennsylvania added a section to its sodomy statute covering fellatio and cunnilingus, until 1925, thirty-six states had either expanded their prohibitions against sexual aberrance by statute or through the state courts.[146] Doubtless physicians viewed with particular pride the Indiana and Wyoming statutes, passed in 1881 and 1890. In both states the legislatures included the following language in their criminal codes: "Whoever entices, allures, instigates or aids any person under the age of twenty-one years to commit masturbation or self-pollution shall be deemed guilty of sodomy."

Iowa, Kansas, Nebrasks, North Dakota, Oregon, South Dakota, and Utah. (Laughlin; St. John–Stevas, pp. 296–309.)

Dr. Harry Laughlin, writing in *Social Hygiene*, the journal of the American Social Hygiene Association, concluded that the sterilization statutes were not nearly as comprehensive as medical science could have wished. In the Model Sterilization Statute that he proposed, the following people would be subject to sterilization: "All persons in the state who, because of degenerate or defective hereditary qualities, are potential parents of socially inadequate off-spring, regardless of whether such persons be in the population at large or inmates of custodial institutions, regardless also of the personality, age, sex, marital condition, race, possessions of such persons. A "socially inadequate" person, for purposes of the act, is defined as "one who by his or her own effort, chronically, and regardless of etiology or prognosis, fails in comparison with normal persons, to maintain himself or herself as a useful member of the organized social life of the state." (Laughlin, pp. 519–20).

146. See Appendix II, pp. 89–94.

Legislation Aimed at Prostitution

Undoubtedly the major thrust of the social purity groups and their successor organizations was directed at stamping out prostitution. Throughout the nineteenth century almost no laws dealt with the practice, and those that did were only nominally enforced. Prostitution was not an offense at common law and, prior to World War I, to be a prostitute was in itself not a crime.[147] No laws existed prohibiting pandering, pimping, procuring, soliciting, or transporting, nor was patronizing a prostitute an offense.[148] This absence of legal restraint, combined with a general sentiment among Americans that the repression of commercialized vice was not particularly desirable, permitted the practice to flourish.[149] During the nineteenth century, prostitution appears to have been so acceptable a part of American life that several attempts were made to license the profession in the 1870s and 1880s. These efforts were ultimately defeated, largely through the agency of the purity groups and a substantial proportion of the medical profession.[150] Yet so rampant was prostitution up to World War I that it was conservatively estimated that the number of prostitutes residing in brothels in the United States in 1912 was no less than 200,000.[151]

In no other area of sexuality did the social hygiene movement eventually prove as effective in its legislative lobbying efforts as in the area of commercialized vice. Beginning in the 1880s and reaching a peak during the war years, each state passed more than a dozen pieces of legislation, prohibiting every aspect of the practice. World War I was of enormous help to the social hygiene crusade against immorality; the suppression of vice became associated in the public

147. Howard B. Woolston, *Prostitution in the United States* 1921: rprt ed., Montclair, New Jersey: Patterson Smith, 1969), p. 25.

148. Ibid., p. 31.

149. See Vern L. Bullough, *The History of Prostitution* (New Hyde Park, New York: University Books, 1964), pp. 187–95; and Fernando Henriques, *Prostitution in Europe and the New World* (London: MacGibbon & Kee, 1963), pp. 268–320.

150. St. Louis had instituted a system of regulation in 1870, but the law was repealed four years later after intense pressure was brought to bear on the Missouri legislature by a coalition of purity groups and physicians. Similar measures were defeated in New York in 1871 and 1875; in Chicago, in 1871; in California, in 1871; in Cincinnati, in 1874; in Pennsylvania, in 1874; and in the District of Columbia, in 1876. For a discussion of these attempts at regulation, see Sheldon Amos, *A Comparative Survey of Laws in Force for the Prohibition, Regulation, and Licensing of Vice in England and Other Countries* (London: Stevens and Sons, 1877), pp. 417–22; William Burgess, *The World's Social Evil* (Chicago: Saul Brothers, 1914), pp. 39–47; id., "Brief History of Regulation of Vice," *Vigilance*, 25 (August 1912):2–9; and Woolston, pp. 26–31.

151. Woolston, p. 38.

mind with the campaign against venereal disease and, hence, with the war effort. Discussing developments in social hygiene legislation during the war years, George Worthington notes that "when the government was suddenly confronted with the necessity of mobilizing for war, it realized at once that to be efficient, its armed forces must be clean. The government's program was based on the realization that the venereal diseases are the greatest scourge to the military forces and that prostitution is the greatest source for their spread."[152] The government was, of course, confronted with two alternate approaches in its battle against venereal infection. It could choose either to medically inspect prostitutes and the men with whom they came in contact or it could prohibit commercialized vice. Under prodding from the medical profession, it opted for suppression.

The result of identifying prostitution with aiding the enemy concluded a process already begun to legislate against almost every element of the prostitute's trade. The publicity attending the reports of the numerous vice commissions established after 1910[153] had already resulted in the passage of the so-called White Slavery Laws, prohibiting enticing females into prostitution, pandering, and pimping. Perhaps the most famous of these was the Mann Act, a federal statute enacted in 1910, which makes it a crime for any person to transport in interstate or foreign commerce any female for immoral purposes.[154] The individual states quickly followed the lead of the federal government. Between 1910 and 1915, practically every state

152. George E. Worthington, "Developments in Social Hygiene Legislation From 1917 to September 1, 1920," *Social Hygiene* 6 (October 1920):557. For a discussion of the contributions of the social hygiene movement to wartime legislation against vice, see, William F. Snow, "Social Hygiene and the War," *Social Hygiene* 3 (July 1917):417–50; and Franklin Martin, "Social Hygiene and the War," *Social Hygiene* 3 (October 1917):605–27.

The antivice campaign even extended to American troops overseas. The official position was contained in a bulletin issued to members of the American Expeditionary Forces by General Pershing, in which he declared that "sexual continence is the plain duty of members of the A.E.F., both for the vigorous conduct of the war, and for the clean health of the American people after the war." Toward this end, U.S. military authorities attempted to close all the brothels in areas of France where American troops were stationed and, when this proved unsuccessful, declared them off limits. (Fred D. Baldwin, "The Invisible Armor," *American Quarterly* 16 [1964]:432–44).

153. Over thirty cities had established commissions to investigate commercialized vice between 1910 and 1915. (Joseph Mayer, *Regulation of Commercialized Vice* [New York: Klebold Press, 1922], p. 11; and, Burgess, *World's Social Evil*, pp. 260–62).

154. The Mann Act was enforced with a vengeance. Between June 1910 and January 1915, more than one thousand "white slavers" were convicted under the law. (Roy Lubove, "The Progressives and the Prostitute," *The Historian* 24 [1961]:313).

in the Union had passed laws against these classes of offenses. Forty-four states made enticing, soliciting, forcing, or transporting a woman into prostitution a crime; forty-five states had forbidden pandering; and thirty-six states had made pimping and living off the earnings of a prostitute unlawful. Only Georgia, Mississippi, and South Carolina had prohibited none of these acts by 1920.[155]

Keeping a disorderly house—or a house of ill fame, as some laws stated—had been indictable as a misdemeanor under common law.[156] During the course of the nineteenth century, however, the concept of the common law crime had weakened considerably, and the criminal law in the various states had become almost exclusively a matter of statute.[157] Yet, before 1890, only twenty-four states had included the offense of keeping a house of ill fame in their criminal codes.[158] Because of the promotional work of the reform movement, however, an additional twenty-two states and the District of Columbia added the crime to their penal codes between 1891 and 1913.[159]

A far more effective weapon for closing houses of ill fame was the Red Light Injunction and Abatement Law, first passed by Iowa in 1909. The law did not involve a criminal action and therefore did not suffer from the restrictions imposed on a prosecution under the criminal code. The Injunction and Abatement Law declared houses of prostitution to be common nuisances and permitted a civil action in a court of equity to be brought in the name of the state by any private citizen to abate the nuisance. A civil action, as opposed to a criminal proceeding, had the advantage of allowing the court to issue

---

155. See Appendix III, pp. 95–97.

156. *Wharton's Criminal Law*, 12th ed., II: 2007–2008 (Section 1722).

157. Friedman, p. 503. Friedman notes:
As of 1900, most states still *technically* recognized the possibility of a common-law crime. But some states had statutes that specifically abolished the concept. These statutes stated bluntly that all crimes were listed in the penal code, and nothing else was a crime. In some states, the courts *construed* their penal codes as (silently) abolishing common-law crime. Where the concept survived, it was hardly ever used; the penal codes were in fact complete and exclusive.

158. Alabama, Arizona, California, Colorado, Connecticut, Florida, Georgia, Idaho, Illinois, Maine, Massachusetts, Michigan, Minnesota, Nevada, New Jersey, New York, North Dakota, Ohio, Oregon, Pennsylvania, Texas, Virginia, Washington, Wisconsin.

159. Arkansas (1897), Delaware (1895), District of Columbia (1912), Indiana (1905), Iowa (1907), Kansas (1913), Louisiana (1912), Maryland (1892), Mississippi (1904), Missouri (1899), Montana (1895), Nebraska (1893), New Hampshire (1895), New Mexico (1901), North Carolina (1907), Oklahoma (1903), Rhode Island (1896), South Dakota (1903), Tennessee (1896), Utah (1898), Vermont (1890), West Virginia (1893), Wyoming (1890). Kentucky and South Carolina had not prohibited keeping a house of ill fame by 1920.

an injunction, including a temporary injunction during the period of the trial, thus closing the house. Further, relief was secured much more rapidly than in a criminal action, and the trial was before a single judge rather than a jury.[160] The law proved so successful in reducing the number of brothels in Iowa that, by 1921, thirty-nine states and the District of Columbia had enacted similar statutes.[161] It is largely through exploiting the Injunction and Abatement Laws that prostitution as a functioning commercial enterprise was eventually abolished in the major American cities.[162]

In addition to the White Slavery Laws, Injunction and Abatement Acts, and prohibitions against keeping a house of ill fame, a number of states passed statutes prohibiting soliciting for purposes of prostitution or lewdness. The prohibitions against soliciting not only made criminal an important aspect of the business of prostitution but, in time, also served the purpose of criminalizing casual homosexual encounters. A large percentage of homosexual offenses have not fallen under the statutes for sodomy but under the more prosecutable one of soliciting—originally a prostitution offense.[163] By 1920, twenty-seven states had added soliciting to their criminal codes.[164]

Finally, the various states and municipalities passed into law a variety of laws and ordinances touching on other aspects of commercialized vice: permitting one's place or conveyance to be used for immoral purposes; receiving or offering to receive another into a place or conveyance for purposes of prostitution; knowingly transporting another to a place of prostitution; acting as a go-between

160. For a fuller analysis of the Red Light Injunction and Abatement Law and its effects in reducing prostitution in Iowa see, Herbert E. Gernert, "Legislation on the Social Evil: The Red Light Injunction Laws of Iowa and Nebraska," *Vigilance* 25 (August 1912):14–29.

161. See Appendix III, pp. 95–97.

162. J..George, Jr., "Prostitution," in, Ralph Slovenko, ed., *Sexual Behavior and the Law* (Springfield, Illinois: Charles C. Thomas, 1965), p. 650. Professor George notes that

so long as the citizen was unable to coerce public officials into enforcement of the laws against prostitution and unable to move against public nuisances in his own right, open prostitution could flourish if the police or public officials so desired; the ballot box was an indirect and usually ineffective way of controlling their activity. It was to meet such a situation that the Red Light Abatement Laws were passed, and it is through their invocation and application that citizens' groups have been able to suppress open and notorious prostitution in almost all cities in the United States.

163. See, among others, Samuel G. Kling, *Sexual Behavior and the Law* (New York: Bernard Geis Associates, 1965), p. 117; and Robert G. Fisher, "The Sex Offender Provisions of the Proposed New Maryland Criminal Code: Should Private Consenting Adult Homosexual Behavior Be Excluded?" *Maryland Law Review* 30 (1970):92.

164. See Appendix III, pp. 95–97.

between a prostitute and her patrons; frequenting, residing in, or occupying a disorderly house; and so on. Perhaps the most far-reaching law enacted by the states was that drafted by the law enforcement division of the Commission on Training Camp Activities of the federal government, for submission to the various state legislatures. Known as the Vice Repressive Law, it prohibited both "giving or receiving of the body for sexual intercourse for hire," and "giving or receiving of the body for indiscriminate sexual intercourse without hire." In addition, solicitation on the part of either party was proscribed by its provisions. The law was so extensive in its coverage that it penalized all commercialized aspects of prostitution, including the activities of the go-between, the keeper of the disorderly house, and so on. The Vice Repressive Law, effectively classifying all sexual intercourse as a species of prostitution, was enacted by ten states by 1920.[165]

If one were to examine the status of the legal regulation of sexual conduct that obtained in the United States in 1948—the year of the publication of Alfred Kinsey's first monumental study of American sexual behavior—he would be confronted with laws prohibiting almost all sexual conduct other than normal sexual intercourse between husband and wife and solitary acts of masturbation. These laws, Morris Ploscowe observed, "make potential criminals of most of the adolescent and adult population."[166] So sweeping are the restrictions on sexual activity contained in the various criminal codes and so out of keeping are they with the realities of actual behavior that Dr. Kinsey estimated that "the persons involved in these activities [which contravene the law], taken as a whole, constitute more than 95 percent of the total male population."[167]

Although it is true that some of these sexual offenses have their roots in the English common law and in the early American Puritan tradition, it is significant that the majority of these prohibitions date from a period no earlier than the last two decades of the nineteenth century. Only a fraction of the sexual behavior that in 1948 was proscribed by law had been prohibited in the United States seventy years earlier. Thus, mutual masturbation, fellatio, cunnilingus—all manner of "lewd and indecent" acts when committed in private— single acts of fornication (in all but a handful of states), relations with prostitutes, consensual intercourse with females over the age of

165. A complete draft of the law together with a brief discussion of its provisions is contained in Worthington, pp. 561–64.

166. Ploscowe, p. 217.

167. Alfred C. Kinsey, Wardell B. Pomeroy, and Clyde E. Martin, *Sexual Behavior in the Human Male* (Philadelphia: W.B. Saunders Company, 1948), p. 392.

ten or twelve, soliciting another for a sexual act—all were beyond the reach of the law as late as 1880.

The shift in American criminal law at the end of the nineteenth century that subjected so much sexual conduct to legal restraint was occasioned not by a reawakening of religious zeal but by the intrusion of medicine and psychiatry into the legislative process. When, during the nineteenth century, doctors and psychiatrists had scientifically established the medical necessity of a life of sexual restraint, they had confined the implementation of their findings to their patients and to the unfortunates committed to their care in hospitals and asylums. By the 1880s, however, the profession was prepared to forcibly remold the entire society in the interests of mental health. In this respect physicians, and particularly psychiatrists, exhibited the same presumptuousness in meddling in the private affairs of people as was shown by others active in the reform movements of the period. Their meddlesomeness came comparatively easily, however. As John Burnham observes, since "as doctors they dealt with matters of life and death, and as psychotherapists in daily practice they undertook to interfere in and change the attitudes and ways of life of their patients, . . . they were accustomed to the responsibilities of leadership."[168] Moreover, the role of leadership for the morals of the nation had been a traditional one for physicians.

When, in 1917, the General Medical Board of the Council of National Defense declared that "continence is not incompatible with health" and the House of Delegates of the American Medical Association unanimously approved the sentiment,[169] doctors in the United States were only affirming a principle that lay at the root of their investigations into sexuality begun a century earlier by Benjamin Rush. Incontinence—and its solitary manifestation, masturbation—were found to be the spring from which issued a spectacular array of diseases, both of the mind and of the body. With respect to the social organism, a wanton and lascivious population, given to unbridled sexuality, undermined the moral fiber of a nation, perverted its character, and destroyed its sense of manliness, womanliness, purity, love, honor, marriage, the home, the family, and the state. Physicians had, throughout the whole of the nineteenth century, been alone in asserting the scientific truth of these observations. Psychiatrists, experts in the area of mental disorder, had proven with cold and detached objectivity that unrestrained sexuality would bring in its

---

168. Burnham, "Psychiatry, Psychology, and the Progressive Movement," p. 462.

169. Snow, pp. 428, 439–40.

wake the decay, first of the mind, and finally of the body. On a national scale, it would, if unchecked, lead to nothing less than the collapse of organized society. The medical profession saw with pristine clarity the necessity of keeping licentiousness in check if mental disease were not to become rampant.

By the end of the century, physicians and psychiatrists had proved their sexual theories to a receptive public. It was no longer necessary to rely on the unverifiable conclusions of moralists and theologians respecting the propriety of inhibiting one's sexual appetite. Science had demonstrated beyond all shadow of doubt that masturbation incontinence, oral-genital contacts, homosexual encounters, even prostitution, were mental perversities, brought about through disobedience to nature's inexorable laws as uncovered by medical science. "The laws of society and physical hygiene are immutable," wrote one psychiatrist,

> and any infringement of them is followed by penalties that must be paid for. The person that does aught to improve the morals of our race and inculcate and secure obedience to nature's immutable laws adds a bulwark to the nation's safety and the nation's greatness; but he that does aught to degrade the morals of our generation and breaks nature's laws commits a crime against the whole nation, because he throws poison into a stream from which we all must drink.
>
> Greece, exalted with her matchless learning and art, and Rome—imperial Rome—with the wealth and power of empires within her grasp, crumbled and went down in ruin when the morality of those nations was eclipsed by sensuality and vice.[170]

The task of sparing America the fate of Greece and Rome belonged to men of vision and dedication such as comprised the medical profession, men who saw that American society, for too long, had disregarded nature's laws and had permitted sensuality and vice to flourish. Armed with new laws to protect the sexual purity of the nation, they joined hands with an emerging bureaucracy[171] to build that bulwark against iniquity and lust of which physicians and psychiatrists wrote. They had discovered that the penitentiary was as viable a therapeutic weapon for sexual disorder as was the asylum.[172]

170. J.H. McCassey, "Disobedience as a Cause of Insanity," *Cincinnati Lancet-Clinic* 76 (July 11, 1896):35.

171. The bureaucratization of American life during the Progressive period is extensively discussed by Robert H. Wiebe, *The Search for Order: 1877–1920* (New York: Hill and Wang, 1967).

172. By 1950, the identification of asylum and penitentiary had been completed. A concurrent process had been under way for some years aimed at

Footnote continued

substituting therapeutic sanctions for the sanctions of the law. This movement culminated in the passage of the sexual psychopath laws in a number of states and marked psychiatry's major inroad into legal doctrine in the area of sexual behavior. The sexual psychopath laws provided for a civil commitment procedure by which two psychiatric experts could commit a "sexual psychopath"—usually defined as one lacking the power to control his sexual impulses—to an asylum for an indefinite period. Criminal conviction of a sexual offense was not, in most states, a prerequisite for commitment. These laws are discussed at length in Alan H. Swanson, "Sexual Psychopath Statutes: Summary and Analysis," *Journal of Criminal Law, Criminology and Police Science* 51 (1960):215–35. See, also, St. John–Stevas, pp. 228–30.

APPENDIX I

Age of Consent*

State	1886	1895	1917
Alabama	10	10	14
Arizona (a)	10	18	18
Arkansas	"puberty"	16	16
California	10	14	18
Colorado	10	18	18
Delaware	10	7†	16
District of Columbia	10	16	16
Florida	10	10	18 (chaste) 10 (unchaste)
Georgia	10	10	10
Idaho (b)	12	14	18
Illinois	10	14	16
Iowa	10	13	15
Kansas	10	18	18
Kentucky	12	12	16
Louisiana	12	12	18
Maine	10	14	16
Maryland	10	14	16
Massachusetts	10	16	16
Michigan	10	14	16
Minnesota	10	16	18
Mississippi	10	10	18 (chaste) 12 (unchaste)
Missouri	12	14	18 (chaste) 14 (unchaste)

Appendix I. continued

State	1886	1895	1917
Montana (c)	10	16	18 (chaste) 15 (unchaste)
Nebraska	12	15	18 (chaste) 15 (unchaste)
Nevada	12	12	16
New Hampshire	10	13	16
New Jersey	10	16	16
New Mexico (d)	10	14	16
New York	10	18	18
North Carolina	10	10	14 (chaste) 10 (unchaste)
North Dakota (e)	10	16	18
Ohio	10	14	16
Oklahoma (f)	10	14	18 (chaste) 16 (unchaste)
Oregon	10	16	16
Pennsylvania	10	16	16‡
Rhode Island	10	16	16
South Carolina	10	10	14
South Dakota (e)	10	16	18
Tennessee	10	12	21 (chaste) 12 (unchaste)
Texas	10	15	15
Utah (g)	10	13	18
Vermont	11	14	16
Virginia	10	12	14
Washington § (h)	12	16	18 (chaste) 15 (unchaste)
West Virginia	12	14	14
Wisconsin	10	14	21 (chaste) 18 (unchaste)
Wyoming (i)	10	18	18

(Notes overleaf)

Appendix I. Notes

(a) Arizona Territory until 1912.	(f) Oklahoma Territory until 1907.
(b) Idaho Territory until 1890.	(g) Utah Territory until 1896.
(c) Montana Territory until 1889.	(h) Washington Territory until 1889.
(d) New Mexico Territory until 1912.	(i) Wyoming Territory until 1890.
(e) Dakota Territory until 1889.	

Sources: Benjamin DeCosta, "Age of Consent Law—1886," *Philanthropist* (February, 1886), p. 5; Helen Gardner, "Sound Morality," *Arena* 14 (October 1895):410; Herbert E. Gernert, "Legislation on the Social Evil: The 'Age of Consent' Laws," *Vigilance* 25 (September 1912):8–13; Timothy Newell Pfeiffer, "The Matter and Method of Social Hygiene Legislation," *Social Hygiene* 3 (January 1917): 51–73; George E. Worthington, "Developments in Social Hygiene Legislation from 1917 to September 1, 1920," *Social Hygiene* 6 (October 1920):557–68. In addition, the statutes themselves have been consulted.

Notes: * The age set by statute below which consent by a female is not a defense to a prosecution for rape.

The table shows the age of consent as of January 1, 1886; June 30, 1895; and December 31, 1917.

† The 1883 statutes of Delaware do not indicate an age of consent and the courts of that state held that the common law age of ten prevailed. However, an amendment to the 1883 statutes several years later stipulated an age of consent of seven years. In late 1895 the state legislature changed the age to sixteen.

‡ In Pennsylvania, if a jury found that the female, even though under the age of sixteen, were of previously unchaste character and consented to sexual intercourse, the accused was to be acquitted of the charge of rape and convicted of the lesser crime of fornication.

§ During World War I, Washington established an age of consent for *males*, making it an offense for a woman to have sexual relations with a boy under the age of eighteen despite his consent. The primary motive for this law seems to have been "to restrain prostitutes and other lewd women from catering to young boys." (Worthington, p. 565n.)

APPENDIX II

Legislative Enactments and Court Decisions Expanding the Sodomy Statutes, 1879–1925

1879	Pennsylvania	A section was added to the Pennsylvania criminal code expanding the definition of sodomy to include oral intercourse. [11 June 1879, P.L. 148, §1]
1881	Indiana	Indiana did not have a sodomy law until 1881. In that year the Indiana legislature enacted a statute prohibiting coitus per anum and including within its definition of sodomy "whoever entices, allures, instigates or aids any person under the age of twenty-one years to commit masturbation." [Rev. Stats. 1881, §2005] In 1913 the Indiana courts held that the statute prohibited fellatio. [Glover v. State, 179 Ind. 459, 101 S.E. 629 (1913)]
1886	New York	In 1886 the New York legislature decided that the language of its original sodomy law—prohibiting "the crime against nature"—was inadequate. The new law prohibitied oral intercourse and necrophilia in addition to coitus per anum. [N.Y. Laws 1886, c. 31, §6]
1887	Massachusetts	The Massachusetts legislature added a statute to its criminal code—supplementing its sodomy law—which prohibited the commission of "any unnatural and lascivious act with another person." [L. 1887, c. 436, §1]
1889	Ohio	Ohio did not have a sodomy law until 1885. Four years later the statute was amended to cover oral intercourse. [L. 1889, p. 251, §1]
1890	Wyoming	Wyoming amended its sodomy statute to encompass oral intercourse. In addition, a clause was added to the statute defining the crime of sodomy to include "whoever entices, allures, instigates or aids any person under the age of twenty-one years to commit masturbation or self-pollution." [L. 1890, p. 139, §87]

Appendix II. continued

1895	North Dakota	The language of the North Dakota statute was amended to include oral intercourse and necrophilia. [Rev. Code, 1895, §7186]
1896	Louisiana	The Louisiana statute prohibiting sodomy was amended to include oral intercourse. [Acts 1896, no. 6, §1]
1897	Illinois	The Illinois statute was interpreted by the Illinois courts to include all acts "of bestial and unnatural copulation." [Honselman v. People, 168 Ill. 172, 48 S.E. 304 (1897)]
1898	Wisconsin	The Wisconsin legislature added a clause to its sodomy statute covering "penetration of the mouth of any human being by the organ of any male person." [Stats. 1898, §4591]
1899	New Hampshire	New Hampshire has no specific statute prohibiting sodomy nor did the state ever enact one. However, in 1899 the legislature passed an "offense against chastity" that prohibits the commission of any "unnatural and lascivious act with another person." [L. 1899, c. 33, §1]
1902	Iowa	The Iowa legislature passed its first sodomy statute in 1892. Ten years later it revised the law to include oral intercourse and bestiality. [29 G.A., c. 148, §1, (1902)]
1903	Michigan	In 1892 the Michigan courts held that, to constitute the offense of sodomy, the sexual act must be committed anally. [People v. Hodgkin, 94 Mich. 27, 53 N.W. 794 (1892)] Partly as a result of this ruling, the Michigan legislature enacted a statute in 1903 making felonious acts of "gross indecency" committed in public or private between one male and another. [L. 1903, c. 198, §1] Similar statutes prohibiting gross indecency between females and females were enacted in 1939. [L. 1939, c. 148, p. 294] In addition, in 1897 a bill to protect boys under the age of fifteen years from homosexual advances was enacted. [L. 1897, c. 95, §2]

1904	Georgia	The state courts ruled that Georgia's sodomy statute covered fellatio. [Herring v. State, 119 Ga. 709, 46 S.E. 876 (1904)]
1909	Minnesota	The Minnesota statute prohibiting sodomy was amended to make its language explicit with respect to oral intercourse and necrophilia. [L. 1909, c. 270, §1]
1909	Washington	Washington did not have a sodomy statute until 1893. In 1909 the law was amended to include oral intercourse and necrophilia within the scope of the sodomy statute. [L. 1909, c. 249, §204]
1910	South Dakota	South Dakota's statute was declared by the South Dakota courts to cover copulation *per os*. [State v. Whitemarsh, 26 S.D. 426, 128 N.W. 580 (1910)]
1911	Missouri	The Missouri legislature revised its sodomy statute to explicitly include copulation *per os*. [L. 1911, p. 198, §1]
1913	Nebraska	The original Nebraska statute prohibiting sodomy was passed in 1875. In 1910 the Nebraska Supreme Court ruled that the law did not prohibit acts of fellatio. [86 Neb. 234, 125 N.W. 594 (1910)] As a result of this ruling, the Nebraska legislature enacted a new statute explicitly prohibiting bestiality and all carnal copulation "in any opening of the body except sexual parts." [L. 1913, p. 203]
1913	Oregon	Oregon's original statute was revised in 1913 to cover oral intercourse or "any act or practice of sexual perversity." [L. 1913, c. 21, p. 56] In 1928 the Oregon courts held that the statute prohibited mutual masturbation. [State v. Brazell, 126 Ore. 579, 269 P. 884 (1928)]
1914	Alabama	The original Alabama statute was construed by the Alabama courts to include fellatio. [Woods v. State, 10 Ala. App. 96, 64 So. 2d 508 (1914)]

Appendix II. continued

1914	Nevada	The Nevada statute was held by the courts of that state to cover "all unnatural acts in whatever form or by whatever means perpetrated." [*In re* Benites, 37 Nev. 145, 140 P. 436 (1914)]
1914	North Carolina	The North Carolina statute, first passed in 1837, was held by the state supreme court to prohibit all sexual acts *per os.* [State v. Fenner, 166 N.C. 247, 80 S.E. 970 (1914)]
1915	Alaska	The Alaska criminal code defined sodomy as "the crime against nature." In 1915, the language of the statute was revised to explicitly prohibit oral intercourse. [L. 1915, c. 22, §1]
1915	California	The California statute was held by the state courts in 1897 not to include sexual acts *per os.* [People v. Boyle, 116 Cal. 658, 48 P. 800 (1897)] As a result of this decision the California legislature, in 1915, enacted a new section to its criminal code explicitly making felonious, acts of fellatio and cunnilingus. [Stats. 1915, p. 1022]
1915	Delaware	The Delaware statute was held to include sexual acts *per os* by the Delaware courts in 1915. [State v. Maida, 6 Boyce 40, 29 Del. 40, 96 A. 207 (Ct. Gen. Sess. 1915)]
1915	Montana	The Montana courts construed the state's sodomy statute as covering sexual acts *per os.* [State v. Guerin, 51 Mont. 250, 152 P. 747 (1915)]
1916	Idaho	The language of the sodomy statute was ruled to cover fellatio and cunnilingus by the Idaho courts in 1916. [State v. Altwater, 29 Idaho 107, 157 P. 256 (1916)]
1916	Maryland	The Maryland legislature added a statute to its criminal code making felonious oral intercourse or the commission of "any other unnatural or perverted sexual practice with any other person or animal." [L. 1916, c. 616, §1]

1917	Arizona	In 1912 the territorial courts ruled that Arizona's sodomy statute did not cover fellatio. [Weaver v. Territory, 14 Ariz. 268, 127 P. 724 (1912)] As a result of this decision, the Arizona legislature passed an additional statute in 1917 prohibiting the commission of "any lewd or lascivious act upon or with the body of (or) any part or member thereof, of any male or female person." [L. 1917, c. 2, §1]
1917	Florida	In 1917 the Florida legislature enacted a statute—supplementing its sodomy law—prohibiting the commission of "any unnatural or lascivious act with another person." [Acts 1917, c. 7361, §1] The Florida sodomy statute, originally enacted in 1868, was interpreted by the Florida courts to cover sexual acts *per os* in 1921. [Ephraim v. State, 82 Fla. 93, 89 S. 344 (1921)]
1917	Oklahoma	Oklahoma's statute was ruled to cover fellatio by the state courts. [*Ex parte* De Ford, 14 Okla. Crim. 133, 168 P. 58 (1917)]
1922	Hawaii	The territorial courts held that fellatio was covered by the Hawaii sodomy statute. [Territory v. Wilson, 26 Hawaii 360 (1922)]
1923	Utah	In 1913 the Utah courts ruled that sexual acts *per os* were not covered by the language of the state's sodomy statute. [State v. Johnson, 44 Utah 18, 137 P. 632 (1913)] As a result of this decision, the Utah legislature amended its sodomy law in 1923 to explicitly prohibit oral intercourse and bestiality. [L. 1923, p. 21, §8121]
1924	Virginia	In 1923 the Virginia courts held that the language of the state's sodomy statute did not cover sexual acts *per os*. [Wise v. Commonwealth, 135 Va. 757, 115 S.E. 508 (1923)] As a result of this decision the Virginia legislature revised the language of its statute to explicitly proscribe oral intercourse. [Acts 1924, c. 358, §4551]

Appendix II. continued

1925	West Virginia	The West Virginia legislature enacted a revised sodomy statute identical in wording to the Virginia statute of 1924. [W. Va. Code 1925, 61–8–13]
1925	Kansas	The Kansas statute was held to prohibit sexual acts *per os* by the Kansas courts. [State v. Hurlbert, 118 Kan. 362, 234 P. 945 (1925)]
1899	Vermont	Vermont has never enacted a sodomy statute. However, in 1899 the state courts held that sodomy, coitus per anum, was indictable as a common law crime. [State v. LaForrest, 71 Vt. 311, 45 A. 225 (1899)]

Sources: Norman St. John–Stevas, *Life, Death and the Law* (London: Eyre & Spottiswoode, 1961), pp. 310–24; Walter Barnett, *Sexual Freedom and the Constitution* (Albuquerque: University of New Mexico Press, 1973), pp. 21–51; "Homosexuality and the Law—An overview," *New York Law Forum* 17 (1971): 273–303; "Note: Sodomy Statutes: The Question of Constitutionality," *Nebraska Law Review* 50 (1971): 567–75; "Note: Victimless Sex Crimes: To the Devil, not the Dungeon," *University of Florida Law Review* 25 (1972–73): 139–59; "Note: The Crimes Against Nature," *Journal of Public Law* 16 (1967): 159–92; James R. Spence, "The Law of Crime Against Nature," *North Carolina Law Review* 32 (1954): 312–24. In addition, the statutes themselves have been consulted.

APPENDIX III

Year of First Adoption, by State and Territory, of Four Laws Against Prostitution (to 1920)

State	White Slavery[1]	Injunction and Abatement[2]	Soliciting	Vice Repressive[3]
Alabama	*	1919	. . . . .	. . . . .
Arizona	1913[abc]	1913	. . . . .	. . . . .
Arkansas	1913[abc]	. . . . .	. . . . .	. . . . .
California	1911[abc]	1913	. . . . .	. . . . .
Colorado	1909[bc]	1915	1908	. . . . .
Connecticut	1911[abc]	1917	1888	1919
Delaware	1911[abc]	1919	. . . . .	1919
District of Columbia	1910[ab]	1914	1916	. . . . .
Florida	1911[ab]	1917	. . . . .	. . . . .
Georgia	. . . . .	1917	1918	. . . . .
Idaho	1911[abc]	1915	. . . . .	. . . . .
Illinois	1909[abc]	1915	1915	. . . . .
Indiana	1913[abc]	1915	. . . . .	. . . . .
Iowa	1913[ab]	1909	. . . . .	. . . . .
Kansas	1913[ab]	1913	1913	. . . . .
Kentucky	1916[abc]	1918	. . . . .	. . . . .
Louisiana	1910[abc]	1918	1918	. . . . .
Maine	1913[abc]	**	. . . . .	1919
Maryland	1910[abc]	1918	. . . . .	1920
Massachusetts	1910[abc]	1911	1910	. . . . .
Michigan	1911[abc]	1915	. . . . .	. . . . .
Minnesota	1909[abc]	1913	1913	. . . . .
Mississippi	. . . . .	1918	. . . . .	. . . . .
Missouri	1913[abc]	1921	. . . . .	. . . . .
Montana	1911[abc]	1917	1895	. . . . .
Nebraska	1911[abc]	1911	. . . . .	. . . . .
Nevada	1913[abc]	. . . . .	1912	. . . . .
New Hampshire	1911[abc]	**	. . . . .	1919
New Jersey	1910[abc]	1916	. . . . .	. . . . .
New Mexico	1913[ab]	1921	. . . . .	. . . . .
New York	1911[abc]	1914	1910	. . . . .
North Carolina	1911[ab]	1913	. . . . .	1919
North Dakota	1909[abc]	1911	. . . . .	1919
Ohio	1910[ab]	1917	. . . . .	1919
Oklahoma	1910[ab]	. . . . .	. . . . .	. . . . .
Oregon	1911[abc]	1913	. . . . .	. . . . .
Pennsylvania	1911[abc]	1913	. . . . .	. . . . .
Rhode Island	1910[abc]	. . . . .	1910	1919

Appendix III. continued

State	White Slavery[1]	Injunction and Abatement[2]	Soliciting	Vice Repressive[3]
South Carolina	. . . . .	1918	. . . . .	. . . . .
South Dakota	1912[abc]	1913	. . . . .	. . . . .
Tennessee	1917[ab]	1913	. . . . .	. . . . .
Texas	1911[ab]	**	. . . . .	. . . . .
Utah	1911[abc]	1913	1909	. . . . .
Vermont	1911[abc]	. . . . .	. . . . .	1919
Virginia	1910[abc]	1916	1918	. . . . .
Washington	1909[abc]	1913	1909	. . . . .
West Virginia	1911[abc]	. . . . .	. . . . .	. . . . .
Wisconsin	1911[abc]	1913	1915	1919
Wyoming	1915[abc]	1921	. . . . .	. . . . .

Sources: Herbert E. Gernert, "Legislation on the Social Evil: The White Slave Traffic Laws," *Vigilance* 25 (June 1912): 2–9; Timothy Newell Pfeiffer, "The Matter and Method of Social Hygiene Legislation," *Social Hygiene* 3 (January 1917): 51–73; George E. Worthington, "Developments in Social Hygiene Legislation from 1917 to September 1, 1920." *Social Hygiene* 6 (October 1920): 557–68; Joseph Mayer, *The Regulation of Commercialized Vice* (New York: The Klebold Press, 1922), pp. 28–32; David Lawrence, "Washington—The Cleanest Capital in the World," *Social Hygiene* 3 (July 1917): 312–21. In addition, the statutes themselves have been consulted.

Notes: 1. The White Slavery Laws have reference to three classes of offenses, indicated by the superscripts a, b, and c after the year of adoption, viz.:

[a]enticing, transporting, or forcing a female into prostitution;
[b]pandering:
[c]pimping and living off the earnings of a prostitute.

The table indicates the date of passage by the various states of a comprehensive law prohibiting these acts. In some instances these laws superseded previous statutes proscribing more specific aspects of these offenses, such as enticing a female under a particular age to a house of ill fame.

2. The Injunction and Abatement Laws permitted a civil action to enjoin the operation of a brothel as a public nuisance. The table covers legislation to 1921.

3. The Vice Repressive Law is a comprehensive statute prohibiting, among other things, keeping, setting up, maintaining, operating, occupying, permitting someone to occupy, transporting to, directing someone to, residing in, entering, remaining in, any place, structure, building, or conveyance for the purpose of prostitution, lewdness, or assignation; soliciting for the purpose of prostitution, lewdness, or assignation;

Notes. continued

"giving or receiving of the body for sexual intercourse for hire"; and, "giving or receiving of the body for indiscriminate sexual intercourse without hire."

*Alabama did not pass a White Slave Law by 1920. However, in 1897 its legislature passed a statute directed against procuring or employing a female over ten and under eighteen for purposes of prostitution. It later amended its vagrancy statute to cover pimps and prostitutes.

**Maine, New Hampshire, and Texas enacted statutes that classified bawdy houses as nuisances prior to Iowa's passage of its Red Light Injunction and Abatement Law in 1909. The dates of passage are: Maine, 1891; New Hampshire, 1899; and Texas, 1907.

✳ *Chapter 3*

Psychiatric Diversion in the Criminal Justice System: A Critique

Thomas S. Szasz M.D.

> It is of the essence of the demand for equality before the law that people
> should be treated alike in spite of the fact that they are different.
>
> F.A. Hayek[1]

I

I shall use the phrase "psychiatric diversion in the criminal justice
system" to refer to any of the interventions of psychiatry that occur
in connection with individuals identified as convicted offenders, with
defendants charged with crime, or with persons suspected of lawbreaking or of legally permissible misbehavior by authorities empow-
ered to invoke the criminal process. Psychiatric diversions from the
criminal justice system thus range from such specific acts as exempt-
ing a criminal sentenced to death from execution by claiming that he
is psychotic to civilly committing a person because he is deemed to
be a suicidal risk. Between these extremes, as it were, psychiatric
diversion includes all the countless interpositions of psychiatry in
the criminal justice system, such as the pretrial examination of defendants for fitness to stand trial, the insanity plea, the insanity verdict,
criminal commitment, civil commitment instead of prosecution for
a crime, and, last but not least, the judicial imposition of various
psychiatric instead of penal sentences on persons formally diverted
from the criminal process by treating them as incompetent patients
rather than as competent lawbreakers.[2]

1. F.A. Hayek, *The Constitution of Liberty* (Chicago: University of Chicago
Press, 1960), p. 86.
2. See generally, T.S. Szasz, *Law, Liberty and Psychiatry* (New York:
Macmillan, 1963); id., *Psychiatric Justice* (New York: Macmillan, 1965); id.,

II

Although, in principle, psychiatric diversion is a matter of political philosophy, jurisprudence, and forensic psychiatry, and may therefore be appropriately discussed in the abstract vocabularies of those disciplines, it is in practice a brutal fact of everyday life and hence must also be discussed in the ordinary language of everyday life. I shall do so, to begin with, mainly by citing and briefly commenting on contemporary American examples of psychiatric diversion. [3]

A recent article, revealingly titled "Presidential Assassination: An American Problem," by Edwin A. Weinstein, a professor at Mount Sinai Medical School and an acknowledged expert on such matters, begins with the following two sentences: "Assassinations of Heads of State of foreign countries have usually been carried out by organized political groups seeking to overthrow the government or change its policies. In the United States, on the other hand, Presidential assassinations have been the work of mentally disturbed individuals." [4]

To demonstrate the depravity of this sort of writing, let me rephrase these sentences from the point of view of a hypothetical Soviet mental health expert: "Emigrations from capitalist countries have traditionally been the acts of poor and persecuted people seeking better opportunities for themselves elsewhere. Emigrations, and attempts at emigration, from the Soviet Union, on the other hand, are the acts of mentally disturbed dissidents."

It is essential to keep in mind that there is no moral neutrality in this kind of account, that there cannot be any, and that we should not pretend that there can be. Weinstein's account implies that those persons who have killed foreign heads of state had valid reasons for doing so, whereas those who have killed American heads of state lacked such reasons. My sarcastic Soviet modification of it implies that it is reasonable to leave capitalist countries, but not communist countries. Certain classes of acts and actors are thus diverted, literally with the stroke of a pen, from matters of moral, political, and judicial discourse into matters of psychiatric diagnosis and disposition.

Ideology and Insanity (Garden City, New York: Doubleday Anchor, 1970); and id., *Psychiatric Slavery* (New York: Free Press, 1977).

3. Examples from the past and from other countries abound. I will not consider them here, save for a few allusions to Russian psychiatric practices, as my emphasis in this chapter is on the incompatibility between the principles of the free society in contemporary American thought and the practices of psychiatric diversion in the present-day administration of American criminal justice.

4. E.A. Weinstein, "Presidential Assassination: An American Problem," *Psychiatry* 39 (August, 1976): 291.

Ironically, when psychiatric diversion is now practiced in the Soviet Union, it provokes indignant condemnation by Western observers and by Alexander Solzhenitsyn. For example, in his *Warning to West*, Solzhenitsyn writes: "In Odessa, Vyacheslav Grunov has been arrested for possessing illicit literature and put into a lunatic asylum."[5]

If we replace illicit books with illicit drugs, and change the scene to the United States, Solzhenitsyn's sentence reads: "In Chicago, John Jones has been arrested for possessing illicit drugs and put into a lunatic asylum."

However, many thinkers—Ludwig von Mises among them[6]—have suggested that books are more dangerous than drugs. Hence, if it makes sense for the government to ban dangerous drugs, it makes even more sense for it to ban dangerous books—and to incapacitate the persons who disagree with such policies. I do not see how we can have it both ways: that is, how we can support the proposition that the American use of dangerous drugs constitutes a form of mental illness and that those who use such drugs may appropriately be controlled by means of psychiatric sanctions—and oppose the symmetrical Russian proposition about dangerous books. Yet, as I shall show, it is precisely this sort of inconsistency that characterizes the position on psychiatric diversion of the foremost American intellectuals, including those who otherwise support market mechanisms and the rule of law.

So much for hypothetical cases of psychiatric diversion, which, of course, are hypothetical only in the sense that I have named no names. It is time now to cite cases, to name names.

The most famous modern American victim of psychiatric diversion is undoubtedly Ezra Pound. Pound, it may be recalled, lived in Italy during the second World War. Allegedly he made some broadcasts over the Italian radio that were treasonous. After the war he was arrested and charged with treason. However, instead of being tried, he was declared to be schizophrenic and hence unfit to stand trial. As a result, he was locked up at St. Elizabeth's Hospital, in Washington, D.C., for thirteen and one-half years.[7]

The chief characteristic of psychiatric diversion, as of all departures from the rule of law, is capriciousness. Pound was incriminated and punished by means of it. The woman whose brief story I shall next cite was exonerated and allowed to go unpunished by means of it.

5. A. Solzhenitsyn, *Warning to the West* (New York: Farrar, Strauss and Giroux, 1976), p. 118.

6. L. von Mises, *Human Action* (New Haven: Yale University Press, 1949), pp. 177–194.

7. See Szasz, *Law, Liberty and Psychiatry*, ch. 17.

On April 11, 1976, Melissa Morris killed her three month old son by beating him to death. She claimed she did it to rid him of the devil. On September 15, 1976, she was released from a Maryland mental hospital "after a judge found 'no clear and convincing evidence that she presents a danger to herself or society.' The decision by a Montgomery County Circuit judge, John Mitchell, followed a murder plea of not guilty by reason of insanity by Melissa Morris, 19, of Wheaton."[8]

Here is a case that was making the headlines as I was preparing this chapter. In October 1976, Joseph Kallinger, a Philadelphia shoemaker, was tried in New Jersey for murdering a nurse and robbing several women. He pleaded insanity. In the court room Kallinger acted so crazy that, at one point, the judge ordered him removed. Kallinger's lawyer put Mrs. Kallinger on the stand to tell the jury how crazy Kallinger was. She testified that "he beat his children, worried about his sexuality, never had a friend, and bowled in his bedroom at 2 A.M. 'It was like hell [Mrs. Kallinger said]. I wouldn't want to have that kind of life again.' " Mrs. Kallinger also testified that she would go to bed each night at 7 P.M. because Kallinger would wake her up before dawn to make him a cup of tea. 'And sometimes he wouldn't even drink it.' "[9]

Kallinger's attorney maintained that his client was insane and not responsible for his crimes. The district attorney argued that Kallinger was faking insanity to escape punishment. The jury decided against psychiatric diversion. " 'We took a vote and we all said he was guilty,' stated Joseph Fragala, a Paramus telephone company employee. 'I think he's crazy, but he's not insane legally,' said Joseph Baeli of New Midford. . . . When asked whether Kallinger's moaning, grimacing, and arm-waving during the trial affected the jury, Fragala said: 'It made me laugh.' "[10]

Laughter is indeed the proper response to such antics. But is laughter not also the proper response to the antics of a person who fancies himself an expert on forensic psychiatry and claims to be able to distinguish between "craziness" and "legal insanity"—all by virtue of serving on a jury?

I am focusing deliberately on the capriciousness of the judgments that go into the decision to psychiatrically divert or not divert a case, since, as Hayek has emphasized, it is arbitrariness, rather than bru-

8. "U.S. woman is freed in 'exorcism' murder," *International Herald-Tribune,* 17 September 1976, p. 5.

9. "Housewife tells of '18-year hell,' " *Syracuse Herald-Journal,* 5 October 1976, p. 9.

10. "Kallinger convicted," *Syracuse Post-Standard,* 13 October 1976, p. 1.

tality, that is the hallmark of a totalitarian system of criminal law.[11] Accordingly, I shall next cite the case of a man who not only acted crazy and committed a crime, but who nevertheless escaped both psychiatric and legal punishment, while his victim, whose freedom he infringed, was punished (through his insurance company). On the night of July 4, 1975, Robert Henry went bar hopping with friends on Long Island. Off Montauk Highway, he stripped naked, "finding it [according to the judge] a fine night for a stroll. . . ." The police sighted him, started after him, and shouted to him to halt. Instead of obeying that order, Mr. Henry tried to avoid arrest by dashing across the highway. As a result, he was hurt by a truck driven by Richard Rusillo. Henry sued for damages, and a Long Island judge upheld an award of $2,030 to him and $525 to his lawyer, payable by the Great American Insurance Company.[12] In this case, then, "streaking" (that is, running around naked), crossing a highway illegally, obstructing traffic, and resisting arrest all went unpunished and unpsychiatrized.

The above case stands in sharp contrast to television star Louise Lasser's recent encounter with psychiatric law. Miss Lasser was apprehended for possessing cocaine, a criminal offense. Unlike Mr. Henry, Miss Lasser harmed no one. Her act—that is, possessing cocaine—was quintessentially private. Nevertheless, she could have been legally punished for it. But she was not. In fact, she was not even tried. Instead she was "placed in a drug diversionary program, consisting of seeing her psychiatrist. . . . In ordering the program [explained the newspaper story of the case], which is common for first-time drug offenders instead of trial, Beverly Hills Municipal Court Judge Leonard Wolfe set December 1 for Miss Lasser's return to court. Charges could be dropped at that time."[13] (They subsequently were dropped.)

That is psychiatric diversion in pure culture. Here is another case, illustrating the use of psychiatric detention in lieu of incarceration in jail:

> JoAnne Brown, who was acquitted last February [1975] in the slaying of Burr C. Hollister . . . has been ordered confined to the Nassau County Medical Center for further psychiatric examination. Mrs. Brown, who was found not guilty by reason of mental disease or defect, was accused of

---

11. Hayek, especially pp. 12, 152–53.

12. "Court backs award to injured streaker," *The New York Times*, 24 September 1976, p. A–23.

13. "About people," *Syracuse Herald-Journal*, 9 June 1976, p. 2.

shooting Mr. Hollister in September, 1974. Last week, the State Department of Mental Hygiene declared that she was now capable of release. However, Judge Bernard Tomson of Nassau County Court said that he would not release Mrs. Brown without another psychiatric opinion being made within the next 60 days. He also said she would not be released unless conditions were established that she have psychiatric therapy or chemotherapy.[14]

This story speaks for itself. Imprisonment in a building called a "medical center." Chemotherapy for murder. Cases such as the one above are, of course, both characteristic and common. Here is one from a recent Syracuse newspaper:

A Baldwinsville woman who admitted slashing her sons' throats was sentenced today to continue treatment at Hutchings Psychiatric Center as a condition of five years probation. Assistant District Attorney David S. Howe said that although Mrs. Joan M. Rice, 34, of 8992 Oswego Road, is responding well to treatment, "she won't be back with her family. Those days are over."

On August 9 [1976], Mrs. Rice pleaded guilty to first degree reckless endangerment, a felony, for attacking her sons Michael and Robert with a butcher knife. Judge Patrick J. Cunningham today told the defendant, "under ordinary circumstances, it would be necessary for us to put you in jail." . . . Mrs. Rice currently resides in a Baldwinsville halfway house, attends the Outreach program two days a week, and receives inpatient care at Hutchings three days a week. . . . "It seems you are doing about as well as you could do," Judge Cunningham told her.[15]

There must be a misprint in the last sentence: Cunningham is identified as "Judge" instead of as "Doctor." It makes one wonder what sort of psychiatric treatment Cain and Abraham would have been sentenced to if the God of the ancient Jews had only been as enlightened as our judges and psychiatrists are.

III

Having offered an overview of the anatomy of psychiatric diversion, I shall continue with some brief remarks about its physiology, that is to say, its function. How and why has psychiatric diversion come into being, and why is it now so popular? We cannot intelligently

14. "New mental tests ordered in slaying," *The New York Times*, 30 July 1976, p. B–2.

15. "B'ville woman ordered to undergo treatment," *Syracuse Herald-Journal*, 13 September 1976, p. 27.

oppose psychiatric diversion—assuming that that is what we want to do—without being able to answer the foregoing question.

Commitment to the rule of law places a heavy moral burden on the citizens of a free, or would-be free, society. Indeed it does so for two reasons, one of which has received much more attention than the other. First, such a commitment implies that the majority of the citizens, through the government, will eschew infringing on the freedom of those of their fellows who obey the law, even if the latter annoy or offend the sensibilities of their neighbors. That, essentially, is what we have come to mean by the phrase "the rule of law."

The rule of law has, however, another implication as well that constitutes an important additional burden for those who commit themselves to it. That burden has to do with the enforcement of the laws and with the dilemma of the citizen—especially as legislator, judge, district attorney, or juror—faced with laws he regards as stupid, unjust, or evil. I refer here to the obvious—but often neglected—fact that the rule of law requires not only that the innocent be left at liberty, but also that the guilty be punished. This often makes those entrusted with implementing the law feel guilty. Thus arises the question: What can a people, and especially its law enforcement authorities, do when they are confronted with acts or actors that they do not want to punish as severely as the law prescribes or that they do not want to punish at all? Actually, they have only a few options. They can look the other way. They can acquit. They can repeal the offensive law. Each of these options is used in the administration of the criminal law. But each suffers from a serious defect—namely, that it impairs the collective sense of security that the impartial administration of the law is supposed to provide. It is precisely at this point that psychiatric diversion comes into play: it provides a mechanism that simultaneously allays the citizens' guilt for punishing certain acts and actors and satisfies their need for security by depriving certain acts of their legitimacy and certain actors of their liberty. An historical example illustrates this core function of psychiatric diversion. The example I shall use—namely, the crime of suicide and its punishment in eighteenth century England—reveals not only the true function of psychiatric diversion, but also the fact that this procedure actually antedates psychiatry (in its modern sense).

To set the matter before us in its historical context, I want to remark briefly on the history of the legal status of suicide and madness in English law. According to Henry Fedden, the secular prohibition of suicide in England can be pinpointed quite accurately, as follows: "Bracton, the legal authority of his time, writing in the thirteenth century, does not rank suicide as a felony. Thus fifty years after the Magna Carta, the suicide was not yet legally a criminal in England. His fate, however, was in the melting-pot. Many of Bracton's contemporaries had not agreed with him, and by the middle of the next century, in spite of Bracton's ruling, the person who intentionally took his life had become guilty of *felo-de-se* (self-murder)."[16] Suicide, which had long been considered to be a sin against the church, now became a crime against the crown as well, and the penalty for it was accordingly very severe: the deceased person's body was buried without Christian rites at the crossroads of a public highway, perhaps with a stake driven through it, and his "movable goods" were confiscated and went to the crown.

With respect to insanity, the starting point from a historical point of view is the ancient position, which did not regard insanity as having any bearing upon criminal guilt. According to Rollin M. Perkins, "Principles of criminal liability dating prior to the Norman Conquest persisted into the thirteenth century and a 'man who has killed another by misadventure, though he deserves a pardon, [was considered to be] guilty of a crime; and the same rule applies . . . to a lunatic. . . .' "[17] In the thirteenth century, the issuance of such a pardon to lunatics who committed homicide came to be granted "as a matter of course."[18] In the time of Edward III (1327—1377), "madness became a complete defense to a criminal charge."[19] Inasmuch as suicide was considered to be a species of murder, lunacy was, after the fourteenth century, a complete defense against it also. However, it appears—although the records concerning this matter are sketchy—that such a verdict was issued quite rarely in cases of suicide before the seventeenth century.

The earliest reliable records concerning deaths by suicide in London go back to 1629. From then on we can trace the incidence of both "suicide (in nonlunatics)" and "suicide in lunatics." They reveal that by the seventeenth century, the traditional penalties against the offense had not been rigidly enforced, the body often being buried privately or at least without indignities. In the early part of the eighteenth century, there seems to have been an increase in the incidence of suicide in England, and with it there occurred an important change in the behavior of the persons who sat on coroners' juries.

"The rise in suicide in 1721"—according to Sprott's fine study of

16. H.R. Fedden, *Suicide: A Social and Historical Study* (London: Peter Davies, 1938), p. 137.

17. R.M. Perkins, *Criminal Law* (Brooklyn, New York: The Foundation Press, 1957), p. 738.

18. Ibid.

19. Ibid., p. 739.

English suicide "From Donne to Hume"—may have been occasioned by the bursting of the South Sea Bubble in the previous year; in the eighteenth century financial failure probably became one of the common 'entrances' into the deed. . . . At the same time [as suicide increased] . . . coroners' juries brought in more and more verdicts of lunacy."[20] Uncontaminated by modern psychiatric doctrines, Sprott describes the process of "discovering" that the person dead by suicide was insane as a phenomenon that points to what went on in the minds of the jurors rather than in the minds of those destined to be posthumously diagnosed as lunatics:

> In the eighteenth century juries increasingly brought in findings of insanity in order to save the family from the consequences of a verdict of felony; the number of deaths recorded as "lunatic" grew startingly in relation to the number recorded as self-murder, whereas in the previous century, according to a modern legal authority, ninety percent of self-killers sat on by coroners' juries had been returned as having made away with themselves. Devices were employed to save or bestow the goods of the deceased, and by the 1760's confiscation of goods seems to have become rare.[21]

Fifty years later English sentiment overwhelmingly favored the view that "Every human being must wish to soften the rigour of our laws respecting suicide."[22] Nevertheless, the law decreeing the suicide's burial at the crossroads was repealed only in 1823, and that decreeing the confiscation of his property was repealed only in 1870.[23] But that gets me a bit ahead of this short story of suicide in eighteenth and nineteenth century English law.

The more heavily the punishment of suicide weighed on the shoulders of the jurymen who had to bring in the verdict, and the more brazenly they discarded the burden by declaring the diseased person a lunatic, the more passionately clergymen denounced suicide as a sin, and the more earnestly legal scholars denounced posthumous diagnoses of lunacy on the part of suicides as subversions of the rule of law. John Wesley, for example, recommended that the suicide's body be gibbetted, and Caleb Flemming declared " 'suicism' unnatural, depraved, impious, and inhuman . . . [an] act of high treason against the laws of human society."[24] To deter suicide, Flemming recommended that "the naked body [be] exposed in some public

20. S.E. Sprott, *The English Debate on Suicide: From Donne to Hume* (LaSalle, Illinois: Open Court, 1961), p. 99.

21. Ibid., p. 121.

22. Ibid., p. 158.

23. Ibid., pp. 157–58.

24. Ibid., pp. 136–38.

place: over which the coroner should deliver an oration on the foul impiety; and then the body, like that of the homicide, be given to the surgeons."[25] It is sobering to recall until how very recently having a body autopsied or dissected was considered to be a punishment even more horrible than burying it at the crossroads.

To be sure, not all clergymen were so sanguine, some supporting the tactic of declaring the suicide *non compos mentis* as moral progress. According to Sprott, the earliest instance of clerical support for this strategy was John Jortin's endorsement of it in 1772: "In all dubious cases of this kind, it is surely safer and better to judge too favourably than too severely of the deceased; and our Juries do well to incline, as they commonly do, on the merciful side, as far as reason can possibly permit; and the more so, since by a contrary verdict the family of the dead person may perhaps suffer much."[26]

Such psychiatric bootlegging of humanism carried a very high price, however. Veritably, eighteenth century Englishmen sitting on coroner's juries diagnosing suicides as lunatics sowed the wind, and we are reaping the whirlwind. They had laid the legal foundations for a forensic-psychiatric maxim that has, for obvious reasons, become dear to the hearts of modern mad-doctors—namely, that a person suspected of lunacy is insane until proven otherwise. Put that way, it is obvious that such a legal-psychiatric rule is the very opposite of the legal-punitive rule that a person accused of crime is innocent until proven guilty. Nevertheless, for two centuries people in English-speaking countries have been puzzled by the so-called abuses of institutional psychiatry and have sought, vainly, to remedy them. But the abuses of our psychiatric system flow as inexorably from the claim that a person is crazy unless he can prove to his diagnosticians that he is not, as flow the abuses of the inquisitorial criminal systems from the claim that a defendant is guilty unless he can prove to his prosecutors that he is not.

These evasions of the laws punishing suicide were, of course, too obvious to deceive legal scholars. Thus, Blackstone realized at once that if a finding of lunacy could be contrived to nullify the laws against suicide, it could just as easily be contrived against every other crime. That, of course, is precisely what men like Karl Menninger and Ramsey Clark have done, believing all the while that they have "discovered" that crime is mental illness and that criminals ought to be treated rather than punished![27]

25. Ibid., p. 138.
26. Ibid., p. 140.
27. See, for example, T.S. Szasz, "Justice in the Therapeutic State," *Indiana Legal Forum* 3 (Fall 1969): 14–34; and id., "The ACLU's 'Mental Illness' Cop-out," *Reason* 5 (January 1974): 4–9.

I shall conclude this brief review of the historical origins of psychiatric diversion by citing Blackstone's restatement of the reasons that justified, in his mind and in his time, prohibiting suicide as a crime, and his objections against evading the law punishing suicide by declaring the deceased a lunatic.

> The law of England [wrote Blackstone] wisely and religiously considers that no man has the power to destroy life, but by commission from God, the author of it; and as the suicide is guilty of a double offence, one spiritual, in evading the prerogative of the Almighty, and rushing into His immediate presence uncalled for, the other temporal, against the sovereign, who has an interest in the preservation of all his subjects, the law has therefore ranked this among the highest crimes, making it a peculiar species of felony committed on one's self.[28]

Noting that for suicide to be a crime, the person who commits it must be "in his senses," Blackstone continues: "But this excuse [of lunacy] ought not to be strained to that length to which our coroner's juries are apt to carry it, viz., that the very act of suicide is an evidence of insanity; as if every man who acts contrary to reason had no reason at all; for the same argument would prove every other criminal *non compos*, as well as the self-murderer."[29]

Sprott cites a part of this passage and emphasizes Blackstone's "disgust" with the behavior of jurors who so conduct themselves.[30] I need hardly belabor here that precisely what then disgusted Blackstone now delights every intellectual, scientist, and right-thinking person: although suicide is no longer a crime, it is in all "civilized" societies a violation of the mental hygiene laws and, if it is unsuccessful, is punishable by appropriate psychiatric sanctions.[31] It is clear, I hope, how well this arrangement satisfies simultaneously the need to condemn suicide and control suicidal persons as well as the need to avoid feeling guilty for doing so.

Mutatis mutandis, the same considerations now apply to virtually all prohibitions and punishments. Cut adrift from religion and natural law, modern man floats without a compass on an existential sea of choices, unsure of what he should condemn and how he should punish. The result is the massive escapism into the embrace of what I

28. W. Blackstone, *Commentaries on the Laws of England: Of Public Wrongs* (1755–1765) (Boston: Beacon Press, 1962), pp. 211–12.

29. Ibid., p. 212.

30. Sprott, p. 157.

31. See, T.S. Szasz, "The Ethics of Suicide," in *The Theology of Medicine*, ed. T.S. Szasz (New York: Harper & Row, 1977), ch. 6.

have called the Therapeutic State.[32] In such a state, there is no evil, only sickness; there is no punishment, only treatment.[33]

I trust that the example I have cited demonstrates that psychiatric diversion has, in fact, nothing to do with psychiatry. It is not the result of, and does not depend on, the modern understanding of the mind or of mental diseases, as its contemporary proponents claim; instead, it is the result of, and depends on, its psychosocial utility, especially in a free and democratic society, for managing the guilty conduct of certain persons and the guilty consciences of those who sit in judgment on them.

IV

Psychiatric interference with the rule of law in the name of individualized justice and therapy is precisely the sort of thing that, as we might expect, would appeal to statists of all persuasions—as the contemporary literature on "psychiatric justice" in fact reveals.[34] However, the fact that psychiatric justice is also embraced by antistatists—by classical liberals, conservatives, and even libertarians— is, on the face of it, rather surprising. It illustrates, as I shall try to show, that, like nearly everyone in modern society, the antistatists too are sometimes the unwitting victims of a psychiatric-therapeutic world view.

Because Ludwig von Mises is justly considered to be a pioneer recreator, in its contemporary version, of free market economics and of the moral philosophy on which it rests, I shall begin my review of the capitulation of antistatists before the onslaught of modern psychiatry by remarking briefly on his comments relevant to our subject.

The crux of Mises' mistake about psychiatry is simple: he accepts that there exists a class of persons whom certain medical experts, called "psychiatrists," can reliably identify as insane, and that such persons cannot be treated as moral agents. "The anarchists," writes Mises, "overlook the undeniable fact that some people are either too narrow-minded or too weak to adjust themselves spontaneously to the conditions of social life. Even if we admit that every sane adult is endowed with the faculty of realizing the good of social cooperation and of acting accordingly, there still remains the problem of the infants, the aged, and the insane."[35]

---

32. See, generally, Szasz, *Ideology and Insanity* and *The Theology of Medicine.*

33. See, typically, K. Menninger, *The Crime of Punishment* (New York: Viking Press, 1968).

34. See, generally, Szasz, *Psychiatric Justice* and *Psychiatric Slavery.*

35. Mises, p. 149.

Mises here places the very young, the very old, and the very odd in the same class—all characterized by their supposed inability to cooperate with their fellow human beings. What is wrong with this? Everything. I will show this by examples, rather than by exposition. The argument I shall construct may be a little simplified, but it is, I believe, entirely accurate.

A month old infant cannot cooperate. It cannot contract for care, but can only feel hunger or pain, scream, and thus coerce relief. The same goes for a senile person, especially if he is a bed-ridden invalid, who is, save for one big difference, much like an infant. The difference is that whereas the helpless infant "waits" to live and others wait for him to live, the helpless old person "waits" to die and others wait for him to die.

How does an insane person resemble them? The answer depends on what one means by an "insane person." If one means an individual whose brain has been destroyed by syphilis, who is demented with paresis, then what is true for the old invalid is also true for the insane. But it is inconceivable that in 1949 that is what Mises meant by "insanity." It is more likely that by "insanity" he meant the sort of (mis)behavior that psychiatrists call schizophrenia, exemplified by the "patient" declaring that he is Jesus. Such a person, I contend, is not incapable of cooperating and contracting; he chooses, instead, to coerce by means of dramatic, deceptive, and self-aggrandizing claims about himself. He is more like a counterfeiter than like a child. He is defiant, rather than defective.[36] Mises completely ignores that possibility, treating the "insane" person as if he were utterly incapable of cooperating.

"We may agree," continues Mises, "that he who acts antisocially should be considered mentally sick and in need of care."[37] Mises here compounds the confusion between bodily defect and personal defiance, medical disease and moral deviance. It is distressing, too, to see someone like Mises use a vague and potentially vicious term like "antisocial" so cavalierly. How could he so casually psychiatrize the protestor as psychotic and consign him into the crushing embrace of the psychiatrist? There can be only one answer: by accepting the principles and practices of psychiatry as intellectually valid and morally sound. This conclusion is borne out by his next statement: "But as long as not all are cured [of insanity], and as long as there are

---

36. See, T.S. Szasz, *The Myth of Mental Illness* (New York: Hoeber-Harper, 1961); id., *The Second Sin* (Garden City, New York: Doubleday, 1973); and, id., *Schizophrenia: The Sacred Symbol of Psychiatry* (New York: Basic Books, 1976).

37. Mises, p. 149.

infants and the senile, some provision must be taken lest they jeopardize society."[38]

Mises keeps persisting with his catastrophic classification of infants, invalids, and the insane as members of the same class. Of course, I agree with Mises that infants, children, very old persons, and those disabled by incapacitating illness require special protection and represent special problems that threaten the well-being of those members of society that support the very existence of that society. That is why, on the one hand, such persons receive special protections from society, and on the other hand are excluded—either by law, as are children, or by biology, as are invalids—from many of the rights and privileges granted to the healthy, adult members of society. However, I disagree strongly with Mises about his placing insane persons in the same class with infants and invalids, and about the sort of societal response that would, in a free society, be most appropriate for dealing with them.

Infants, incapable of caring for themselves, are also incapable of rejecting the protections offered them. Whether so-called insane persons are capable of caring for themselves is, sometimes, debatable; that they are capable of rejecting the help offered them—indeed, that they often go to extreme lengths to reject it—is, however, painfully obvious. Mises suggests that in the face of such behavior, psychiatric coercion is a legitimate and necessary societal option. I believe it is neither legitimate nor necessary. If so-called insane persons refuse the protection that is offered them, a right that no society can deny them, and remain free, then I believe we should adopt a moral perspective and a social policy toward such persons that is more consistent with the principles of the rule of law than is recourse to psychiatric coercion. I propose that we regard "insane" individuals as deviant or defiant persons rather than as diseased or demented patients; and that we treat them the same way we treat the so-called normal members of society—that is, by leaving them alone so long as they obey the law, and by prosecuting and punishing them if they break it.

V

Friedrich von Hayek has articulated the political philosophy of individual liberty and responsibility more fully than anyone else. Nevertheless, he has the same blindspot when it comes to psychiatry that we encountered in Mises. I shall try to show that Hayek's views on

---

38. Ibid.

individual liberty are inconsistent and incompatible with his own views on the legitimacy of its psychiatric curtailment.

Psychiatric diversion comes into being mainly in response to the need for social protection from all sorts of difficulties that are conveniently attributed to madness or to madmen. Because such diversion arises out of a conflict between liberty and security, it is logical to begin with Hayek's own candid acknowledgment of this phenomenon as a general social problem. "It is very probable," he writes, "that there are people who do not value the liberty with which we are concerned, who cannot see that they derive great benefit from it, and who will be ready to give it up to gain other advantages; it may even be true that the necessity to act according to one's own plans and decisions may be felt by them to be more of a burden than an advantage."[39]

This is an essential point for our understanding of the problems so-called psychiatric illness pose for the political philosopher, the lawmaker, and the judge. That is because a great many people who, in effect, define themselves as mad—by acting crazy, by inviting (overtly or covertly) psychiatric interference in their lives—do so because they loathe liberty. These are persons who, so to speak, do not know what to do with themselves and with their lives. They are incompetent, helpless, aimless, and dependent on others; they try to unload their problems of making a life for themselves onto the shoulders of others. Unless they manage to find a husband or wife willing to assume this burden for them, such persons often get defined as psychiatric patients. As a result, a sort of psychiatric matrimony comes into being, in which liberty is sacrificed for another, higher, good: the patient sacrifices his own liberty for security; and the psychiatrist sacrifices the patient's liberty (and often some of his own as well) for the domination he gains over him.[40]

As a rule, institutionalized mental patients rank liberty low on their scale of values. Such persons pose a difficult problem for the philosopher of freedom, as indeed do all those who loathe liberty. How should he treat the person who instead of wanting to be free, wants to be enslaved? Who instead of wanting to be an adult, wants to be a child? Both Mises and Hayek treat such a person as if he were, in fact, incapable of being free because, like the infant or the imbecile, he lacks responsibility. But responsibility is not something like a spleen that a person may literally possess or fail to possess. Instead, it is something that a person assumes or fails to assume, or

39. Hayek, p. 18.
40. See Szasz, *Schizophrenia*, ch. 4.

something that we ascribe or do not ascribe to him. The point is that individuals who complain of mental symptoms or irresistible impulses feel or claim to feel unfree with respect to certain experiences or desires; whereas individuals confined in mental institutions actually lose some of their liberty. In both cases—more obviously in the latter —the "victim" is, however, "compensated" for his loss by a commensurate relief from the responsibility of having to lead his own life.

It is in confronting this obvious and universal social-psychological phenomenon and the problems it poses for political philosophy that Hayek's analysis, too, exhibits a serious weakness. It lies, essentially, in his treating insanity as if it were a biosocial condition, like infancy, rather than an individual-ethical strategy, like imitation.[41] It is worth noting here that psychiatry's assault on the philosophy of liberty has traditionally been concentrated at this very point—at that philosophy's veritable Achilles' heel—that is, on the notion of personal responsibility. For centuries alienists, mad-doctors, and psychiatrists have claimed that, like infants and imbeciles, insane persons are not responsible for their behavior; and people in all walks of life—professionals and laymen alike—have increasingly accepted that claim. Therein lie the ideological foundations for the widespread acceptance —among liberals, conservatives, and even libertarians—of the legitimacy of psychiatric diversion from liberty. Thus, Hayek writes:

> The complementarity of liberty and responsibility means that the argument for liberty can apply only to those who can be held responsible. It cannot apply to infants, idiots, or the insane. It presupposes that a person is capable of learning from experience and of guiding his actions by knowledge thus acquired; it is invalid for those who have not yet learned enough or are incapable of learning. A person whose actions are fully determined by the same unchangeable impulses uncontrolled by knowledge of the consequences or a genuine split personality, a schizophrenic, could in this sense not be held responsible, because his knowledge that he will be held responsible could not alter his actions. The same would apply to persons suffering from really uncontrollable urges, kleptomaniacs and dipsomaniacs, whom experience has proved not to be responsive to normal motives.[42]

The proposition that so-called kleptomaniacs and dipsomaniacs "suffer from uncontrollable urges" is, however, conceptually faulty and unsupported (and indeed unsupportable) by evidence. Concep-

41. Hayek, p. 71.
42. Ibid., p. 77.

tually, Hayek here falls into the linguistic trap of psychiatry: he seems to think that because a word ends with the Greek suffix "maniac," it designates a medical (psychiatric) illness, presumably characterized by irresistible impulses to commit a particular act. Thus, the person who likes to steal becomes a "kleptomaniac," the person who likes to drink becomes a "dipsomaniac," the person who likes to commit arson becomes a "pyromaniac," and the person who likes his own single-minded obsession becomes a "monomaniac." However, there are obvious dangers in that direction. Would calling cigarette smokers "nicotinomaniacs" make them into mental patients suffering from an uncontrollable urge to smoke? Just how grievously short-sighted and self-serving such ostensible diagnoses are is illustrated by the term "drapetomania" which, a little over a century ago, was considered to be a mental disease characterized by the slave's uncontrollable urge to escape from bondage and seek liberty.[43]

As I showed elsewhere, the language of psychiatry serves the purpose of making men seem like madmen, exhibiting behaviors they do not "will" and for which they are not "responsible."[44] Hayek adopts this language when he speaks of "schizophrenics . . . whose actions are fully determined." The trouble with this sort of statement is, first, that there is no objective way of knowing who is and who is not a schizophrenic; and second, that if an action were fully determined, it would cease to be an action and would become a movement or reflex. Both of these considerations are crucial, especially in the context of Hayek's own argument, since Hayek himself insists that freedom under law requires the impartial application of rules applicable equally to all, and that responsibility is not an attribute but an ascription. Let me briefly elaborate on each of these points.

When Hayek speaks of a "schizophrenic" as a person whose actions are not altered by his knowledge that he will be held responsible for them, he is simply mistaken. I say this partly because the conduct of schizophrenics is susceptible to influence, albeit perhaps of a different sort from that which would be effective with others; partly because there is, as I noted already, no satisfactory way of dividing people into two groups, schizophrenics and nonschizophrenics; and partly because his argument about schizophrenics contradicts one of his most important caveats—namely, that "in public life freedom

---

43. See, T.S. Szasz, "The Sane Slave: An Historical Note on the Use of Medical Diagnosis as Justificatory Rhetoric," *American Journal of Psychotherapy* 25 (April 1971): 228–39.

44. See Szasz, *The Myth of Mental Illness*; id., *The Second Sin*; and id., *Heresies* (Garden City, New York: Doubleday Anchor, 1976).

requires that we be regarded as types, not as unique individuals, and treated on the presumption that normal motives and deterrents will be effective, whether this be true in the particular instance or not."[45] I assume that by types Hayek here means categories such as "persons accused of speeding" or "persons convicted of murder," and not categories such as "Jews" or "Catholics," "fat persons" or "thin persons." Since in its official psychiatric use, the term "schizophrenia" denotes a personal characteristic, like Jewishness or obesity, rather than an illegal act, it is not clear how Hayek would reconcile his recommendation to treat people as types in precisely that public life in which psychiatrists and their supporters insist that schizophrenics (as indeed all mental patients) ought to be treated as unique individuals.

Actually, Hayek's well-reasoned insistence that, in a free society, laws should promulgate abstract or general rules is itself enough to invalidate all psychiatric coercions. "Because the rule is laid down in ignorance of the particular case," explains Hayek in a passage that could have been written specifically to refute the justifications for psychiatric methods of social control, "and no man's will decides the coercion used to enforce it, the law is not arbitrary. This, however, is true only if by 'law' we mean the general rules that apply equally to everybody. . . . As a true law should not name any particulars, so it should especially not single out any specific persons or groups of persons."[46] Commitment laws and other regulations mandating psychiatric diversion do precisely what Hayek here says genuine laws should not do—namely, they single out specific persons or groups of persons whose behavior is to be judged differently from that of other members of society.

Moreover, Hayek explicitly—and I believe correctly—excludes nonpunitive sanctions from among the legitimate powers of the government in a free society. "Under the rule of law," he writes, "government can infringe a person's protected private sphere only as punishment for breaking an announced general rule."[47] This proposition actually contains two parts, only one of which Hayek emphasizes. The part he emphasizes has to do with "breaking an announced general rule": that is, if a person breaks no announced general rule, he ought to be left unmolested by the government. But his proposition contains another important part: that is, the "government can infringe a person's protected private sphere only as punishment." In

45. Hayek, p. 78.
46. Ibid., pp. 153–54.
47. Ibid., p. 206.

other words, it cannot do so as diagnosis or treatment. Since jurists and psychiatrists never tire of asserting that psychiatric coercions are not punitive but therapeutic, such interventions have, by Hayek's own criteria, no legitimate place in a free society.

VI

Edward Banfield—who may be included among the contemporary critics of statism but whose position on political philosophy otherwise defies categorization—is so unreserved in his support of psychiatric methods of social control that in this regard his position is indistinguishable from that of the psychiatric statists who created psychiatry at the beginning of the nineteenth century and have dominated it ever since. Although I am familiar with the characteristic cant of institutional psychiatry, I find it somewhat astonishing to hear it reechoed, without the slightest doubt or criticism, by a person of Banfield's acumen. By psychiatric cant I mean statements such as the following: "However, much of the violence in lower class life is probably more an expression of mental illness than of class culture. The incidence of serious mental illness is greater in the lower class than in any of the others."[48] And further:

In the chapters that follow, the term *normal* will be used to refer to class culture that is not lower class. The implication that lower class culture is pathological seems fully warranted both because of the relatively high incidence of mental illness in the lower class and also because human nature seems loath to accept a style of life that is so radically present-oriented.[49]

I am surprised that Banfield has not yet been awarded the order of merit by the American Psychiatric Association. Perhaps he has not because his statements about mental illness are more extreme than even the APA would now dare to offer. Banfield's assigning all persons who share in the lower class culture to the category of the mentally ill is reminiscent of the Spanish Inquisition's declaring, in the second half of the sixteenth century, the entire population of the Netherlands to be heretics and sentencing it, en masse, to death.[50]

Such ideas and opinions are, however, not matters for merriment. They are serious in the extreme, since—as I have tried to show in my

48. E.C. Banfield, *The Unheavenly City Revisited* (Boston: Little, Brown and Co., 1974), p. 63.

49. Ibid.

50. See T.S. Szasz, *The Manufacture of Madness* (New York: Harper & Row, 1970), p. 297.

work—mental illness is today one of the main justifications for the scapegoating and persecution of individuals and groups. Banfield's own further remarks about mental illness support this contention. Although he writes as if madness were a descriptive term, he actually deploys it as the dispositional weapon it is:

> There are individuals whose propensity to crime is so high that no set of incentives that it is feasible to offer to the whole population would influence their behavior. They may be compelled, but they cannot be deterred. The only effective way of *compelling* someone not to commit crimes is to lock him up—in the most extreme case, in solitary confinement. Society does this even if the individual has not committed a crime when it is considered almost certain that he cannot be prevented in any other way from committing very serious crimes. No one would doubt the wisdom or justice of confining indefinitely a madman who, if released, would rush to attack anyone he saw—and this even if he had not yet seriously injured anyone.[51]

I would doubt the wisdom and justice of such a course of action, and so would many other people. It is important to note that Banfield here endorses psychiatric diversion both as a general principle that is allegedly unchallenged and unchallengeable intellectually and as a social practice without any rules or guarantees for protecting persons from being placed in the class of madman mistakenly or maliciously. The casual assurance with which Banfield supports psychiatric coercion is a stark reminder of how profoundly this method of social control has subverted the classic principles of the rule of law.

VII

The sort of psychiatric diversion from the criminal justice system that characterizes our present American situation constitutes a genuinely fresh danger to individual liberty in the history of man and society. It therefore calls for appropriate new correctives.

Traditionally, societies have been tyrannical. Those who wished to secure liberty or to enlarge its scope were thus occupied with efforts to curb the powers of the rulers, whether they be theocratic, aristocratic, or democratic. From Montesquieu and Jefferson to Mises and Hayek, the magic formula has been limited government. That made sense in the context of its underlying premise: the rulers wanted to do too much (especially in the way of coercing others); hence the

51. Banfield, pp. 207–208.

thing to do was to make it difficult or impossible for them to do certain things (especially coercing others not guilty of lawbreaking). Thus was constitutional government born.

Today, however, we are confronted with some societies, in particular with American society, in which that classic premise is no longer valid, or rather is not valid in its original form.[52] The American government is now a threat to the freedom of its own people not because it punishes the innocent, nor because its punishments are too harsh, but rather because it does not punish the guilty. One result is an ever-increasing army of thiefs and thugs, muggers and murderers, abroad in the land, preying on a people unprotected by their own police and judiciary. Another result is an ever-increasing tendency not to punish those who are evil and who commit evil acts but instead to treat them for nonexistent illnesses.

I only state the obvious when I now say that our personal liberty is as easily threatened by a desperado as by a despot, by a mugger as by a monarch. We all know that. Why, then, do we keep asking stupid questions, such as: Why is crime increasing? Why do so many people rob and kill?

One answer to these questions lies in inverting the patently false adage that "crime does not pay." Crime indeed pays, and in more ways than one—that is, it pays not only for the criminals but also for the criminologists (by which term I refer here to all those who make a living confining, diagnosing, treating, rehabilitating, and otherwise managing and studying offenders). And it pays each of them both economically and existentially—that is, by putting money in their pockets and meaning into their lives. We cannot reduce crime until we recognize these facts. And even when we do recognize them, we shall be able to reduce crime only in proportion as we either make noncriminal pursuits more attractive for would-be criminals, or make criminal activities less attractive for them, or both. We are not likely to do any of these things so long as we look to professional criminologists (and other statist reformers) to solve a problem of which they themselves are so important a part.

---

52. It is important to reemphasize that psychiatric classification and constraint is basically compatible with, and is indeed exceedingly suitable for, political systems that debase individual liberty in favor of equality (of condition) and collective security. In other words, psychiatric diversion is perfectly suited to the Russian style of social control, whether exercised by a czarist or a communist autocrat. *Mutatis mutandis*, it is completely incompatible with the American style of social control which repudiates paternalism and is committed to the principle of treating each person as a moral agent entitled to both the protections and punishments of the rule of law.

In summary, it seems to me that however complex the nature of our present crime problem in America might be, it has at least one obvious cause, for which there is at least one obvious remedy. That cause is the unwillingness of the American people—as individual citizens and as members of the government at every level—to shoulder the responsibility for punishing men, women, and children who deprive other individuals of their life, liberty, or property. And that remedy is to reject the ethic of a fake psychiatric therapeutism masquerading as the rehabilitation of offenders, and to reembrace the ethic of a truly dignified system of criminal sanctions consisting of minimal but fitting punishments meted out as inexorably and as fairly as possible. I believe that such a system of criminal justice is no more utopian than is a system of constitutional government. In proportion as limited government has been realized, people have been safe from tyranny. In proportion as a decent punitive penology would be realized, people would be safe from crime.

✳ *Chapter 4*

The Challenge of Habilitation*

Stanton E. Samenow

In many segments of society, the belief that criminals can
be rehabilitated is dying. But the alternatives have been
regarded by many as so unpalatable that hope has not been
totally extinguished. Incarceration has been viewed at best as protecting society by warehousing criminals and at worst as a degrading
experience in a dehumanizing environment that serves as a "school
for crime." There has been growing conviction that confining a criminal does nothing to change him and only makes him more hardened,
embittered, and antisocial. On the other hand, alternatives to simply
locking him up have met with little success.

Attempts to rehabilitate the criminal either in confinement or in
the community have not been as successful in reducing crime as
people had hoped. In fact, criminals have exploited such opportunities. Many have participated in a variety of programs (job training,
education, work-release, halfway houses, etc.) and conveyed the
impression that they were changing while, in fact, they continued
their crime patterns. Society is discovering that a criminal's holding a
job or utilizing community programs for self-improvement does not
per se assure that he will function responsibly. Helping the criminal
find a place in society does not alter the inner person; it does not
change what he wants out of life or how he lives his life. There is
hope in some quarters that mental health professionals can significantly alter the psychological makeup of offenders. Some, how-

---

*The views expressed by the author do not necessarily reflect the opinions,
official policy, or position of Saint Elizabeth's Hospital; the National Institute of
Mental Health; the Alcohol, Drug Abuse, and Mental Health Administration; or
the U.S. Department of Health, Education, and Welfare.

ever, are outraged at the commission of further crimes by criminals that mental health professionals have discharged from their care as "improved." With sociologically and psychologically inspired approaches failing to meet expectations, there has been a gathering cloud of despair, cynicism, and nihilism. The belief that criminals can change if they are given the opportunity has been severely undermined, and this has nurtured the conclusion that little can be done to change the lives of antisocial individuals who have repeatedly inflicted harm on their families, neighborhoods, communities, and on society at large. As the rehabilitative ideal dies, a process of polarization is occurring. On the one hand, there are those who speak out against retributive justice and continue to urge that criminals be helped into the mainstream of society. On the other, there are those who advocate removing the criminal from society, contending that society has already done too much for him. Those who defend rehabilitation are not necessarily naive. Some, while they know all to well the failure of current efforts, are still unwilling to conclude that a human being is a lost cause. This is especially true when youthful offenders with long lives ahead of them are involved. A significant segment of society refuses to dispose of rehabilitation, searches for new approaches to this goal, and continues to hope.

In this chapter, reasons for the growing disenchantment with rehabilitation will be discussed. We contend that rehabilitation was actually a misconception to begin with. A sixteen-year, government-supported study of the criminal, begun in 1961 by the late Dr. Samuel Yochelson, has resulted in the conclusion that prior attempts to rehabilitate criminals were based on a misunderstanding of the offenders they were dealing with.[1] Having spent thousands of hours studying and trying to change hard core criminals, we are in a position to present new findings and to offer a new perspective on the issue of rehabilitation.[2] Before closing, I shall discuss society's dilemma in dealing with criminals who reject all attempts to help them function responsibly.

One element in the failure of many rehabilitative efforts is that they have been conceived and launched in an atmosphere of crisis. Citizens were locking their doors, fearing to walk the streets; cities became a no man's land after dark. There was a virtual stampede to

1. This study has been funded by Saint Elizabeth's Hospital in Washington, D.C., under the auspices of the parent agency, the National Institute of Mental Health. Dr. Yochelson began the study in 1961 and Samenow joined him in 1970.

2. Findings of our study are presented in two volumes: *The Criminal Personality: A Profile for Change* (New York: Jason Aronson, 1976), and *The Criminal Personality: The Change Process* (New York: Jason Aronson, 1977). A third volume will be published on the criminal drug user.

do something, rather than sit back helplessly. This atmosphere was and still remains conducive to doing anything that anyone thinks might help. Consequently, ad hoc, ill-conceived programs have often been hastily set up and poorly administered. Little, if any, systematic evaluation of results has been attempted, and followups have been mostly cursory. While enthusiasm for many of these crash efforts has been initially high, this has usually been followed by near total disenchantment as more money was spent and expectations were not fulfilled.

Rehabilitative measures have generally been tied to their sponsors' beliefs about what causes crime. Those who have thought that the environment causes crime have argued for changes in the environment as both remedial and preventive. Poverty, broken homes, the schools, the mass media, the alienating aspects of highly developed technology, discrimination, the social malaise attending materialism and affluence, and the values of a "sick society" were among the multitude of factors regarded as contributory. The 1960s saw a plethora of social programs enacted to remedy these ills. Opportunities for jobs and education were expanded, much substandard housing was torn down, schools revised curricula and beefed up guidance departments, progress was made in civil rights, and other adverse social conditions were the target of new programs. Proponents of these programs believed that crime reduction would be one outcome of offering improved conditions of life.[3] However, despite all this, crime remained.

Some searched for the answers in psychology. It was hoped that criminality could be "treated," much in the way other maladaptive behavior had been treated. Psychological techniques that were successful in treating disturbed but responsible people were utilized with criminals. This was understandable, since criminals were thought to be basically little different from the rest of humanity and therefore amenable to the same form of treatment as other patient groups.[4]

3. The President's Commission on Law Enforcement and Administration of Justice (1967, p. 60) declared: "Before this Nation can hope to reduce crime significantly or lastingly, it must mount and maintain a massive attack against the conditions of life that underlie it." See the commission's report, *The Challenge of Crime in a Free Society* (Washington, D.C.: U.S. Government Printing Office).

4. Law professor Weihofen cites a 1952 study by psychiatrists Cruvant and Waldrop, who said:

Mentally ill people who have committed violent and serious offenses against society are not a group apart from other mentally ill persons who have not translated their emotional conflicts into overt assault upon others. They run the same gamut of psychiatric disorders as psychiatric patients in general. Moreover, psychotic murderers respond to the same methods of care and treatment as other mental hospital patients.

The 1960s saw an acceleration in the development of programs in forensic psychiatry. Various forms of psychotherapy and counseling, both group and individual, proliferated in correctional facilities as well as in psychiatric hospitals. Indeed, the first four years of our investigation were spent taking extensive detailed histories from, and working hundreds of hours with, criminals. Because our objective was to discover the psychologic roots of criminal behavior and to help criminals achieve insights that would result in change, we uncovered their oedipal complexes, castration anxieties, and other aspects of psychosexual development. After literally thousands of hours in this undertaking, we found ourselves with criminals who had well-developed psychiatric insight rather than criminals who lacked such insight. They remained criminals and continued their violating patterns. They had examined us as we were examining them and had fed to us what they thought we wanted to hear. They seized upon any adversity in life to justify their continuing criminality. In the course of our studies, it became evident that much of the psychological understanding that we and others had gained was based on the self-serving stories that the criminal relates when he is held accountable and therefore in jeopardy. Society has accepted as true a large part of what has been said under such circumstances by criminals who had everything to gain by blaming others.

Over the sixteen years, we have spent up to 8,000 hours with 255 criminals from all backgrounds—poor and affluent members of both broken and intact families, urban residents and suburbanites, whites and blacks, grade school dropouts and college graduates. Half have been criminals referred to us through the courts and community agencies; the other half have been patients in a psychiatric hospital's forensic division. When we stopped searching for causes and ceased focusing on the sociological and psychological factors that criminals used as excuses, new vistas opened. We began to study how criminals think and found that there is indeed a criminal *personality*. We focused upon the extreme group of criminals who inflict the greatest injury upon society. (This is a small minority of the population who are "career criminals.") Our profile of the extreme criminal applies across educational levels, social class, family structure, and race. It also holds true across different kinds of crime. We had expected to discover different profiles of criminals according to type of crime— property, sex, and assault. We found that all participants in our study, regardless of their modus operandi and particular objectives in crime, share the same thinking patterns. Thus, the so-called "white collar criminal" and the so-called "street criminal" have far more similarities than differences in their approach to life.

We found that ever since he or anyone from his family whom

we interviewed could remember, the criminal had made a series of choices to take a path in life different from others in the family and different from that of most of his peers. He chose to become "somebody" by doing the forbidden and scorning those who were responsible. He went counter to the expectations of his family, his contemporaries, his school, and his church, carving out a way of life antithetical to the skills and values that his peers acquired. Lying was a way of life. He rarely planned long range, except to scheme about making a "big score" in crime. Relationships were based on conquest, not friendship. He rejected the idea of overcoming adversity and achieving success by effort. He fully expected to emerge on top in any undertaking. If he was not "number one," he quit. Rather than learn from failure, he was put down and angered by it. Rather than benefit from the experience of others, he believed he knew it all and tried to be a big shot. He pursued power for its own sake, invariably at the expense of others. Whenever the world did not accede to his desires, he angrily attempted to reassert his control, hurting others in the process.

Some of our observations of the criminal's functioning have, of course, been made by others. For example, Edward C. Banfield[5] discusses the relationship between "present-orientedness" and crime. Our contribution is to consider the criminal's time perspective by focusing on his thinking about past, present, and future. By delineating *cognitive patterns*, we go beyond the traditional descriptions of psychopathic (or criminal) traits and behavior. Our profile of the criminal in terms of his thinking patterns has two advantages. It allows the responsible person to see the world from the criminal's point of view, and it provides the data that is vital for the process of changing criminal thinking to responsible thinking.

We identified fifty-two thinking patterns present in all criminals, regardless of what environment they came from. From the standpoint of responsible functioning, these are thinking errors. To be sure, many of these errors are occasionally made by responsible people, but the degree to which each of these thinking patterns is present in the subjects of our study is extreme—all fifty-two patterns are present to a large degree, invariably resulting in a life of crime.[6] These pat-

---

5. Chapter 5, pp. 133–142.

6. An example is lying. On the one end of the continuum is the person who almost always is truthful. On rare occasions, he tells a lie to avoid embarrassment or to protect someone from being hurt. On the other end is the extreme criminal for whom lying is a way of life. He lies not only to escape detection or to get out of difficulty, but he lies for the sake of lying, thereby shrouding himself in secrecy and making fools out of others. He derives enormous power and control from lying.

terns were not inherited, but were developed early in life to fulfill specific objectives.

It took us close to five years of intensive work to realize who the criminal really was. We had been prisoners of our earlier training and experience in treating responsible people and of preconceptions in our approach to criminals. Finally, we concluded that rehabilitation was a misnomer. "Rehabilitation" entails restoring a person to an earlier condition, usually a constructive one.[7] For example, a stroke victim is helped to walk again and to take care of his needs. However, there is no prior condition to which to restore the criminal, because he has never developed the thinking patterns necessary to live responsibly.

Our objective from the beginning has been to effect changes in the criminal. We discovered that the task was more sizable than we had ever believed. Not only had we underestimated it, but clearly so had society. Those who argued that a criminal would give up crime if he were equipped to function at a job and in other legitimate enterprises had miscalculated. Even if he worked or went to school, the criminal did not want to give up his criminal excitement. A genuine change required that he be converted to a way of life about which he knew nothing. To accomplish this, it is necessary that the fifty-two thinking errors be eliminated and be replaced by a new set of correctives— the thinking patterns necessary for responsible thinking and action. The criminal had to be habilitated, not *re*-habilitated.

Our profile of the criminal is new. In presenting a detailed description of his thinking patterns, we go beyond the diagnostic dimensions of psychiatry or the popular characterizations of the novelist and the media. Once we knew with whom we were dealing—once we were knowledgeable about the thinking patterns of the criminal—we were able to determine the parameters of the change process and to develop a set of techniques to engage in that process.

We have piloted a program that has been successful in achieving change in some extreme criminals. We initially interview a criminal for three hours, at a time in his life when he has failed even as a criminal; that is, he has been apprehended and is in jeopardy. We do not take a history or ask open-ended questions, because these are procedures that only give him the opportunity to try to lead the interviewer astray. Rather, he is informed from the beginning that we know a great deal about him and that we are in a position to help him help himself. A discussion of our techniques is beyond the scope

---

7. Rehabilitate: "1a: to restore to a former capacity. . . . 2b: to restore to a condition of health or useful and constructive activity." *Webster's New Collegiate Dictionary* (1976), p. 974.

of this paper.[8] In essence, we have developed a program in which choice and will (defined in terms of enduring the consequences of choice) are paramount, and morality is the cornerstone. The criminal learns to observe and report his thinking in detail every day. Using a rational approach in a group format, we identify thinking errors and teach correctives as well as instruct him in a set of increasingly sophisticated processes to deter criminal thinking and action. This occurs in the context of daily experience, rather than through didactic presentations. By proceeding from a specific thought or event and introducing a corrective that can be applied in comparable situations, we teach a *concrete* thinker to become a *conceptual* thinker about a responsible living. *We do not regard emotions as the primary cause of behavior and therefore of crime. The focus remains on thinking. When thinking is altered, emotional responses follow suit.*

The criminal begins to function in the responsible world much as an infant does. He learns what the restraints in life are and what initiatives he must take. He comes to recognize that life entails meeting a series of problems that he has to struggle to solve in a responsible manner. Growing self-disgust and a sense of the futility of his former course in life are necessary to the initial choice to change. The criminal has been intolerant of fear and guilt. Now he must be fearful of and guilty for his potential for injuring others. Moral values develop when the criminal acquires something honestly and prizes it, whether it be the gratitude and affection of family, the respect of co-workers, or the accumulation of material possessions honestly earned. No longer does he dwell in a tiny corner of the world, looking over his shoulder for the policeman. He is functioning with integrity, is accountable to others for time and money, and is implementing automatically the new thinking patterns of responsibility. In short, we utilize our profile of the criminal's thinking to help him correct his thinking and put into practice a new set of concepts that are essential for him to live responsibly.

To be sure, our concepts and techniques still must be replicated by others if the program is to have maximum impact and be ultimately validated. Furthermore, there is some question as to how many criminals will respond positively to such a program if it is adopted for use in the community or in institutions. Nevertheless, if a minority of the criminals who are the frequent repeaters were to be habilitated in such a manner, the savings to all concerned would be incalculable.

---

8. The techniques are described in *The Criminal Personality: The Change Process*.

What then of the majority of criminals who are not willing to participate in such a rigorous program of habilitation? Those theorists and professionals in the criminal justice field who address themselves to the problem of how to deal with this group are invariably concerned with issues of punishment, restitution, and retribution. Many segments of society view punishment as odious. Indeed, some have contended that punishment as it has been administered by the criminal justice system is itself a crime. Karl Menninger called for the abolition of punishment that was, in his view, a "long continued torture." He advocated penalties, such as restitution, rather than punishment.[9] Whether done in the name of rehabilitation or treatment, it was still impossible to escape the fact that confinement in a prison or commitment to a psychiatric facility was still punishment. Some have argued that the latter is worse because it is arbitrary and indeterminate. Now the climate of opinion is such that people are saying that punishment justly administered is a legitimate end in itself.

One controversy is whether punishment can be proportional to the seriousness of the crime. As John Hospers points out, " 'treatment in accord with desert' is probably the most frequently encountered definition of the term 'justice' itself."[10] If one understands the criminal in terms of our findings, it is difficult to see how there can be "just deserts" for such an individual who has inflicted incalculable damage on society.[11] If one considers entire criminal output, there never can be just deserts for criminals who have committed thousands of crimes but are caught for very few (or sometimes for none at all). Whether one refers to a particular crime or a lifetime of crime, as Walter Kaufmann observes, "the past is not a blackboard, punishments are not erasers, and the slate can never be wiped clean, and what is done is done and cannot be undone."[12] With respect to the hard core criminal, this conception of "just deserts" neither changes him nor "wipes the slate clean."

The criminal regards punishment as an injustice. Behind bars, he is, of course, the same person as on the street. He may use confinement (his punishment) as another opportunity for criminality. He may cooperate with the institution's authorities by good behavior

9. Karl Menninger, *The Crime of Punishment* (New York: Viking Press, 1968).

10. Chapter 8, p. 183.

11. There is also the argument that it is extremely difficult, if not impossible, for there to be "just deserts" for particular crimes, such as rape, child molestation, or homicide.

12. Chapter 9, p. 230.

to expedite his release and, at the same time, indulge in as much criminal excitement in thought, talk, and action as he can. Or else, in a show of power, he may confront the establishment in a disruptive, belligerent manner. If further punishment follows, it is yet another opportunity to demonstrate his toughness by showing that he can take it. What of the effect of punishment on later criminal output? Criminals in our study who did not successfully participate in our program invariably returned to crime and often to prison, although usually only after they had committed hundreds of additional crimes. In instances where the taste of the penitentiary was fresh, some just-released criminals resolved to stay out of the "action," but their intentions were not sustained. The oxygen of the criminal's life has been excitement seeking, and it is only a matter of time before he returns to his former mode of existence. For the hard core criminal, the threat of punishment and actual punishment are not enduring deterrents.

This is not to conclude that punishment should be abolished, nor is it to say that punishment has no deterrent effect on less extreme criminals. Deterrence does work for some offenders. Some youngsters have asserted that they stopped shoplifting after they had been caught and punished. Rarely is it possible to determine who has been deterred by specific measures because, of course, the person who restrains himself does not come to the attention of the authorities. How many shoppers resist stealing clothing because they know that they are marked with metal tags? How many prospective vandals are deterred by television surveillance of an apartment complex? The more society beefs up security and establishes more severe penalties, the greater the restraints for some criminals, but the more this poses a challenge to the ingenuity of the extreme criminal. The threat of apprehension and punishment undoubtedly prevents many crimes and reduces the seriousness of some that are actually committed, but it is the extreme criminal who is deterred the least.

In the criminal justice system, the criminal has been the object of attention, while his victim usually has been overlooked. Recently, the field of "victimology" has emerged, and there is increasing interest in making restitution to victims of crime. Murray N. Rothbard contends that if restitution becomes a primary objective of the criminal justice system, the major goal of prisons would be "to force the criminals to provide restitution to their victims," not to simply pay a debt to society by spending time incarcerated.[13] Randy E. Barnett describes a system of "pure restitution" in which the criminal would

13. Chapter 11, p. 261.

not be punished and thereby be made to "suffer for his mistake." All that would be necessary would be that he "make good that mistake."[14] Compensation by the criminal to his victim may well be feasible when a price tag can be affixed for property damage or theft. It is difficult to imagine how restitution can be made to victims of mugging, rape, child molestation, or in cases where the monetary loss is so great that the criminal could not manage repayment by honest means. Burt Galaway suggests that a restitution schema "will contribute to a more cohesive, integrative society."[15] He believes that the criminal's self-esteem may be raised by his compensating his victim. Unfortunately, the makeup of the criminal's personality argues otherwise. The criminal does not desire to be integrated into responsible society. Furthermore, we surmise that restitution may well give the hard core criminal a license for further crime. No matter how many crimes he has committed or how many prison terms he has served, every criminal regards himself as fundamentally a decent person, not a criminal. He may base this on his appreciation of art, his musical talent, his tenderness toward babies and old people, his fondness for animals, his charity to the handicapped, his dedication to humanitarian causes, or his religious sentiment. Every positive deed that he does reinforces this view of himself. If he were to make restitution to his victim (whom he does not perceive as a victim, because *he* is the victim for having been caught), this would be another feather in his cap. It contributes to building up his opinion of himself as a good person and thus gives him more room to commit crime.

The restitution paradigm is unsatisfactory if it is to be applied to the hard core criminal. It might have positive (deterrent) value with less extreme criminals. As Barnett suggests, the criminal would be "master of his fate" in that the length of his sentence would be commensurate with how quickly he makes restitution.[16] He might well pay off his debt (possibly through proceeds of further crimes), but there is no reason to assume that doing so would change his thinking patterns and his objectives in life. The victim would be better off; the criminal would remain unchanged. The latter is irrelevant if society adopts the position, as does Barnett, that "Our goal is not the sup-

---

14. Chapter 16, p. 364. It is important to be careful in terminology. We believe that in speaking of the hard core criminal use of the word "mistake" instead of calling a crime a "crime" is itself a mistake. Certainly, from the criminal's point of view, crimes are not mistakes. Rather, they are the outcomes of his objectives—his thrusts for power and control, his desire to be "somebody" in this world.

15. Chapter 15, p. 341.

16. Chapter 16, p. 370.

pression of crime; it is doing justice to victims."[17] Of course, it is possible, and conceivably desirable, to accomplish two purposes at once—compensate victims and habilitate criminals. But, in our view, the process of restitution per se does not constitute habilitation.

Finally, the question emerges—if a criminal rejects habilitation, if there are no "just deserts," if restitution helps only some of the victims, and if punishment only embitters the career criminal or gratifies society's desire for vengeance, what is to be done with this small segment of the population that continues to commit so many crimes? It is not our intention here to formulate a social policy, but only to mention several alternatives that have been suggested.

One recommendation is to impose harsher penalties—to remove criminals from society for a longer time period and hope that this will have a deterrent and disabling effect. (The controversy over reinstating capital punishment is largely an outgrowth of this position.) Another suggestion is to permit these individuals to function in the community under strict daily supervision. At this time, such a proposal is unrealistic. Parole and probation officers have enormous caseloads, a consequence of which is that their clients often receive only the most perfunctory evaluation and followup. Leonard Liggio writes of the age-old practice of excluding criminals from society by transporting them to found new social units (e.g., from England to colonize Australia and the United States). He states: "The system of transportation of criminals deserves a central place in discussion of alternatives to the collapsed existing systems."[18] Sol Chaneles suggested a contemporary means to operationalize the transportation concept. He recommended establishing "open prisons" by permitting urban convicts to turn abandoned ghost towns into rural communities.[19]

Invariably, citizens wonder if something cannot be done to improve techniques of early identification and prevention. Conceivably, our very detailed profile and new techniques can be used to help educators, parents, and youngsters change thinking and action that might otherwise emerge into a criminal career, in much the same way that early intervention is used to identify, prevent, and correct reading problems, learning disabilities, and other conditions. Most likely, there is widespread consensus that crime prevention is a desirable goal. In fact, there may be substantial agreement that the schools are

17. Ibid., p. 373.

18. Chapter 12, p. 294.

19. Sol Chaneles, "Open Prisons: Urban Convicts Can Turn Ghost Towns into Rural Communities," *Psychology Today*, April 1974, p. 30.

a reasonable place in which to begin.[20] However noble the goals, many problems are inherent in research of this type. Much thought must be given to how to enlist the cooperation of all participants. Even those who may not object to youth evaluation and counseling will be concerned about methods, interpretation of findings, and utilization of results. Children must be safeguarded so that they are not inappropriately labeled and thereby stigmatized for life. Nor is it desirable to coercively remove them from their environment as a part of the research. It seems to us that such research is valuable and desirable, providing that individual rights and civil liberties are safeguarded.

Our work has been welcomed in most quarters because it provides more detailed information about the criminal's patterns of thought and action than previously has been available. Once society understands the nature of the criminal with whom it has to deal, some problems can be solved, and others are placed in better perspective. Illusions can be dispelled and unproductive approaches discarded. The complexities lie in resolving difficult moral and philosophical questions. These involve what society is to do with those who have injured others from a very early age, who resist all efforts at habilitation, and from whom we can expect in the future only more of the same. We hope that our findings of the past sixteen years will be useful to policymakers in their attempts to resolve this social problem.

20. The National Council on Crime and Delinquency (1975) asserted, "Apart from the family, the school should be the most important social structure in preventing delinquency" (*The 1975 Thrust of The National Council on Crime and Delinquency* [Hackensack, New Jersey: an in-house publication]).

✳ *Chapter 5*

Present-Orientedness and Crime

Edward C. Banfield

Since the seventeenth century, political philosophers have maintained that an irrational bias toward present as opposed to future satisfactions is natural to both men and animals and is a principal cause of crime and, more generally, of threats to the peace and order of society.[1] It is to protect men against this irrationality that civil government exists. Hume makes the fullest statement of the case. All men, he says, have a "natural infirmity"—indeed a "violent propension"—that causes them to be unduly affected by stimuli near to them in time or space; this is the "source of all dissoluteness and disorder, repentence and misery," and because it prompts men to prefer any trivial present advantage to the maintenance of order, it is "very dangerous to society." Government is the means by which men cope with this defect of their nature.

1. Most men, Hobbes wrote in *The Citizen* (ch. 2, paragraphs 27 and 32), "by reason of their perverse desire of present profit" are very unapt to observe the dictates of reasons (which are also the laws of nature). If they did observe them, he said in *Leviathan* (pt. 2, ch. XVII) there would be no need for civil government "because there would be peace without subjection."

Spinoza agreed: ". . . in their desires and judgments of what is beneficial they are carried away by their passions, which take no account of the future or anything else. The result is that no society can exist without government and force, and hence without laws to control and restrain the unruly appetites and impulses of men (*Tractatus Theologico Politicus*, ch. V).

For Locke, the "great principle and foundation of all virtue and worth" is placed in the ability of a man "to deny himself his own desires, cross his own inclinations, and purely follow what reason directs as best, tho' the appetite lean the other way. One who does not know how to resist the importunity of present pleasure or pain for the sake of what reason tells him is fit to be done "is in danger never to be good for any thing" (*Some Thoughts Concerning Education*, paragraphs 33 and 45).

133

Here, then, is the origin of civil government and society. Men are not able radically to cure, either in themselves or others, that narrowness of soul which makes them prefer the present to the remote. They cannot change their natures. All they can do is to change their situation, and render the observance of justice the immediate interest of some particular persons, and its violation their more remote. These persons, then, are not only induced to observe those rules in their own conduct, but also to constrain others to a like regularity, and, enforce the dictates of equity through the whole society.[2]

The philosophers' perspective is useful for the present purposes for at least three reasons:

1. It emphasizes a fact—now well-established by experimental psychology—that there is an innate (i.e., biologically given) tendency to choose, as between rewards that are otherwise the same, the one that is nearer in time.[3] Although not of equal strength in all organisms of the same species, some degree of present-orientedness is apparently present in all. That the tendency is innate does not, of course, prevent it from being greatly affected by cultural or other nonbiological forces.

According to Rousseau, the passage from the state of nature to the civil state forces man "to consult his reason before listening to his inclinations"; in the civil state man acquires (*inter alia*) "moral liberty, which alone makes him truly master of himself; for the mere impulse of appetite is slavery." The judgment that guides the general will must be ". . . taught to see times and spaces as a series, and made to weight the attractions of present and sensible advantages against the danger of distant and hidden evils." This makes a legislator necessary. The legislator ought ". . . to look forward to a distant glory, and, working in one century, to be able to enjoy the next" (*The Social Contract*, bk. I, ch. VIII; bk. II, chs. VI and VII). In *A Discourse on the Origin of Inequality* he explains (in Part One) that the savage is "without any idea of the future, however near at hand" and (in Part Two) that "as men began to look forward to the future, all had something to lose, everyone had reason to apprehend that reprisals would follow from any injury he might do to another." In this situation men "had just wit enough to perceive the advantages of political institutions, without experience enough to enable them to foresee the dangers. The most capable of foreseeing the dangers were the very persons who expected to benefit by them. . . ." Law and property, Bentham maintained, exist to restrain and protect "the man who lives only from day to day . . . precisely the man in a state of nature." "To enjoy quickly—to enjoy without punishment—this is the universal desire of man; this is the desire which is terrible, since it arms all those who possess nothing, against those who possess anything. But the law, which restrains their desire, is the most splendid triumph of humanity over itself" (*Principles of the Civil Code*, ch. 9 [Works, vol. 2]).

2. David Hume, *An Enquiry Concerning the Principles of Morals*, 1777 ed., sec. 6, pt. 1, paragraph 196. Other quotations are from the *Treatise of Human Nature*, 1740, bk. 3, pt. 2.

3. George Ainslie, "Specious Reward: A Behavioral Theory of Impulsiveness and Impulse Control," *Psychological Bulletin* 82 (1975): 463–96.

2. It calls attention to the diversity of the ways in which present-orientedness may injure the society. Crime is perhaps the most conspicuous of these, but behavior that is antisocial without being illegal, or that is merely unsocial, also arises from present-orientedness and may represent a greater threat to the "quality of life" or, as it used to be called, civilization. However much the social bond is harmed by assaults, robberies, rapes, and the like, it may be even worse harmed by behavior that is merely regardless of others' wishes, needs, interests, and rights.

3. It raises the question of how society may be protected against the consequences of present-oriented behavior and, especially, of the role of government in that connection.

PRESENT-ORIENTEDNESS AS PSYCHOPATHY

For at least three-quarters of a century, psychiatric literature has discussed "the kind of person who seems insensitive to social demands, who refuses to or cannot cooperate, who is untrustworthy, impulsive and improvident, who shows poor judgment and shallow emotionality, and who seems unable to appreciate the relation of others to his behavior. Such persons are commonly called 'psychopaths.' "[4] That extreme present-orientedness is conspicuous among the traits of the psychopath is evident from the following:

> . . . psychopaths are characterized by an over-evaluation of the immediate goals as opposed to remote or deferred ones; unconcern over the rights and privileges of others when recognizing that they could interfere with per-

4. Harrison G. Gough, "A Sociological Theory of Psychopathy," *American Journal of Sociology* 53 (March 1948): 365. Gough's theory is strikingly similar to that of Adam Smith in *The Theory of Moral Sentiments*. George Herbert Mead, Gough says, gave what is probably the most acceptable account of the "self" as a link between the individual and the social community, his view being that the self has its origin in communication and the individual's taking the role of the other. Smith's "abstract spectator" comes into being and functions exactly in the manner of Mead's "generalized other." For Smith, as for Mead, it is the internalization of the group's standards that mainly checks impulse. "The pleasure which we are to enjoy ten years hence," Smith writes,

> interests us so little in comparison with that which we may enjoy today; the passion which the first excites is naturally so weak in comparison with that violent emotion which the second is apt to give occasion to, that one would never be any balance to the other, unless it was supported by the sense of propriety [which is the advice, or command, of the abstract spectator]. (pt. IV, ch. II.)

The psychopath, Gough writes, is unable to foresee the consequences of his own acts, especially their social implications, because he is ". . . deficient in the very capacity to evaluate objectively his own behavior against the group's standards" Gough, pp. 364–65).

sonal satisfaction in any way; impulsive behavior, or apparent incongruity between the strength of the stimulus and the magnitude of the behavioural response; inability to form deep or personal attachments to other persons or to identify in inter-personal relationships; poor judgment and planning in attaining defined goals; apparent lack of anxiety and distress over social maladjustment as such; a tendency to project blame onto others and to take no responsibility for failures; meaningless prevarication, often about trivial matters in situations where detection is inevitable; almost complete lack of dependability and of willingness to assume responsibility; and finally, emotional poverty.[5]

What David Shapiro calls "neurotically impulsive styles" involve many of the same traits.[6] Neurotically impulsive people are remarkably lacking in active interests, aims, values, or goals much beyond the immediate concerns of their own lives. Neurotically impulsive people usually do not have abiding, long-range personal plans or ambitions. Durable emotional involvements—deep friendships or love—are not much in evidence. Family interests or even personal career goals are usually not strong. When frustrated they show lack of forebearance or tolerance. Their interests tend to shift erratically in accordance with mood or opportunities of the moment and without being subjected to the critical, searching process that is called judgment. One whose style is impulsive tends to be without moral scruples. He is given to what in others would be called insincerity and lying but in him may be better described as a kind of glibness. He seems free of inhibitions and anxieties. Because his awareness is dominated by what is immediately striking and relevant to his immediate need or impulse, the world of the neurotically impulsive person is seen as discontinuous and inconstant—a series of opportunities, temptations, frustrations, sensuous experiences, and fragmented impressions. This style does not necessarily involve lack of intelligence—it *does* involve lack of concentration and of logical objectivity—but intelligence in the subjective world of the neurotically impulsive can function only to arrange speedy action.

THE PRESENT-ORIENTED CULTURE

That cultures (and subcultures) differ greatly in their tendency to reinforce or weaken the natural disposition of the individual to pre-

5. This is H.J. Eysenck's summary of the article by Gough cited above. It appears in *Crime and Personality* (London: Paladin, 1971), p. 54.

6. David Shapiro, *Neurotic Styles* (New York, Harper Torchbook, 1965). The author says those exhibiting impulsive styles include (among others) most persons usually diagnosed as psychopathic and certain kinds of male homosexuals, alcoholics, and probably addicts (p. 134).

fer present to future rewards has long been noted. Early in the last century, for example, John Rae recorded, albeit impressionistically, a great many evidences of differences in the time preferences of cultures.[7]

The normal or typical individual in some cultures exhibits a set of traits remarkably like those of the psychopaths of our culture. For example, Mayhew in his *The Life and Labour of the London Poor* (1851) notes of the "vagabond":

> ... his repugnance to regular and continuous labour—his want of providence in laying up a store for the future—his inability to perceive consequences ever so slightly removed from immediate apprehension—his passion for stupefying herbs and roots, and, when possible, for intoxicating fermented liquors—his extraordinary powers of enduring privation—his comparative insensibility to pain—[his] immoderate love of gaming, frequently risking his own personal liberty upon a single cast—his love of libidinous dances—the pleasures he experiences in witnessing the suffering of sentient creatures—his delight in warfare and all perilous sports—his desire for vengeance—the looseness of his notions as to property—the absence of chastity among his women, and his disregard of female honor— and lastly,—his vague sense of religion—his rude idea of a Creator, and utter absence of all appreciation of the mercy of the Divine Spirit.[8]

The Appalachian mountaineer as described by Weller (1965) has a cultural style in many respects similar to the neurotically impulsive one.[9] The mountaineer, Weller writes, does not think ahead or plan; disregard of time is part of his makeup. As a child he learns the *feeling* of words and to grasp nuances of personal relations, but he does not learn to grasp ideas, concepts, or abstractions. He is reared impulsively, permissively, and indulgently, seldom being required to do what he does not want to do. As a youth, he holds few realistic hopes or ambitions, is seldom able to articulate goals, and is even reluctant to talk about the future. As an adult he tends to be capricious, vacillating, and volatile. He tends also to lack a sense of who

7. "Statement of Some New Principles on the Subject of Political Economy," first published Boston 1834, reprinted in R. Warren Jones, John Rae, *Political Economy*, vol. 2, University of Toronto Press, 1965.

8. Henry Mayhew, *London Labour and the London Poor* (London: Griffin and Co., 1851), vol. I, p. 4. Frederick Engels, writing at almost the same time (although his book was not published in English until 1887) remarked in *The Condition of the English Working Class*; "The failing of the workers in general may be traced to an unbridled thirst for pleasure, to want of providence, and of flexibility in fitting into the social order, to the general inability to sacrifice the pleasure of the moment to a remoter advantage."

9. Jack E. Weller, *Yesterday's People, Life in Contemporary Appalachia* (Lexington: University of Kentucky Press, 1965). Some of the sentences in the paragraph are Weller's own and others are paraphrases.

he is and where he is going—of being a person in his own right. He is self-centered; all that he does has the self at heart. He does not conceive of a "public good" except as it coincides with his "private good." He sees the government as "they" and expects it to care for him. A fatalist, he has no feeling that he himself is to blame for his lot. His life is pervaded by apprehensions and anxieties, however, arising from a lack of self-confidence. His relations with others, even with members of his family, are difficult and uneasy. Married persons tend to lead separate lives and to have little in common. For the mountaineer work is a necessary evil, not an outlet for creativity or a means of fulfillment.

EFFECTS OF PRESENT-ORIENTEDNESS

Insofar as they are expressed in action, the traits associated with present-orientedness (both psychopathic and culturally given) tend to give rise to a characteristic set of social conditions. These in turn support and perpetuate the traits, the relation being that of a "feedback loop." The principal conditions are listed below along with some of the traits that produce them:

Condition	*Traits*
1. Ignorance (including lack of work skills)	Lack of goals, inability to concentrate
2. Poverty and squalor	Improvidence, untrustworthiness, inability to accept discipline of work, fatalism
3. Unplanned births, illegitimacy	Inability to think ahead or to control impulses; lack of feelings of responsibility, lack of moral scruples
4. Weak or broken family (male absent, lack of parental care of children)	Inability to form deep or durable attachments; inability to tolerate frustration
5. Dependency (welfare, borrowing, handouts, etc.)	Preoccupation with self and with immediate wants; lack of anxiety at failure to achieve
6. Poor health	Impulsiveness (fighting, reckless acceptance of risks); inability to think ahead (failure to secure preventive health care); sensual self-indulgence (abuse of alcohol, tobacco, etc.)

Condition	Traits
7. Nonparticipation	Feelings of personal inadequacy; preoccupation with self; unwillingness to accept responsibility
8. Crime and delinquency	Lack of moral scruples; inability to control impulses, to identify with others, to exercise critical faculty called judgment; freedom from inhibitions and anxieties

As one would expect, these conditions prevail in the Appalachian community described by Weller.[10] The mountaineer acquires social but not other skills. Work is for him merely a means of making a living and he is satisfied with a very meager one—enough food, clothing, and shelter for survival (acceptance of undesirable conditions is part of his way of life). He is content to live in squalor (he has no time to exhume himself from mounting piles of trash, but he can sit on his front porch swing doing nothing). Births are unplanned and the illegitimacy rate is high. Households are seldom female-headed, but husbands and wives have little in common and tend to lead separate lives. Small children are played with, but older ones are left pretty much to themselves. There is an off-hand attitude toward money, almost as if it did not matter, and impulsive buying of household appliances is common. The mountaineer expects the government to care for him. He does not join neighborhood groups or the larger organizations of the city (he may, however, involve himself impulsively in a community group, the style of which is not impersonal). Contrary to what one might expect, there is little delinquency and hardly any serious crime.

CRIME IN PARTICULAR

It would be an error to suppose that present-orientedness (whether psychopathic or culturally given) necessarily leads to crime. The psychopath who lives among normal people may be kept out of trouble by caretakers of one sort or another—relatives, friends, lawyers, and so on. In a society the culture of which is present-oriented, one's knowledge that others are as hot-tempered as oneself is apt to constitute (despite Hobbes and the other political philosophers) an effective social control. In such a culture, people are likely to go to great length to avoid giving even accidental offense to others, out of fear

10. Ibid. Here again some sentences are Weller's and others are paraphrases.

of provoking quick reprisals. (This may explain the low crime rate in the Appalachian communities. Weller stresses the unwillingness of mountaineers to do anything that neighbors might construe as interference with them or that might otherwise stir ill-will.)

It is evident, however, that a cohort of present-oriented persons could as a rule be expected to commit a good many more crimes of certain types than a matched cohort of persons who are not present-oriented. The qualification "of certain types" is important. Present-oriented people are, of course, incapable of crimes that require them to think and plan ahead to create organization or give it leadership, or even to be dependable.

The crime proneness of the present-oriented person has obvious connections with his characteristic traits. His inability to foresee the consequences of his actions or to control his impulses tends to behavior that, without being malicious, is criminally reckless. His inability to enter into the feelings of others and his lack of moral scruples together with the traits just mentioned may prompt him to brutal acts such as assault and rape. His improvidence, together with his inability to tolerate frustration, may lead to his "taking things" for which he has a present need; if what he needs is illegal—e.g., narcotics—or if he can get what he needs most easily by violence or the threat of it, his "taking" is likely to involve other crimes as well.

For most people, Eysenck has maintained, the most effective deterrents to crime are the anticipatory pangs of conscience.[11] Early conditioning, he has pointed out, produces a disincentive—namely, the autonomic anxiety and fear reaction provoked by the idea of the crime—that is felt almost simultaneously with the temptation to the criminal act and before any possible gain can be had from it. The impulsive (present-oriented) person is resistant to early conditioning and has had little of it. Therefore, although he is usually aware of what society deems "right" and "wrong," he does not experience the unpleasant subjective state ("pangs of conscience") that for the person who has had early conditioning is usually a sufficient deterrent. It is possible, Eysenck acknowledges, that a child may be conditioned in the "wrong" direction—that is, toward behavior that society wants suppressed.[12] This, presumably, is common in present-oriented cultures.

The threat of punishment at the hands of the law is unlikely to deter the present-oriented person. The gains that he expects from his illegal act are very near to the present, whereas the punishment that

11. Eysenck, pp. 120–123.
12. Ibid., p. 146.

he would suffer—in the unlikely event of his being both caught and punished—lies in a future too distant for him to take into account. For the normal person there are of course risks other than the legal penalty that are strong deterrents: disgrace, loss of job, hardship for wife and children if one is sent to prison, and so on. The present-oriented person does not run such risks. In his circle it is taken for granted that one gets "in trouble" with the police now and then; he need not fear losing his job since he works intermittently or not at all, and as for his wife and children, he contributes little or nothing to their support and they may well be better off without him.

THE PROSPECT

In countries in which irreligion and democracy coexist, de Tocqueville wrote, the instability of society fosters the instability of man's desires, hiding the future and disposing men to think only of tomorrow.[13] Moralists ought therefore to teach their contemporaries that it is only by resisting a thousand petty passions of the hour that the general and unquenchable passion for happiness can be satisfied. Men in power ought to strive to place the objects of human actions far beyond man's immediate range and, above all, to make it appear that wealth, fame, and power are the rewards of labor, not chance.

Since de Tocqueville's day, moralists have largely succeeded in persuading their contemporaries that, God being dead and existence absurd, what matters is the full and unfettered expression of self. Men in power, meanwhile, have responded to the growth and spread of democracy (why did de Tocqueville not anticipate this?) by placing the objects of human action so as to assure their reelection.

Other forces have combined with irreligion and democracy to make the predominant style of modern culture ever more present-oriented or, if the reader prefers, less future-oriented. The rapid growth and spread of affluence, the transfer to the state of most responsibility for providing for the individual's future, the extension of higher education to the masses (education that exalts self, sentiment, and expression while deriding institutions, reasons, and subordination to a common good)—these influences have been powerful in recent decades and there is every reason to expect them to be so for a long time to come. The sudden and tremendous increase in the number and proportion of young people in the 1960s—young people who had money in their pockets and so were free of all constraints—dramatically strengthened these forces.

13. Alexis de Tocqueville, *Democracy in America*, vol. 2 (New York: Knopf, 1948), ch. 17.

As the predominant cultural style becomes ever more hostile toward authority, discipline, and all constriction of individuality, and ever more indulgent toward self-expression, one must expect to see more frequently displayed the traits and conditions associated with present-orientedness. Except as children internalize "a stringent morality based on fear and trembling," Bettleheim warns, they will live out their lives on a primitive ego, one which prefers the experience that gives immediate pleasure, and, although they may acquire bits of knowledge and skill, they will remain essentially uneducated and uneducable.[14] The more present-oriented the culture, it seems safe to say, the less stringent will be its morality and the less that morality will be based on fear and trembling. In the more relaxed and permissive culture that is coming (if it is not already here), personalities that are now judged psychopathic or neurotically impulsive will be considered normal or, at any rate, not remarkable. As those who have not learned in childhood to control their impulses become more numerous, more caretakers will be required to guide and check their conduct. If a considerable degree of present-orientedness is the norm of the culture, where are these caretakers to be found?

In the society that has overcome all concern for the future, the voice of conscience will be so still and soft as to be nearly inaudible. What for most people is still by far the most important deterrent to crime and, more generally, to socially undesirable behavior will be weakened accordingly. As for the deterrent effect of law and the machinery of law enforcement, that, even in the present state of the public mind, is generally of very little effect. In the society that does not concern itself with the future, even the pretense of such deterrence may be given up. "It is possible to imagine," wrote a prophet of the self-expressive culture, "a society flushed with such a sense of power that it could afford to let its offenders go unpunished. What greater luxury is there for a society to indulge in? 'Why should I bother about these parasites of mine?' such a society might ask. 'Let them take all they want. I have plenty.' Justice, which began by setting a price on everything and making everyone strictly accountable, ends by blinking at the defaulter and letting him go scot free."[15]

---

14. Bettleheim, in Nancy F. and Theodore R. Sizer, *Moral Education* (Cambridge: Harvard University Press, 1970), p. 90.

15. Friedrich Neitzsche, *The Genealogy of Morals* (New York: Macmillan, 1897), Essay 2, sec. 10.

✳ *Chapter 6*

Professor Banfield on Time Horizon: What Has He Taught Us About Crime?

Gerald P. O'Driscoll, Jr.

INTRODUCTION

Although Professor Banfield's *Unheavenly City* [1] is controversial, I find it a very level-headed, carefully argued essay on urban problems. It is a work that is as intellectually stimulating as Jane Jacob's *Economy of the Cities*, that great paean to urban economy. In many respects these two books are complementary, for they combine to present a balanced view of the central place of the city in social and economic development, and to refute those who advocate a rural and agrarian ideal, glorifying a life that men have been fleeing for centuries.

Banfield's treatment of urban crime is surely one of the more controversial parts of this controversial book. I will argue, however, that his theory of the time horizon, which he uses in his analysis of criminal behavior, is well grounded in economic theory. Ironically, my major criticism of Banfield concerns a similarity in his treatment of policy toward crime with that of the recent economics of crime literature.

The first section of this chapter deals with Banfield's treatment of the role time preference plays in criminal behavior. After showing how well grounded in pure economic theory is his approach, I examine the recent economics of crime literature and relate Banfield's theory to this burgeoning subdiscipline in economics. I argue that he is at his best precisely where he keeps his distance from this sub-

1. All references to Banfield are to *The Unheavenly City Revisited* (Boston: Little, Brown and Co., 1974).

discipline; and his arguments are weak insofar as he shares a common conceptual framework with economists of crime. In the final section, I suggest the need for an alternative approach to social policy toward crime.

THE ECONOMIC BASIS OF PROFESSOR BANFIELD'S THEORY

Time Preference and Crime

In treating a wide range of urban problems, including crime, Banfield employs "class" in a special sense. He defines class in terms of a set of attitudes, rather than an income flow. He argues that what members of a social class in the United States share is "a characteristic patterning that extends to all aspects of life: manners, consumption, child-rearing, sex, politics, or whatever."[2] Banfield sought out a principle to explain the "association of the many, heterogeneous traits that have been found to constitute each 'district patterning.' "[3] For his purpose—"analysis of social problems from a policy standpoint"—he found "psychological orientation toward the future" as "the most promising principle."[4] In Banfield's words:

> The theory or explanatory hypothesis . . . is that the many traits that constitute a "patterning" are all consequences, indirect if not direct, of a time horizon that is characteristic of a class. Thus, the traits that constitute what is called lower-class culture or life style are consequences of the extreme present-orientation of that class. The lower-class person lives from moment to moment, he is either unable or unwilling to take account of the future or to control his impulses. Improvidence and irresponsibility are direct consequences of this failure to take the future into account (which is not to say that these traits may not have other causes as well), and these consequences have further consequences: being improvident and irresponsible, he is likely also to be unskilled, to move frequently from one dead-end job to another, to be a poor husband and father. . . .[5]

It is most important to observe here what Banfield is at great pains to remind the reader: "members of a 'class' as the word is used here are people who share a 'distinct patterning of attitudes, values, and

2. Ibid., p. 53.

3. Ibid.

4. Ibid.

5. Ibid., p. 54. Banfield continues: "The working class is more future-oriented than the lower class but less than the middle class, the middle class in turn is less future-oriented than the upper. At the upper end of the class-cultural scale the traits are all 'opposite' those at the lower end."

modes of behavior,' *not* people of like income, occupation, schooling or status."[6]

To understand the relevance of Banfield's class analysis to criminal behavior, one must consider the traits of the lower class person:

> If he has any awareness of a future, it is of something fixed, fated, beyond his control: things happen *to* him, he does not *make* them happen. Impulse governs his behavior, either because he cannot discipline himself to sacrifice a present for a future satisfaction or because he has no sense of the future. He is therefore radically improvident: whatever he cannot use immediately he considers valueless. His bodily needs (especially for sex) and his taste for "action" take precedence over everything else—and certainly over any work routine. He works only as he must to stay alive, and drifts from one unskilled job to another, taking no interest in his work.[7]

Having considered the "pathology" of the lower class person,[8] let us examine his place of habitation: the slum. "The slum . . . is an expression of his tastes and style of life."[9] Banfield describes three characteristics of the slum: It is "a place of excitement," a "place of opportunity," and a "place of concealment."[10] The excitement of the slum is of central importance to the lower class individual because his life is a constant search for action.[11] Moreover, the lower class person is often one who defines his life in terms of the group.

Banfield quotes another source as follows: "The goal of group life is constant excitement. Its behavior is episodic; an endless period of "hanging around," punctuated by short adventures undertaken by the group as a whole or by individuals. Life thus tends to be immediate and sensational; past adventures are continually recalled and the future is not anticipated."[12]

The slum is a "place of opportunity" chiefly for the purchase of illegal goods and the performance of illegal acts. Concealment is valuable as it provides escape from capture and censure.[13] The

6. Ibid., p. 56. Banfield remarks that: "A lower class individual is likely to be unskilled and poor, but it does not follow from this that persons who are unskilled and poor are likely to be lower class. (That Italians eat spaghetti does not imply that people who eat spaghetti are Italian!)"

7. Ibid., p. 61.

8. Ibid., p. 63. Banfield views lower class behavior as pathological. Indeed, he employs "normal" to refer to "class culture that is not lower class."

9. Ibid., p. 71.

10. Ibid., p. 72.

11. Ibid.

12. Ibid., p. 123. Banfield quotes from Peter B. Doeringer and Michael J. Piore, *Internal Labor Markets and Manpower Analysis* (Lexington, Massachusetts: Heath Lexington Books, 1971).

13. Ibid., p. 72.

people of the slum lead lives that tend to make criminal activity attractive relative to a life that is crime free. The episodic and present-orientedness of their lives makes crime, which is often episodic in nature and which offers immediate rewards, seem relatively attractive.[14] Moreover, the attitudes and qualities of lower class slum life reduce employment opportunities in legitimate endeavors.[15] The rewards of criminal activity are relatively high, and the costs, in terms of foregone income in legitimate activities, are relatively low. In short, the slum is conducive to criminal behavior.

My chief concern is with Banfield's emphasis on the high time preference (i.e., the short time horizon) of lower class individuals. Indeed, he has defined classes in terms of their orientation toward the present. In bringing his class analysis to bear on criminal behavior, Banfield sees "an element of calculation—indeed, a very considerable one—in practically all criminal behavior."[16] He then summarizes the increasingly prevalent view of crime: "The present scheme implies that when probable costs exceed probable benefits, an individual will not commit the crime. Indeed, he will not commit it even when probable benefits exceed probable costs if another [noncriminal] action promises to be *more* profitable."[17]

Banfield echoes other work on the economics of crime, such as Isaac Erlich's, which amplifies the choices facing a potential criminal:

Any violation of the law can be conceived of as yielding a potential increase in the offender's pecuniary wealth, his psychic well-being, or both. In violating the law one also risks a reduction in one's wealth and well-being, for conviction entails paying a penalty (a monetary fine, probation, the discounted value of time spent in prison and related psychic disadvantages, net of any direct benefits received), acquiring a criminal record (and thus reducing earning opportunities in legitimate activities), and other disadvantages. As an alternative to violating the law one may engage in legal wealth—or consumption—generating activity, which may also be subject

14. There are undoubtedly crimes that involve great sacrifice of present enjoyment for relatively distant future (criminal) return. But this would obviously not be the type of crime committed by Banfield's lower class. It does not seem that the existence of this type of foresightful criminal behavior requires modification of Banfield's analysis of the type of crime considered by him in *The Unheavenly City Revisited*. He does seem to see lower class crime as the most important kind of urban crime.

15. Ibid., pp. 122–26.

16. Ibid., p. 181.

17. Ibid. Strictly speaking, cost is the highest valued alternative foregone. The noncriminal activity would here represent the relevant economic cost. In this case, then, costs of criminal activity do exceed the benefits.

to specific risks. The net gain in both activities is thus subject to uncertainty.[18]

On one hand, Banfield eschews any reference to a "criminal type."[19] Yet he notes the importance of "class-cultural and personality factors [that] enter into the individual's cost-benefit calculus, making him more or less ready to accept one or another type of criminal opportunity (or criminal opportunity in general)."[20] One of these factors is the individual's time horizon:

> This refers to the time perspective an individual takes in estimating costs and benefits of alternative courses of action. The more present-oriented an individual, the less likely he is to take account of consequences that lie in the future. Since the benefits of crime tend to be immediate and its costs (such as imprisonment or loss of reputation) in the future, the present-oriented individual is ipso facto more disposed toward crime than others.[21]

Banfield notes that a number of the other "elements of propensity" toward crime tend to go together with a short time horizon: diminished ego strength, fondness for risk,[22] and little distaste for doing bodily harm to particular individuals.[23]

Before considering further the implications of Banfield's analysis, I will examine the theoretical foundations of his treatment of the time horizon of various individuals and classes. Among those appealing to the economic motivation behind crime, Banfield is unique in placing so much emphasis on the criminal's attitude toward the future. He does bring in other influential factors (e.g., fondness for risk) that are important in most economists' treatment of crime. But he has placed a great burden on his class analysis in explaining criminal behavior. And his definition of class is dependent on his theory of the time horizon.

18. Isaac Erlich, "Participation in Illegitimate Activities: A Theoretical and Empirical Investigation," *Journal of Political Economy* 81 (May–June 1973): 523.

19. Banfield, p. 181. Cf. Erlich, pp. 521–22.

20. Banfield, pp. 181–82.

21. Ibid., p. 183. The benefits of the episodic crime for those who live the "group life" are especially immediate, and thus this analysis is especially suited to slum life. But see n. 14.

22. Economists typically emphasize the importance of risk preference or risk avoidance in explaining criminal behavior. For instance, see Erlich, pp. 524–29.

23. Banfield, pp. 182–83.

Professor Mises on Time Preference

The comparatively small emphasis that economists place on the role of time in explaining criminal behavior surely reflects the diminished importance of this factor in economics generally. Economists' constructions of pure economic theory are largely timeless. Even where time is considered in economic analysis, it is often treated in an essentially ad hoc manner. But "time" in these constructions does not really change the pure logic of the otherwise timeless analysis. Time does enter in a way that produces consequences that alter economic analysis substantially.

The current state of affairs is in marked contrast to the treatment accorded time in the works of the Austrian School of Economics, from the work of its founder, Carl Menger,[24] down to the present. Perhaps nowhere else is time accorded a more central place than in the work of the late Ludwig von Mises. More to the point, his development of the pure theory of time preference is directly relevant to Banfield's application of time preference analysis.

Mises wished to reconstruct economics so as to dispel the residual feeling, too often shared by economists, that economics is merely the science of wealth. For Mises, economics is "much more than merely a theory of the 'economic side' of human endeavors and of man's striving for commodities and an improvement in his material well-being."[25] Consequently, as Mises argued, "It is no longer enough to deal with economic problems within the traditional framework. It is necessary to build the theory of catallactics upon the solid foundation of a general theory of human action, praxeology."[26]

Being a Kantian, Mises treated time preference as a category of action.[27] All action is future-oriented, as Mises argued in the following passage:

---

24. In his *Principles of Economics*, Menger argued that: "A process of change involves a beginning and a becoming, and these are only conceivable as processes in time. Hence it is certain that we can never fully understand the causal interconnections of the various occurrences in a process, or the process itself, unless we view it in time and apply the measure of time to it." Carl Menger, *Principles of Economics*, trans. and ed. James Dingwall and Bert F. Hoselitz (Glencoe, Illinois: The Free Press, 1950), p. 67.

25. Ludwig von Mises, *Human Action: A Treatise on Economics*, 3rd ed. rev. (Chicago: Henry Regnery Co., 1966), p. 3.

26. Ibid., p. 7.

27. Ibid., p. 100: "It is acting that provides man with the notion of time and makes him aware of the flux of time. The idea of time is a praxeological category." Also: ". . . All human action is necessarily dominated by a definite categorical element which, without any exception, is operative in every instant of action."

Action is always directed toward the future; it is essentially and necessarily always a planning and acting for a better future. Its aim is always to render future conditions more satisfactory than they would be without the interference of action. The uneasiness that impels a man to act is caused by dissatisfaction with expected future conditions as they would probably develop if nothing were done to alter them. In any case, action can influence only the future, never the present that with every infinitesimal fraction of a second sinks down into the past. Man becomes conscious of time when he plans to convert a less satisfactory present state into a more satisfactory future state.[28]

Action involves a plan in response to a present dissatisfaction with expected future conditions. We only act in the present moment;[29] but our action is capable of influencing not the present moment in which we find ourselves, but only the more or less distant future.[30]

Time enters into human action in two ways. Allocation of resources involves provision for the future. But individuals can provide for the future in a variety of ways, some more productive of good than others. A period of preparation is necessary in any endeavor.[31] This period of preparation is what Mises called the "period of production." Thus, the period of production is the investment or construction period.[32] But, as Mises continually emphasized, these purely "economic" concepts are derivative from general categories of action.[33]

There is also a period of provision: "the fraction of future time for which the actor in a definite action wants to provide in some way and to some extent."[34] Some individuals are provident, some

28. Ibid.
29. Ibid. "The present is . . . nothing but an ideal boundary line separating the past from the future."
30. Sometimes the interval of time between an action and its effects is so small as to be ignored in practice. This situation may be what people mean when they say that someone is acting entirely in the present. Cf. Mises, p. 101.
31. Ibid., p. 479.
32. Friedrich A. Hayek, *The Pure Theory of Capital* (Chicago: University of Chicago Press, 1941), p. 69.
33. Mises, p. 480: ". . . The period of production as well as the duration of serviceableness are categories of human action and not concepts constructed by philosophers, economists, and historians as mental tools for their interpretation of events."
34. Ibid., p. 481. Mises discussed yet another time dimension, "the duration of serviceableness"—the durability of an economic good. In reality, this involves no *further* consideration of time than the two already adduced. But the economics of the problem (i.e., the durability of goods) are extremely complex. See Hayek, pp. 66–67.

improvident. In this technical language, the former have a longer period of provision, the latter, a shorter period.[35]

Banfield's concept of the time horizon seemingly comprises both the period of production and the period of provision. Thus the upper class individual "looks forward to the future of his children, grandchildren, great-grandchildren (the family 'line'), and is concerned also for the future of such abstract entities as the community, nation, or mankind."[36] In short, what is being described is an individual with a rather extended period of provision. Moreover, this individual "has strong incentives to 'invest' in the improvement of the future situation—i.e., to sacrifice some present satisfaction in the expectation of enabling someone (himself, his children, mankind, etc.) to enjoy greater satisfactions at some future time."[37] The willingness to invest governs how long a period of production of a good[38] an individual will accept.

At the other end of the class-cultural scale is the lower class individual, who has been described previously. The radical improvidence of the lower class individual, described by Banfield, seems to consist both of a short period of provision, and an unwillingness to invest (i.e., to accept) a long period of production for a good.[39]

Thus far we have observed that Banfield deals with a "more or less" problem: For how far into the future does one provide? For a given future good (which may even be for "the community, nation, or mankind"), how much of a present satisfaction will an individual sacrifice? On the other hand, Mises dealt with the fact that all action is future-oriented, but seemingly not with Banfield's problem. Time preference refers to the general preference, other things equal, for satisfaction sooner rather than later.[40] But there are degrees of this time preference.

35. Words like "provident" and "improvident" have pejorative connotations. Yet they can also be used merely to indicate relative positions on a scale of provision for the future. It is in this latter sense that economists usually employ such terms, and such is my sense. At the conference it was asserted that when Banfield uses such phrases as "radically improvident" to describe lower class behavior, he is expressing his (undefended) values. Whether this is true or not, it would be beyond the scope of this paper to deal with such usage. Suffice to say, such usage need not express approval or disapproval. I am not using the words to do so, and neither Banfield's nor my arguments depend on their value-laden connotations.

36. Banfield, p. 57.

37. Ibid.

38. "Good" here is being used in the most general sense of economics, to refer to anything that is the object of a desire and that consequently yields satisfaction.

39. Ibid., pp. 61–62.

40. Mises, p. 483. "Satisfaction of a want in the nearer future is, other things

The existence of time preference is demonstrated by the fact that men consume at all: "If he were not to prefer satisfaction in a nearer period of the future to that in a remoter period, he would never consume and so satisfy wants. He would always accumulate, he would never consume and enjoy. He would not consume today, but he would not consume tomorrow, either, as the morrow would confront him with the same alternative."[41]

An individual typically does not consume all his resources. The extent to which an individual is willing to defer present satisfaction for future good is a measure of the degree of that individual's time preference. The greater his time preference—that is, the greater the desire for present relative to future satisfaction—the shorter will be the period of production used, and generally, the shorter will be the period of provision. The higher an individual's time preference, the more that individual is like Banfield's lower class individuals. And conversely, the lower his preference for present relative to future satisfaction, the more this individual resembles Banfield's upper class individual.

The higher one's time preference, the less he values future satisfaction, and consequently, the less he is willing to sacrifice for it. In other words, the higher an individual's time preference, the greater is his *discounting* of future events. The greater an individual's discounting of future events, the less do events removed in time impinge on him. In economic terms, such as individual places a lower *present value* on these future events. Banfield's lower class individuals are those who heavily discount the future, and who act accordingly. His upper class individuals discount the future less heavily, and also act accordingly.

Neither Banfield nor Mises need commit themselves to any particular psychological theory of what causes individuals to have a high or low time preference. In particular, Banfield eschews taking a position on the psychological question when he expresses neutrality on the "social heredity" and "social machinery" explanations of behavior.[42]

Banfield has produced an imaginative and fruitful taxonomy that implicitly makes use of the praxeological category of time preference. He has constructed ideal types of lower, working, middle and upper

---

being equal, preferred to that in the farther distant future. Present goods are more valuable than future goods."

41. Ibid., p. 484.

42. Banfield, p. 56. "The time-horizon theory does not prejudge this question. It merely asserts that the traits constituting a culture or life style are best understood as resulting from a greater or less ability (or desire) to provide for the future." See also Mises, pp. 486–87.

class behavior, applying his analysis to a wide range of problems, including urban crime.[43] Precisely because he deals with ideal types, Banfield is innocent of the charge of having engaged in hyperbole.[44] While he has scarcely demonstrated conclusively the empirical importance of these ideal types—chiefly because of the near impossibility of ascertaining the numbers in each class—this is scarcely of great moment for our *understanding* of the tendencies produced by extreme present orientation. Moreover, he is correct in his observation that the patterning of traits is a widely observed phenomenon. If this patterning is not explained by orientation toward the future, it must be explained some other way.[45] Finally, as argued above, Banfield's positive analysis is well grounded in economic theory. Before considering his normative recommendations, I must turn to Banfield's place in the economics of crime literature.[46]

BANFIELD AND THE ECONOMICS OF CRIME

Economists generally avoid appeals to differences in tastes in their analysis of human behavior and focus instead on the incentives facing

43. Banfield, p. 54 (footnote reference omitted): "It must be understood that the perfectly present- and future-oriented individuals are ideal types or constructs; the time horizon theory is intended as an analytical tool, not as a precise description of social reality." On ideal types and praxeological categories, see Mises, pp. 59−64, 251−56.

44. Banfield, p. 158. Save perhaps when he states that the "lower class child's conceptual universe lacks the dimension of time; in such a universe people rarely try to change things."

45. Ibid., pp. 56−57. It is worth noting in passing that Mises hinted at an application of time preference analysis to some of the areas that Banfield addresses. See Mises, pp. 15−17.

46. Recent examples of this literature are: M.K. Block and J.M. Heineke, "A Labor Theoretic Analysis of the Criminal Choice," *American Economic Review* 65 (June 1975): 314−25; Erlich, "Participation in Illegitimate Activities"; id., "The Deterrent Effect of Capital Punishment: A Question of Life and Death" *American Economic Review* 65 (June 1975): 397−417; Richard B. McKenzie and Gordon Tullock, *The New World of Economics* (Homewood, Illinois: Richard D. Irwin, 1975); Llad Phillips, Harold L. Votey, Jr., and Darold Maxwell, "Crime, Youth, and the Labor Market," *Journal of Political Economy* 80 (May−June 1972): 491−504; Thomas F. Pogue, "Effects of Police Expenditures on Crime Rates: Some Evidence," *Public Finance Quarterly* 3 (January 1975): 14−45; David Lawrence Sjoquist, "Property Crime and Economic Behavior: Some Empirical Results," *American Economic Review* 63 (June 1973): 439−46; and Ann Dryden Witte, "Testing the Economic Model of Crime on Individual Data" (Chapel Hill, North Carolina: Photocopy, 1976). Further bibliography is available in each of these. Even Wertheimer adapts this line of reasoning in parts. See Alan Wertheimer, "Deterrence and Retribution," *Ethics* 86 (April 1976): 181−99. The classic article in this literature, which dictated the form of much subsequent research, is Garry S. Becker, "Crime and Punishment: An Economic Approach," *Journal of Political Economy* 78 (March−April 1968): 169−217.

decisionmakers. This professional precept comes very close to being a methodological rule.[47] Economists adopt this procedure for several reasons. Two considerations perhaps dominate. Tastes demonstrably vary among people. Knowledge of this fact is one of the common experiences that we all share and upon which we can draw in our social analysis. Since they vary so much, differences in tastes could conceivably *always* be an important factor in explaining individual behavior, especially "abnormal" (e.g., criminal) behavior. But an explanation that can explain (nearly) everything is of limited scientific usefulness. At the very least, then, economists would fall back on explanations couched in terms of taste differences only as a last resort.

Also relevant is the positivist nature of modern economics. Economists place great emphasis on the ability to predict behavior on the basis of models constructed with relatively few variables, which involve stable relationships between the independent and dependent variables. The variables with which economists deal must necessarily be objective and quantifiable; taste variables are neither.[48] Consequently, economists concentrate on constraint variables, as these are believed typically to be both objective and quantifiable.[49] The desires for scientific explanation and prediction reinforce each other in economic research.[50]

But see also Gordon Tullock, "The Welfare Costs of Tariffs, Monopolies and Theft," *Western Economic Journal* 5 (1967): 224–32.

47. The strongest recent statement of this rule is made in George J. Stigler and Gary S. Becker, *"De Gustibus Non Est Disputandum," American Economic Review* 67 (March 1977): 76–90.

48. Erlich, "Participation in Illegitimate Activities," p. 537. Erlich's approach to the economics of crime is typical of what I am describing: "Since psychic elements cannot be accounted for explicitly in an empirical investigation, it will be necessary to modify equations . . . by separating quantifiable from nonquantifiable variables."

49. Economists thus focus on *cost* differences rather than *taste* differences. Costs are believed to be objective and quantifiable. While this is widely believed among economists, it is not true. Costs reflect tastes rather than objective or technological conditions. See James M. Buchanan, *Cost and Choice* (Chicago: Markham Publishing Co., 1969); Gerald P. O'Driscoll, Jr., "The Problem of Social Cost" (Ames, Iowa: Photocopy, 1976); also see the discussion in the text below. In a much more narrowly focused argument, Block and Heineke offer a criticism of the treatment of costs entirely in monetary terms. See Block and Heineke, pp. 319–23.

50. Yet another, sociological, reason might well be adduced for economists' attitudes on this question. The nonspecialist will tend to attribute seemingly strange or idiosyncratic behavior to individuals' unique preferences. The ability to identify differences in taste requires no specialized knowledge. The ability to identify the relevant constraints, and to analyze their effects on behavior, does require specialized knowledge. Consequently, to write and speak in terms of constraints rather than in terms of tastes serves to identify economists as competent practitioners of their profession to other economists.

For these two major reasons, and perhaps others, economists avoid explanations that appeal to the criminal type. Banfield evidently adopts an economic approach to crime by doing likewise. *The Unheavenly City Revisited* would thus belong in the mainstream of the literature on the economics of crime. But the relationship between this book and the economic research on crime is more superficial than real. For Banfield has presented us with a theory of the criminal type: the lower class slum dweller.[51] This individual lives in an environment that presents him with numerous and daily opportunities for crime. Moreover, Banfield tells us, in opposition to the prevailing view on the subject, the lower class slum dweller lives there because he *prefers* to do so. Lower class individuals do not want middle class life: "The dangers and seductions . . . of the lower class world are life itself."[52] Given their high time preference, their episodic existence, and other traits that render them relatively unfit for the performance of legitimate jobs, lower class individuals have an inherent predisposition or "taste" for criminal life.

We now see why economists have generally avoided reference to the time preference of criminals versus that of noncriminals. To have emphasized any such differences would have gone against the fiction adopted by economists that tastes are the same for all individuals and that individuals merely face different constraints or opportunity sets.[53]

On the other hand, Banfield's analysis makes differences in time preference central to the social analysis of criminal behavior, because class is of central importance in understanding criminal behavior. The radically present-oriented individual is more disposed toward a life of crime than are those with a lower time preference.[54] This disposition affects his calculation of the costs and benefits of crime. In particular, the present orientation of lower class individuals makes them less influenced by the prospect of even severe punishment.

> The threat of even very stiff penalties would not have a deterrent effect upon radically present-oriented individuals. It is likely that even to a nor-

51. The reader is reminded that "lower class" does *not* refer to people of modest means, or to any particular race or ethnic group; the term refers to people of all these groups who possess certain attitudes and tastes.

52. Banfield, p. 238. But this is not true of slum dwellers who belong to other than Banfield's lower class. And he suggests that it may not even be true of lower class women. Moreover, other factors beyond the control of the lower class individual could conceivably be responsible for their "taste" for slum life. This latter is an open question.

53. Stigler and Becker have elevated this fiction to the status of a virtual axiom in economics.

54. This is at least true of the type of crime that Banfield considers. See n. 14.

mal person a punishment appears smaller the farther off in the future it lies. With the radically present-oriented, the distortion of perspective is much greater: a punishment that is far enough off to appear small to a normal person appears tiny, or is quite invisible, to a present-oriented one. His calculus of benefits and costs is defective, since benefits are in the present where he can see them while costs are in the future where he cannot. Accordingly, even if he knows the probability of his being caught is high and that the penalty for the crime is severe, he may commit it anyway; no matter how severe, a penalty that lies weeks or months away is not a part of reality for him.[55]

Two points must be noted. First, if Banfield is correct about the importance of time preference in understanding criminal behavior, then his analysis helps to rationalize the other wise anomalous findings of researchers on the deterrence of punishment. Thus far the tendency has been to suggest that changes in the probability or severity of punishment have differential effects on different types of crime.[56] Banfield's analysis suggests that there are different types of criminals, and that the differences in class, or present orientation, of different types of criminals may be the key factor in the effectiveness of punishment. And, in particular, the archetypal criminal type—the lower class urban slum dweller—will be little affected by the threat of punishment in the relatively distant future, even if there is a high probability of being caught and punished—which demonstrably there is not for almost all crimes.[57] It cannot simply be argued that the lower class will nonetheless respond to marginal changes in the probability and severity of punishment;[58] the relevant punishment may be so far in the future as to be beyond the period of provision of the lower class individual. Or the punishment may be so far away that marginal changes, calculated at the lower class individual's high rate of time discount, may go unnoticed. This is particularly true for crimes that already have severe punishment.[59] Poor and conflicting statistical results in economic studies of crime may very well reflect

55. Banfield, pp. 63, 201. It is true, of course, that the relatively distant future is more heavily discounted, or evaluated as less important, by all individuals than is the present or relatively near future. This follows from the theory of time preference. The reader should remember that for Banfield "normal" is a technical term. It refers to a class culture that is other than lower class. Banfield argues that this definition is not arbitrary, but that it corresponds to our perception of what is acceptable and what is pathological behavior.

56. Erlich, "Participation in Illegitimate Activities," pp. 532, 545; and Witte, pp. 16–19.

57. Banfield, pp. 199–203.

58. Erlich, "Participation in Illegitimate Activities," p. 522.

59. Banfield, pp. 199–200.

this problem that Banfield has brought to our attention. This would be especially likely if certain types of crime attract lower class individuals' participation, while other types of crime do not.

Second, positivist economists to the contrary notwithstanding, it is impossible to explain very much even in economics without recourse to tastes and other subjective categories. When two members of the same income class, apparently facing the same opportunities, etc., engage in mutually beneficial trade, one is virtually compelled to appeal to differences in preferences to explain this exchange. If one such individual borrows and another lends a sum of money, surely this reflects differences in their time preferences.[60] It is simply a fact of life that some true hypotheses in economics are not verifiable in fact, though they may be in principle.[61]

It might also be noted in passing that it is increasingly accepted in economics that what is a constraint—part of the given data—in one situation is an object of choice in another context. It is not unreasonable to argue that we choose many of those conditions—indeed, a large part of our environment—that appear later both to us and to outside observers as binding constraints that influence all future decisions. Certain tendencies in human capital theory, for example, treat virtually all lifetime situations as having been rationally chosen, though these later appear as constraints in subsequent decisions. To focus attention only on the constraints facing an individual at a given moment, without noting that these selfsame constraints are the outcome of past choices (which reflect tastes) does seem out of step with this other tendency.[62]

The practical relevance of these considerations enters when one considers various policies toward social problems. If the way of life of the lower class has little to do with their money incomes, then attempting to alleviate lower class living conditions by means of supplementing earned incomes may very well be a futile gesture.[63] Like-

60. The reader may find it odd that the author is devoting so much effort to demonstrating the "obvious," *viz.*, that different people have different tastes. The author shares the reader's frustration, for it makes little sense to him that scholars would ever have let themselves be boxed into the intellectual corner in which they felt compelled to *deny* what is obvious.

61. F.A. Hayek, *Full Employment at any Price?* (London: Institute of Economic Affairs, 1975), pp. 30–32.

62. I find it especially ironic that Gary Becker, a leading theorist of human capital, should be arguing forcefully for treating people as if they had the same tastes, and that they do not change over time.

63. Banfield, p. 143: ". . . The capacity of the radically improvident to waste money is almost unlimited." In this regard, it seems to be one of the great insights of Victorian social reformers that there are "undeserving poor." To have

wise, if one believes that crime is largely the result of constraints on those who become criminals (e.g., poverty), where these constraints are largely beyond the individuals' control, then one will be inclined to recommend policies considerably at variance with those that one would select if one saw the problem as reflecting pathological attitudes on the part of the criminal.[64] Thus conclusions such as the following make sense or not in a utilitarian framework (a framework that will be challenged in the final section) depending on one's attitude toward the causes of criminal behavior: "With respect to public policy, the findings of this study support a tentative conclusion that criminal activity may be better controlled by reducing poverty and racial discrimination than by increasing police spending and employment and the severity of capital punishment."[65] In short, then, it is being argued that contrary to what he says about his work, Banfield has produced a theory of the criminal type: the lower class slum dweller. He certainly has not overlooked the role of "inducement" to crime. Here his approach is similar to that of most economists of crime. But in emphasizing the factor of time preference, he has gone beyond the literature on the economics of crime.[66] He takes account of the basic factors that they consider, while at the same time emphasizing a factor that they have overlooked. Yet his results cast doubt on the relevance of the standard models of rational calculation. For they suggest that the actions of a substantial portion of the

---

wasted the comparatively meager surplus of the middle class on Eliza Doolittle's father would have left the deserving poor unassisted. This line of reasoning leaves open the question of whether there are historical reasons explaining why certain groups may possess the attitudes that they do, and which make them lower class in Banfield's sense. For a well argued account of such reasons, see Thomas Sowell, *Race and Economics* (New York: David McKay Co., 1975).

64. Once one realizes that attitudes change only very slowly, there is little practical difference whether the "social machinery" or "social heredity" explanation is correct. There is little we can do to change attitudes. Changing the material circumstances of the lower class would then do nothing toward altering their present inclination to crime. See Banfield, p. 238. Moreover, even if we adopt a "long run view" and seek to influence the attitudes of not the present, but future generations, income grants to alleviate poverty may be self-defeating. See Sowell, p. 238.

65. Pogue, p. 40. It should be noted that another study found there to be significant marginal net returns from law enforcement. See Erlich, "Participation in Illegitimate Activities," pp. 556—59.

66. Banfield, p. 181. Banfield's own views on the existence of criminal types are not completely clear. He states: "Criminologists generally agree that there is no such thing as a 'criminal type'; presumably they mean that people decide whether or not to do illegal things in essentially the same way that they decide whether or not to do other things." But he also asserts that "there are individuals whose propensity to crime is so high that no set of incentives that is feasible to offer to the whole population would influence their behavior (p. 207)."

criminal class may not fruitfully be analyzed in such terms. Economic analysis of crime should consider Banfield's work more than has heretofore been the case.[67]

THE JUSTICE OF ALTERNATIVE POLICIES

Surely in one respect, Banfield's *Unheavenly City Revisited* shares a common conceptual framework with most other scholarly work on crime. For his is a utilitarian analysis of crime and punishment. The utilitarian adopts the following procedure. He must first have a clear conception of the nonmoral good (e.g., material possessions). Right action is then defined as that which maximizes the nonmoral good. In other words, the rightness of an action depends on its consequences; and *these consequences are the only relevant consideration in deciding whether an action is morally right or not.*

It would be beyond the scope of this paper and the ability of this writer to give a detailed criticism of utilitarianism as a moral principle. What is relevant, however, is to note that utilitarianism is a very special and controversial moral theory that cannot simply be accepted without justification. Yet this is precisely what most writers on the economics of crime seem willing to do.[68] Moreover, the burden of the argument is really on utilitarians in a very important sense. While utilitarians cannot consistently consider anything but the consequences of an action, all other, nonconsequentialist, moral theories may take into account other considerations as well as the consequences of an action.[69] Suffice it to say, utilitarianism is under attack on many fronts, and, in moral philosophy, nowhere more effectively than in John Rawls' *Theory of Justice.*[70] Specifically, in the area of crime and punishment, utilitarianism is incapable of explaining why the innocent should not be punished if so doing would yield a

67. McKenzie and Tullock do consider the existence of "irrational" criminals. They argue that on an aggregative basis, marginal analysis of criminal behavior as a rational activity would still work. See McKenzie and Tullock, pp. 133–35. They also mention the factor of time discounting in explaining one particular technical issue in the standard literature (p. 152).

68. See Banfield, pp. 205–10.

69. It must be repeated that nonconsequentialist theories of ethics are not generally committed to ignoring the consequences of an action, but merely to not basing their judgments solely on the consequences. Utilitarianism, however, is severely limited to consideration of the consequences only. On the subject of utilitarianism and morality, as well as the wider subject of deontological versus teleological theories of morality, see William K. Frankena, *Ethics* (Englewood Cliffs, N.J.: Prentice-Hall, 1963), pp. 11–46 (especially, pp. 13–16).

70. John Rawls, *Theory of Justice* (Cambridge, Massachusetts: Harvard University Press, Belknap Press, 1971).

net social utility.[71] Moreover, as Professor Alan Wertheimer has recently argued:

> If human behavior were such that punishments would have absolutely no deterrent effect whatever, it would be pointless, from a utilitarian perspective, to establish a system of punishments. If, for example, punishing those who shoplift had and could have no effect whatever on the amount of shoplifting, then such punishments would necessarily yield a net disutility —they would inflict pain and suffering on those punished, the society would bear the cost of detection, prosecution, and punishment, and there would be no compensating gain. I am not, of course, arguing that it would be pointless to punish an individual lawbreaker when doing so would have no deterrent effect, but that a *system* of laws and punishment known to have no deterrent effect could not be justified on grounds of utility.[72]

Wertheimer has pointed out the utilitarian's dilemma. Once the deterrence effect is demonstrated to be weak or nonexistent, it is impossible to defend punishment except by invoking considerations other than the consequences of punishing the criminal. Wertheimer also cites Nozick in briefly raising a particularly thorny problem for the utilitarian moral and legal philosopher. In attempting to calculate net social utility, one surely must justify giving equal weight to (or even including) the suffering of the criminal who is being punished and the suffering of the victim.[73] It is simply not obvious that the disutility of the transgressor should be given equal weight in considering the justice of punishment.

Banfield has questioned the deterrence effects of punishment for at least one class of criminals, and he shares the utilitarian's dilemma. He can only suggest a series of policies for dealing with crime that almost everyone would reject as inconsistent with a free society.[74] For a consistent utilitarian, however, there are no moral grounds for rejecting these proposals. Having a free society might not yield "net social utility."[75] Nor, as Banfield has demonstrated, can any propo-

71. Wertheimer, pp. 181–82.

72. Ibid., p. 182. The hold of utilitarianism can be seen in the case of McKenzie and Tullock, p. 148. They note of those who deny the deterrence effects of punishment: "Indeed, we have never been able to understand how people who believe in the conventional wisdom favor imprisonment at all." It never seemed to occur to them that there are other than utilitarian theories of justice.

73. Wertheimer, p. 197.

74. Banfield, pp. 208–10.

75. Wertheimer, p. 181. A fuller treatment of these issues would necessitate distinguishing between what Wertheimer calls "legislative utilitarianism" and "enforcement utilitarianism." Also, one should distinguish between act and rule utilitarianism. Wertheimer's is a defense of enforcement retributivism from a rule utilitarian standpoint.

nent of punishment who is a nonretributivist consistently oppose preventive detention, and a whole host of other antilibertarian measures.[76] But anyone who sees "Justice as Fairness" must oppose these measures. Yet in proposing (albeit tentatively and reluctantly) these outrageous ways of dealing with crime, Banfield is more consistent than his fellow utilitarian social theorists, whose policies do not always belong to the same system of thought as do their theories.

It is time that scholars reconsider their inclination to utilitarianism in moral and political theory. There are other considerations in moral reasoning beside the consequences of an action. Even more to the point, utilitarian reasoning is deficient in respects that even a nonphilosopher can criticize. The concept of social utility is literally nonsensical. In one of the seminal works in economics of this century, Lionel Robbins demonstrated that interpersonal comparisons of utility are impossible.[77] There simply are not conceivable units in which to carry out such comparisons. Utility is not cardinal but ordinal, and the preference rankings of individuals cannot be compared.

The "social cost" analysis that must be undertaken in the utilitarian calculus is on equally shaky grounds. Economic cost is foregone utility. The only relevant cost is choice-influencing cost. Therefore, cost is the foregone utility affecting each individual decisionmaker. These costs are subjective evaluations of displaced alternatives—alternatives not taken, and, hence, not observable or measurable. Thus costs are not something that can be added up to obtain an aggregate, or social, cost. For such a figure would bear no relation to any magnitude that influenced the separate choices of individuals. And the utilities gained and foregone (i.e., the costs) by each individual are not comparable.[78]

Quite apart from the more philosophic arguments against it, utilitarianism relies on procedures that have no scientific basis. Policy toward crime based on utilitarian moral philosophy is at best without the firm support that its adherents apparently believe it has. Until the economics of crime literature takes more account of these prob-

76. Banfield, p. 209.

77. Lionel Robbins, *The Nature and Significance of the Economic Problem*, 2nd ed. (London: Macmillan & Co., 1935).

78. The denial of the existence of social cost is a far more controversial proposition than the one denying interpersonal comparisons of utility. But I believe the former follows from the latter and from certain other considerations of methodological individualism. Nonetheless, while many economists have chosen to ignore Robbins' brilliant argument against interpersonal comparisons of utility, a surprisingly large number have simply never been acquainted with the parallel arguments against social cost. On the latter, see the references in n. 49.

lems, it can scarcely claim the attention of serious legal and moral philosophers.[79] It is regrettable that in an otherwise brilliant and superbly argued book, Professor Banfield has fallen prey to utilitarian shibboleths.

CONCLUSION

My purpose has been to examine the relation of Banfield's treatment of the time horizon to the economic theory of time preference. The work of Ludwig von Mises, who developed the theory of time preference more extensively than any other economist, provides a firm theoretical underpinning for Banfield's analysis. It is perhaps ironic that in this sense Banfield's approach takes more account of an important aspect of economic theory than does any of the standard economic literature on crime. Where this literature and Banfield's approach are in opposition, I have come down tentatively on Banfield's side. My chief criticism of his approach is that it shares the utilitarian bias of much of the literature on economic policy. Even some economists who purport to do only positive economics implicitly accept the presuppositions of utilitarians. Briefly noting the philosophic case against utilitarianism as a moral philosophy, I pointed out some of the scientific errors it makes.

One can conclude, then, that shorn of certain of its normative presuppositions, the *Unheavenly City Revisited* is one of the most important books recently written on a complex subject. Though he apparently had no acquaintance with the major work on the theory of time preference that I cited,[80] Professor Banfield's analysis in no way suffered.

79. In all fairness, it must be observed that many writers on the economics of crime draw no direct policy conclusions, though their work is nonetheless suffused with utilitarian presuppositions. But for sins of commission, see, for example, Erlich, "The Deterrence Effect of Capital Punishment," pp. 397–417, whose circumspection does not hide his normative conclusions. Becker, in "Crime and Punishment: An Economic Approach," is perhaps the most egregious offender.

80. Were I writing a detailed history of the concept of time preference, I would have mentioned the work of a number of other figures. Frank A. Fetter is particularly important among these. Fetter's work on the subject will be included in *Capital, Interest and Rent: Essays in the Theory of Distribution*, ed. Murray N. Rothbard (Kansas City: Sheed, Andrews & McMeel, 1977).

REFERENCES

Banfield, Edward C. *The Unheavenly City Revisited*. Boston: Little, Brown and Company, 1974 (A Revision of *The Unheavenly City*. [Boston: Little, Brown and Company, 1970]).

Becker, Gary. S. "Crime and Punishment: An Economic Approach." *Journal of Political Economy* 76 (March—April 1968): 169—217.

Block, M.K. and Heineke, J.M. "A Labor Theoretic Analysis of the Criminal Choice." *American Economic Review* 65 (June 1975): 314—25.

Buchanan, James M. *Cost and Choice.* Chicago: Markham Publishing Co., 1969.

Erlich, Isaac. "Participation in Illegitimate Activities: A Theoretical and Empirical Investigation." *Journal of Political Economy* 81 (May—June 1973): 521—65.

_____. "The Deterrent Effect of Capital Punishment: A Question of Life and Death." *American Economic Review* 65 (June 1975): 397—417.

Frankena, William K. *Ethics* (Englewood Cliffs, N.J.: Prentice-Hall, 1963).

Hayek, Friedrich A. *The Pure Theory of Capital.* Chicago: University of Chicago Press, 1941.

_____. *Full Employment at any Price?* London: Institute of Economic Affairs, 1975.

Jacobs, Jane. *The Economy of Cities.* New York: Random House, Vintage Books, 1970.

McKenzie, Richard B. and Tullock, Gordon. *The New World of Economics.* Homewood, Illinois: Richard D. Irwin, 1975.

Menger, Carl. *Principles of Economics.* Translated and edited by James Dingwall and Bert F. Hoselitz. Glencoe, Illinois: The Free Press, 1950.

Mises, Ludwig von. *Human Action: A Treatise on Economics.* 3rd ed. rev. Chicago: Henry Regnery Co., 1966.

O'Driscoll, Gerald P., Jr. "The Problem of Social Cost." Ames, Iowa: Photocopy, 1976.

Phillips, Llad; Votey, Harold L., Jr.; and Maxwell, Darold. "Crime, Youth, and the Labor Market." *Journal of Political Economy* 80 (May—June 1972): 491—504.

Pogue, Thomas F. "Effects of Police Expenditures on Crime Rates: Some Evidence." *Public Finance Quarterly* 3 (January 1975): 14—45.

Rawls, John. *A Theory of Justice.* Cambridge, Massachusetts: Harvard University Press, Belknap Press, 1971.

Robbins, Lionel. *The Nature and Significance of the Economic Problem.* 2nd ed. London: Macmillan & Co., 1935.

Sjoquist, David Lawrence. "Property Crime and Economic Behavior: Some Empirical Results." *American Economic Review* 63 (June 1973): 439—46.

Sowell, Thomas. *Race and Economics.* New York: David McKay Co., 1975.

Stigler, George J. and Becker, Gary S. "*De Gustibus Non Est Disputandum.*" *The American Economic Review* 67 (March 1977): 76—90.

Tullock, Gordon. "The Welfare Costs of Tariffs, Monopolies and Theft." *Western Economic Journal* 5 (1967): 224—32.

Wertheimer, Alan. "Deterrence and Retribution." *Ethics* 86 (April 1976): 181—99.

Witte, Ann Dryden. "Testing the Economic Model of Crime on Individual Data." Chapel Hill, North Carolina: Photocopy, 1976.

✳ *Chapter 7*

Time Preference, Situational Determinism, and Crime*

Mario J. Rizzo

Edward Banfield has presented a provocative thesis that "present-orientedness" is responsible for much behavior that is blatantly antisocial in character. "The more present-oriented an individual," Banfield tells us, "the less likely he is to take account of the consequences that lie in the future. Since the benefits of crime tend to be immediate and its costs (such as imprisonment or loss of reputation) in the future, the present-oriented individual is *ipso facto* more disposed toward crime than others."[1] The immediate plausibility of this view masks some very fundamental confusions and ambiguities that, because they have rather broad consequences for the analysis of crime, it will be our task to investigate. Furthermore, the methodological roots of this position pose a number of interesting problems many of which, it should be noted, are not peculiar to Banfield's work but, rather, represent very widespread tendencies in the social sciences.

There are two quite different notions of "present-orientedness" between which Banfield fails to distinguish. The first is "present-orientedness" as an *explicandum*, or what we shall call relatively

*I am indebted to the Scaife Foundation for financial support of my research, to Professor L.M. Lachmann of New York University for stimulating many of the ideas in Section III, and to Professor I.M. Kirzner of New York University for a number of helpful comments. I also wish to thank Mr. Michael Becker of Brown University for encouragement.

1. Edward C. Banfield, *The Unheavenly City Revisited* (Boston: Atlantic–Little, Brown, 1974), p. 183.

present-oriented behavior. It is the task of theory to explain this phenomenon. The second sense is "present-orientedness" as an *explicans*, i.e., the subjective state that explains the existence of certain behavior. This notion we shall refer to as high time preferences or a high internal rate of discount (schedule). Concern with only relatively present-oriented *behavior* rather than high time preferences leaves the former inexplicable by any sort of "time orientation." To be sure, we are not contending that time preferences exist in a kind of disembodied world apart from real action or behavior. On the contrary, differences in time preferences are *imputed* to an individual or group of individuals on the basis of action under certain *ceteris paribus* conditions. Unless these conditions are precisely specified, confounding of the two senses of present-orientedness is the likely result.

In the purely behavioristic sense, present-orientation is obviously a matter of degree: the existence of some present orientation is a necessary prerequisite for the emergence of any human action at all.[2] To put it another way, the existence of human action entails some "preference" for the present or else every action would always be postponed to some never-arriving future. Note that we have not used the words "consumption" or "savings" here. This is because we are interpreting "action" in its broadest possible sense, including behavior directed toward the attainment of the present desire to ensure future consumption. However, certain human physiological requirements make it impossible that we shall ever observe an optimal zero present consumption level. Hence, the relative character of present-oriented behavior reflects itself in the varying degrees of provision for consumption today versus consumption tomorrow.

Referring to what is obviously the preference or *explicans* sense of present-orientedness, Banfield says of the lower class or high time preference individual that "His calculus of benefits and costs is *defective* . . ."[3] [emphasis added]. The sense in which a decisionmaking calculus can be "defective" is not clearly spelled out. Surely, if there were some aspect of an individual's decision framework that brought about a systematic frustration of his *own* ends then we might, in a *wertfrei* manner, talk of a "defective" calculus. However, no claim that high time preferences systematically thwart the actor's own goals can possibly be sustained. Time preferences constitute an integral *part* of those goals, e.g., a pint of strawberries today is preferred (under certain conditions) to two pints of strawberries tomorrow.

2. Ludwig von Mises, *Human Action*, 3rd. ed. (Chicago: Henry Regnery Company, 1966), p. 484.

3. Banfield, p. 201.

Hence, if high time preferences cannot be inappropriate from the point of view of the individual's purposes, the appelation "defective" must be viewed from some other vantage point. *If* it is true, as Banfield claims, that this "defective" calculus results in criminal behavior, then might we not be justified in saying that high time preferences are in some sense "irrational"[4] from *society's* point of view? This formulation is, of course, naked holism.[5] Society can have no viewpoint apart from its individual members, and "rationality" is a term that has meaning only in the context of an individual's means-ends framework. To be sure, some or even most individuals will disapprove of the resultant criminal behavior. Yet people disapprove of many things. Shall we then call any decisionmaking framework that results in (majority) disapproved behavior "defective"? Clearly, the issue cannot be resolved on the basis of time preferences alone, for it is the behavioral consequence that is of paramount importance.

In this regard, we are told that a radically present-oriented culture or lifestyle is not "normal" or is "pathological."[6] This "seems fully warranted both because of the relatively high incidence of mental illness in the lower class and also because *human nature* seems loath to accept a style of life that is so radically present-oriented."[7] The second point is devoid of literal meaning and, unfortunately, I am unable to find any coherent meaning in it at all. Therefore, only the first point shall be discussed. Here, Banfield fails to make an important distinction.

Even if psychopathological individuals engage in more present-oriented behavior than the rest of us, it does not follow that all or even a significant number of highly present-oriented people are psychopaths. Indeed, Banfield presents no evidence that any substantial proportion of highly present-oriented (*explicandum* sense) people are, by any generally accepted psychological standards, "pathological." Hence, the invocation of "mental illness" may be of no usefulness as an explanation. Of course, one may claim that "radical" present-oriented behavior is itself a sufficient condition for psychopathology. Then, however, the issue is reduced to a tautology. Finally, it may be claimed that the term "pathological" actually refers to sociopsychopathological behavior. This usage is, however, to

4. See the transformation of the term "irrational" into the quasi-medical "psychopathological" below. While the former appears to be a matter of judgment, the latter *seems* to be a statement of fact.

5. F.A. Hayek, *The Counterrevolution of Science* (New York: Free Press, 1955), ch. VI; and Karl R. Popper, *The Poverty of Historicism* (New York: Harper Torchbooks, 1964 (Reprint of 1957 edition)), pp. 17–19.

6. Banfield, p. 63.

7. Ibid. (emphasis added).

be criticized on two grounds: (1) it is strictly improper to use the term "pathological" in a sense other than one referring to an individual's homeostatic system; and (2) the term "psychopathological" is an example of an unhelpful analogy run wild—in what sense does it mean anything other than "defective," and in what sense does the latter mean anything but "disapproved"?

To refer to some time preferences as "defective" and some kinds of behavior as "pathological" diverts our attention from the survival properties that implicit rules of behavior can have in given contexts. [8] Admittedly, this presupposes an equilibrium or optimal adjustment of individuals to their environments. If this were not the case, then the decision and behavior patterns need not have survival value. Nevertheless, there must surely be *some* presumption that long-enduring characteristics of a culture or subculture have utility in promoting the survival of its members in a certain context. For example, in a society where, because of political instability (e.g., continual agression by a foreign power), the future is highly uncertain, extreme present-oriented behavior can indeed be rational (i.e., appropriate to the achievement of given individual ends).

Until now we have concerned ourselves with what is, in a way, merely a prelude to Banfield's application of the time-orientedness theory. In his explanation of (much?) criminal behavior, Banfield stresses the importance, as we have previously noted, of differential internal rates of discount. Some, or many, or most individuals who commit crime do so because on average they discount the future costs of their acts more heavily than do noncriminals. [9] A major difficulty with this conjecture is that the evidence adduced to support it does not adequately distinguish between Banfield's view and an equally plausible alternative hypothesis.

Let us hypothesize that the main explanation for criminal behavior lies in the differences in the rates of trade-off between present and future consumption faced by different members of society. For example, assume that all of the costs of criminal behavior lie in the future (say, one year from now) and that the future is certain. Fur-

---

8. F.A. Hayek, "Notes on the Evolution of Systems of Rules of Conduct," in *Studies in Philosophy, Politics and Economics* (Chicago: University of Chicago Press, 1967), pp. 66–81.

9. In more technical language, the effect of high time preference on present-oriented behavior *in general* can be formulated in the following way. Let us postulate a two period model where the money value of present consumption is measured on the horizontal axis and the money value of the next period's consumption along the vertical axis. Then, a person with high time preferences (or a high time preference pattern) is one whose indifference curves are relatively steep. Given the same interest rate and wealth constraint, an individual with high time preferences will consume more today than one with lower time preferences.

ther assume that there are two individuals, both of whom would receive the same payoff from the commission of a given criminal act (say, $1,000). On the one hand, individual A has high opportunity costs of time, and imprisonment would cost him in terms of foregone income $1,040 one year from now. On the other hand, individual B has lower opportunity costs of time and the cost of the criminal act is for him only $1,020 one year from now. If both individuals discount the future by exactly the same rate—3 percent—individual A will find commission of the crime too costly, while individual B will leap at the opportunity. In this stylized example, we have explained criminal behavior without any recourse to differential degrees of present-orientedness (or future discounting) and relied entirely on differential costs. Banfield's evidence does not, I believe, adequately distinguish between these two (equally) plausible hypotheses.

Now, of course, Professor O'Driscoll's point elsewhere in this volume becomes quite relevant. "Tastes," we are told, "*demonstrably* vary among people. Knowledge of this fact is one of the common experiences that we all share, and upon which we can draw in our social analysis."[10] Here, I'm afraid, we have a terminological difficulty. It is not *tastes* that demonstrably vary but, rather, it is choices or acts of individuals that so vary. Differences in tastes may or may not explain differences in choices. For example, two individuals may be in the same wealth position and may face the same trade-off between present and future consumption and yet one may save more than the other. In *this* case, we can say that their time preferences or tastes as between present and future consumption differ. If, however, they faced different rates of trade-off, could we make the same statement with equal confidence? Not, to be sure, unless we recognize no distinction between the terms "choices" and "tastes" even when choices are made in differing circumstances. This last consideration provides the reason why even Professor Rothbard's notion of "demonstrated preferences" will not be adequate to defend O'Driscoll's viewpoint.[11]

Returning to our alternative explanation for criminal behavior, it might be argued (in Banfield's defense) that the reason individual B has lower opportunity costs of time in legitimate activities is because of his high present-orientedness. Of course, now we have shifted the context of the analysis from a purely static to a dynamic one. In the latter context, the argument would run something like this: individ-

10. Chapter 6, p. 153 (emphasis added).

11. Murray N. Rothbard, "Toward a Reconstruction of Utility and Welfare Economics," in *On Freedom and Free Enterprise*, ed. Mary Sennholz (Princeton: D. Van Nostrand, 1956), pp. 225–32.

ual B's legitimate opportunities next year are poor because last year his intense preference for present consumption made him unwilling to invest in the acquisition of skills that would have increased the market value of his time. Again, there is plausibility in this argument, but what evidence has Banfield presented for it that would enable us to decide between this hypothesis and other (equally) plausible ones? To be more precise, how can we differentiate among differences in natural intellectual endowments, attitudes toward risk, legal constraints, and social and racial discrimination as alternative hypotheses? Banfield's evidence does not distinguish among them.

It should be possible, at least in principle, to determine whether certain groups are characterized by higher time preferences than average. If we control for the after tax rate of return on assets and the level of real wealth, we could attribute differences in the savings-consumption ratio to time preferences.[12] It is these differences that might be usefully viewed as a proxy for the height of the time preference pattern. *A priori* it is not clear that significant differences would be found, nor if they are, how important they will be relative to other causes of crime.

II

Whatever the role of time orientation in the explanation of criminal behavior, it has a clear place in the explanation of government activities. To see this, consider first the position of a private corporation. Owners of such a corporation can capture, through its stock, the present value of the firm, and hence have an incentive to concern themselves with its long-run profit situation.[13] The appropriability of present value by owners creates pressure on the firm to set up an incentive structure adequate to ensure efficient behavior on the part of both managers and the board of directors.[14] This does not mean that managers, for example, will perfectly reflect the wishes of the owners but, rather, that such control will be *optimal*, subject to the costs of monitoring.[15] Furthermore, maximization of the firm's pres-

12. In practice the issue is more complicated than this because the form in which real wealth is held may have an effect. Where human wealth cannot easily be transformed into nonhuman wealth the ratio of the former to the latter will be of significance.

13. Roland McKean and Jacquelene Browning, "Externalities from Government and Non-Profit Sectors," *Canadian Journal of Economics* (November 1975): 580.

14. On these issues, see Henry Manne, "Mergers and the Market for Corporate Control," *Journal of Political Economy* (April 1965).

15. Armen A. Alchian and Harold Demsetz, "Production, Information Costs, and Economic Organization," *American Economic Review* (December 1972): 777–95.

ent value will be independent of the personal time preferences of the owners. This is because once they have maximized the present value of their income stream they can (within some limits) arrange their consumption pattern to suit their time preferences. Hence, "present-orientedness" on the part of some owners is not important.

On the other hand, voters cannot capture or appropriate the present value of the state's action (or inaction). Therefore, unless their own future self-interest is affected, they are unlikely to worry (very much) about distant benefits or losses.[16] Moreover, high voter information costs and the necessity to choose candidates on the basis of many issues at once compound the problem. This is because legislators are therefore quite unlikely to capture the present value of their deeds in the form of voter approbation or disapprobation (except in special cases). The absence of appropriability of future benefits distorts the rate of trade-off between present and future goods in favor of the former. Therefore, a voter or legislator will exhibit greater present-oriented behavior in the political sphere than he would in the private sphere where there is more complete appropriability. Consequently, the greater present-orientation of the state is not the result of high time preference individuals being attracted to statecraft but, rather, to the distorted present-future trade-off that characterizes much of the political sphere.

There are many ways in which the present-oriented behavior of the state manifests itself. We shall concern ourselves here with only two. In the first place, it is now well understood[17] that government borrowing to finance deficits distorts the voluntary savings-consumption pattern established by the market. Issuance of bonds to finance the deficit will, of course, drive interest rates upward. At the new higher rates, some private investment will be "crowded out" by the new government demand for savings. This means that there will be a substitution of government consumption for the investment in real capital that would have occurred in the absence of the deficit. The higher current consumption level today implies a lower consumption level tomorrow, and hence a change in the allocation of consumption over time established by the nongovernment sector.

The second example of present-oriented behavior is somewhat paradoxical. Let us suppose that the monetary authorities increase the quantity of base money and that the banks increase loans to businesses. The greater availability of loans will lower the market rate of interest below the natural rate (i.e., the rate at which real

16. McKean and Browning, p. 580.

17. Franco Modigliani, "Long-Run Implications of Alternative Fiscal Policies and the Burden of the National Debt," *Economic Journal* (December 1972): 730–55.

savings equals real investment *ex ante*).[18] *If* this lower market rate is expected to endure, then there will be an increase in the relative profitability of investment projects with a longer time horizon. It will appear *as if* real savings have voluntarily increased and that people wish to engage in more time-consuming (and more productive) methods of production. Hence, it may seem as though there has been an all-around increase in the *future* orientation of the economic system. This way of looking at matters is, however, quite misleading. When the market rate of interest rises again some (though not all) of the longer investment projects will be abandoned due to a decrease in their relative profitability.[19] The previous misallocation of resources is revealed, business losses ensue, and unemployment rises. The earlier future orientation of the production structure is, from the point of view considered here, really irrelevant. What the credit expansion has brought is a boom *today* (especially in the capital goods industries) at the expense of a recession *tomorrow*. If it were possible to compel the state to bear the full burden of this resource misallocation (i.e., if the losses were appropriable by the monetary authorities), then the "cycle effect" would be unprofitable from its own point of view. A Hayekian business cycle effect yields no net benefits and hence reduces the present value of the "system."

What we have seen is that, in our society at least, the State is a *source* of relatively present-oriented behavior. Since legislators cannot appropriate or own the distant future benefits of long-sighted action, their activities will be characterized by more immediate concerns. Professor Murray Rothbard has cogently summarized this situation in *Power and Market*:

> It is curious that almost all writers parrot the notion that private owners, possessing time preference, must take the "short view," while only government officials can take the "long view" and allocate property to advance the "general welfare." The truth is exactly the reverse. The private individual, secure in his property and in his capital resource, can take the long view, for he wants to maintain the capital value of his resource. It is the government official who must take and run, who must plunder the property while he is still in command.[20]

Though it may be conceded that the State through its officials has a clear *incentive* to act in a relatively present-oriented manner, one

18. F.A. Hayek, *Prices and Production*, 2nd ed. (New York: A.M. Kelly, 1967 (Reprint of 1935 edition)), Lecture III.

19. F.A. Hayek, *Profits, Interest and Investment* (New York: A.M. Kelly, 1975 (Reprint of 1939 edition)), pp. 3–82.

20. Murray N. Rothbard, *Power and Market* (Menlo Park, California: Institute for Humane Studies, 1970), p. 140. See also id., pp. 47–52.

might, in a defensive posture, claim that these officials do not, in fact, act in accordance with that incentive. They resist the temptation, as it were, and promote *our* true interests. This, of course, is based on the artificiality of assuming that men in the private sphere act in accordance with self-interest but, once they are channeled into the so-called public sphere, they do not. There is growing evidence of many sorts that this is untrue.[21]

There is an aspect of the Rothbard quote that may give us pause. This is the reference to the State's officials as plundering and running. Ought we to interpret this language as permissible hyperbole? Does not the present-oriented behavior of the State consist of a kind of mere benign immediate concern? The answer to these questions depends very much on the moral views one holds. The State may do nothing *illegal* when it taxes (at least to pay interest on government bonds) and consumes, but what, if any, is the relationship between the current high rates of taxation and theft? I am *not* referring to the question (important though it may be) of whether high taxes create an incentive for theft, but rather, I am asking whether they are *morally* equivalent to theft. The answer ought not—in an exploratory collection of papers such as this—be taken for granted or considered obvious.

III

There are more things in heaven and earth, Horatio,
Than are dreamt of in your philosophy.

Hamlet, Act I, Sc. V

The view that some individuals commit crime because of their relatively high time preferences is a particular instance of a more general mode of analyzing criminal behavior that, in turn, stems from an even more fundamental perspective in the social sciences. This mode of analysis is what Spiro Latsis has recently called "situational determinism."[22] Human action, from this viewpoint, is a species of "highly constrained *re*action."[23] Hypothesize an individual with stable tastes and a situation with some constraints as well as different

21. See, for example, George J. Stigler, *The Citizen and the State* (Chicago: University of Chicago Press, 1975).

22. Spiro J. Latsis, "Situational Determinism in Economics," *British Journal for the Philosophy of Science* (1972): 207–45.

23. Spiro J. Latsis, "A Research Programme in Economics," in *Method and Appraisal in Economics*, ed. S.J. Latsis (Cambridge: Cambridge University Press, 1976), p. 17 (emphasis added).

relative costs of alternate paths of behavior. Introduce, then, the "trivial animating law"[24] of narrowly conceived rationality, and actions assume the character of mechanistic reactions to shocks. Present-orientedness plus A, B, and C determine a set of reactions D. Explanation of human behavior takes on the character of mere computation or logical deduction. This was realized quite early in the development of contemporary economic theory by Pareto. Speaking of indifference curves (preference functions), Pareto said, "The individual can vanish now, provided that he leaves us this photograph of his tastes."[25] If an individual's (or an ideal type of an individual's) tastes are given, then the *objective situation* (i.e., income and relative prices) determine his choices. There have been elaborations of this basic structure: the substitution of permanent income for current income as the relevant constraint, or the introduction of a time price as well as a money price, etc. Yet Pareto's essential insight as to the mechanistic or logically deterministic character of equilibrium economics (and much contemporary social science) remains accurate.

Fritz Machlup, in a recent article[26] on Latsis' work, has adopted a position that is important for us to consider. In effect Machlup claims that all well-constructed models yield perfectly determinate results.[27] In general, "*any* model designed to present [exhibit] a causal connection between an independent variable and a dependent variable under given conditions . . . must display the dependent variable as a *logical* consequence of all the premises in the model."[28] That this is a characteristic of the *model* and not necessarily of the real *world* is granted: ". . . the applicability of the model with its determinate conclusion is always open to question; it is *never* certain . . . ."[29] Nevertheless, all of this tells us what we presumably have known all along, *viz.*, that the full meaning of a model consists in its use. If the constructor of a mechanistic model claims that it essentially explains some specified instance of human behavior, then he is asserting the determinate character of (most of) that behavior. Furthermore, it is indeed unfortunate that much model building is intimately connected with attempts to make *specific* historico-temporal predictions, because this ignores the important

24. Ibid., p. 21.

25. Vilfredo Pareto, *Manuel D'Economie Politique* (New York: AMS Press, 1969 (Reprint of 1909 edition)), p. 170.

26. Fritz Machlup, "Situational Determinism in Economics," *British Journal for the Philosophy of Science* (1974):271–84.

27. Ibid., p. 283.

28. Ibid., p. 280 (emphasis added).

29. Ibid. (original emphasis).

role of a more general form of explanation. To explain the *principle* of certain forms of human behavior may do no more than "predict" the overall *pattern* of, say, market response to a change in a given variable.[30] This may exclude certain types of response, but it leaves a variety of alternatives open as possible consequences of the given change.

The relevance of the foregoing discussion to our general concern with time preference and crime is this: if criminal behavior is determined by high time preferences along with several other variables, then in what sense is criminal behavior voluntary? To put the issue another way, in which sense are criminals *responsible* for what they do if their behavior is determinate? Here it is important to distinguish between two types of variables that can be said to determine (criminal) behavior. They can be broadly classed into objective and subjective variables. It might be reasonably contended that determination by subjective factors is not really determinism at all because these factors are, in effect, what constitutes the individual. Unfortunately, this view cannot be directly used to salvage the notion of individual responsibility. Only the objective variables can be observed, and hence the subjective ones must be viewed through their objectifiable proxies. Therefore, it appears *as if* objective phenomena determine (criminal) behavior. Indeed, many investigators may wish to omit any reference whatsoever to (directly) unobservable subjective factors in the name of Occam's razor. So we are back to our dilemma: whither individual responsibility in a world of puppets?

One possible solution to this problem is to emphasize that men *choose* their ends, i.e., that tastes or preferences of all sorts are to be considered voluntary. Determinism, then, exists only with reference to the given framework of ends and means. In such a framework, the maximization of utility requires (necessitates) certain behavior. So the necessity here is of a conditional nature: *if* men seek to fulfill particular ends, given the availability of x, y, and z means, then they must do a, b, and c. However, men are free not to choose those particular ends.

The proposed solution is really a compromise which apparently permits the retention of both situational determinism and genuine choice. Yet this cannot be. The simplicity and plausibility of this solution unfortunately masks a number of significant complications discussed by G.L.S. Shackle. "In order to have recipes of action for attaining his ends, a man," Shackle tells us, ". . . must also know

30. F. A. Hayek, "The Theory of Complex Phenomena," in *Studies in Philosophy, Politics and Economics* (Chicago: University of Chicago Press, 1967), pp. 22–42.

what actions of other people his own act will accompany."[31] The determinateness of behavior in a given means-end framework is for one individual thus dependent on the ends chosen by other individuals. To put the issue succinctly: ". . . if we claim that men can choose their ends in some substantial meaning of the word 'choose,' how can any man know what ends, and therefore what actions, others are *simultaneously* choosing. . . . If there is choice of ends, there are no complete laws prescribing the means of attaining ends. There is no complete rationality."[32] There are no problems of this sort for Robinson Crusoe, since for him there are no other individuals whose actions might affect how Crusoe will use available means to attain his given ends (once chosen). In a multiperson world, complete determinateness of an individual's behavior demands "pre-reconciliation"[33] of individual plans. Therefore, our proposed solution to the dilemma of determinism implicitly concedes too much. It is incorrect to say that once an individual chooses his ends there are strict laws determining his behavior. This is not enough for determinism. The choices of others must be either eradicated or pre-reconciled. The former requires that we treat only one individual as free, an exception to a general rule for which no plausible argument could be adduced. Pre-reconciliation, on the other hand, is not an empirical feature of societies as we know them.

It is important to stress here the kind of uncertainty on which the case for indeterminism rests. If the choices (of ends) and hence the actions of others are merely uncertain in the actuarial sense, then there is no *real* uncertainty. In this case, if an individual's decisions depend on the behavior of a large number of people or if he can insure, then actuarial risk can be converted into a fixed cost.[34] This form of uncertainty is susceptible to elimination and therefore does not affect the "complete rationality" of the decision-making process. The kind of uncertainty we have in mind is one most often ignored by economists and other social scientists, *viz.*, Knight's "estimates" or "true uncertainty."[35] In this case, ". . . there is no possibility of forming *in any way* groups of instances of sufficient homogeneity to make possible a quantitative determination of true probability."[36]

31. G.L.S. Shackle, *The Nature of Economic Thought* (Cambridge: Cambridge University Press, 1966), p. 71.

32. Ibid., p. 72 (original emphasis).

33. G.L.S. Shackle, *Epistemics and Economics* (Cambridge: Cambridge University Press, 1972), pp. 53–54.

34. Frank H. Knight, *Risk, Uncertainty and Profit* (Chicago: University of Chicago Press, 1971 (Reprint of 1921 edition)), p. 213.

35. Ibid., pp. 225, 232.

36. Ibid., p. 231 (original emphasis).

The mental processes involved in decision-making under true uncertainty are even today not well understood, and nonrational factors (e.g., intuition) may be of considerable importance here. In any event, the determinateness of an action given certain objectively specifiable data is out of the question. It is this kind of uncertainty that is important in matters of entrepreneurship, and may well be the main uncertainty faced in most decisions.[37] Real world uncertainty is doubtless often a complex of actuarial risk and Knightian true uncertainty. Yet it is only the latter that is, in principle, ineradicable and gives rise to the main problems of an uncertain world. Decision-making under this mode of uncertainty requires that we *go beyond* the objective data because in these cases such data is, by definition, insufficient.

The argument up to this point has shown that choice of ends where that choice is truly uncertain negates the possibility of situational determinism. Hence, even *given* the ends of an individual, his actions cannot be viewed as determinate. Even in a world in which the only uncertainty is actuarial risk (or in which all behavior could be "explained" *as if* it were merely risky) the givenness of ends still does not yield a pure form of determinism. To see this, we must inquire into the precise nature of human ends.

Thomas Aquinas implicitly argues against the view that if ends are taken as given, human acts are determinate. He reports the (incorrect) view in the following way: "But the principle of human acts is not in man himself, but outside him, since man's appetite is moved to act by the appetible object which is outside him, and which is as a *mover unmoved*."[38] In his reply to this view, Aquinas emphasizes two things: (1) movement toward an end is movement according to an intrinsic principle (i.e., the *actor* desires); and (2) movement toward an end requires knowledge. He states: ". . . the voluntary is defined not only as having *a principle within* the agent, but also as implying *knowledge*. Therefore, since man especially knows the end of his work, and moves himself, in his acts especially, is the voluntary to be found."[39] An illuminating extension of Aquinas' second argument is possible. What is knowledge of an end? Clearly, it is not knowledge of something that now exists. It is "knowledge" or anticipation of a future "sensation" that moves men to act. Hence, the goal toward which action is directed is not a (current) real world perception or sensation but, rather, an imagined one: an idea. Without inquiring as to where ideas come from, we shall follow common sense and say

37. Ibid., p. 226.
38. Thomas Aquinas, *Summa Theologica*, I–II, q. 6 (a.1).
39. Ibid. (original emphasis).

that a person's ideas are his own. Therefore, the givenness of ends does not imply determinism in any but a formal sense.

In a recent article, Stigler and Becker attempt to extend Pareto's dispensing of the individual by claiming that much human behavior can be explained without assuming "that tastes . . . change capriciously [or] differ importantly between people."[40] This is an attempt to extinguish altogether the notion of choice in any meaningfully free sense. In effect, Stigler-Becker individuals are *endowed* with certain basic tastes and then seek to maximize utility in the usual way. A main difference between this and the conventional approach is that the tastes are here defined over very basic (unobservable) commodities such as love, power, etc. The choice among observable market goods is determined by shadow prices (including time price) and an income constraint. Differences in market goods purchases are then never (or almost never) due to differences in tastes, but rather to differences in the true prices of these goods (which satisfy the constant tastes) or to differences in full income. "On our view," they propose, "one searches, often long and frustratingly, for the *subtle* forms that prices and incomes take in explaining differences among men and periods."[41] The assumption of lifelong constancy of tastes (including time preferences[42]) does not in itself imply a pure situational determinism,[43] but it pushes us much farther along that road.

A detailed examination of the Stigler-Becker view would be inappropriate here so we shall discuss only two general points. In the first place, the constancy of tastes must, in a broader sense, include the constancy of the entire means-ends framework.[44] If the individual's *perception* as to what constitutes an appropriate means to a given end changes exogenously, then behavior will change without alteration in tastes, prices, or income. The perception of a means-ends framework is a necessary prerequisite for application of the entire constrained utility maximization apparatus. This perception will necessarily be affected by the *undeliberate* acquisition of knowledge or information.[45] Hence, the alteration of "extra-economic" factors

40. George J. Stigler and Gary S. Becker, *"De Gustibus Non Est Disputandum,"* American Economic Review (March 1977):76.

41. Ibid. (emphasis added).

42. Ibid., p. 89.

43. We would at least have to confine all uncertainty to the actuarial risk variety. For other qualifications, see below.

44. For a discussion of the importance of the perception of the means-ends framework, see Israel M. Kirzner, *Competition and Entrepreneurship* (Chicago: University of Chicago Press, 1973), ch. 2.

45. Israel M. Kirzner, "Knowing About Knowledge: A Subjectivist View of the Role of Information" (Unpublished paper, New York University, 1977).

will affect responsiveness of behavior to economic variables, and produce an element of indeterminateness.

Second, a leap from the constancy of tastes view to pure determinism can occur only in the context of maximizing behavior. "Outside" forces do not *compel* individuals to maximize utility, although it is consistent with the "rational" pursuit of happiness. If individuals do not engage in maximizing behavior, then changes in, say, relative prices might produce no effect or, perhaps, a perverse effect on their relevant actions. If, on the other hand, we say that it is man's nature to be "rational," we misuse the concept of determinism to call the derived actions "determinate." To do so would come perilously close to saying that any behavior that can be explained is not free.[46]

The discussion in this section might seem somewhat belabored to those who take the common sense view that men (especially criminals) are free and hence responsible for their actions. Yet contemporary social science—especially economics—is becoming less and less congenial to this view. Thus, it has been necessary to examine the determinist implications of the economic approach to the explanation of behavior. One fundamental point ought to be kept in mind, however. The perception of man in everyday life is that his actions are free, that he really chooses among alternatives, and that he could have done otherwise. For this reason alone, the *notion* of truly free choice is one that doubtless affects the way men behave, as it colors their perception of the relevant actions of other men. Consequently, it seems reasonable to construct our models so as to include the very basis of that which makes us human.

46. None of the above discussion implies that the constancy of tastes "hypothesis" (or, more exactly, positive heuristic) is invalid or useless. When these qualifications and limitations are kept in mind, the framework can serve useful purposes.

Part II

Criminal Responsibility: Philosophical Issues

Any assessment of crime and criminals necessitates moral judgement. We speak of the "culpable" offender, the "guilty" defendant, and the criminal "violator." Utilitarian or majoritarian philosophy notwithstanding, such terms require an understanding of the ethical dimension of criminal justice and the acts that we seek to sanction. What gives some the right to assess the acts of their fellow men and to punish accordingly? The papers in this section attempt to approach this question from several perspectives.

John Hospers' outlines a retributive justification for punishment. He views punishment as properly directed toward the "just deserts" of criminal offenders, that is, their moral worth. Central, then, to his formulation is an assessment of criminal intent and the acts that evidence that intent. Walter Kaufmann objects to such a project and argues that, since the past is unalterable, any justification of punishment as "balancing the books" is a dangerous and misleading fiction.

Richard Epstein attempts to rationalize the traditional distinction between the criminal law and tort law. His formulation of the object of criminal law remarkably resembles Hospers' concept of just deserts. Murray N. Rothbard shifts the focus of inquiry from the criminal to an assessment of criminal *acts* as violations of the rights of victims for which the criminal should be assessed a proportionate penalty. Rothbard's essay, with its emphasis on the victim's rights, and even the criminal's right to proper punishment, is a significant and provocative departure from traditional retribution theory which, perhaps, merits a new label.

✳ *Chapter 8*

Retribution: The Ethics
of Punishment

John Hospers

The question of what considerations justify the infliction of
punishment on a person who is guilty of a crime has been a
subject of disagreement among philosophers throughout
the history of Western philosophy. I shall attempt in this chapter to
present the merits of a view of punishment that is currently somewhat out of fashion—the retributive theory. But I shall defend retribution in a somewhat milder form than some theorists have done,
with the result that those who favor "sterner" versions of the theory
may not be satisfied with it.

I shall restrict my discussion on several counts.

1. I shall consider only legal punishment for crimes (crimes being
   acts contrary to law), and not consider other forms of punishment, e.g., the punishment of children by parents.
2. I shall assume that the crimes for which punishment is justified
   are "genuine" crimes, not, e.g., "victimless crimes" such as prostitution. The reasons why these should not be considered crimes is
   beyond the scope of this chapter.
3. I shall not consider the question of which persons or which institutions should administer the punishment. In fact it is the state
   that in all civilized societies today administers punishment, but I
   shall neither attempt to defend the state as the institution authorized to administer punishment nor exclude other institutions
   from this role—and thus I shall not raise the question of who
   should administer punishment in an anarchist society.

I

In defending the retributive theory I shall not travel the "high priori road" by defining any other possibility than the retributive out of existence. For example, in a recent column in *Newsweek*,[1] George Will writes: "The silliest argument is that [punishment] is wrong because it is retributive. *All* punishment is retributive. . . . The point is a logical [one]. It is that the word 'punishment' is only properly used to describe suffering inflicted by authority in response to an offense. Punishment is always 'to retribute,' to 'pay back for' guilt."

But of course this doesn't settle the traditional battle between retributive and utilitarian theories. Utilitarians will simply respond that in that event people should never be punished, only incarcerated, isolated, treated, or in some other way be made to give up their freedom so that others may be deterred. If a man is imprisoned for ten years just to set an example to others or to stop a crime wave, and we say to him, "Of course, you're not really being punished, since punishment is necessarily retributive, and we're not exacting retribution," he is not likely to be very much consoled by this reflection. What words we attach to it, he may say, doesn't really matter; he is still being locked up for ten years and as far as he's concerned that's punishment. The question *why* we should fine or imprison people is a substantive moral question not to be disposed of by semantic sleight of hand.

There are several views popularly associated with the term "retributive theory" that I shall not defend. First, I shall not defend the idea of retribution as *vengeance*. Ordinarily the term "vengeance" refers to the actions of the aggrieved party to "get even" with the aggressor outside the jurisdiction of laws and courts. One disadvantage of this is that the acts of aggression tend to be indefinitely perpetuated (e.g., the Hatfields and the McCoys). Another is that in the absence of law there are no rules known in advance specifying the limits of punishment for each offense: a person could respond to birdshot with machine guns in the name of vengeance.

Second, I shall not defend the concept of retribution as *lex talionis*, visiting upon the aggressor a punishment identical with (or even similar to) the offense of which he was guilty. ("An eye for an eye" was not even taken literally in the Old Testament.) According to this view, the punishment should be a kind of mirror image of the crime: the murderer should himself be killed as punishment. Lacking an exact similarity between the two, the aggressor should be made to suffer a punishment that is felt to be peculiarly fitting or appropriate

1. George Will, *Newsweek*, 19 November 1976.

to his crime—such as Mussolini being hanged by his toes in a public square, the same punishment to which he condemned so many others. But such a narrow view of justice, besides raising questions as to why it should be applied at all, cannot in any case be applied to all offenses. What punishment would be sufficient for a Stalin who condemned not one but millions to torture and death? His is only one life, and the lives he took number in the millions. And if being killed is the proper punishment for killing, what is the proper punishment for rape? Or for a toothless aggressor who knocks someone else's teeth out?

The term "retribution" is, indeed, so rife with misleading associations that I would prefer not to speak of "the retributive theory" at all, but rather "the *deserts* theory." The only form of the so-called retributive theory that I would defend at all is its most general one, the one that marks off the theory itself without being committed to any special versions such as the ones I have described: namely, the view that each person should be treated (and in the case of crimes, punished) *in accordance with his desert.* Thus formulated, there is no implication that desert must take the special form of *lex talionis*, although desert might well take that form in specific cases.

Now, "treatment in accord with desert" is probably the most frequently encountered definition of the term "justice" itself. And indeed I gladly accept this definition of "justice"—partly because it is already in common use and already familiar; partly because it is brief, terse, and relatively clear; and more important, because it is sufficiently general, and other proffered definitions tend to cover only parts or aspects of it. For example, Mill in Chapter 5 of *Utilitarianism* discusses five definitions of "justice," of which this is only one; but some of those he lists, such as "injustice is breaking faith with someone," appear to be special cases of the general definition. Finally, I accept it because it sets in bold relief the contrast (and potential clash) between justice and utility, which I shall discuss later; and this concept suffices as neatly as any other, with the possible exception of "rights," to show why "utility is not enough."

Other views may have some points in their favor, but if they yield justice when applied, they do so only in those cases in which the deserts theory and the other theories coincide in practice. The deserts theory is in fact the only one primarily concerned with justice. The philosopher Francis H. Bradley has given the theory its classical formulation.

Punishment is punishment, only when it is deserved. We pay the penalty because we owe it, and for no other reason; and if punishment is inflicted for any other reason whatever than because it is merited by wrong, it is a gross immorality, a crying injustice, an abominable crime, and not what it pretends to be. We may have regard for whatever considerations we please —our own convenience, the good of society, the benefit of the offender; we are fools, and worse, if we fail to do so. Having once the right to punish, we may modify the punishment according to the useful and the pleasant; but these are external to the matter; they cannot give us a right to punish, and nothing can do that but criminal desert.[2]

To many, in fact, the statement "It is fitting that a person who has committed a crime against others should be made to suffer for it" will seem as close to a self-evident moral truth as is to be found. To those who desire something more specific, the justification presented by Professor Herbert Morris in his essay "Persons and Punishment" will be helpful. It is to the interest of everyone in a society, says Professor Morris, to have

> . . . rules that prohibit violence and deception, and compliance with which provides benefits for all persons. These benefits consist in non-interference by others with what each person values, such matters as continuance of life and bodily security. The rules define a sphere for each person, then, which is immune from interference by others. Making possible this mutual benefit is the assumption by individuals of a burden. The burden consists in the exercise of self-restraint by individuals over inclinations that would, if satisfied, directly interfere or create a substantial risk of interference with others in proscribed ways. If a person fails to exercise self-restraint even though he might have and gives in to such inclinations, he renounces a burden which others have voluntarily assumed and thus gains an advantage which others, who have restrained themselves, do not possess . . .
> . . . A person who violates the rules has something others have—the benefits of the system—but by renouncing what others have assumed, the burdens of self-restraint, he has acquired an unfair advantage. Matters are not even until this advantage is in some way erased. Another way of putting it is that he owes something to others, for he has something that does rightfully belong to him. Justice—that is, punishing such individuals—restores the equilibrium of benefits and burdens by taking from the individuals what he owes, that is, exacting the debt.[3]

II

At first glance the position seems simple enough: each person should be treated in accord with his or her desert—whether it is a grade for

2. Francis H. Bradley, *Ethical Studies*, 2nd ed. (London: H.S. King and Co., 1876), pp. 26–27.

3. Herbert Morris, "Persons and Punishment," in *Human Rights*, ed. A.I. Melden (Belmont, California: Wadsworth Publishing Co., 1970), pp. 113–14.

achievement in a course, wages for work performed, or punishment for crimes committed. But of course there are difficulties. Professor Walter Kaufmann, in his book *Without Guilt and Justice*,[4] finds so much difficulty here that he would throw out the concepts of justice and desert entirely. For example, "It is quite impossible to say how much income surgeons, lawyers, executives, or miners deserve."[5] Professor Kaufmann includes both "retributive justice" and "distributive justice" (justice in punishment and justice in rewards) in his criticism. It is, he says, just as impossible to say what punishment an armed robber or a rapist deserves as it is to say what rewards people in different trades and professions deserve for their labor.

He makes a detailed and powerful case for the view that no person or committee in a college or university administration can say truly what a given assistant professor deserves by way of salary increase or promotion.[6] To what extent shall we consider teaching to be a criterion of desert? And what if he is a popular teacher at the undergraduate level but impossible for graduate students (or vice versa)? How much shall we consider publications? How strongly should quantity of publications be weighed in relation to quality (and who is to judge the quality)? How important is unpublished research? How important is work on committees and other administrative work, which someone has to do if a university is to function? What about rapport with colleagues and exchange of ideas with them? People can disagree endlessly about the various weights to be attached to each item, and also about the extent to which a given instructor fulfills the criteria in each category. Cases like this, and countless others, present us with bewildering complexities. What are we to say of them?

It is true that in view of the large number of variables (possibly their indeterminate number), and problems about the weights to be attached to each, that it is impossible to arrive at a mathematically precise outcome that one could call just. But I do not find this any more so in discourse about justice than about other kinds of moral discourse, e.g., about which alternative act one ought to perform, or which specific goals are most worth aiming at. The resultant duties that emerge from Sir David Ross' list of *prima facie* duties[7] is equally indeterminate: one has to weigh, for example, the *prima facie* duty

4. Walter Kaufmann, *Without Guilt and Justice* (New York: Peter H. Wyden, 1973).

5. Ibid., p. 71.

6. Ibid., pp. 75–78.

7. William David Ross, *The Right and the Good* (Oxford: The Clarendon Press, 1930), ch. 2.

of beneficence against the *prima facie* duty of fidelity—and according to Ross if we could achieve 1000 units of net good by keeping a promise and 1001 by breaking it we should keep the promise even if doing so achieves less good; if, however, we could achieve a million units of good by breaking it we should do so. At what point of increasing good achieved by breaking the promise should we break it? Ross provides no answer; and if the answer were given, "Break it if more than 13,749 units of good are thereby achieved," this wouldn't help, because (1) we wouldn't be able to identify this cutoff point if we found it, and (2) we would still want to know why this cutoff point was chosen rather than some other.

But, it will be objected, this difficulty is encountered because in Ross' ethics, as indeed in other systems of deontological ethics, we are trying to weigh incommensurables against one another. So let's try a simpler ethical theory, utilitarianism. In utilitarianism our only duty is to achieve maximum possible intrinsic good; but if we hold that there is a plurality of intrinsic goods, e.g., happiness and knowledge, then we still have the same problem of incommensurables as before. So let's take the simplest form of utilitarianism, hedonistic utilitarianism, in which the only thing to consider is happiness. Even here, however, we encounter insuperable difficulties. (1) There is the familiar point that happiness is unquantifiable—I can't say that today I am 3.7 times happier than a year ago at this time. (2) And even if happiness were quantifiable we could not achieve the quantification in fact in every case in which we would have to compare the degrees of happiness of various people. Even if I could say that I enjoy chocolate ice cream just twice as much as vanilla, I could not know that I enjoy chocolate just twice as much as you do. So the impossibility of arriving at an exact result bedevils utilitarianism, even in its simplest form, just as much as it does deontological systems of ethics. In spite of all this I never hear the objection that discussion about right and wrong should be abandoned. Still, the difficulties of trying to weigh various factors against one another in the case of right action, or various kind of values against one another in the case of goodness, are no less severe than the difficulties in estimating desert. We just have to do the best we can with what we have.

Example: should one reveal under torture the names of one's friends in the underground? One would ordinarily say no, it would be wrong to do so. But what if you know that there is a limit to the torture you can withstand, that if you don't give the information now you will be pushed beyond that point anyway, so that the added suffering you will endure will be pointless? And what if you have reason to believe that even if they don't get the information from you they will get it from one of your friends, someone who is also being interrogated and has a lower torture threshold than you do? And what if you have excellent reason to believe that the war is nearly won anyway, the Allied invasion of Normandy is imminent, and any information you divulge is likely (but not certain) to be of little use? How much weight is to be attached to such considerations? One could easily list several dozen others that would have a bearing on the question of what you should now do. There is no doubt that this makes moral decisions extremely difficult—but it is precisely because of difficulties like this that moralists have distinguished between objective duty and subjective duty (or as Russell put it in his essay "The Elements of Ethics,"[8] between the *most fortunate act* and the *wisest act*): the act that *does* achieve the most good (which only the eye of omniscience could discern at the time), and the act that *at the time of acting* appears on the basis of all the available evidence to be (on the whole, on balance), the one most likely to achieve it. It is only the latter for which we can be praised or blamed as moral agents, until such time as we receive the gift of omniscience. This conclusion—that the situation is too vastly complicated to admit of an answer that is either precise or certain—is widely accepted in matters of good and bad, right and wrong. Why then should it not equally be accepted in matters of justice and desert? I conclude, then, that the idea of desert need not be scrapped on the grounds that Professor Kaufmann proposes; and that if it should, so on the same grounds should goodness and rightness and most concepts in the sphere of ethics.

It seems to me that, both in the area of right and wrong and in the area of justice and desert, there are certain paradigms that govern our moral judgments. We may dispute endlessly, and with good reason, whether a given proposed act is right or wrong[9]—but not whether it is wrong to inflict suffering on others without reason. We may dispute endlessly whether this man deserves a prison sentence and for how long—but not whether an innocent person should be imprisoned, and not whether a person guilty of a trivial offense such as stepping on somebody's toe should be imprisoned for twenty years. Such paradigm cases seem to me as clear in the case of deserts as in the case of right and wrong.

Complex though particular judgments of desert can be, it seems to

8. Bertrand Russell, "The Elements of Ethics," in *Readiness in Ethical Theory*, 2nd ed., eds. Wilfred Sellars and John Hospers (Englewood Cliffs, New Jersey: Prentice-Hall, 1970), pp. 3—29.

9. The dispute may center on moral points, e.g., what constitutes sufficient reason, or on empirical points, e.g., what are the facts of the specific case at hand?

me that Professor Kaufmann makes them even more complex than they are. In the case of the assistant professors, he includes what a given candidate *desires* and what he *needs* as relevant to the estimate of what he deserves. I do not see how these factors are relevant at all. Surely one's desert (in the case of the promotion or the raise) depends on one's past performance, and on one's future potential as reflected in one's past performance. When one considers also whether the assistant professor has independent means, or whether he has a large family to support, one is considering what he needs but *not* what he deserves. The fact that one candidate is a millionaire who doesn't need the promotion (at least not for financial reasons) and another is the sole support of a large family, is simply irrelevant to his desert as a teacher. If the ability and performance of the millionaire are somewhat better, and the promotion is given to the other candidate anyway, this is surely an admission *not* that need is relevant to estimates of desert, but that one is using criteria *other* than desert (or in addition to desert) in deciding whether teachers should be promoted. And so, I think, the decision procedure as regards desert is actually simpler than Professor Kaufmann has pictured it, since he has intertwined factors relevant to desert with others that have nothing to do with it.

III

Are there any guidelines we can fruitfully adopt in attempting to punish offenders in accord with their desert?

Emile Durkheim once claimed that a proper measure of ill-desert was the degree of public indignation or resentment caused by the act. "In cases," he said, "which outrage the moral feelings of the community to a great degree, the feeling of indignation and desire for revenge which is excited in the minds of decent people is, I think, deserving of legitimate satisfaction."[10] I do not, of course, know what he meant by "decent people." But I fail to see how the degree of public indignation, which may be irrational and misguided and depends largely on how and whether the media fan the flames, is any measure of desert. It has to do with public reaction to the act, not the degree of culpability attaching to it.

A more fruitful suggestion, made by Professor John Kleinig in his book *Punishment and Desert*,[11] is to list each crime in order of sever-

10. Emile Durkheim, *The Division of Labor in Society*, trans. George Simpson (Paris, 1893; Rpt. New York: The Free Press, 1933), bk. 1, ch. 2.

11. John Kleinig, *Punishment and Desert* (The Hague: Martinus Nijhoff, 1973), pp. 118–24.

ity, then list an equal number of penalties in order of severity beginning with the smallest penalty it is feasible to give (say a $10 fine or a day in jail) and ending with the most severe, and then match the items on the two lists. There would then be a one-to-one correlation between the seriousness of crimes and the gravity of the punishments. This procedure would at least make sure that a person who committed a less serious offense would never get punished more than a person who committed a more serious one.

There are certainly worse schemes than this; yet this one raises problems. (1) Not everyone would agree on which offenses are the most serious. (2) Even if they did, they might not agree on the severity of the punishment appropriate to each—some might begin with ten days in jail and proceed with rapidly increasing severity to capital punishment, although the rank ordering of crimes and gravity of punishments would remain the same. (3) But most of all, it is surely a "fallacy of misplaced abstractness" simply to list offenses in order of seriousness, by type, without regard to the circumstances in which they were committed, whether intentionally or not, etc.—all of which would have to be taken into consideration in estimating desert. In some circumstances, a theft may be worse than a mugging: you can't consider merely the *type* of offense, you must consider the individual circumstances of each case. This makes things much more difficult, but justice requires no less than this.

These problems are indeed difficult, but not, I think, insuperable. As to the first point, there is much more agreement than might at first be apparent on which offenses are the most serious. Does anyone really believe that petty theft is worse than murder? When you steal from someone you take away something he owns, which he may be able to replace; if you take his life you take from him everything. The long tradition of natural law theory testifies to a large measure of agreement on which offenses are the most serious. Killing someone is, in general, worse than maiming him; maiming him is worse than giving him a temporary injury or pain; injuring is worse than stealing his wallet or trespassing on his yard. And there would, surely, be much more agreement than there is if people would engage in calm rational give and take discussions ("in a cool hour") of each issue, rather than simply repeating without thought, as many do now, whatever prejudices they have been taught to perpetuate.

As to the second point, undeniably there are people of lenient temperament and people of severe or "retributive" temperament, and every possible stage in between. But this situation could be ameliorated considerably if each person asked himself (á la Kant and Hare), "What would I wish done to me if I committed this offense?"

A person with a hypersensitive ego would gladly electrocute someone for the crime of stepping on his toe; but it is unlikely that he would be willing to have the same thing done to him if the circumstances were reversed, and consequently he would be reluctant to approve a *general rule of conduct* prescribing such punishment for such behavior. The mother of the hoodlum, who pleads for clemency for her dear boy who has just knifed a classmate to death in the street, would probably have a different view if she put herself in the place of the mother of the boy who was murdered—and vice versa.

On the third point, it is of utmost importance that each case be seen in all its concrete particularity, with whatever features distinguish it from other cases falling within the same category. I believe that if this were done (and it is not always easy to do), the measure of agreement on desert would be vastly increased. Since deserts are individual, and individuals differ in merit and demerit, we must not say in general that some types of offenses are always worse than others. Once we know not only the *kind* of offense a person has committed, but the circumstances in which it was performed, whether he did it deliberately, the kind of pressures on him when he did it, his whole psychological "set," and a host of other factors, we have much more data for deciding what he deserves than when we know only the type of crime he committed and then attempt to correlate the gravity of that type of crime with the gravity of the punishment. A person who steals food from a store may well be adjudged less deserving of punishment if he was hungry and had tried repeatedly to find work but failed—although the offense still falls into the same category, theft. When we know the concrete particulars of the individual case, people (at least people whose minds are not entirely closed and who are willing to discuss the issue rationally at all) will usually be much more inclined to agree about what an individual deserves than at the initial stage when the case is simply subsumed under a certain heading and is described no further.

IV

There *is* a difficulty about punishment and desert that is more troublesome than any of those I have discussed, although this one has been little noted. It is that in punishing someone, we are forcibly *imposing* on him something against his will, and of which he may not approve. It's not like the case of tolerating conflicting lifestyles (which we gladly do), but a matter of imposing on others penalties against their will and without their sanction.

Libertarians are especially sensitive about this issue, for they really wish to impose nothing forcibly on anyone else; they would prefer to live and let live. Liberals (twentieth-century sense), by contrast, shouldn't mind too much—they do it, or at least vote for doing it, all the time. They are constantly forcing their ideals on everyone else in the form of voting to make everyone cough up more tax money to pay for the implementation of those ideals. The unadmitted but pervasive formula underlying their actions is "I'm so convinced that my ideals are worthy ones that I'll force you to pay for them with added tax money whether you believe they're worthy or not." The wheels of liberals are already generously greased in this direction, from constant practice in forcing their ideals upon others (via the State) in the economic area; they tend to have a messianic delusion about their ability and their authority to manage and legislate the lives of others. If they feel wise enough to prescribe panaceas and force them on everyone in the social and economic spheres, it is not surprising to find that they feel themselves endowed with the same infinite wisdom in the area of what punishments (or treatments) to inflict. But libertarians above all don't want to be caught in this kind of situation; to force their ideals upon others, whether in the form of extracting taxes from others or regulating their lives or their businesses, is absolutely anathema to them, and utterly contradicts their first principle, "The lives of other human beings are not yours to dispose of."

There is, of course, a built-in qualification in this libertarian view. Libertarians consider it immoral for any individual to interfere forcibly in the life of another *unless* that other person has first forcibly imposed his will on someone. When that happens, the victim is entitled to respond according to the rule ("The use of force is permissible") that the aggressor himself has implicitly laid down. And in the case of genuine crimes, as opposed to "victimless crimes," this is what has happened: in murder, manslaughter, rape, mugging, robbery, embezzlement, plunder, etc., someone has initiated a forcible intrusion into the life of someone else, and that someone else need not then "take it lying down" by letting the aggressor's blade plunge into his heart. There is nothing contrary to libertarian doctrine in an act of self-defense.

And yet there is a problem, and a very serious one, in the infliction of punishment: some person (judge or parent) or some group (jury, council of elders) sits in judgment on someone else and determines what punishment if any the aggressor shall be made to suffer. Not everyone, not even everyone of good faith, would agree that the punishment pronounced is the right one, yet some punishment must be given. The only alternative is to abandon punishment entirely and let aggressors go free. *Someone* must decide what the punishment shall be. And as far as I can see, short of letting all aggressors go free, there is absolutely no way around this: someone has to make the decision, whether a judge or a jury, whether the State or a private agency, whether by a code of law or custom or by the whims of an emperor. But please note that this is a problem that attends not only the deserts theory but *any* theory of punishment (or for that matter of compulsory "treatment"): whenever you punish, for whatever reason, under the banner of whatever theory, you sit in judgment on someone else, playing God with his life, determining how his life (or his income) is to be disposed of. Only a just and omnipotent God could do this without error, and none of us is omnipotent or wholly just. And there lies the problem. If you want a problem, not only for the deserts theory but for any theory of punishment, this is it.

V

According to the deserts theory, at least in the form in which I would defend it, guilt is a *necessary* condition for punishment, but not a *sufficient* condition for punishment. In other words, if a person is not guilty he should never be punished, but if he is guilty it does not follow that he should be punished. (I would not say, "Do justice though the heavens fall.") The decision that A has committed the offense does not automatically carry with it a prescription to punish A, for there are conditions that if present will suffice to break the connection.

First, there are conditions that if present negate the claim to desert. I shall mention two obvious ones:

1. *Coercion.* If the agent was coerced into performing the act, this negates the claim that the agent deserves punishment for it. But unfortunately the matter is not so simple as this. Coercion is a matter of degree, and much depends on the degree of coercion exercised. At one end of the spectrum is the case of the man who is bigger and stronger than you who forces you to pull the trigger by laying his fingers on yours; in such a case of course it is he who deserves punishment and not you—in fact it is not your act at all but his—he is the agent, you the patient. Normally, however, coercion involves not a physical act by another but the *threat* of harm to you if you fail to do something the coercer wants; in such cases it is still up to you whether you will do the act or not. And here the situations range from extremely dire threats to relatively trivial ones. In the case of revealing the names of your colleagues in the underground, you

might well merit ill-desert if you named them even under torture, since the lives of many others are at stake and you knew the risks when you volunteered for the job. Most cases of coercion, however, are less extreme than this. "If you don't let me marry your daughter, I'll beat you up" is coercion, but you can still freely decide whether it's better to be beaten than to give him your daughter in marriage; in spite of the coercion, you still have some control over the situation. "If you don't do what I want, I'll leave you," said by your wife, still has an element of coercion in it—there is a threat, but since it is not a threat to your life or limb, many would deny this example the status of coercion; yet having her with you (in spite of her disposition to utter such threats) might mean more to you than your life or limb, so the threat could still be devastatingly effective. On the other hand, "If you don't do as I say, I'll sneeze" would not be construed as coercion at all: essential to the notion of coercion are extremely unwelcome consequences to you for not submitting, and in this case you would probably say, "Go ahead—sneeze!" And if your mother-in-law said "If you don't do what I want, I'll move out," this could even be construed not as a threat but as a promise.

2. *Insanity.* This one is even messier, because of the vagueness of the term "insanity." (a) According to the M'Naghten Rule, a person is insane if he is ignorant of "the nature and quality of his act" and "the fact that it was wrong." Besides being extremely vague, such a criterion considers only the impairment of one's rational functions and leaves the volitional untouched. (b) If one says that a person is insane if "he is unable to understand what he is doing and to control his conduct at the time he commits a harm forbidden by criminal law,"[12] we are involved in endless disputes about whether on the particular occasion he could or could not have controlled his conduct, and to what extent. (There is a troublesome problem of degree here: almost everyone can control his conduct to a certain extent, in certain circumstances but not others—e.g., at gunpoint but not under pressure of more ordinary stimuli.) (c) If one applies as a test whether "he could have done otherwise at that moment," there is no clear way to resolve the contrary to fact conditional statement that *if* certain conditions had been fulfilled (an exact repetition of those he did confront?) *then* he would have acted otherwise than he did. No matter which formula we try to apply, we seem in the end to fall back on a highly intuitive test: "Is he just plain crazy or not?"

12. Jerome Hall, *General Principles of Criminal Law*, 2nd ed. (Indianapolis: Bobbs-Merril Co., 1960).

Dr. Thomas Szasz has made a powerful and (it seems to me) convincing case for the view that if a person has not committed a crime he should not be forcibly incarcerated, either in jail or in a mental institution.[13] But the case confronting us now is a different one: assuming that he *has* committed a crime, should a plea of insanity ever be admitted to enable him to escape an otherwise mandatory prison sentence? I am far less certain about the answer to this one: I am inclined to say Yes, but there is (a) so much vagueness about what constitutes insanity, and (b) so much skulduggery by psychiatrists themselves (one testifying that the defendant is insane, the other that he is not), that it is difficult to think of any concrete case in which the plea of insanity is clearly justified.

Second, there are conditions that if present do not negate desert, but only the obligation to punish, in spite of the fact that desert is present. I shall mention two:

1. Sometimes a person may deserve punishment but there are special reasons why it should not be carried out. For example, an old man guilty of a serious crime is dying of cancer and there is no longer any point in punishing him. (Some would say "He's been punished enough"—though scourges of nature can hardly be called punishment.) So he receives a suspended sentence—which of course is not the same as finding him innocent or exonerating him. The same might be said for an expectant mother whose imprisonment might jeopardize the health of her unborn child. (There are, of course, severe limits to all this. If a murderer is not apprehended until thirty years later, I do not see how the mere passage of time does anything to lessen his ill-desert.)

2. No matter how much a person might deserve a given penalty, it should be administered only if it has been arrived at through a fair trial, by prescribed procedures, and by impartial and competent judges. Suppose for example that a person deserves a certain penalty and that it was indeed pronounced, but that the judge or jury or attorneys suppressed evidence or broke laws to obtain the evidence, witnesses perjured themselves, or a confession was arrived at through bullying and beating the defendant. Then it is at least arguable that the punishment should not be carried out, no matter how richly it was deserved.

13. See Chapter 3.

VI

I have endeavored to defend the deserts theory only in its most general form, and have frankly admitted the difficulties that attend it in practice, as indeed similar difficulties attend all ethical theories when put into practice. But my principal reason for holding to it nonetheless is the really insuperable difficulties that attend any alternative to it.

The principal alternative, of course, is the utilitarian theory (more aptly called the "results" theory). "The past is past," says the utilitarian—and he intends this to be taken in the non-tautological sense, such as "What's past should be forgotten"; even if he said, "What's past cannot be changed," this too is a necessary truth. In the matter of punishment, as in all other moral matters, says the utilitarian, we should consider only how we can help make the future better. This is a plausible enough appeal, since presumably we all want to help make the future better. The question is (1) how—whether we can do this by considering, in the matter of punishment, only the future consequences of punishing and not the nature of the past deed (and doer) for which the punishment was administered, and (2) whether in any case making the future better is the only goal relevant to the situation, particularly when doing so ignores considerations of justice.

The utilitarian theory has sometimes been called the deterrence theory, but this is a mistake. One function of punishing, according to the utilitarian theory, is indeed to deter potential lawbreakers, but it is only one of several, and it can in fact be overriden by the others. The consequences of punishing that the utilitarian must consider seem to be at least four:

1. Consequences to the aggressor. The aim of punishing should be to make him a better person—to reform him, or at any rate to rehabilitate him—so that he will emerge in such a state as never to repeat his offense.
2. Consequences to potential aggressors. This aim is deterrence—to show people what happens if you commit crimes, and thus to discourage you from trying to commit them.
3. Consequences to society in general. The aim here is to protect the public from dangerous persons by isolating them, in prisons or work farms or whatever, from the rest of society during the period that they constitute a threat.
4. Consequences to the aggrieved party, i.e., the victim. The aim of punishing here is not to "undo the crime"—that is impossible—

but to make restitution to the victim (or in the case of murder, the victim's family) by improving his lot in some way, such as working for him or making his life more pleasant or in some way producing for him good consequences out of the bad situation that he caused. The traditional utilitarian theory is ordinarily limited to the first three kinds of consequences, although there is no reason why, in his consideration of consequences, the utilitarian should not consider the victim also—not only as a member of "society in general," but specifically as the aggrieved party to whom good consequences should accrue.

When this fourth kind of consequence is considered exclusively, we have what is called the "restitution theory of punishment." But we must be careful: all depends on how it is formulated. If the theory asserts, not that we should aim to produce good consequences for the victim, but that the victim *deserves* recompense for the agression against him, then the restitution theory becomes retributive (deserts)—but with this special twist, that it considers not the desert of the *aggressor* but the desert of the *victim*.

It is quite improbable that all of these aims will be fulfilled in any particular case of utilitarian punishment. First, imprisonment seldom rehabilitates lawbreakers; if that were the sole purpose of punishing, prisons should close up shop tomorrow. Most prisoners learn about crime and are far more oriented toward it after they emerge from prison than before they go in.

The second aim, deterrence, is somewhat more effective: many people who would otherwise kill and steal are deterred from doing so by the thought that they may get caught. Unfortunately, however, deterrence is only sporadically effective. It is much more effective for minor offenses, such as overparking and shooting game out of season, than for major crimes like murder. Most murders are committed "in the heat of passion," with no thought of future consequences at the time, and at that moment no severity of threatened future punishment would be sufficient to deter them. Deterrence then is a mixed bag.

But even if deterrence fails in a particular case, the third aim may be achieved: the protection of others. Even if the offender is not improved by punishment, and even if no one else is deterred from crime by his being imprisoned, at least while he is out of circulation other people are protected from further acts of aggression by him. This third utilitarian aim is really the most important one; even if the other two don't work, other people must be protected, and it is more important to protect the innocent than to protect the freedom of the offender to do what he wants.[14]

An unwelcome fact for the utilitarian, but a fact nonetheless, is that very often the utilitarian functions of punishing work against each other. What deters others may not improve the offender or protect society, and where protection is most needed, deterrence or reformation are often least effective. Utilitarians tend to assume that the greatest degree of deterrence and protection of society is needed for the most serious crimes. But this is far from being the case. A man has done what he felt he had to do, namely, kill his wife; apart from that one act he has no aggressive tendencies whatever; society does not need to be protected from him because he is not dangerous to anyone, nor is he any more likely than you or I to initiate any further acts of aggression. If he were let loose today he would be no threat to anyone—not nearly as much as petty thieves, whose offenses are less grave but who are much more likely to repeat their acts over and over again. Would the utilitarian, in view of this, have the courage of his convictions and recommend that the petty thief remain imprisoned indefinitely and that the murderer be released?

"But other people need to be *deterred* from acts of murder, and this can be done only by imprisoning the murderer, to make an example of him." So apparently it is not the murderer's ill-desert that counts, it is how his imprisonment may affect *other* people. And this, of course, is to use the offender simply as a means to an end—someone else's end; it makes him a sacrificial lamb on the altar of other people's (real or supposed) well-being. Besides, the effectiveness of deterrence is least in major crimes like murder; at the moment he commits the deed, the killer is not deterred by threats of punishment or by any other considerations of "rational egoism" as the overparker is. Many persons guilty of murder, then, (1) don't need to be "rehabilitated," (2) are less likely to deter others through his imprisonment than any other type of offender, and (3) don't need to be imprisoned to protect society, since he has no dangerous proclivities that society needs to be protected from.[15] The one consider-

14. Even this aim, however, is not achieved by the prison system. Even the most hardened prison wardens agree that 80–85 percent of the people in prisons don't belong there, and that if the entire prison population of the United States were released tomorrow, Americans would be just as safe (or unsafe) as they are now: most of the dangerous people are not in prisons but right around us, in the streets. See Jessica Mitford, *Cruel and Usual Punishment* (New York: A.A. Knopf, 1973).

15. Besides, the effectiveness of deterrence depends not on *whether* he is punished, but on *how much publicity* attends his punishment, i.e., on how many people know about it. If no one knows he is imprisoned, no one is likely to be deterred by that fact.

ation that would justify punishing the murderer, namely that he has committed the most serious of crimes and accordingly *deserves* it, is a consideration that the utilitarian excludes from consideration.

The utilitarian, aiming still at the production of good consequences, is likely to throw out *punishing* the offender and substitute *treating* him. "Treatment, not punishment"—this is supposed to be "the wave of the future" in penal systems. (He need not, of course, favor it in every case: many prisoners are quite immune to any "treatment.") "Don't punish him, that's barbaric—treat him, mold his personality so that he will never commit offenses in the future"—this is now the watchword; it all sounds very attractive, very enlightened, very humanitarian.

Yet this manifestation of the utilitarian theory is the most ominous of all, as the reading of Bruce Ennis' *Prisoners of Psychiatry*[16] or virtually any of the books by Dr. Thomas Szasz will quickly demonstrate. First, there is a vast difference between *voluntary* and *compulsory* treatment. Therapy voluntarily entered upon may often achieve the desired ends; compulsory treatment is far less effective, and, when it is, its effect is to mold him in directions that other people want for him rather than what he himself wants. Second, even when treatment is not strictly compulsory, great pressure—such as depriving him of access to prison facilities or locking him up in solitary for months on end until he decides to "cooperate"—can be brought to bear to make him engage in it. Third, by what standards will the treatment be conducted? What is to be the criterion of "improvement?" It is almost inevitable that the prisoner will be considered "unimproved" or "unrehabilitated" until he has conformed to the image the therapist desires for him. Fourth, how long will it last? A prison sentence is for a definite maximum period of months or years, and then at last he is free. But in treatment, he stays in until the therapist certifies that he is "cured," which may be ten days, ten years, or for the rest of the prisoner's life. Even if he is in for a trivial offense, his period of treatment may not be short: the therapist may find so many things wrong with his psyche that it will take years to "cure" him. (And if he can meanwhile be used as cheap labor to do jobs in the institution, he will not be treated at all but simply left in year after year to do the menial jobs.) The man is the therapist's prisoner, and if he doesn't respond in the way the therapist wants he can be in forever. In Soviet Russia, where the fashion is to place dissenters in mental institutions, they are subjected to deprivation,

---

16. Bruce Ennis, *Prisoners of Psychiatry* (New York: Harcourt Brace Jovanovich, Inc., 1972).

shock, cold, and a variety of injected chemicals until they "see the error of their ways" or until the prisoner dies of the therapy. In this respect, American prisoners and psychiatric institutions are not far behind. C.S. Lewis put the matter eloquently in his essay "The Humanitarian Theory of Punishment":

> They are not punishing, not inflicting, only healing. But do not let us be deceived by a name. To be taken without consent from my home and friends; to lose my liberty; to undergo all those assaults on my personality which modern psychotherapy knows how to deliver; to be re-made after some pattern of "normality" hatched in a Viennese laboratory to which I never professed allegiance; to know that this process will never end until either my captors have succeeded or I have grown wise enough to cheat them with apparent success—who cares whether this is called punishment or not? That it includes most of the elements for which any punishment is feared—shame, exile, bondage, and years eaten by the locust—is obvious. Only enormous ill-desert could justify it; but ill-desert is the very conception which the humanitarian theory has thrown overboard.[17]

VII

The utilitarian theory of punishment (or treatment) is a failure both in theory and in practice. Some of its inadequacies have apparently been perceived, for there have been several attempts to "combine" the deserts and the results (utilitarian) theories in order to arrive at a satisfactory "compromise" theory.[18]

It has been suggested that the deserts theory is acceptable in providing a *justification* for punishing at all (unless the person has committed a crime he should not be punished, no matter how socially beneficial punishing him might be); the deserts theory *sets a limit* on who may be punished. But once a person has been adjudged guilty, then the results (utilitarian) theory takes over: the sole purpose from that point on should be to produce good consequences.

The "deserts" part of this compromise theory seems to me acceptable, the "results" part not. Granted that we are not to incarcerate the innocent (though on the utilitarian theory it is far from clear why we should always accept this proviso); once guilt has been deter-

17. C.S. Lewis, "The Humanitarian Theory of Punishment," *Res Juridicae* 6 (1953): 224–30. Reprinted in W. Sellars and J. Hospers, *Readings in Ethical Theory* (Prentice-Hall, 1970).

18. I have discussed these points, as well as some of those in the following section, in "Punishment, Protection, and Retaliation," in *Justice and Punishment*, eds. J. Cederblóm and W. Blizek (Cambridge, Massachusetts: Ballinger Publishing Co., 1977), pp. 9–30.

mined, we are to consider only future consequences. When this is done, of course, considerations of desert must be abandoned. What if the offender is a perennial public nuisance of a minor sort (always annoying people, engaging them in unwanted conversations, etc.) and the welfare of society would be promoted in this case by keeping him locked up for many years; shouldn't this be done, if the total well-being of the 500 people he would otherwise bother is greater because of his incarceration than the total discomfort visited upon him? He is one and society is many; many individuals find him to be a thorn in their flesh, and moreover he is immune to any known techniques of therapy on the outside. If we are to consider only future effects, the "incurable" petty offender should certainly receive a longer sentence than the "model prisoner murderer" who will never do it again and whose future incarceration (from the point of view of producing good consequences) would be pointless. Would the compromise theory really accept this consequence?

It has been suggested by John Rawls[19] that each of the two theories has its proper place, but in a somewhat different way. When we ask what is the justification for punishing a particular person we should be desert theorists: we say, *because* you were tried and found guilty of committing armed robbery. But when we ask what offenses should be punished and how much, and what laws should be passed forbidding which types of acts, then we should be utilitarians, and consider only the consequences of prescribing various punishments for various types of offense.

This compromise view seems at first to give each party its due, plus the impression that each of them was right all along; each settles for a piece of the pie. But I do not find this compromise theory any more satisfactory than the previous one. *Why* should the legislator be a utilitarian about punishment any more than the judge? Why should they not *both* consider what range of punishment is *deserved* for the given offense? Why should the legislator's eye, as opposed to the judge's eye, be solely on the results of punishing? Why must the legislator but not the judge turn a blind eye to deserts? Consider our previous case: Suppose it is determined with high probability that incarcerating the minor but "incurable" nuisancemaker for forty years has highly desirable consequences for society as a whole, and that to punish a one time murderer (the kind who'll make a model prisoner and needs no rehabilitation) is not. Is this consideration to be taken as decisive? Is one then to pass a law incarcerating such

19. John Rawls, "Two Concepts of Rules," *Philosophical Review* 64 (1955): 3–32.

nuisancemakers for years, or indefinite sentences, and giving this kind of murderer a suspended sentence? If you consider only what the results of punishing would be, you might very well come up with this legislative plan. It is popularly taken for granted that the worse the crime (the more deserving of punishment), the more severe will be the sentence, even on utilitarian grounds, since there's that much more to be deterred and to protect ourselves against; but as we have already observed, this is not so: there is simply *no correlation* between the gravity of an offense and the utilitarian consequences of punishing it. Once this lack of correlation is clearly perceived, and we *then* ask, "Why should we punish a less serious offense more severely," our question now stands out naked, as it were, shorn of its utilitarian trappings; and now it is by no means obvious that we should still answer, "We should assign the heaviest punishments to whatever offenses will produce the best consequences to punish." In fact, the very asking of the question should now make it clear that legislators should *not* go about passing laws with only utilitarian considerations in mind.

VIII

The fact is that between the deserts theory and the results theory there lies an unbridgeable gulf:

1. Utilitarianism (results theory) is future-looking, whereas deserts (and justice) are past-looking. According to utilitarianism, each of us has but one kind of duty, to produce optimific (i.e., the best possible) consequences in each particular case; and this is as true, according to the utilitarian, in the specific area of punishment as in all other areas of human action. The past is of no importance except insofar as consideration of it may affect future consequences. Desert, by contrast, is past-looking; what you deserve depends on your past record. This is true in all deontological ethics: you keep a promise because you have made it (not in order to produce optimific consequences, though it may sometimes do that too). You pay for repairs to the house you have damaged, even though you might achieve more total good by repairing the poor man's house next door (which you did not damage) with the same money. You owe special consideration to those who have benefited you, even though more total good might be achieved by ignoring your benefactors and helping those who have never lifted a finger for you. And one punishes *because* offenses against justice have occurred in the past: if punishing also does some good to somebody or other, that is a fringe benefit.

2. Desert is *individualistic*; utilitarianism by contrast is *collectivistic*. This point is less obvious but ever so much more important. The utilitarian is always concerned with the *total amount* of good to be brought about, not with a just *distribution* of it.

If maximum social utility were to result from an innocent person being railroaded ("telished") for a crime he did not commit, as long as others were deterred by his imprisonment, the community felt secure, etc., the utilitarian would in all consistency have to approve this deed, as long as it had optimific social effects. True, the innocent man wouldn't be very happy about it, but his happiness is but a small weight in the balance against the great weight of social good that would be achieved by sacrificing him. If, now, one says that this wouldn't actually happen because the real criminal might turn up (thus losing all the recently restored confidence in the efficiency of the police department), we could easily doctor up the scenario so that this wouldn't happen—e.g., by having the judge and no one else know that the real culprit was dead. Anyway, is *that* the only reason why we shouldn't railroad the innocent? If other people don't know it happened, does that make it better? Surely the reason we shouldn't do it is simply that he isn't guilty, and thus doesn't deserve the sentence; nor would the social good to be achieved by sacrificing him, which might under some circumstances (e.g., during a crime wave) be very great indeed, justify punishing him for what he did not do. Once again we would be using him as a means to other person's ends—sacrificing him to some (real or imaginary) "greater social good." We would not be concerned at all with justice, but only with "social engineering." Anyone who is tempted by that prospect should read Solzhenitsyn's *The Gulag Archipelago*.

Kant was surely right about this—that one should treat other human beings as ends, never merely as means toward someone else's end. And if this is accepted, the morality of punishing someone not because he deserves it but to achieve some "greater social 'good' " stands condemned at its very inception. That is most importantly what is wrong with utilitarianism—that it would permit such a thing. It considers the *total*, but not the *individual*. The individual counts, but only as an infinitesimally small fraction of the total. Rawls himself has put the finger on this Achilles' heel of utilitarianism:

> The most natural way . . . of arriving at utilitarianism . . . is to adopt for society as a whole the principle of rational choice for one man. . . .
> In this conception of society separate individuals are thought of as so many different lines along which rights and duties are to be assigned and scarce means of satisfaction allocated in accordance with rules so as to

give the greatest fulfillment of wants. The nature of the decision made by the ideal legislator is not, therefore, materially different from that of an entrepreneur deciding how to maximize his profit by producing this or that commodity, or that of a consumer deciding how to maximize his satisfaction by the purchase of this or that collection of goods. In each case there is a single person whose system of desires determines the best allocation of limited means. The correct decision is essentially a question of efficient administration. This view of social cooperation is the consequence of *extending to society the principle of choice for one man*, and then, to make this extension work, *conflating all persons into one* through the imaginative acts of the impartial sympathetic spectator. *Utilitarianism does not take seriously the distinction between persons.* [20]

Having emphasized the individualistic character of desert as opposed to utility, I must now attach a qualifier for purposes of practical application: that sometimes it is justifiable to be collectivistic because one cannot know or cannot reasonably determine what each individual deserves. For example, automobile insurance premiums are much higher for unmarried males under twenty-five. This is so because this group as a whole has the highest accident rate. Yet there are many unmarried males under twenty-five who are extremely safe drivers, with perfect records, who are unjustly penalized because they are in the same category as a large number of others who are not. The high premiums are surely unjust to them—they pay more because *others* in their group have more accidents. Suppose we now object that insurance companies are behaving unjustly, and that they should scrutinize every case individually. The companies reply that if they did this, it would take so much work time and require the addition of so many employees that everyone's rates would have to go up.

Whether this is so in this particular instance I do not know: but there are surely cases where the cost and effort that would have to go into the evaluation of each individual case simply are not worth the trouble—that the case is not worth all that effort, and that in such cases individual deserts must be sacrificed. If there is a grand total of $1 for bonuses to be distributed among twenty employees, it isn't worth spending many dollars to figure out who deserves 25¢, who deserves 10¢, who 5¢, and who nothing at all.

This concession, then, and only this, I am willing to make to collectivism: that sometimes to discover deserts in each individual case is impossible, or not feasible, or simply not worth the trouble

20. John Rawls, *A Theory of Justice* (Cambridge: Harvard University Press, 1971), pp. 26–27 (emphasis added).

and expense. Obviously this applies only to cases of less than life or death importance. In a criminal trial, where a man's life (or years of his life) is at stake, it is obviously of great importance to uncover the truth and the whole truth about each individual case brought before the court, even though doing so is extremely costly and time-con-suming. The same, I would add, is true of admissions offices in col-leges and universities: when many would like to be admitted but only some can be, it is of great importance to take pains to discover who does and who does not merit admission. Going beyond a certain point with this, like spending $10,000 per student, wouldn't be worth the cost and would soon bankrupt the college. But very often admissions boards are collectivistic out of laziness—because it is so much easier to admit candidates by group quotas, based on race or sex or high school grades (never mind *which* high school), rather than to go into the laborious business of estimating the deservingness of each individual candidate. Yet his fate for years to come may depend on this decision. If it is always unjust to imprison an innocent man, it is also unjust to admit a less deserving student (regardless of age or sex or race) in preference to a more deserving one.

IX

Some of the same causes of concern that I have discussed in connec-tion with the utilitarian theory apply also to the *restitution* theory. True, the restitution theory is not collectivistic; its concern is for the individual victims of the crime. It is also concerned (at least in one formulation of the view, already mentioned) with the deserts of the victim. But it is not equally concerned with the deserts of the offender. I shall consider just two kinds of cases.

1. One man purposely inflicts $10,000 worth of damage or in-jury; another man does it inadvertently, perhaps in spite of his best efforts to avoid doing it. The amount of damage or injury is the same, and so presumably the amount of restitution required in the two cases would be the same. But this seems to me a rather discom-fiting consequence of the theory, for the two offenders' *deserts* are not the same. Whether the offender did it deliberately does enter into a consideration of his desert. There is a difference between mur-der and manslaughter, and everyone agrees that murder should be more harshly punished. But the damage done may be exactly the same; and when death is involved, the victim is equally dead both ways. On the restitution theory, should not the amount of restitu-

tion be equal? I find this disturbing because no consideration is given to the offender's desert.

2. Even more disturbing are cases involving unsuccessful attempts at crime. If I try to kill you but don't succeed because I'm a bad shot, I am morally as guilty as if I had succeeded; if I didn't succeed, it isn't because I didn't try. Legally, however, we do not punish unsuccessful attempts as much as we do successful ones, because in fact the attempted deed was never completed. Just the same, we don't let attempted murders go unpunished. For attempting to kill I merit considerable ill-desert. Attempting to kill, of course, is different from *intending* to kill; for intending to kill you, in spite of moral ill-desert, I am not legally punishable at all (who of us would go free if we were punished for our intentions?). An intention is not yet a deed: I might change my mind when the time came.

Now how do things stand with the restitution theory? If the attempt does not succeed, there is nothing to make restitution for. If you know that I am going to make the attempt, I might have to make restitution to you for scaring you or causing you fear or panic, but if you don't know, then there is no damage or injury to you at all, and presumably no restitution. In other words, there would be restitution required only if attempts succeeded. I confess to being unhappy about not penalizing attempts. If you don't penalize attempts, more attempts will be made, and more of them are likely to succeed. Besides, the man who attempts to kill you deserves a penalty; some would even say he deserves as great a penalty as if he had succeeded.

Consider now the opposite case: if I do something unknowingly or accidentally, not meaning to hurt you or damage your property, I may nevertheless be liable for huge damages. Mrs. O'Leary's cow upsets a lantern, which lights fire to the barn and through a chain reaction destroys the whole city of Chicago—so at least goes the legend. Does she deserve to be made to pay for that huge loss, which she couldn't do in a hundred lifetimes of hard labor? Perhaps that is why New York City has had a law on the books for over a century providing that if you inadvertently (never intentionally) start a fire in a building, the damages for which you are liable are limited to the building in which the fire starts. Perhaps this is to keep people from having to pay for large damages they inadvertently cause beyond their desert. This particular law, of course, has its problems too: if you are going to start a fire indoors in New York, make sure you do it in a small building.

Does a person who causes damages or injury accidentally, or fails through negligence to do something he should have done, deserve any penalty at all? Surely he may, depending on whether he could have taken steps to avoid the act or omission. I didn't mean to leave the bicycle on the sidewalk, I was going to take it into the garage in a few minutes, but meanwhile a blind man passed by, tripped over it, and was injured; surely I do merit some ill-desert for my negligence. The trouble is that the actual damage caused may have very little relation to the degree of my culpability. I may be extremely negligent or reckless and nothing happens, and I may be trivially negligent or reckless and through some fluke a huge catastrophe occurs.

The problem of relating damage to desert is an acutely practical one. The problem stems from the fact that damage or injury did occur, and someone has to pay for it. Since it would be unjust for the victim who suffered the injury to have to pay for it (he has already suffered the injury), and since it would also be unjust for every taxpayer to have to help pay for it, the only solution seems to be for the person who caused the injury or damage in the first place to pay for it (who else are we going to get hold of to do it?), even though the amount he has to pay is way out of line with his desert. I suppose some people would say that it was quite just for him to be made to pay for it all, no matter how large the amount or how unintentional the offense; but in that case justice would depend far too much on factors that are accidental, whimsical, outside your or my control. The person who pleads that this solution is just is probably simply extending the term "just" ad hoc to cover this case since he doesn't know how else to handle it. Such a solution, however, smacks of intellectual dishonesty. I would much prefer to say that there *is* no just solution in such cases. I would say that if someone accidentally struck you and bloodied your nose, and didn't know you were a hemophiliac and might consequently bleed to death, and nevertheless is made to pay $50,000 in hospital bills and for expensive blood transfusions, this solution, whether or not it is a practicable one, is not a just one. The trouble is that every other available solution is even less just.

X

Both the utilitarian and the restitution theories are defective to the extent that they fail to consider desert. I see no help for it: there are times when we have to be concerned with matters of desert, however much complexity and vagueness may plague us in the determination of it. When we compare the worthiness of various goals, we need to talk about goodness and value. When we consider alternative courses of action, we need to talk about right and wrong. And when we believe that someone isn't being fairly treated, we need to talk about justice and desert. We cannot eliminate these terms from our moral vocabulary.

A thug on the city streets, looking for a new source of kicks, beats up an old lady with a shopping bag on the way to the market, slashes her face to ribbons, rapes her, and then clubs her to death. Yes, I want to see him punished, not only to deter others, not only because we must be protected against him and his kind, but because to do nothing in this case is to flout justice. I not only want him to mend his ways, I want him to feel guilty—guilty as hell—so that he can comprehend the enormity of his crime. Even if I knew that punishing him would deter no others, I would still say he deserved to be punished.

But much less dramatic cases than these will suffice. When Howard Hughes had been in the hands of the "Mormon Mafia" for several years, although his already well-developed tendencies toward secretiveness and paranoia were reinforced by the men around him, there were still times when he apparently yearned to escape from that psychological vise. On one occasion, when Hughes and his entourage had moved to Bayshore Inn overlooking Vancouver Bay,

> When they took Hughes up the elevator to the suite they had picked out for him, Hughes went over to the window and looked out, instead of scuttling into his bedroom.
>
> "The aides had picked the big middle room for The Office," Margulis said. "The boss gazed out the window a little while and watched a seaplane landing in the harbor. He said he liked the view.
>
> "The aides didn't like that one bit," said Margulis. "They told me to get him away from the window and into his bedroom.
>
> "Then something happened that really frosted me. The boss said he liked the big room and the view and said it would make a nice sitting room for him. He hadn't had a sitting room for years, and he'd always had the windows taped and never looked out.
>
> "They warned him that somebody could fly past the sitting room in a helicopter and shoot his picture with a telephoto lens. 'Here's *your* room,' they told him, and took him into another little blacked-out bedroom, with the draperies all taped down tight. He just went along with them, and they had him back in the cave again. After a while he got into bed, and called for a movie, and everything was just the way it had been for years."[21]

21. *Time*, 13 December 1976, p. 36.

When I read that passage I felt a strong sense of *moral outrage.* Here was a sick recluse who showed glimmerings of desire to escape from his condition, and here they were pushing him back into sickness again. "But nobody forced him!" I can hear someone say. "Hughes went back into the taped-up room of his own free will." And it's true they didn't exactly force him, they conned him. They were afraid that if he went public again they would be out of jobs, their importance to him would be over and so would their extravagant salaries; so they did what they could to keep things working to their advantage. No, they didn't force him physically—they worked on him mentally at what they knew was a weak spot and it worked.

One could say that Hughes was crazy, at least in some segments of his complex personality. But even if true, that would be nothing to the purpose. The point is that *they* weren't crazy: they knew exactly what they were doing. They made sure that they kept on controlling him, never letting him out of their grasp, perhaps simply to retain power, perhaps ultimately to get hold of his money, but at any rate they knowingly and deliberately frustrated any attempt by him to get himself out of his cocoon. I don't know what they deserved, I can't even say they deserved legal punishment, but I had the overwhelming feeling of enormous ill-desert on their part. What I felt was not covered by the idea that they could be made better persons, or that others should be deterred from doing what they were doing, or that society should be protected against the machinations of such men. I would not particularly deny any of these things, but they were perfectly distinct from (and far less strong than) the overwhelming conviction of their ill-desert. The other convictions were not even related to it as first cousins.

I would rest the case with two questions, substantially the same questions that J.D. Mabbott posed in his classic essay "Punishment."[22] (1) Suppose a person is punished for a heinous crime, but that the punishment did not improve him, that no one was deterred by his imprisonment, and that no one was protected because of his isolation from them. Does this show, or even tend to show, that his punishment was unjust? The answer seems to me obviously no. (2) Suppose a person is punished, and emerges a changed and bettered person; that countless others have been deterred from crime by his example; and that many more have felt (or truly have been) protected because he was imprisoned—but that in fact he never committed the deed at all for which he was convicted. Would any or all of these benefits show, or even tend to show, that his punishment was just? The answer again is obviously no.

22. J.D. Mabbott, "Punishment," *Mind* 48 (1939):152–67.

XI

Suppose a student has been lazy the whole term, had done no work, and absorbed nothing from the course. But suppose that he would be happier if he got an A, in fact he needs the A to improve his grade average and go on to school, that the teacher would be happier if he accepted the student's bribe of $100 for giving him the A, and that nobody else would ever know the difference. Would this lead us to believe that he should receive the A? No, for the simple reason that he didn't deserve it. The utilitarians on punishment are analogous to those who agree to give the undeserving student an A. The good results would not justify giving the undeserved grade; and the good results of "telishment" would not justify punishing the innocent. That is the profound but simple truth underlying the deserts theory.

If, finally, one wishes to say that the general *practice* of giving As only to those who deserve them is a good practice, in that on the whole the effects of adhering to the practice turn out to be the best, I would agree that this is, or tends to be, so. And if one wishes to say that the general practice of rewarding or punishing in accord with desert produces the most good in the long run—not in every individual case, but only as a general rule—then I will agree once more that this *tends* to be the case. If this is construed as assent to rule-utilitarianism as opposed to act-utilitarianism, at least in one meaning of the dozens of senses of these terms that philosophers have now spun out, so be it—I shall not object. But that is simply a consequence or by-product of my conviction, not the heart of it. My reason for saying that the thing should not be done, the grade of A in one case and the punishment of the innocent in the other—is simply that the individuals concerned do not deserve it. That is enough by itself, just as it stands. All the rest is a fringe benefit. In moral philosophy it is always the simple and obvious truths, long since recognized by the common man, that we in the ivory tower seem to lose sight of first.

✳ *Chapter 9*

Retribution and the Ethics of Punishment

Walter Kaufmann

The wording of the topic assigned to me may suggest that retribution constitutes the ethical factor in punishment.

This is certainly what many people believe, although this view is less prevalent in discussions of punishment during the second half of the twentieth century than it was fifty or a hundred years ago. Still, it is widely held that punishment can be viewed in a variety of perspectives, considering, for example, its efficiency, but that these approaches are nonethical and that only retribution makes punishment moral. I have been asked to speak on this topic because I have criticized this view.[1] Let us begin by asking:

WHAT IS PUNISHMENT?

Punishment involves at least two persons (call them A and B) and two acts. A holds a position of authority in relation to B, claims that B has done some wrong, and by virtue of his authority causes something unpleasant to happen to B in return for (as a punishment for) this claimed wrong. This is what is meant by punishment. If A does not claim that B has done some wrong, one speaks of maltreatment or torture, not of punishment; and if A does not hold a position of authority one speaks of revenge.

1. *Without Guilt and Justice* (New York: Peter H. Wyden, 1973; New York: Dell Publishing Co., A Delta Book paperback, 1975). The present paper is based on this book and especially on Chapter 2, "The Death of Retributive Justice." The following section is actually quoted with a few small changes from Section 17 in Chapter 2.

B could be an animal, but only if A treats B more or less as a person. Thus B could well be a dog or a cat; but we do not call it punishment when we kill a mosquito that has just bitten us. If A and B are one and the same person and we say, "Why do you keep punishing yourself?" we are using the term figuratively but still in a manner that is wholly consistent with our explication: B assumes the role of A and punishes himself. Finally, A could be a deity, who in that case would act more or less like a person—specifically, like a father, a judge, or possibly a teacher.

What is the purpose of this institution of punishment? It is encountered in many, if not all, societies and is used not only by political authorities but also by parents and teachers and even in games. Its ubiquity makes a mockery of any search for "the purpose," as if there were always one purpose only, the same everywhere. In different societies, contexts, and ages, punishment served various functions. Its entertainment value was more important in some places than in others. But the desire to see justice done, to do to the offender what he deserved, was never the primary reason for instituting punishments. The primary purpose of proclaiming a penal code is to prevent some evil. But this does not mean that the penalties are intended solely for deterrence. In Deuteronomy 19, "eye for eye" is actually introduced: "The rest shall hear and fear, and shall never again commit any such evil in your midst." Deterrence is very important indeed, but often understood far too narrowly.

A penal code deters people from committing crimes not only (1) by engendering fear but also (2) by inculcating a moral sense. A trivial penalty (say, a five cent fine) suggests that an offense is trivial, while a severe penalty conveys the sense that the crime for which it is decreed is grave. The code may also deter people simply (3) by informing them of what is forbidden. At first glance, it may seem to be overly subtle to distinguish this function from the first two. In fact, in many cases one is neither frightened nor led to feel that anything is immoral, and it is quite common for people to know that certain acts are forbidden without having any idea what penalties have been decreed for offenders. In such cases the third function is in evidence, but not the first two. But crimes occur in spite of all this, and the penalties are intended to undo, or at least to minimize, the damage. How?

(4) By preventing private vengeance, lynchings, and a general breakdown of order. Often the offense injured others who, in the absence of a penal code, might have taken the law into their own hands.

(5) By seeing to it that the breaking of a law does not become

an invitation to other men to emulate the lawbreaker. The punishment is meant to deter others and thus to reenforce the code. The offender has weakened the law and come close to annulling its deterrent effect; now the punishment is meant to undo this negative consequence and thus to restore the deterrent effect.

(6) By providing a safety valve for the unlawful desires that smolder below the surface and are fanned to the danger point by the commission of a crime. Many people have wanted to do what the criminal did but were kept from doing it by the law or by their conscience. Now he makes them look silly; they were timid, he was bold; they were weak, and he was strong—if he gets away with it. And he seems to have gotten away with it. Hence many people are burning to do what he did. The penal code provides an outlet for this criminal desire. He has killed someone, and now you—many of you—also want to kill. All right; kill him! He has maimed someone, and now many of you also want to maim someone. All right; maim him! Thus the desire for talion—for doing to the criminal what he has done to someone else—does not evidence any profound sense of justice or a primordial conviction that this is clearly what the criminal deserves.

These last three functions (4—6) interpenetrate. But the desire to proportion punishments to crimes is not born of the feeling that anything *less* than this would not be justice; it represents an attempt to keep cruelty in bounds. For as soon as people are invited to vent their criminal desires on the criminal, the same dangers reappear that we have just considered (under 4 and 5): as long as he is to be killed in any case, why merely kill him? Why not hang him first, then take him down alive, cut out his entrails. Why not have an orgy? Historically, the call for talion has generally signified a great advance over wanton cruelty.[2]

The fourth and fifth functions still come under the heading of deterrence. The sixth might be called cathartic, to use an ugly word for an ugly fact. Punishment purges the society—not, as often claimed, by removing some mythical pollution, but in a more palpable psychological sense. The purge, of course, affords only temporary relief, and unfortunately there is evidence that it is addictive. But this function of punishment has often been mistaken for a demand for retributive justice.

The traditional distinction between three functions of punishment

2. Cf. Paul Reiwald, *Die Gesellschaft und ihre Verbrecher* (Zurich: Pan-Verlag, 1948), pp. 268f., 273, 294, and also 16ff. where it is pointed out that in eighteenth-century England the punishment for treason began with hanging; then the offender was taken down while still alive and his entrails were cut out and burned before his eyes; and then he was beheaded and quartered.

—deterrence, reform, and retribution—is not subtle enough. One should distinguish ten functions—four more in addition to the six considered so far.

(7) Punishment is often justified as a means of reforming the offender. Thus a child is punished to teach him a lesson and to make him a better person. Lawbreakers have been pilloried, whipped, sent to prison, branded, maimed, and fined to reeducate them. Hardly solely for that purpose, but we need not doubt that this was often held to be one aim of punishment—and more rarely also one function of punishment.

(8) Recompense or restitution is scarcely a punishment as long as it is merely a matter of returning stolen goods or money. But suppose one has insulted another person and is required to make a public apology, or one has to make up to someone else some form of humiliation, inconvenience, or suffering. When the offender is humiliated, inconvenienced, or made to suffer in turn because this is held to be some recompense for the offended party, we enter the realm of punishment. Similarly, when it is claimed that the lawbreaker has harmed society and must now pay his debt to society, recompense is invoked as the purpose of punishment. The point is not that the offender deserves to suffer; it is rather that the offended party desires compensation. Again, the various functions often interpenetrate

(9) Expiation is also a form of recompense, but here the underlying idea is that some god has been offended and must be appeased. The notion of expiation depends on religious beliefs and makes no sense apart from them. Here I am sticking closely to the traditional meaning of "expiation." If it were objected that the notion also makes sense in relation to a sovereign, a parent, or anyone at all who sees himself as standing in God's place, I should say that such cases are best included under number 8.

(10) Finally, there is the claim that justice requires retribution, and that justice is done when, and only when, the offender is punished: he deserves to be punished, and until he actually is punished he fails to get what he deserves. This claim, which figures prominently in the rhetoric about punishment, is open to several criticisms;

(a) The notion of desert is questionable.

(b) The first seven functions are clearly future-oriented. The eighth (recompense) is at least partly future-oriented, but it also hinges on the notion of desert. The ninth (expiation) is a variant of the eighth that introduces the supernatural. But retribution is past-oriented and frequently based on the claim that a past event needs to be—and can be—undone. This is a superstition. The past is not a blackboard, punishments are not erasers, and the slate can never be wiped clean: what is done is done and cannot be undone.

(c) The intuitive certainty that nevertheless often accompanies the belief that an offender fails to get what he deserves until he is punished can be explained psychologically.

Before we develop some of these objections, it is important to consider the matter of ethics.

ETHICS IN HISTORICAL PERSPECTIVE

We usually take for granted that there is a discipline called ethics, and we rarely if ever ask what it amounts to. But when discussing "the ethics of punishment," we should know what we are talking about. Asked to define ethics, one might say that it is the science of right and wrong. If pressed about the word "science," one might speak instead of systematic or, perhaps better, sustained reflection. If questioned whether ethics really concerns itself with every kind of right and wrong, including, for example, right and wrong chess moves or right and wrong answers to problems in arithmetic, one might qualify these two terms and speak of "moral" right and wrong. But at that point one would beg the question, inasmuch as "moral" is used simply as a synonym for "ethical." And to say that ethics is the study of ethical right and wrong does not tell us what ethics amounts to. But at this point it may suffice to say merely that ethics is the study of what makes human actions right or wrong.

Specifically, what are we doing when we discuss the ethics of punishment? We have defined punishment and seen that this institution serves a variety of purposes. Perhaps we can even agree that it would be very unsatisfactory to discuss punishment at length and ignore ethical questions. But what are the "ethical" questions that need to be taken into account?

Ethics was born among the Greeks in the fifth century B.C. When one person is singled out as its founder, this is generally Socrates. Actually, his immediate forerunners include not only some of the Sophists but also Aeschylus, Sophocles, and Euripides. In the *Oresteia*, most notably in the last play of this trilogy, the *Eumenides*, we encounter sustained reflection on rival claims of right and wrong, and similar issues were central in many other Greek tragedies.[3] It remains startling that this kind of reflection has not been a feature of all

3. For more detailed discussion, see Kaufmann, *Tragedy and Philosophy* (Garden City, New York: Doubleday, 1968; Anchor Books, 1969).

times and climes. Nevertheless it is possible and illuminating to see it against the background of some earlier stages and to distinguish five stages in all.

1. Originally, "right" meant conforming to tradition, and "wrong" was what violated tradition. At this point, or rather during the ages when this attitude prevailed, there was no distinctively moral sense of "right" or "wrong." One might therefore speak of a *preethical stage*, and in many ways the *Iliad* is still preethical in this sense.[4]

2. The second stage is reached when tradition clashes with tradition. In a tightly knit society whose members stay put in one place and have few contacts with other societies this need never have happened, especially during the millennia before the art of writing was invented. But as outside influences multiplied, tradition ceased more and more to speak with a single voice. Literacy did its share to facilitate comparisons. When individuals arise to criticize convention by appealing to a rival tradition, as the Hebrew prophets did, we reach the *protoethical stage*. In Greek tragedy we see how this stage gives rise to the next. The characterization just given fits the *Eumenides* and *Antigone*, but in these plays and in many of Euripides' we encounter a delight in argument that offers a stark contrast to the Hebrew prophets.

3. The next stage is reached when some of the Sophists discover that arguments cannot prove that a convention is right. Skepticism emerges and results in *ethical relativism*. If ethics is understood as sustained reflection, it begins with the Sophists, and this is the oldest ethical position. For the Hebrew prophets did not engage in sustained reflection or in a more or less systematic study of right and wrong. Socrates may have concentrated on conduct more exclusively than the major Sophists did, and to that extent he may be the father of ethics, but the main reason why he is so often singled out in this way is surely that Plato, the first philosopher known to us from complete works and not merely fragments, acknowledged Socrates as his master; and in the earliest complete works on ethics that we know— some of Plato's dialogues—Socrates leads the discussion. Yet we do not know for sure to what extent, if any, the historical Socrates developed a response to ethical relativism.

4. What Plato and many subsequent moral philosophers tried to do was precisely this: to counter ethical relativism. Plato's way of

_____

4. For a striking example, see *Iliad*, 6:57ff.

doing this is still with us in the twentieth century. It is illuminating to distinguish three elements in his strategy, which in essentials has also been the strategy of Kant and many others. First, he presents himself as the champion of a tradition and the opponent of the relativistic critics of that tradition whom he sees as moral nihilists. Second, he is actually far from endorsing any one tradition in toto; like later theologians, he selects and reinterprets without realizing fully how this procedure is open to the criticisms of the ethical relativists. Finally—and this is why, like Kant, he has been revered as a great philosopher—he offers arguments in defense of his *ethical absolutism*. Upon close examination, his arguments, like Kant's, do not stand up. And having discovered that, one finds that philosophers of this kind actually offer bad reasons for an expurgated version of the moral code on which they were brought up.

To understand this position, it is essential to recognize the three moves on which it depends. The contrast of a hallowed tradition with moral nihilism provides some sanction by authority as well as a powerful threat, as if this version of ethical absolutism were all that stood between us and disaster. We are lulled into forgetting that there are many traditions and many versions of ethical absolutism. In typical Manichaean fashion, the absolutist poses as a savior from moral chaos—no, not as *a* savior but as *the* savior, as if he provided the one and only alternative to moral nihilism. We do not ordinarily think of Plato and Kant as Manichaean, but their dualism is palpable and involves them again and again in ignoring significant alternatives. Absolutists with widely different positions abound, and it is sustained reflection on this fact and on divergent codes that leads to ethical relativism. The first element of Plato's strategy thus involves a crucial mistake. In Plato's case we cannot be altogether sure that he himself failed to realize this, for he defended the "noble lie" and argued that one has to deceive people in order to save them.[5]

The second element of this strategy involves a common form of self-deception. It consists in what I call "exegetical thinking," which is to say that a tradition or a text is endowed with authority; that one then reads one's own ideas into it; and that one gets them back endowed with authority.[6]

The third and last element of this strategy bears the burden of giving this whole enterprise the name of philosophy. We are offered arguments, often even alleged proofs. Plato scholars, however, no

5. *Republic*, 414, et passim.
6. For more detailed discussion, see, e.g., *Without Guilt and Justice*, Section 6, and the chapter on "The Art of Reading" in Kaufmann, *The Future of the Humanities* (New York: Reader's Digest Press. 1977).

longer accept Plato's arguments, and Kant scholars are appalled by what a close study of Kant's arguments in his books on ethics shows.[7]

The reason for singling out Plato and Kant is, of course, that they are widely considered as great as any philosopher of any time. To prove the case against them in detail and to show how the same analysis applies to Christian absolutists, some utilitarians, and various contemporary writers would obviously be impossible in a short essay. That the absolutist position is based on reason, and ultimately on authority, if only that of the thinker's own moral intuitions, seems plain. I am suggesting that it is also based on a more or less sweeping disregard for rival authorities and different moral intuitions.

5. The last stage to be mentioned here is *critical ethics*, meaning critical reflection on alternatives. Perhaps representatives of critical ethics can claim Socrates as a forerunner with at least as much right as Plato had to do this. But my own ethics being of this type, I have no wish to invoke any authority. What is remarkable is rather how little ethics of this kind is to be found before the nineteenth century.

Critical ethics does not involve the absurd view that any ethic is as good as any other. On the contrary, that view is thoroughly uncritical. Nor does critical ethics entail a lack of moral convictions. It does entail what Nietzsche once called "the courage for an *attack* on one's convictions."[8] Far from treating one's own ultimate intuitions as authoritative and finding corroboration in the consensus of like-minded individuals, past or present, one asks systematically what speaks for and against one's own views, and what speaks for and against various alternatives. In the process, many positions are discovered to be confused, inconsistent, or based on shoddy evidence or arguments, while a few—sometimes only one but often more than one—seem tenable.

When we place the ethics of punishment in this framework, two points emerge. First, those who defend retribution as the ethical function of punishment are generally absolutists who consider it intuitively obvious that certain crimes call for certain punishments and who ignore history, which shows how many brilliant writers felt

7. See, for example, Lewis White Beck, *A Commentary on Kant's Critique of Practical Reason* (Chicago: The University of Chicago Press, 1960); and Robert Paul Wolff, *The Autonomy of Reason: A Commentary on Kant's Groundwork of the Metaphysics of Morals* (New York; Evanston, Illinois; San Francisco; and London: Harper & Row, 1973).

8. In a posthumously published note, *Gesammelte Werke, Musarionausgabe* (Munich: Musarion Verlag, 1920–29), vol. XVI, p. 318.

no less sure that the same crimes called for very different punishments. Second, by no means all absolutists have been retributivists. In fact, retributivism does not occupy a privileged position in any of the five stages considered here.

RETRIBUTION IN HISTORICAL PERSPECTIVE

It might be neat to distinguish the same five stages just considered. But it meets the eye that neither the Sophists nor Plato defended retribution, and even Aristotle ignored retribution in his careful analysis of justice. We shall therefore concentrate on the first two stages and on some non-Greek versions of ethical absolutism.

A.S. Diamond has shown that in early penal codes homicide was punished with fines; and in the many more or less primitive tribes he studied, pecuniary fines for homicide outnumbered capital punishment by a ratio of better than five to one: 73 percent versus 14 percent; and in the remaining 13 percent the punishment was also a fine: the slayer had to turn over to the victim's family a number of women, children, or slaves. It is only in what Diamond calls "Late Middle and Late Codes (including England, 1150 and onwards)" that intentional homicide is taken to require capital punishment.[9]

The belief that wrongs call for retribution is not primordial, instinctive, and universal—a timeless truth inscribed in the hearts of all men that only moral nihilists and relativists dare to question. It is rather a belief that developed in historical times. Of course, that does not prove it to be false, but it does refute one argument on which retributivists often rely, the appeal to the *consensus gentium*, the consensus of all nations. In addition to eliminating this prop, historical study also shows how shaky the appeal to moral intuition is.

In the Code of Hammurabi, around 1700 B.C., capital punishment is invoked rather frequently, but for the most part the reason for it would not seem to be retribution, much less an attempt to approximate the punishment of the crime. To be sure, if a noble has destroyed the eye of another noble, his eye shall be destroyed; if he has broken the bone of another noble, "they shall break his bone"; and if he has knocked out a tooth of a noble "of his own rank, they shall knock out his tooth."[10] If the victim is not a noble, the punishment is a fine, and this is also the case when a commoner has struck the

9. A.S. Diamond, *Primitive Law* (London: Longmans, 1935; Methuen, 1971), especially p. 316. See also *Iliad*, 9:632ff.

10. *Ancient Near Eastern Texts Relating to the Old Testament*, 2nd ed., ed. James B. Pritchard (Princeton: Princeton University Press, 1955), pp. 163–80.

cheek of a commoner. But what needs emphasis is that the cases in which the punishment is so similar to the crime that we may think that the underlying principle is surely retribution are the exception, not the rule, even in the section of the code on which we have concentrated. If a noble has struck the cheek of a noble of higher rank, he is to receive sixty lashes with an oxtail whip in the assembly. If he has struck the cheek of noble of his own rank, he is to pay a fine. If a slave has struck the cheek of a noble, they cut off his ear; if a son has struck his father, they cut off his hand.

In other sections of this code it is even more obvious that it does not rest on the principle of retribution. It may suffice to cite two consecutive laws (§154f.). If a noble has had intercourse with his daughter, they shall make him leave the city. If he has chosen a bride for his son, and the son has had intercourse with her, but later he himself has lain in her bosom and he is caught, they shall bind that noble and throw *him* into the water. The translator has "him" but says in a footnote: "Through a scribal error the original has 'her.' " One may wonder whether this was a scribal error, and, if it was, how many women may have died on its account. Either way, whether he or she was drowned, it will come as a surprise that this offense was considered so much more serious than incest between father and daughter. In any case, retribution is not invoked as the basic principle.

Even Hammurabi may be assigned to the protoethical stage rather than to the preethical stage, if it is assumed that the point of such a codification of law is that convention occasionally clashed with convention and it was necessary for that reason to determine clearly which traditions were to be binding. When we consider the Hebrew Bible, the so-called Old Testament, this is plainly so. Here an awareness of alternatives is stressed from the start. Moses is said to have been schooled in the wisdom of Egypt, and his laws are meant to give shape to a different way of life—different not only from that of Egypt but also from that of other nations.

It has often been claimed that the Law of Moses is based on the principle of an eye for an eye and a tooth for a tooth, but anyone who has studied Exodus, Leviticus, Numbers, and Deuteronomy knows that this is not so, although this phrase occurs three times. Even where it does occur, exceptions are noted, and it is not by any means suggested that retribution is what is sought. Indeed, in one of the three passages (Deuteronomy 19), as we have seen above, the phrase is actually introduced: "The rest shall hear and fear, and shall never again commit any such evil in your midst."

Perhaps the Book of Job is best understood as belonging to a later

stage. Here we find sustained reflection and argument, and traditional views are called into question. But the author's view cannot be
categorized as ethical relativism. In a way, then, this book does not
quite fit into the scheme I have outlined. The reason for bringing it
up nevertheless is that it represents an attack on the views of Job's
friends who understand human suffering as divine retribution for
human wrongdoing. Job maintains, and so does the author of the
book, that Job, who suffers grievously, has done no wrong, and in
the final chapter God says twice that Job has spoken the truth while
his friends have not. In a theological context one would have to
stress that Job and the author of the book deny God's goodness and
justice.[11] In the present context it is more important to insist that
they reject the view, apparently widespread even then, that the good
and evil fortunes of men may be understood as the result of divine
retribution.

Looked at superficially, this may seem to be irrelevant to "the
ethics of punishment." In fact, beliefs about divine justice are as
relevant as Plato's beliefs about the idea of justice, for in both cases
it is assumed that what is at stake is *the paradigm of justice*. Moreover, those who believe that all suffering is deserved and more or less
directly due to divine retribution will feel, as Augustine and many
outstanding Christians after him did and taught, that compassion for
those God chooses to punish is sinful. The ethical implications of the
Book of Job, on the other hand, include the view that it is entirely
appropriate to feel compassion for the unfortunate. Their suffering is
not necessarily deserved.

It has often been claimed falsely that the friends of Job represent
the mainstream of old Testament thought. In fact, the Book of Job,
in which Job's "friends" are rebuked and repudiated, is at one with
the ethic of Moses and the prophets and specifically with the insistence on compassion for widow, orphan, stranger, and slave and the
refrain that the children of Israel, having been slaves in Egypt, should
understand how it feels to be oppressed. Isaiah 53, on the suffering
servant, is also close to the Book of Job.

11. Of course, this is not the way the Book of Job has usually been read. See
The Dimensions of Job: A Study and Selected Readings, presented by Nahum N.
Glatzer (New York: Schocken Books, 1969). In addition to a long introductory
essay, Glatzer presents, with short prefatory notes, thirty-two interpretations.
My own (pp. 237–45, reprinted in abbreviated form from *The Faith of a Here-
tic*, 1961) he introduces as "one of the boldest and most incisive and sensitive
reflections on the Joban problem. His analysis stresses Job's protest against divine injustice and his denial of God's goodness—issues carefully avoided by theological moralists." I mention this only because my reading might strike some
people not versed in biblical scholarship as eccentric.

In the Old Testament, retribution had never achieved the central importance that it assumed in the New Testament. In the New Testament men's laws, society, and this world are depreciated radically, and justice is to be found only in the divine judgment that consigns a few to heaven and the mass of men to hell and eternal damnation. In this divine judgment all other functions of punishment drop away. As Pope Pius XII noted in his address to the Sixth International Congress of Penal Law, October 3, 1953,[12] "The Omnipotent and All-Knowing Creator can always prevent the repetition of a crime by the interior moral conversion of the delinquent"—or, we might add, in any number of other ways. "But the supreme Judge, in His Last Judgment, applies uniquely the principle of retribution." This shows, according to the pope, that "modern theories" are wrong when they "fail to consider expiation of the crime committed . . . as the most important function of punishment."

Liberal Protestantism has spread a very different but historically untenable conception of the Gospels. In fact, the notion that retribution is the crucial ethical function of punishment is rooted in the New Testament, at least as far as Western civilization is concerned. This is no small matter, for it did not remain for a twentieth century pope to exhort Christians to an *imitatio Dei* in these matters. The belief in a God who was held to punish relatively trivial offenses with eternal tortures was taken to justify cruelties that have no parallels in the codes of Moses or Hammurabi. Moreover, Jesus neither counselled nor showed compassion for the damned, and Augustine among others taught expressly that one must not feel compassion for them.

Of the other religions in which similar doctrines prevailed it will suffice to mention Hinduism with its doctrine of reincarnation. Here the wisdom of Job's friends poisoned a whole society. The widow, the poor, and the oppressed are held to deserve their fates and to suffer just retribution for the wrongs they did in previous lives. Again, compassion would be sinful.[13]

The notion that just retribution is possible was not born of philosophical reflection and much less of the experience of human legislators. It was born of the unsupported claim that—in the words of Jesus cited by Pius XII—"the Son of Man will come with his angels in the glory of his Father, and then he will repay every man for what he has done"[14]; or of the equally unsupported claim that there is a

---

12. *The Catholic Mind*, February 1954.

13. The views presented here are defended much more fully in some of my other writings, especially in *Religions in Four Dimensions* (New York, Reader's Digest Press, 1976).

14. Matthew 16:27, cited by the pope along with Romans 2:6 and 13:4. The

law, *karma*, that governs the transmigration of souls, insuring that after death everybody gets what he deserves.

Two of the most impressive men of the enlightenment still tried their hands at attempts to emulate God's alleged justice. In his first inaugural address, Jefferson proposed nothing less than "Equal and exact [!] justice to all men." For him this did not entail the abolition of slavery; but in 1779 he had actually drafted "A Bill for Proportioning Crimes and Punishments," whose provisions are likely to strike a modern reader as grotesque: "Whosoever shall be guilty of rape, polygamy, or sodomy with man or woman, shall be punished, if a man, by castration, if a woman, by cutting through the cartilage of her nose a hole of one half inch in diameter at the least." And:

> whosoever on purpose, and of malice forethought, shall maim another, or shall disfigure him, by cutting out or disabling the tongue, slitting or cutting of a nose, lip, or ear, branding, or otherwise, shall be maimed, or disfigured in like sort; or if that cannot be, for want of the same part, then as nearly as may be, in some other part of at least equal value and estimation, in the opinion of the jury, and moreover shall forfeit one half of his lands and goods to the sufferer.

Kant stated that:

> Whoever steals makes everybody else's property insecure; he thus robs himself (in accordance with the law of retribution) of the security of all possible property; he has nothing nor can acquire anything but still wants to live, which is not possible unless others feed him. But since the state will not do this for nothing, he has to place his powers at the disposal of the state for whatever labor it deems fit. . . .

And, Kant also said:

> Even if civil society were to dissolve with the full agreement of all its members (e.g., a people on an island resolved to scatter all over the world), the last murderer still confined to prison would first have to be executed in order that everybody received what his deeds deserved, lest a blood guilt should stick to the people that had not insisted on this penalty. . . .[15]

The major critics of retributivism (for example, Bentham, Nietzsche, and Shaw) have been more or less militant anti-Christians,

---

RSV lists the following parallel passages: Matthew 10:33; Luke 12:9; 1 John 2:28; Romans 2:6; Revelations 22:12. It would be easy to lengthen the list.

15. See *The Complete Jefferson; Containing his Major Writings, Published and Unpublished, except his Letters*, ed. Saul K. Padover (New York: Duell, Sloan and Pearce, 1943), pp. 90–102; and Immanuel Kant, *Metaphysische Anfangsgründe der Rechtslehre* (1797), § 49E.

but by no means moral nihilists. On the contrary, the turn against retributivism has been motivated ethically for the most part.

OBJECTIONS TO RETRIBUTION

It is arguable that this whole chapter should have concentrated on this topic, recapitulating all the major arguments. But it is a mistake to think of philosophy only or mainly as the amassing of arguments. It is important to gain perspective on a problem or position and to perceive its relation to other problems and alternative positions. That is what has been attempted here so far. It is important to realize that retribution is not one of the three functions of punishment, along with deterrence and reform, but rather one function among many more, of which ten have been considered here. It is also crucial to realize how it is a relative latecomer, and how small a role if any it has played in many codes. Finally, we can hardly begin to understand its place in the modern world until we grasp its relation to Christianity.

Instead of recapitulating all or even most of the arguments to be found in a vast literature, I should like once again to concentrate on a few especially important points that need more discussion.

1. What has hurt retributivism more than any argument is the conjunction of three cultural developments: the eclipse of Christianity; the spread of humanitarianism, to which some of the greatest nineteenth century novelists contributed; and the emergence of depth psychology. The type of psychology that is at issue here is tied above all to four names: Dostoevsky, Tolstoy, Nietzsche, and Freud. I shall say no more about the first two developments, but it may be useful to indicate at least briefly how depth psychology has contributed to the marked decline of faith in retribution. One simply cannot understand the change in the whole climate of opinion about punishment without paying some attention to the rise of depth psychology.

It has become a commonplace that criminals are not essentially different from law-abiding citizens. Manichaeans do not see their enemies as essentially like themselves, and most Christians had not thought of the damned as essentially like the saved. The insistence of the new psychology that criminals are not profoundly different from other men went well with the spread of humanitarianism. But Freud and Nietzsche also attacked from the opposite side the sharp division between respectable society on the one hand and the abnormal and criminal on the other. They exposed the unedifying motives and emotions of the normal and respectable and thus showed us punishment in a new light. Even when the cathartic function of punishment described above has not been perceived as clearly as I have sought to present it, capital punishment and the claim that retribution is required are no longer seen today as they were seen by Kant and Hegel, T.H. Green and Bernard Bosanquet.

Green still claimed that "Indignation against wrong done to another has nothing in common with a desire to revenge a wrong done to ourself."[16] This claim was crucial not only to *his* defense of retribution as the distinctively ethical factor of punishment. Yet it is psychologically naive in the extreme. The Buddha knew that in the sixth century B.C., but before Nietzsche and Freud very few other people did. On January 28, 1804, the British *Morning Herald* could still publish the following report that Green, who was born some thirty years later, might still have taken at face value, while many, if not most, readers today will consider it a vivid refutation of Green's view of indignation:[17]

> The enormity of Thomas Scott's offence [*sic*], in endeavouring to accuse Captain Kennah, a respectable officer, together with his servant, of robbery, having attracted much public notice, his conviction, that followed the attempt, could not be but gratifying to all lovers of justice. Yesterday, the culprit underwent a part of his punishment: he was placed in the pillory, at Charing Cross, for one hour. On his first appearance, he was greeted by a large mob with a discharge of small shot, such as rotten eggs, filth, and dirt from the streets, which was followed up by dead cats, rats, etc., which had been collected in the vicinity of the Metropolis by the boys in the morning. . . .

If we are immune to all attempts to convince us that what Thomas Scott received was what Jefferson called "exact justice," this is surely not because such a claim could not be supported by arguments at least as good as Jefferson's and Kant's arguments for other punishments. Scott had tried to undermine respect for Captain Kennah, and it could be argued that retributive justice demanded that he be subjected to loss of respect.

Branks were iron frames placed over a woman's head, with a sharp metal bit entering the mouth, and were used to punish scolds. Surely it could be argued that this punishment fitted the crime and was not wholly disproportionate. Yet nobody nowadays takes seriously the

16. T.H. Green, *Lectures on the Principles of Political Obligation* (London: Longmans Green, 1937), p. 184. First published posthumously in 1895.

17. The report is quoted by William Andrews, *Old-Time Punishments, 1890* (London: Tabard Press, 1970), p. 84f. The chapter on "The Pillory" shows that the scene described was typical.

claim that retributive justice demands such punishments as branks or pillories, or gags and ducking stools, or branding and maiming. And one of the most important reasons for these changes is an awareness of the motives that find expression in such punishments.

It may be objected that being a scold or falsely accusing a man of armed robbery are not crimes at all, or that at least they involve no direct physical harm, and that any physical punishment is therefore obviously disproportionate. But that is really beside the point at issue here. What requires explanation is that attempts to devise ingenious punishments that could perhaps be defended as proportionate have all but disappeared and hardly anyone in the Western world advocates *public* punishments of any kind. This does not necessarily mean that we have become more humane. But it has come to be felt widely that the "lovers of justice" who feel gratified by watching and contributing to the punishments of wrongdoers are not so different from these wrongdoers and anything but admirable. Hence the tendency has been to prevent such spectacles as that described in the *Morning Herald* by no longer punishing offenders in public. This change of procedure also has the advantage that *we* do not see what is done and hence are not haunted by the vision of brutal warders and inhuman prison conditions. We know that punishment in action is not fit for the daylight—and keep it out of the light; and even most of the judges who send people to prison refrain from ever setting foot in a prison lest they see what they do.

2. The most important argument against retributive justice is that punishments can never be deserved. This means that a punishment can never be wholly proportionate. The admission that some punishments are more disproportionate than some others does not entail that there is one punishment that is perfectly proportionate any more than the claim that X is warmer or softer than Y, or more beautiful than Y, entails that there must be a perfectly warm, soft, or beautiful entity (Plato's error). Most retributivists are Platonists without realizing it. They even extend his ancient error to punishment, as he did not.

It is surely obvious that for many, indeed most, crimes there is no wholly proportionate punishment; for example, seducing a child, raping a child, arson, treason, traffic violations, genocide, embezzlement, fraud, forgery. Nevertheless some people still believe that at least in some cases there are perfectly proportionate penalties that make retribution feasible. The prime example has always been homicide or at least premeditated murder. Yet it meets the eye that being killed suddenly, unexpectedly, is altogether different from a protracted trial and a long period of imprisonment under the sentence of death; and usually the mode of execution bears no resemblance to the method of the murder. To this one might also add the difference in the family circumstances, the age, and the attitude toward life of the original victim and the criminal. I am not arguing against the death penalty at this point but only against the claim that capital punishment for murder is a wholly proportionate penalty and thus an example of just retribution.

My thesis that punishments can never be deserved also means that the notion of desert is a confused notion and that on closer examination we find that desert cannot be calculated. This point is equally relevant to distributive justice and retributive justice, and I have developed it at length elsewhere, mainly in the context of "An Attack on Distributive Justice."[18]

I have also tried to show how the origin of the idea of justice, which I equate with the idea that a reward or a punishment is deserved, is to be found in a promise that if X does *this*, X will receive that reward or punishment. When the promise is not fulfilled, or its fulfillment is delayed, one feels that X has a reward or punishment coming to him, that X deserves it; and only when the promise is fulfilled does one feel that justice has been done. The promised reward or punishment need not be presented as perfectly proportionate, and it may even be capricious, provided only that the person who makes the promise is viewed as having some authority. This analysis applies both to the historical past and to our childhood in which we develop notions of justice. (Guilt feelings are the sense that we deserve to suffer, that we have a punishment coming to us. "Guilty" means at bottom "deserving of suffering.")

At a later stage, when conventions are examined critically and one begins to look for inconsistencies, one is struck by the occasional rhetoric of proportionality and the discovery that actually punishments as well as rewards are not proportionate. Instead of admitting at this point that desert is incalculable and that people cannot be given what they deserve in this more refined sense of the term, which

---

18. *Without Guilt and Justice*, ch. 3. Chapter 4 is "The Birth of Guilt and Justice." John Hospers believes that if we scrapped the idea of desert, then "on the same grounds should goodness and rightness and most concepts in the sphere of ethics" (Chapter 8, p. 187) be scrapped. I cannot agree. We can give examples of what we consider good, loving, honest, and courageous; but most people who defend justice are unable to specify just punishments and distributions. And whenever someone does make bold to give examples, which is unusual in the 1970s, most of the other advocates of "justice" who are present are quick to disagree. This shows how "just" is very different from "courageous," "honest," and many other moral terms.

involves not merely the fulfillment of a promise but proportionality, some great religious teachers, notably including Jesus or the evangelists, have claimed that after death everybody will receive precisely what he deserves. Hence Jefferson still believed in the possibility of "exact justice," or at least paid lip service to it and lent it his immense prestige. Speculation about the proportionate punishments after death gave rise to a veritable pornography of punishment and allowed the sadistic imagination rather free rein. Speculation about proportionate rewards, on the other hand, has remained a rather barren affair.

We simply cannot determine who deserves what. "Exact justice" and "simple justice" are chimeras; and what one generation considers simple justice often strikes the very next generation as simply outrageous. This would long have become a commonplace if it were not for the prestige of glib religious claims that after death all of us receive our just deserts and that divine or perfect justice consists in exact retribution.

Philosophers have been confused further by the Platonic error that if X is softer than Y, there must be something that is perfectly soft. But I can admit that if a child steals a penny and her father beats her to death for it after first torturing her for a week, this punishment is more disproportionate, undeserved, and outrageous than it would have been for him to torture her for four days and to stop beating her before she was dead; but from this it does not follow that there is a punishment for stealing a penny that would be truly proportionate and deserved, or another one that would be "perfectly" outrageous. As Gerard Manley Hopkins said in the opening words of one of his best poems: "No worst, there is none." And we might add: No best either.

3. Even if a punishment could be proportionate, it would not follow that it ought to be imposed. Clearly, hanging Eichmann was a less proportionate punishment for the crime of which he was found guilty than it would have been to all but kill him again and again, millions of times, and always to bring him back at the last moment to be subjected to a similar procedure. From the fact that most of us would object to the more proportionate punishment *on ethical grounds* it follows that the attempt to make punishments proportionate—that is, the retributive factor—cannot be the distinctively ethical factor of punishment.

It may be objected that most of us are simply mistaken and that Eichmann ought to have been tortured for years. For my purposes here it is sufficient to note that the view that retribution is the distinctively ethical factor of punishment does entail this conclusion.

While I find this conclusion odious (and actually asked Ben Gurion to commute Eichmann's sentence and let him go free), I must admit that the plea for torture in such cases is less inhumane and much more rational than the words of Jesus in the first three Gospels, comforting his disciples with the assurance that "if anyone will not receive you or listen to your words . . . it shall be more tolerable in the day of judgment for the land of Sodom and Gomorrah [that is, for the greatest evildoers of all time] than for that town."[19]

It may be asked on what grounds I would oppose torturing Eichmann. The answer is simple. If anyone deserved torture, he and Himmler, Beria, Stalin, and Hitler would have been prime candidates. But I hold that no human being deserves torture, that the attempt to determine what a human being deserves is misconceived and hopeless, and that a society that condemns all forms of torture might diminish human cruelty. But there are times and cases that lead one to wonder whether this last hope is too optimistic.

4. It should be abundantly clear, but it may be well to say so expressly, that I have not argued for the abolition of punishment. As indicated in the opening section of this chapter, punishment has many functions. We cannot dispense with punishment. We need rules and laws, and these require sanctions in the form of penalties. In our penal codes we have reduced the staggering variety of *Old-Time Punishments* or *Curious Punishments of Bygone Days*, to cite the titles of two old books (1890 and 1896) to mainly two or three: fines, imprisonment, and in some places also capital punishment. The deceptive charm of fines and prison terms is that both permit neat quantification and measurement and thus go well with the old conceit that desert is calculable. Actually, of course, it is common knowledge among those who have reflected on these matters that a $20 fine is not the same for a rich man and a poor man, nor is the same prison sentence for two people necessarily the same punishment. Since we cannot dispense with punishment, it is important to bring some imagination to the modes of punishment. In this connection it may be well to conclude with a word about restitution.

RESTITUTION

This subject is considered at length by other contributors to this symposium, and I cannot deal with it in depth at the end of this chapter. Only a few very brief observations are in order here.

I am all for a future-directed orientation and believe that those who have wronged others should ask themselves how they can make

19. Matthew 10:14 and 11:34; Mark 6:11; and Luke 10:10ff.

it up to them or, if that is impossible, as it often is, how they can make it up to humanity. To some extent, the courts might encourage and help offenders to find appropriate ways and means. But this path is strewn with difficulties.

The central problem is the one I have tried to develop in this chapter. "Restitution" is a chimera like "exact justice." The term is based on and invites the same superstition that I have attacked earlier.[20] The past is not a blackboard, the slate cannot be wiped clean, and what is done cannot be undone. As I try to show in a forthcoming book, *Time is an Artist*, most people are loath to admit irrevocable change. Their attitudes toward history and death, toward other men and even more so women, and toward so-called restorations of works of art and archaeological sites show this in a multitude of ways. So do many beliefs about retribution and restitution. In fact, there is no proportionate punishment for seducing a child, raping a child, treason, traffic violations, or genocide, and there cannot be any "restitution" in such cases. If we should decide nevertheless to speak of "restitution," we should at least realize how misleading this term is. Like fines and prison terms, it seems to allow for quantification and measurement and thus invites the old superstition that we can have exact justice and perhaps even restore the *status quo ante*. In this way "restitution" may lead us back into the ancient errors that I have criticized here.

That is not all. If we recognize these errors and permit the courts to exercise a great deal of discretion in decreeing how a particular offender is to make "restitution," we invite arbitrariness and monstrous inequities. Goethe's Mephistopheles calls himself

> Part of the force that would
> Do evil evermore and yet creates the good.[21]

Conversely, those who would do good often create evil. Good and humane intentions are not adequate safeguards.

In spite of these caveats, we must explore alternatives to our present penal system, because that is a horror. And we cannot write off the suggestions that are often lumped together under the heading of "restitution" either because that term is unfortunate or because of the other difficulties mentioned. The problems of punishment are exceptionally thorny, and *all* paths are strewn with difficulties. Our task is to develop a system that is better than what we have now. No best, there is none.

20. See 10b, pp. 214–215.

21. *Goethe's Faust: The Original German and a New Translation and Introduction* by Walter Kaufmann (Garden City, N.Y.: Doubleday, 1961, Anchor Book, 1962) lines 1335f.

✳ *Chapter 10*

Crime and Tort:
Old Wine in Old Bottles

Richard A. Epstein

The relationship between crime and tort is much vexed in the judicial and academic literature. Most people recognize that the two systems of individual responsibility have much in common, but that much, too, separates them. In this essay I wish to investigate the reasons why the two rules of tort and crime should overlap and diverge, and then, having established the general framework, to show how it applies to key substantive questions about individual responsibility that must be confronted in both systems. With the general part of the explanation completed, I want to turn to the question of under what circumstances, if any, the victim of a crime should be entitled to compensation (sometimes called "restitution") in a criminal proceeding from his assailant.[1]

---

1. In this essay I shall discuss only the issue of restitution, and not the related question of "compensation." These two terms have in the specialized literature somewhat technical meanings that are clearly brought out in Stephen Schafer, *Compensation and Restitution to Victims of Crime*, 2nd ed. (Montclair, New Jersey: Smith, Patterson Publishing Co., 1970), p. x:

> Compensation is an attempt to counterbalance the victim's loss resulting from a criminal attack. It represents a sum of money awarded to him for the damage or injury caused by a crime. It is an indication of the responsibility assumed by society; it is, in essence, civil or neutral in character and thus represents a non-criminal goal in a criminal case. Restitution differs in that it allocates the responsibility to the offender. The restoration or reparation of the victim's position and rights that were damaged or destroyed by the criminal attack become, in effect, a part of the offender's sentence.

See, for a discussion of the compensation issue, the Symposium in *Minn. L. Rev.* 50 (1965):213–310.

I. OVERLAP AND DIVERGENCE

A moment's glance should convince even the most casual observer of the obvious points of both similarity and difference in the tort and the criminal law. It has been observed more than once that the ordinary street mugging is properly conceived of as both a crime and as an (intentional) tort; and it is generally understood that the action of the state in prosecuting the criminal offense does not bar the private claim for civil damages, and that, of course, the civil action does not bar the criminal prosecution. Yet it is also clear that in many typical situations there is either a crime but no tort or a tort but no crime: a conspiracy that works no harm is regarded as criminal but not tortious; and the same is the case with an unsuccessful attempt to commit a crime that works no harm to its intended victim or to any third party. Likewise, the ordinary traffic case, sounding in negligence, that gives its victim a civil action for damages does not under any view constitute a crime, even if criminal negligence is treated as a form of criminal responsibility.[2] Given the clear differences between the two systems, moreover, it follows that they cannot be regarded as complementary, if separate, parts of a comprehensive whole. It has often been said, for example, that both the law of crime and tort are directed toward the control of antisocial behavior, and that both are ultimately based upon some type of deterrence theory.[3] It still remains the case that such a theory is inadequate, for if the tort law is solely a means of reinforcing penal sanctions, or vice versa, then what

---

2. The clear opposition between the civil and criminal standards of negligence can be easily illustrated. Civil negligence rests upon objective considerations, and the question asked always is whether the defendant as the man of ordinary skill and prudence, exercised reasonable care under the circumstances. And cases too numerous to mention have stressed that the test is the due care of the reasonable man, and not of the plaintiff with his own frailties and weaknesses. The criminal standard is quite different, as the language of the Model Penal Code suggests:

§ 2.02. General Requirements of Culpability
(2) Kinds of Culpability Defined
(d) Negligently

A person acts negligently with respect to a material element of an offense when he should be aware of a substantial and unjustifiable risk that the material element exists or will result from his conduct. The risk must be of such a nature and degree that the actor's failure to perceive it, considering the nature and purpose of his conduct and the circumstances known to him, involve a gross deviation from the standard of care that would be exercised by a reasonable man in his situation.

3. Oliver Wendell Holmes, *The Common Law* (Boston: Little, Brown and Co., 1964), Lecture II.

are the functions of each body of rules when their substantive commands diverge?

There has been in the literature only sporadic and ineffectual efforts to account for the differences (let alone the similarities) between the tort and the criminal law. The late Dean Prosser captured the customary view by identifying the difference between the two systems "in the interests affected and the remedy afforded by the law."[4] Thus the crime is treated as the offense against the state and public at large, while the tort is treated as an offense against the particular individual who seeks compensation and redress through the legal system. Likewise, the object of the tort law is thought (the question of relief to one side) to be the award of compensation to deserving injured parties, while the object of the criminal law is thought to be the punishment of the criminal, be it by death, incarceration, or fine, whether for purposes of retribution, deterrence, or even rehabilitation.

The traditional bases for distinction are devoid of accuracy and analytic power. First, as will be discussed in greater detail, it is by no means clear that different interests are involved in the law of crime and tort, as both interests presuppose the invasion of individual rights in person and property. It is true that there are some circumstances in which the conduct of a given individual will give rise to private actions, while other situations call for the invocation of the public force. But this observation, however true, only restates the question: when should the state, with its exclusive franchise, intervene on behalf of the public, and when should redress be left to the injured party? *A fortiori*, the distinction does not tell us anything about our central question: why the persistent substantive distinctions between criminal and civil actions? The mere statement that the interests affected are different gives no clue whatsoever to applicable principles at work in either or both areas.

Similar observations can be immediately made about the second purported difference between tort and crime—that one looks to the punishment of the accused and the other looks to the compensation of the victim. The problem with this test, quite simply, is that at best it tells us only the *consequences* that flow once certain conduct is described as criminal and/or tortious. Yet the object of the inquiry is to determine, not the consequences of the distinction, but the reasons why it should be drawn in the first place. This proferred distinction between the two systems therefore begs the very question that

---

4. William L. Prosser, *Handbook on the Law of Torts*, 4th ed. (St. Paul, Minnesota: West Publishing Co., 1971), p. 7.

we have asked, because it assumes what we seek to learn—why the principles of punishment differ from those of compensation.

II. HOLMES AND THE UNIFICATION OF TORT AND CRIME

One possible response to the failure to find a suitable account of the differences between tort and crime is that no such account can be found because no such distinction in fact exists. In effect the argument is that the two systems are at bottom governed by the same principles because they serve the same social ends. The implications of this are of course immense, for if the position is correct, it marks a fundamental repudiation of our traditional legal view, and requires us to reorganize the substantive principles in either, or more likely both, areas. It is therefore of importance to examine the arguments in some detail, in order to isolate the source of their confusion and error.

One of the major theoretical efforts to unify the law of tort and crime is that of Oliver Wendell Holmes in *The Common Law*, which almost 100 years after its publication still retains, because of its vigor and in spite of its errors, a central place in our legal culture. Holmes always sought to work out the relationships between legal categories upon a grand scale, and one of his chief ambitions was to show why and how the law of tort and crime could be reduced to a single set of principles.

For Holmes the central concept making possible the unification of crime and tort is that of "reasonable foresight," foresight based upon circumstances known to the wrongdoer or discoverable by him through the exercise of reasonable care. In order to establish the dominance of foresight within his system, Holmes made searching critiques of both tort and crime. In dealing with the law of tort, Holmes noted an uneasy truce amongst the fashionable theories of responsibility. There is first strict liability, described by Holmes as the theory that an individual "acts at his peril." There is next the theory of Austin, the "criminalist," that tortious liability can be imposed only in those circumstances in which there is an identifiable culpable mental state—the want of actual care under the subjective theories of negligence. And last there is general theory of objective negligence, which Holmes did so much to promote and to advance.[5]

In order then to demonstrate the superiority of his chosen alternative, the objective test, Holmes proceeded in fine Aristotelian style

5. Holmes.

to show how it overcame the weaknesses of the first two positions.[6] One of the great (indeed consuming) attractions of the old strict liability theory was its protection to innocent bystanders against the harmful conduct of their neighbors. The great (perceived) advantage of the subjective theories of negligence was the importance it attached to the personal responsibility of the defendant in determining legal liability. Each position, however, lays bare the weaknesses of the other: the strict liability theory was harsh on individual defendants, and the subjective theory of negligence made innocent persons bear the "slips" of "a man born hasty and awkward,"[7] of neighbors who were forever doing damage to those who came near them. The test of reasonable foresight split the difference between the two positions. It held individuals to act at their "proper"[8] peril (and thereby smuggled a judgmental premise into a legal conclusion) while recognizing that some mental element, if only the foresight of the man of ordinary prudence and intelligence, was still required for tortious liability.

Holmes used a different route to establish criminal responsibility bottomed on reasonable foresight.[9] Originally, Holmes noted, a primitive sense of justice mistakenly placed criminal responsibility only on those persons who acted maliciously, in the strong sense of acting with specific hatred or ill-will toward the plaintiff. Actual malice as the test of criminal responsibility is of course too restrictive, because it permits deliberate infliction of harms upon strangers if done with the best of motives. It would be intolerable if, for example, terrorists could escape punishment for the killing of innocent people because they killed not out of the specific dislike of their victims, but only to make dramatic social protest for their cause, however just. Malice, then, cannot be the test, and we are therefore driven back, says Holmes, to the notion of intention to harm, which does permit punishment of the terrorist with noble motives. Yet Holmes says that intention itself cannot be the ultimate test. Here we need only consider the case where one individual knows that one necessary consequence of his deliberate choice is the harm to another person, harm that the wrongdoer both knew and foresaw. Consider only the individual who sets off a bomb in order to take down an abandoned building, but does so with the knowledge that other individuals within the building or neighborhood are certain to be injured

6. Ibid., pp. 107–10.
7. Ibid., p. 108.
8. Ibid.
9. Ibid., pp. 52–56.

by the explosion. Once it is knowledge rather than specific intent that is decisive, then it becomes possible to take the final short step and to say that it is not the defendant's knowledge that counts in a criminal proceeding, but the knowledge attributable to the reasonable man acting in the same circumstances as the accused. And so the test of reasonable foresight under the circumstance governs responsibility under the criminal law as well as under the tort law.

The force and eloquence of Holmes' presentation should not conceal its major defects.[10] It is easy enough to move from actual malice to intention to harm, from intention to harm to certain or substantial knowledge that harm will result, and from there to recklessness about whether a certain harm will come to pass. Yet the gap between these conceptions and the test of reasonable foresight raises insuperable problems because we are never told why we should equate those bases of responsibility that appeal to the accused's mental state with a distinct version of responsibility that does not. While the obviousness of harmful consequences and manifest dangers associated with certain activities may well be evidence that an accused did possess the requisite mental state, it should remain open to the accused to present evidence in rebuttal. Revert for a moment to a variation of Holmes' own example:[11] if a workman on a scaffold drops a plank that strikes and kills a pedestrian below, there is no criminal offense (putting aside statutory offenses of a strict liability nature), even though he knows of the dangers inherent in his work, so long as he could establish that the falling was attributable only to simple inadvertence or neglect. No amount of reliance upon the test of reasonable foresight could displace that evidence if it is believed and acted upon by the jury. Indeed, we can make the point even stronger, for suspicion of criminal conduct will arise only if there was some special relationship between the workman and the injured party, say a personal feud, that provides a motive for a criminal conduct. Objective standards may be important upon questions of proof, but if the issue is theory and principle, then the position of Holmes must be, as it properly is, rejected.

10. See also, the powerful critique in Jerome Hall, "Interrelationships of Criminal Law and Torts," *Columbia Law Review* 43 (1943):760–75.

11. Holmes, pp. 55–56. In this case Holmes actually speaks of a workman who "throws" a heavy beam into what he knows to be a crowded street. Here the case is easily treated as one of wanton conduct because of what the workman both knows and does. Let the beam drop and it will be difficult to escape tortious liability, yet the case for criminal responsibility is reduced to the vanishing point.

III. THE DISTINCTION BETWEEN TORT
AND CRIME RECONSTRUCTED

We have thus arrived at an impasse. Holmes' efforts to find a theoretical base for the distinction between tort and crime have failed, as have those designed to collapse tort and crime into a unitary structure. It is therefore time for a fresh start, to explain anew the different profiles of tort and criminal law. My hope is not to present a novel conclusion, but to give some support for a position generally, if uneasily, held. At the outset we must beware of pressing too far the distinction between tort and crime, for the similarities of language and approach are as important as the differences.[12] Let me first, then, speak to the points of identity, and then to the points of difference.

The first point shared by the law of tort and crime is a common method of legal argumentation—the method of presumptions.[13] With both, the essential task of substantive legal theory is to identify all those conditions and circumstances that justify withholding or imputing individual responsibility. Yet there is no logically complete statement of the conditions for responsibility that is without unstated qualifications and exceptions. The inability to develop logically complete rules of responsibility is not and should not be taken as an invitation to abandon the pursuit of order and structure in legal thought. In effect the idea of substantive presumptions—think only of the literal meaning of the phrase *prima facie* case—is treated as a way to organize legal thought that falls midway between logical completeness and total disorder. Under a system of presumptions, the facts are taken one at a time (the order and selection are, of course, crucial) and incorporated in a system that with constant elaboration and expansion begins to approximate the desired complete statement of the conditions for individual responsibility. And if, thankfully, most cases are dominated by routine features, effective resolution of a few central questions should allow easy determination of a large number of cases. The content of the presumptions is not—and should not be—the same in tort and criminal law, but the difference in substantive principles should not obscure the identity in legal

---

12. Hall, pp. 753–56.

13. For a detailed elaboration and defense of the method, see Richard Epstein, "Pleadings and Presumptions," *U. Chi. L. Rev.* 40 (1973):556; for the application of the method in the torts context, see my three articles, id., "A Theory of Strict Liability," *J. Legal Studies* 2 (1973):151; id., "Defenses and Subsequent Pleas in a System of Strict Liability," *J. Legal Studies* 3 (1974):165; and id., "Intentional Harms," *J. Legal Studies* 4 (1975):391.

method, particularly between two bodies both concerned with different facets of the single question of individual responsibility.[14]

There are substantive as well as formal similarities between the law of crime and tort. These concern, on the one side, the nature of the protected individual interests, and on the other, the need for human conduct and behavior as a prerequisite for imposing any kind of legal responsibility. We consider them in order.

Previously in this essay we noted the case for distinguishing tort and crime on the ground that each sought to protect different "interests" from the wrongful conduct. At this point I want to elaborate the argument in order to press the point one step further, by urging that criminal and tort law can only be understood by recognizing that both vindicate precisely the same set of individual interests. Begin, for example, with the tort law. It is traditional to identify several different types of interests over which the plaintiff is entitled to exclusive possession and control. The first of these proprietary interests is the interest that each individual has in his own person; that is, an interest, however odd the terminology may sound today, that belongs to each individual by natural right, in the sense that he is not obligated to take any affirmative steps to secure that interest.[15] Closely connected is the interest in freedom of locomotion, protected by the action for (false) imprisonment. There is next the protection of the interest in property possessed or owned, no matter how acquired. And lastly, there is the class of so-called "relational" interests, as when the plaintiff asserts his right to make offers to contract with others with whom he chooses (subject to their right to accept or decline) or claims the benefit of an obligation of contract, status, or statute in another to support and maintain him. The last class of interests involves both possible advantageous commercial relationships, and the familial between the decendent and the members of his family.

Now it seems tolerably clear that these are precisely the same interests that are protected under the criminal law. The crimes of assault and battery, rape, and the like are all concerned with the inviolability of the person and contemplate, via different substantive theories, invasions of exactly the same interest as that protected by the tort law. Likewise, the crimes of arson and the many forms of

---

14. The passage in the text is not meant to suggest that the method of presumptions cannot apply to other substantive areas, such as contracts. To the contrary, I believe it can and does: one should usually keep his promises, constituting the basic moral premise at the bottom of a very complex structure.

15. "[E]very man has a property in his own person; this nobody has any right to but himself." John Locke, *Of Civil Government—Second Treatise*, ch. 5, § 27.

larceny, robbery, and the like are all concerned with external things that are also protected under the tort law. The only apparent cleavage between tort and crime arises with death cases and relational interests, as there is no criminal analogue to the survivor's wrongful death actions in tort. This is, however, easily explainable, since the criminal punishment for murder or manslaughter is not destroyed in its inception by want of a suitable private plaintiff to press a claim; the state in its public capacity can maintain an action even if the decedent cannot. The destruction of the survivor's relational interests thus no longer need be the subject of an analogous criminal action. It is fully vindicated in the prosecution of the greater offense of manslaughter or murder, which of course has no precise equivalent in tort.

There are other types of interest that might be thought to break the symmetry between tort and crime. Here treason and counterfeiting serve as the two stock examples. It would, however, be a mistake to conclude that the interests implicated in these crimes have no tort analogues. Indeed, these offenses involve interests—the protection of the state against force or in the integrity of its currency—for which the state has sole entitlement, both qua private owner and qua state.[16] Thus the state could preserve the currency of the realm by preventing insane or ignorant individuals from printing or circulating counterfeit bills. Likewise it could confiscate counterfeit bills from private parties who in good faith came into possession of them. Similarly, certain acts, such as not observing blackout regulations during wartime, could and should be treated as civil wrongs even if done out of ignorance or by inadvertence; yet those same actions could well be treasonable if done to give aid and comfort to the enemy. Properly understood, these cases present no more difficulty to the general conclusion that the protected interests in tort and crime are the same than does the case of the government mail truck destroyed by a private person.

The common features of tort and criminal law also can be approached from the point of view of the defendant's conduct that invades (or that threatens to invade)[17] that interest. Under both the

16. There is a delicate question of whether the state should be required to compensate any person who in good faith paid value for counterfeit money. Treating the question under private law principles, the counterfeiter could not give better title than he had even to an innocent person. That point in turn suggests that no compensation should be payable, leaving the third party with dubious remedy against the person who gave him the counterfeit cash in the first instance.

17. The parenthetical qualification is obviously needed to deal with attempts under the criminal law. See *infra* at pp. 248–249.

tort and the criminal law, all damage to property or injury to life is not the proper subject of legal intervention. Thus, where one person is killed by lightning or maimed by a wild animal, there may be need of redress on the one side, but clearly no right to demand it either of a tort defendant or of a criminal accused. In order to establish any nexus between plaintiff's harm and defendant's conduct, it is universally necessary, as a minimal condition, to point to some individual conduct on the part of the person charged with wrongdoing. The types of conduct subject to further investigation under both branches of law are two: (1) actions; and (2) the failure to act, but only in situations where there is a duty to act. In both tort and crime some concept of volition, however difficult to define, is essential to distinguish the class of human behavior from the class of natural events, including those that involve bodily motions not attributable to human actions. Thus in an early trespass case,[18] it was stated, because there is no human action, there is no liability, "as if a man take my arm by force and strike another." And the want of liability in the tort law is, moreover, marked by an equivalent want of responsibility under the criminal law, and for the same reason: the motion was not an action for there was no possible description of the person whose arm moved (we cannot say actor) under which that motion could be attributed to him and not to another. As we have not crossed the line from natural events to human action, the question whether a person's conduct supports charges of tortious or criminal responsibility cannot arise.

Similar issues are raised in connection with failures to act. Here the major conceptual problem is that responsibility does not depend in any straightforward way upon the conduct of the individual to be charged. To escape this problem the conduct theory seeks, both in tort and in crime, to go back one step in the chain of events and focus on the individual's assumption of a particular duty, usually created by entering into some form of voluntary relationship with, or for the benefit of, the person to whom the duty is owed. The prior assumption of duty thus functions as a substitute for the act causing or threatening harm. This theory is somewhat strained whenever the affirmative obligations are imposed by virtue of status. But here the formation of the relationship (e.g., being the parent of a child) normally is sufficient conduct upon which to impose subsequent duties to act. Yet awkwardness remains when we treat prior conduct as creating a duty for which there is not an explicit assumption, as with the unwanted child. The statute case is even more em-

18. Weaver v. Ward, Hobart 134, 80 English Reports 284 (1616).

barrassing, for there the "out" employed in status cases is unavailable, leaving us reduced to the assertion that the individual is bound not by his conduct, but by the conduct of his publicly chosen agent. The upshot is that here we should exercise real caution in selecting the types of obligations to impose, and in choosing the penalties for noncompliance. Similarly, the criminal law of omissions also places a special duty upon the state to give actual notice of the obligation upon which the individual is to be charged. Thus the better view of the subject has it that an individual cannot be charged with a criminal omission where he knows the external circumstances that under the statute call forth the duty but does not know of the duty itself. Here, as in the case of crimes of commission, it is impossible to argue that the very nature of the act gives the actor the sense of its inherent wrong.[19]

These, then, are the elements of commonality between the tort and the criminal law. They are the elements, moreover, that speak to

19. Henry Hart, "The Aims of the Criminal Law," *Law and Contemp. Probs.* 23 (1958):401, 413:

[A]lmost every one is aware that murder and forcible rape and the obvious forms of theft are wrong. But in any event, knowledge of wrongfulness can fairly be assumed. For any member of the community who does these things without knowing that they are criminal is blameworthy, as much for his lack of knowledge as for his actual conduct. This seems to be the essential rationale of the maxim, *Ignorantia legis neminem excusat.*

We must, however, beware of pushing Hart's argument too far. Ignorance of the law itself is clearly no offense, however blameworthy, in anyone who does not commit murder, forcible rape, or theft. And if it was an offense, it would not be an offense punishable with the same severity as the associated crime. The rule is troublesome because it rejects the importance of mental states concerning the question of whether the accused knows his conduct constitutes a criminal offense when it is assumed that there must be knowledge or intention to do each element of the offense. The basis for its widespread acceptance rests, however, not upon its theoretical compatibility with theories of criminal responsibility, but upon the administrative convenience, indeed necessity, of the rule. We know that the overwhelming proportion of individuals who engage in these forms of conduct know them to be both wrongs and prohibited. To allow the tiny proportion of individuals who may not know to prove their case on this issue will allow the others to deflect attention from the central issues in their cases. The price for the pure theory is simply too high. The argument contains its own limitations. Where we deal with the nonperformance of affirmative obligations that can only be described as *malum prohibitum*, the overpowering probability of knowledge will no longer apply. See, e.g., Lambert v. California, 355 U.S. 225 (1957), where for constitutional reasons of notice and due process, the Supreme Court created an exception to the maxim of "ignorantia legis" for the "wholly passive" conduct of failing to register in California after being convicted elsewhere of crimes that would be felonies in California. Note that where legal requirements are more broadly known, the administrative case for *ignorantia juris* reasserts its grip, even with omissions, as in driving an automobile without a license.

the language, approach, and method, if not the ultimate purposes that each is designed to serve. To complete the program of analysis, it is now necessary to turn to the way the two systems diverge. To establish that divergence, we begin with an analysis of the relationship between the plaintiff's *prima facie* case in tort law, and the state's *prima facie* case in a criminal prosecution. Once the differences are established, and the reasons for them made clear, I hope it will be possible to give satisfactory explanations of tort and crime and the relationship between them.

In most discussions of the relationship between crime and tort, it is taken for granted that the plaintiff's tort action is made out merely by showing that the defendant deliberately caused harm to plaintiff's person or property or that the defendant could not have prevented the harm so caused by the exercise of reasonable care. In effect, therefore, the standard point of departure treats the defendant's causation of harm, standing alone, as insufficient to establish a *prima facie* liability; proof of negligence or wrongful intention is required as well. True, it has been understood that the tort law recognizes isolated pockets of strict liability, say for ultrahazardous activities[20] but these have, at least until recently, been regarded as primitive forms of liability that have resisted, perhaps because of institutional conservatism or inarticulate public policy, incorporation into the general system of tort law based upon individual fault.

The characterization of the general rule of tortious liability has had an unfortunate influence on the discussion of the relationship between tort and crime. Once it is clear that strict (causal) liability does not represent the basic position of the tort law, distinguishing between tort and crime is a more troublesome task, for we are asked to identify the differences between two systems, both of which demand some form of individual "fault." The problem is difficult enough when objective negligence is contrasted with the *mens rea* of the criminal law, and it becomes well-nigh intractible with subjective negligence—which is largely a reflection of the criminal law concern with personal responsibility. The basic problem, moreover, is made still more acute under either objective or subjective view if the general liability rule gives way to a softer standard of judgment for infants and insane persons—the very persons for whom special rules are furnished under the criminal law. The problems with negligence are yet further compounded when we are pressed to explain how intentional torts should be distinguished from crimes, since the individual mental state of the party charged is of central concern for

20. See, American Law Institute *Restatement (Second) of Torts*, §§ 519, 520. Siegler v. Kuhlman, 81 Wash. 2d 448, 502 P.2d 1181 (1973).

both tort and criminal law. Finally, the problem scarcely looks better when we turn to strict liability. Here there is not only some support for the doctrine as a tort principle, but much support, too, in the criminal law, particularly with the wave of public welfare or regulatory offenses. If both tort and crime admit all possible substantive theories of responsibility, how can any clear distinctions be made between them?

The major problem with the traditional approach to this issue is that its purported account of the differences in tort and crime is made on the assumption of the soundness, at least in broad outline, of the substantive doctrines in both areas. In my view, the nub of the problem is the substantive confusion present in both areas. The basic point throughout, I believe, can be stated as follows: in the tort law alone the fundamental question is always, which of the two parties to the lawsuit should bear the loss, where a decision in favor of the one necessarily precludes a decision in favor of the other? The equities between parties must, therefore, be resolved on a comparative basis, in which it is possible that the most marginal distinctions between them will be decisive on the liability question. That constraint is not the only determinant of the rules of tortious liability, for it operates within a system of rules that as a substantive matter permits recovery only for the defendant's invasion of a recognized interest in person and property. The constraint, however, is crucial in helping construct a complete liability system out of the building blocks of the substantive law. The criminal law stands in sharp opposition, for it does not labor under such a comparative constraint. If two parties are involved in a dispute, each will escape punishment only if the state's prosecution is frustrated, and vice versa. But the state can choose to dispose of the case of each individual party to a private dispute in a manner that does not prejudice the treatment of the other. In criminal cases, therefore, it is possible to measure the conduct of each individual against an ideal standard of judgment, rather than by constant comparison to the conduct of another party. The difference, then, between the two systems persists across the length and breadth of both areas of law. The discussion has, so far, been perfectly general, and it is now essential to show, first, how in the tort law this constraint permits the organization of the standard theories of strict liability, negligence, and intention, and second, how in the criminal law it invites treating *mens rea* as a fundamental prerequisite of criminal liability. It is then necessary to show how the difference in orientation carries over to other substantive issues, particularly those involving defenses that depend upon the choice of basic legal theories.

Let us begin our revisionist enterprise with a review of the basic principles governing tort actions.[21] The typical tort case involves an injury to one party for which redress is sought from another. The question that must be resolved by the court is whether compensation for the hurt, however measured, should be compelled from one party for the benefit of the other. When the question is put in that manner, it is clear that the plaintiff must show some kind of damages in order to claim redress, for without hurt nothing should be recovered because nothing has been lost. Yet more than plaintiff's injury is required to make out a case, as any defendant could demure with ease (say "so what!") to a *prima facie* case that simply stated, "I am hurt," as this case fails to connect plaintiff's hurt with the defendant. It is in this simple fashion that the tort law necessarily raises the issue of causal connection between the defendant's conduct and the harm to the plaintiff's person or property. In the simplest case, the connection is established by the direct and immediate application of force by the defendant to the person or property of the plaintiff. It is possible, moreover, in all systems to identify more complicated causal connections that take into account not only the defendant's conduct but also the actions of the plaintiff, or of a third party, as well as of course natural events, sometimes called acts of God.[22] The exact parameters of the causal argument, the exact relationship between direct and indirect harms, and the precise limitations and uses of "proximate cause" raise problems that, I believe, permit fairly precise common sense answers. For purposes of this treatment, however, it is sufficient to assume that these complications created by an extended causal chain have been solved one way or another. To determine the appropriate basis of liability in torts, we must focus on the easiest of stranger situations—those involving the direct use of force: hitting, shooting, etc. of another.

On this last issue, as noted above, three separate and distinct theories have continually vied for supremacy in the tort literature: strict (causal) liability, negligence, and intentional harms. My basic position is that the *prima facie* case is always one of strict liability in all tort actions involving physical harm. *As between* two parties, the one that has caused harm to the person and property of another should, *prima facie*, bear the loss for the harm so inflicted. Holmes' account of strict liability, for example, is indeed stronger than his rejection of it.

---

21. I have covered this ground in much greater detail in my three articles on tort theory, *supra* n. 13.

22. See my *Theory of Strict Liability*, pp. 160–89.

Every man, it is said, has an absolute right to his person and so forth, free from detriment at the hands of his neighbors. In the case put, the plaintiff has done nothing; the defendant, on the other hand, has chosen to act. As between the two, the party whose voluntary [read: volitional] conduct has caused the damage should suffer, rather than one who has no share in producing it.[23]

Holmes rejected the position because he felt, wrongly, that it could not be contained within proper or workable causal limits, and because he did not understand the defenses that limit the principle that a man always acts at his peril. Here, in my view, the principle of fairness "as between the parties" which requires comparing the plaintiff's conduct to the defendant's conduct is relevant throughout. What the defendant did to the plaintiff makes out the *prima facie* case; what the plaintiff did to the defendant makes out the (*prima facie*) defense. If it be urged, for example, that the defendant should not be liable because he struck the plaintiff by accident only because he himself was attacked by a third party, the complete response is that it is better that the defendant seek his remedy (if it has value) from that party than to use the fact of his own necessity to force a wholly innocent plaintiff (one who has done nothing), to bear the loss, comforted only by an uncertain right of redress. The impact of the third party's conduct does not address the equities between the two parties to the case; it is properly treated as the gist of the injured party's action against the third party, which states, "you made me hit X."

The same plaintiff's argument cannot be made, however, when the defendant argues that he struck the blow in response, say, to threats of force from the plaintiff. Here the defendant can indeed say that as between himself and the person who made him strike the blow (now no longer a third party) he should be entitled to prevail; he made the plaintiff do nothing, while the plaintiff made him act. The plaintiff should, without regard to his negligence or intention, be held responsible for the consequences of his own conduct, which here include the actions of another that he compelled, on exactly the same grounds that strict liability applied to the defendant. The choice must be made between these two parties: the plaintiff, far from being wholly passive, performed those very acts that made the defendant strike and harm him. Note Holmes' argument for strict liability, and the reason why on its own terms it no longer applies. The central limitations upon responsibility in a strict liability system depend not upon proving a defendant's lack of negligence or intention,

23. Holmes, p. 84.

but upon showing that the *plaintiff's own conduct disentitles* him to relief that would otherwise be his.

Having thus far established the basic strict liability principle, we need now to account for both intention and negligence. Let us take negligence first.

In my view, the issue of negligence, fairly conceived, can arise only when there is a special relationship between the parties (whether or not it is one that rises to the level of a formal contract, e.g., gratuitous bailment) that supports some obligation of the defendant to care for the plaintiff. Thus the negligence issue should not arise for example in routine automobile accidents between strangers, as these are best decided in accordance with the causal contributions of the two parties to the accidents, under a system of strict liability with defenses discussed above. Negligence may well be, however, of real importance in actions brought by visitors on the land against its owner or occupier, by users or consumers of a particular product against its seller or manufacturer and in professional liability actions, particularly against physicians or hospitals. There, as the plaintiff wishes to share in the benefit of a joint enterprise, it is often appropriate, unless otherwise agreed, that he share in its burdens as well as its benefits. One simple illustration is that of medical malpractice, where it would be quite inconceivable that a plaintiff should recover for the pain and hurt of successful surgery that he had requested of the defendant.[24] Unlike the stranger cases considered above, the plaintiff treats the pain of the procedure (and the risk of yet greater loss) as the price for those benefits he hopes to get from the operation. Yet the assumption of risk provided by the medical agreement does not cover all the possible risks of treatment to which it seems thus far to apply. In general it has been held, and held correctly, that those harms that could have been avoided or prevented by the exercise of reasonable care are, unless otherwise agreed, not included in the harms for which the defendant escapes liability. As between the two parties, the party who agrees to bear the loss must do so. Negligence is important not as an abstract principle of justice, but only as a test for distributing by implied agreement the risks between the parties.

There is next the question of how intentional torts should be treated under the tort law. Here I have no wish to argue that inten-

---

24. Note that the negligence standard also works in cases of omission, as with the failure to perform certain diagnostic tests, for here the assumed undertaking by the physician establishes whatever duty to act is required. For a more detailed discussion, see Richard Epstein, "Medical Malpractice: The Case for Contract," *Am. Bar. Found. Res. J.* 1 (1976):87, 102–103.

tion is an unintelligible concept in tort cases, for such would preclude a principled defense of *mens rea* in the criminal law. Nor do I want to argue that intention to harm has no place in the overall structure of the tort law. To the contrary, it has a central role to play, but one unconnected with the *prima facie* case. To make the point concrete, assume that A strikes B's car after B has (without any imputation of negligence) driven across the midline of a highway, to avoid some greater danger that lurks on the other side of the road. Thus far no reference to the precise mental state of either party is made, for none is necessary to say each has acted. If the case turned only on the facts given, B's own conduct should serve as a causal bar to recovery. If, moreover, A by counterclaim seeks to recover his collision damages, he can prevail on the same causal principles sufficient to defeat the B's primary action. Now change the situation with one additional fact. Assume that A saw the plaintiff's car across the road, and decided to continue at high speed, deliberately inflicting harm upon the plaintiff. Here courts in every jurisdiction would (and should) hold that the defendant's dominance on causal principles should yield, given the proof of the additional mental element in the case. The element of intention (here A's) does not appear as part of the original *prima facie* case, but only serves as a way of overcoming any affirmative defense based upon plaintiff's (here B's) conduct, at least—and the limitation is crucial—to the extent that the damages were both caused and intended by the defendant.

We must now look to the way in which these three types of theories should function in the criminal law system. The proper treatment of strict liability, negligence, and intentional harms assumes very different dimensions within the criminal law system, for here we are freed from the necessity of tying decisions about the fate of one party to decisions about the fate of the other. There is, of course, no *necessary* reason why, once freed from the constraints of the zero sum game, criminal judgments cannot adopt tort standards of liability. One could punish for murder the automobile driver who killed a pedestrian when faced with a hazard not of his own making, even though he did what he could to avoid the harm, and even if he spared the life of others whom he might have killed. We could punish as a thief the man who absent-mindedly walks off with the book belonging to another, or punish as a vandal the man who breaks the neighbor's window while playing a game of catch. Yet there is a pervasive social sense that something must be deeply wrong in a system that is prepared to sacrifice the life or liberty of one individual when the harm inflicted upon him is not for the benefit of another, particularly since redress by tort remedies is already available to the injured party. That sense is born of the view that we should distinguish between accidental and deliberate harms, and not rest content with the observation that anyone who does anything knows that it could go awry, or knows that he could have done it better. There is, in short, the sense that even though we are not logically committed as a society to take a nontortious view of responsibility when faced with the question of punishment, we are well advised to do so. One can and must, therefore, understand and defend the position of those who, like Jerome Hall and Henry Hart,[25] always thought that the criminal law works best when it deals with conduct of the defendant that the law thinks worthy of moral condemnation, and that it works worst when in the name of effective social control it modifies its standards by judging actors at their peril. At bottom, I think, lies a sense that enormous caution is needed before criminal liability is imposed and that the individual subjected to punishment should by virtue of what he has done be *deserving* of that punishment. The theory is, I think, retributive, even though I for one do not choose to put too much stress upon the word.

IV. APPLICATIONS

We are now in a position to see the way in which the basic differences between the theories of tortious and criminal responsibility work themselves out in the context of particular rules. The most obvious place in which these differences assert themselves is on the question of the proper relationship between the actual harm of the victim and the mental state of the party charged with that harm.

Briefly put, the position must be that the intention to harm is immaterial (to the *prima facie* case) in the tort law, whereas the actual harm itself is immaterial to the criminal law. Common acts, such as street muggings, may well be actionable as torts and punishable as crimes. Yet that fact should not obscure the essential point that the grounds for punishment and the grounds for liability are never the same. The act itself may be a unitary phenomenon, but the descriptions under which it is judged in the two systems do and should diverge.

The law of attempts follows necessarily from the view that the state should punish any person whose own conduct is worthy of moral condemnation. It cannot make any difference whether or not the accused who shot at his target hit it or, for reasons totally fortui-

---

25. See Jerome Hall, *General Principles of Criminal Law*, 2nd ed. (Indianapolis: Bobbs-Merrill Co., Inc., 1960), ch. 3; and Hart, pp. 522–25.

tous, missed. Hitting or missing is at best morally neutral, as it is not to the accused's credit that he did not succeed for reasons beyond his control. Under the criminal law, human *conduct* (for while attempts necessarily involve mental states, they also presuppose public and overt physical conduct) is judged by descriptions that do not take into account contingencies external to the will. The elimination of the comparative judgments between persons will in some cases work in a relaxation of standards or responsibility by the inclusion of mental elements. In other cases it will toughen those standards by factoring out those features of conduct—notably its success or failure—that do not entitle a person to either credit or blame. The treatment of attempts in criminal law illustrates that the criminal law standard of responsibility is not necessarily lower than the tort standard.

The sharp, separate profiles of tortious and criminal responsibility are not only brought into relief by the law of attempts, but also by the efforts to do away with the *mens rea* requirement through the creation of the so-called strict liability offenses of the criminal law. As a matter of principle, these strict liability offenses are totally contrary to the general theory of criminal responsibility—barring, as they do all defenses based upon mistake, knowledge, good faith, intention, or reasonable care—and only the strongest possible case can maintain their legitimacy.[26] These statutes are usually designed to facilitate the deterrence of certain types of institutional behavior that would escape public regulation and control if the accused were given the protection of the general principles of criminal responsibility. Yet examination of the typical situation governed by these statutes should make it apparent that they are all better understood not as criminal remedies, but as disguised tort (or contract) provisions, applicable where private remedies are inadequate.

Private actions for selling goods at short weight are plainly insufficient to stop the practice because the trifling amounts involved in each case do not make it worth anyone's while to sue. And suits to recover for injuries caused by dangerous products or toxic substances are, even if successful, less desirable than the prevention of these harms, in some cases by collective public action. This limited justification for public remedies—the ineffective protection of admitted individual rights by private remedies—implies that the state acts not to vindicate a public sense of moral responsibility, where it can summon on its behalf the special rights of the sovereign, but as a self-appointed agent for aggrieved private parties. As essentially private

26. See Hart.

actions, these cases belong outside the criminal law, for the state ought to be able to resort to private remedies only when it limits itself to the types of sanctions normally available to private parties. Fines are thus acceptable as substitutes for private damage judgments, and cease and desist orders a substitute for injunctions and other forms of specific relief. Yet incarceration is unacceptable for the very reason that it is not a remedy available to the private parties whom the state represents. And civil disabilities associated with punishment —the loss of the voting franchise, etc.—are likewise inappropriate. The procedures, moreover, should be governed by civil and not criminal conceptions on all matters relating to, for example, discovery, privilege, and burden of proof. Public protection is fully achieved by tort techniques, even with public suits. And the condemnation of individual defendants should rest on the same principles applicable to ordinary criminal cases, it being strictly necessary to prove the usual mental conditions relating to knowledge or intention.

The differences between tort and crime affect not only the treatment of the *prima facie* case, but also of the possible defenses that could be raised to it. The point is well made in connection with mistakes of fact, whether they go to the question of whether the party charged has invaded or threatened the interests of another, or to the question of *whether he has* any possible excuse or justification for an admitted invasion. Although the cases lack a proper uniformity and clarity on the point, the mistake of a defendant, even if reasonable and in good faith, should not constitute an affirmative defense to a tort action brought by a stranger, unless that stranger induced that mistake.[27] As between the two parties, the plaintiff should be disentitled to a recovery only by his own action, which is not involved where the plaintiff is not the source of the defendant's error. Thus the man who cuts timber he believes to be his own must answer to the owner if his cutting was done in the best of faith or for the noblest of motives.

In criminal cases the accused often takes advantage of the mistake doctrine by saying that if the state of affairs was as he believed them to be, his actions would not constitute a crime, and, if proved, the claim is indeed a fair one. Yet there is no reason why this doctrine, when applied as a neutral principle of judgment, cannot work in favor of criminal responsibility, even where no tort action is possible. Where the accused believed the state of facts to be such that, if true, his conduct would have amounted to a criminal offense, then there is no reason in principle why he should escape liability because the

27. See Holmes, p. 97; Courvoisier v. Raymond, 23 Colo. 113, 57 P. 284 (1896); Siegel v. Long, 169 Ala. 79, 53 So. 753 (1910).

facts turned out to be such that no offense was in fact committed. Thus if the accused believes that property he is about to take belongs to another, it should make no difference in the application of the criminal law that by some fluke or confusion the property is unowned, that the accused happens to own it, that a gift was about to be made, or that the owner has not communicated a subjective consent to allow the accused to use it. The consent point illustrates the difficulty of importing tort conceptions to the criminal law. To make the action turn on the fortuitous consent of a third party means that we can no longer judge the accused on the strength of its own conduct, as we must now investigate as well the mental state of another individual. What possible reason is there under the criminal law for the conviction of A to depend upon whether B lost, say by reason of infancy or insanity, the competence to allow A to use his car? The insanity of the accused is surely relevant to criminal responsibility, but why the insanity of another party?[28]

The same principles should apply not only to completed acts, but to attempts as well. If it is attempted murder to shoot at and miss a human being, it should make no difference to the theory if the accused shoots at and misses a scarecrow whom he believes to be a human being. Any impulse to retreat in practice from the rigors of a rule that judges the accused's conduct on the strength of his perceptions of the relevant facts cannot rest on theoretical grounds. It must rely instead on the simpler point that it is not worth the time and effort of the state to ferret out cases of this sort, when the evidence supporting the improper mental state of the accused is apt to be fragile and incomplete. Yet this administrative argument itself might not be conclusive, for it could well turn out that the best accommodation of theory and practice is to allow the rules of criminal responsibility to be settled on theoretical grounds, leaving it to prosecutors with discretion to move only when the evidence in a particular case appears to support conviction. The temptation to work evidentiary problems into the fabric of the substantive law is better avoided, if not in practice, then surely in theoretical discussions.[29]

---

28. For a contrary view, see Fletcher, "The Right Deed for the Wrong Reason: A Reply to Mr. Robinson," *U.C.L.A. L. Rev.* 23 (1975):293.

29. There are of course proof difficulties that might move us toward an abandonment of the theoretical position in cases involving both mistakes and attempts. In Oviedo v. United States, 525 F.2d 881 (5th Cir. 1976), the court relied upon these proof complications to overturn the conviction of the accused who had attempted to sell to a federal agent what he believed to be heroin, but which was in fact a harmless substitute, procaine hydrochloride. The decision is disturbing because the court conceded that in the case at bar the extensive evidence was sufficient to support the conviction. It therefore rested its case upon the general fears of abuse, which were, however, never substantially documented.

The difference between crime and tort extends not only to the *prima facie* case, but also to defenses. Thus the defenses to strict liability in tort, based upon plaintiff's causal conduct, or plaintiff's assumption of the risk of accidental harm, or plaintiff's trespass upon defendant's property have no place within the criminal law. Since *mens rea* is part of the *prima facie* case in the criminal law, the defenses that in tort law are overridden by showing the deliberate nature of the defendant's infliction of harm need never be raised in criminal contexts at all. Instead, the question to be faced will be that of *justification*, a common problem for intentional harms in both tort and criminal law. Yet here too there are, of course, points of difference that bring us back to the question of mistake. Under tort law a defendant may wish to plead that he deliberately harmed the plaintiff because he was in the mistaken but good faith belief that he was being attacked by the plaintiff; he may be able to show, too, that his mistake was eminently reasonable and induced by some third party for whose conduct the defendant is in no sense responsible. The purported justification fails, for the defendant cannot show that his mistakes were induced by the plaintiff, who is wholly innocent; the proper remedy therefore is an action against the third party (who could of course be directly sued by the injured party). Yet with criminal law the arguments are quite different, for now the question is the mental state of the defendant, and, without the constraints of tort law, it is possible to make judgments about that state taking into account only the bona fides of the belief and not its source. The elements of duress and coercion can be brought into the case and considered wholly apart from their source. Though we need not excuse A for the harm he deliberately inflicted upon C while acting under threats from B, where only property damage has occurred, that position is surely attractive. Where personal injury has resulted, however, it may well be that *mitigation* of offense is preferable to the complete excuse.

There is, of course, the converse situation, where the facts surrounding the act may be sufficient if known to justify or mitigate such actions, but the accused has acted without such knowledge. Thus assume, to borrow an example from Professor Fletcher,[30] that the accused, while hospitalized, harbors a grudge toward his physician, and resolves to kill him during the next examination. He does so, not knowing at the time that the physician, who also harbored a grudge, was about to kill the patient by secretly injecting air into his veins. The patient's action was in fact done in self-defense, and that

30. See Fletcher.

alone should protect him from tortious liability even if he was utterly unaware of the justification at the time he acted. The key to analyzing tort liability is the physician's forfeiture of rights by his wrongful conduct, not the patient's knowledge of his own justification. Yet, by the same token, the patient's conduct is of the sort worthy of moral condemnation when considered in isolation and on the strength of the facts as he perceived them. There is, therefore, in principle no reason to exonerate him from criminal liability on account of the good fortune that the physician acted as he did.

The differences in tort and criminal theory carry over to the treatment of the insanity issue. In a tort system based upon negligence there is some temptation to treat the defendant's insanity as a relevant consideration in determining whether his conduct satisfied the reasonableness standard, and no less an authority than Holmes was prepared to allow it as an independent defense, at least in extreme cases. Under a strict liability theory, however, insanity has no place in cases of accidental harms between strangers. However much insanity has influenced the defendant's condition, it cannot be treated on a par with plaintiff's conduct, and thus cannot work a forfeiture of the plaintiff's valid *prima facie* case based only upon the defendant's causing him harm. As between the two parties, the defendant must bear the costs associated with his own condition.

In the criminal system, however, it is clear in principle at least that insanity does and should bear upon the question of responsibility. Note some extreme forms of madness appear to be easy to decide in principle, however difficult they may be to prove in fact. The case that first comes to mind is that of a person who kills another person, all the time thinking that he is slicing a loaf of bread. The accused's insanity is strictly speaking not even an independent defense, as it only serves as a powerful means of proving that the accused did not have the requisite *mens rea* for murder or manslaughter. There are of course still other cases where it is conceded that the accused intended to kill his victim. To these the insanity defense functions, where accepted, to excuse the accused as lacking the capacity to govern his own conduct. Concerns of this sort are captured for example in statements of the insanity defense which speak of conduct which is the "product of a mental defect"[31] or that is attributable to

---

31. See Durham v. United States, 214 F.2d 862 (D.C. Cir. 1954), overruled in Brawner v. United States, 471 F.2d 969 (D.C. Cir. 1972), where the court, noting the abuses in the case of expert testimony, adopted the test of the Model Penal Code, § 401(1): "A person is not responsible for criminal conduct if at the time of such conduct as a result of mental disease or defect he lacks substantial capacity to appreciate the wrongfulness of his conduct or to conform his conduct to the requirements of the law."

an "irresistable impulse." And much the same logic applies where it is said that the accused "couldn't help" doing what he did because of his insanity. Behind all rules of this character is the sense that conduct controlled by forces from within the accused but nonetheless beyond the influence of his will, cannot be treated as free or voluntary. As the *source* of coercion is not an ultimate issue in criminal cases, the defense of internal compulsion serves as well as external compulsion and, perhaps, even better, since it undermines the capacity for rational judgment.

It is easy, however, to be suspicious of the fraud and abuse to which only insanity defense is subject to in practice, given our inability to make judgments about whether the requisite conditions for its application have been satisfied. As has been observed more than once, it is difficult to litigate a distinction between "irresistible impulse" and "an impulse that has not been resisted." And a note of skepticism is rightly raised, when, as Dr. Szasz repeatedly points out, the individual who insists that he could not make his conduct conform to law is the very person clever enough to plan a killing or a robbery. Given the difficulties of proof and the frailties of social institutions, criminal and tort law are both under constant pressure to make compromises between what is desired as a matter of legal theory and what is attainable as a matter of practice. When such compromises are raised it is quite easy to treat them as representing ultimate legal or moral judgments and to lose sight of the larger theoretical structure of the legal system. These practical problems are, no doubt, quite acute in criminal cases where the insanity defense is raised, and may well demand, as Dr. Szasz insists, the removal of the insanity issue from criminal cases, no matter what pure theory might require.

We could, I believe, extend the basic analysis to cover other issues faced by both tort and criminal law, and do so in a manner that preserves the hard-edged and systematic distinctions between them. That distinction is blurred all too often by the analytic confusions and the administrative compromises that are part and parcel of any ongoing legal system. Legal rules and their underlying principles cannot be responsible for the errors of commission and omission made by those who work on and write about them. My initial purpose of identifying the points of differences and the points of similarity between tort and crime has, I believe, been done, and done as our basic intuitions would have it done. The old instincts are correct; and we should drink old wine in old bottles.

V. CRIME AND RESTITUTION

To complete our task, it is necessary to turn our attention to the specific problem that provoked this analysis in the first place—the issue of restitution from the individual criminal to his victim.

There is a compelling intellectual case to be made for allowing the victims of crimes to recover civil damages from their aggressors. In most cases, even though the two bodies of law are developed from divergent assumptions about individual responsibility, the same conduct that supports criminal prosecution usually supports a civil suit, even if the converse is not always true. The real issue, however, is not the *entitlement* question—should civil damages be allowable to victims of crimes—but the procedural question—should the tort action be brought as part and parcel of the criminal proceedings? Here the differences in both substantive and procedural rules preclude any easy unification of the two systems into a single trial. There may still, however, exist the possibility of some limited awards to victims, under some special rules, which do not seek to track the general principles of tort law.

Unification is most difficult where the victim seeks full tort damages from a criminal assailant. How in a unified system should we treat the routine mugging that raises issues of both criminal responsibility and tortious liability? If we argued that restitution to victims of crimes presupposes a determination of criminality, then we must first complete the criminal phase of the case before turning to its civil aspects. But note the perils in that course of action. One obvious point is that the death of the accused terminates the criminal aspects of the case, but not the civil aspects. But that theoretical point aside, there are others that go to the logistics of the case. For example, how should a private attorney for the injured plaintiff coordinate his behavior with the activities of the government prosecutor, not only at trial but before trial as well? Plea bargaining does not resemble civil settlements and may be impaired if a criminal concession is treated as creating a civil right. Private discovery may drag on long after the criminal case is ready for trial. Suppose, too, that the accused is acquitted for failure to prove *mens rea*, or by reason of insanity. Judgments of that sort (unlike a judgment that the accused did not do the mugging) should have no effect upon any civil suit against the wrongdoer, for issues of causation and damages (including economic loss and medical expenses) are the very stuff of which ordinary civil actions are made. What then should be done? Since the civil action remains, should the case be transferred out of the criminal division into the civil division, or should the trial judge who heard the criminal side of the case be retained, perhaps for days or weeks, to hear the civil suit as well? The first alternative undercuts the specialization of the bench and the bar. The second makes the criminal trial an unessential "preliminary canter" for the civil suit. Finally, we cannot escape those same problems even with a conviction in the criminal case: the choice of forum is still intractable, and the thorny issues of damages still remain to be tried.

The legal problems extend not only to substantive issues, but to procedural issues as well. The criminal and the civil law have different burdens of proof on crucial common questions of fact. In a criminal case, the state must establish the elements of the offense beyond a reasonable doubt, whereas the plaintiff in a civil action can prevail by a simple preponderance of the evidence. Thus, where the jury thinks it only likely that the accused attacked the injured victim, it must acquit the defendant of criminal liability, even though it must decide the civil case for the plaintiff. Does the restitution ideal envision the criminal standard of guilt as controlling in the civil action? If so, there is a real disadvantage to the injured party of going this route instead of suing in tort. If not, then there are real questions as to how the jury is to be instructed.

The differences in legal structure involve far more than the proper burden of proof. The two systems have different rules on admissibility of evidence, different rules of discovery, and different rules on privilege, as exemplified by the nonapplicability of the self-incrimination privilege to civil cases. The question of competence to stand trial also differs between the two systems. There is no need to elaborate the differences here, as they vary from state to state and from crime to crime. The very existence of these differences, whatever their precise form in any given jurisdiction, is, I believe, a strong indication of the inherent dangers of compressing two totally divergent types of cases into a single lawsuit in order to exploit their common factual core.

These remarks are directed toward the effort to make a full scale tort action part and parcel of a criminal case. All these difficulties do not apply, however, where an effort is made to provide some simple form of relief that might well be appropriate to a criminal prosecution. In the simplest example, an accused is convicted of the theft of a television set, which is now in the hands of the police. There is no reason why the victim of the theft should have to initiate a separate civil action to recover the television. It should be in the power of the court to order it returned to its rightful owner, as is doubtless done today. Where the property taken is destroyed, the problem is of course more complicated, and here the best approach might be to impose a civil fine equal to the property's value, at least if the property has a readily determinable market value. Where it does not, it may be best to impose some form of fine payable to the victim to impress upon the criminal the fact that his actions have both private and public ramifications. In all of these situations there is no real possibility that the differences between tort and crime will assert themselves; and avoided is the common danger that victims, required to bear the cost of a private action, will find it too expensive to pursue as a matter of course.

Most criminals are judgment proof, and few injured parties will sue for meager rewards from insolvent defendants. Some fine imposed after the criminal proceedings, a fine that in no sense attempts to measure the true value of the injury, could be made payable to the victim, and might, in principle, have a desirable effect, particularly if immediately collected. The precise measure of the fine is difficult to determine, but one guesses (cautiously) that it should be measured by the nature of the offense and the severity of the injuries. Where such a fine is imposed, moreover, the coordination between the civil and criminal case can be maintained, by allowing the accused, in the event that a tort judgment is entered against him, to credit the fine against civil damages to be paid. A system of this sort should not require the presence of a separate tort action for the injured party, nor of specialized tort counsel for the defendant. Its effect is partially compensatory and essentially symbolic.

The real problem with limited restitution is how to proceed in the event that the criminal does not have the funds to discharge the civil fine. It seems difficult to require the plaintiff to maintain civil actions for collection at some later time. By the same token it is cumbersome for the criminal justice system—the court or correction authorities—to bear the burden of enforcing the monetary obligation long after the criminal trial is done with, particularly as they are already overburdened with tasks that are not effectively performed. The project may well be worth a try, although there is good reason to have strong doubts about the entire matter.

As those brief remarks suggest, the entire matter is from a practical point of view far from clear. The substantive division between tort and crime will of course persist for the foreseeable future, no matter how fervently some might wish to collapse the one area into another. The changes that are desirable must be made on an incremental basis, and by those whose knowledge is not only of what ought to be, but what in fact is.

✳ *Chapter 11*

Punishment and Proportionality

Murray N. Rothbard

Few aspects of libertarian political theory are in less satisfactory state than the theory of punishment.[1] Usually, libertarians have been content to assert or develop the axiom that no one may aggress against the person or property of another; what sanctions may be taken against such an invader has been scarcely treated at all. We have elsewhere advanced the view that the criminal loses his rights *to the extent* that he deprives another of his rights: the theory of "proportionality." We must now elaborate on what such a theory of proportional punishment may imply.

In the first place, it should be clear that the proportionate principle is a *maximum*, rather than a mandatory, punishment for the criminal. In the libertarian society, there are only two parties to a dispute or action at law: the victim, or plaintiff, and the alleged criminal, or defendant. It is the plaintiff that presses charges in the courts against the wrongdoer. In a libertarian world, there would be no crimes against an ill-defined "society," and therefore no such person as a "district attorney" who decides on a charge and then presses those charges against an alleged criminal. The proportionality rule tells us *how much* punishment a plaintiff *may* exact from a convicted wrongdoer, and no more. It imposes the maximum limit on punishment that may be inflicted before the punisher himself becomes a criminal aggressor.

1. It must be noted, however, that *all* legal systems, whether libertarian or not, must work out some theory of punishment, and that existing systems are in *at least* as unsatisfactory a state as punishment in libertarian theory.

Thus, it should be quite clear that, under libertarian law, capital punishment would have to be confined strictly to the crime of murder. For a criminal would only lose his right to life if he had first deprived some victim of that same right. It would not be permissible, then, for a merchant whose bubblegum had been stolen to execute the convicted bubblegum thief. If he did so, then *he* the merchant, would be an unjustifiable murderer who could be brought to the bar of justice by the heirs or assigns of the bubblegum thief.

In libertarian law, there would be no *compulsion* on the plaintiff or his heirs to exact this maximum penalty. If the plaintiff or his heir, for example, did not believe in capital punishment, for whatever reason, he could voluntarily forgive the victim part or all of his penalty. If he were a Tolstoyan, and was opposed to punishment altogether, he could simply forgive the criminal, and that would be that. Or—and this has a long and honorable tradition in older Western law—the victim or his heir could allow the criminal to *buy his way out* of part or all of his punishment. Thus, if proportionality allowed the victim to send the criminal to jail for ten years, the criminal could, if the victim wished, pay the victim to reduce or eliminate this sentence. The proportionality theory only supplies the upper bound to punishment—since it tells us how much punishment a victim may *rightfully* impose.

A problem might arise in the case of murder—since a victim's heirs might prove less than diligent in pursuing the murderer, or be unduly inclined to let the murderer buy his way out of punishment. This problem could be taken care of simply by people stating in their wills what punishment they should like to inflict on their possible murderers. The believer in strict retribution, as well as the Tolstoyan opponent of all punishment, could then have their wishes precisely carried out. The deceased, indeed, could provide in his will for, say, a crime insurance company to which he subscribes to be the prosecutor of his possible murderer.

If, then, proportionality sets the upper bound to punishment, how may we establish proportionality itself? The first point is that the emphasis in punishment must be, not on paying one's debt to "society," whatever that may mean, but in paying one's "debt" to the victim. Certainly, the *initial* part of that debt of *restitution*. This works clearly in cases of theft. If A has stolen $15,000 from B, then the *first*, or initial, part of A's punishment must be to restore that $15,000 to the hands of B (plus damages, judicial and police costs, and interest foregone). Suppose that, as in most cases, the thief has already spent the money. In that case, the first step of proper libertarian punishment is to force the thief to work, and to allocate the

ensuing income to the victim until the victim has been repaid. The
ideal situation, then, puts the criminal frankly into a state of *en-
slavement* to his victim, the criminal continuing in that condition of
just slavery until he has redressed the grievance of the man he has
wronged.[2]

We must note that the emphasis of restitution-punishment is diametrically opposite to the current practice of punishment. What happens nowadays is the following absurdity: A steals $15,000 from B.
The government tracks down, tries, and convicts A, all at the expense
of B, as one of the numerous taxpayers victimized in this process.
Then, the government, instead of forcing A to repay B or to work at
forced labor until that debt is paid, forces B, the victim, to pay taxes
to support the criminal in prison for ten or twenty years' time.
Where in the world is the justice here? The victim not only loses his
money, but pays more money besides for the dubious thrill of catching, convicting, and then supporting the criminal; and the criminal
is still enslaved, but *not* to the good purpose of recompensing his
victim.

The idea of primacy for restitution to the victim has great prece-
dent in law; indeed, it is an ancient principle of law that has been
allowed to wither away as the state has aggrandized and monopolized
the institutions of justice. In medieval Ireland, for example, a king
was not the head of state but rather a crime-insurer; if someone committed a crime, the first thing that happened was that the king paid
the "insurance" benefit to the victim, and then proceeded to force
the criminal to pay the king in turn (restitution to the victim's insurance company being completely derived from the idea of restitution
to the victim). In many parts of colonial America, which were too
poor to afford the dubious luxury of prisons, the thief was inden-
tured out by the courts to his victim, there to be forced to work for
his victim until his "debt" was paid. This does not necessarily mean
that prisons would disappear in the libertarian society, but they
would undoubtedly change drastically, since their major goal would
be to force the criminals to provide restitution to their victims.[3]

In fact, in the Middle Ages generally, restitution to the victim was
the dominant concept of punishment; only as the state grew more

2. Significantly, the only exception to the prohibition of involuntary servitude in the Thirteenth Amendment to the U.S. Constitution is the "enslave-
ment" of criminals: "Neither slavery nor involuntary servitude except as a punishment for crime whereof the party shall have been duly convicted, shall exist
within the United States, or any place subject to their jurisdiction."

3. On the principles of restitution and "composition" (the criminal buying
off the victim) in law, see Stephen Schafer, *Restitution to Victims of Crime*
(Chicago: Quadrangle Books, 1960).

powerful did the governmental authorities encroach ever more into the repayment process, increasingly confiscating a greater proportion of the criminal's property for themselves, and leaving less and less to the unfortunate victim. Indeed, as the emphasis shifted from restitution to the victim, from compensation by the criminal to his victim, to punishment for alleged crimes committed "against the state," the punishments exacted by the state became more and more severe. As the early twentieth century criminologist William Tallack wrote, "It was chiefly owing to the violent greed of feudal barons and medieval ecclesiastical powers that the rights of the injured party were gradually infringed upon, and finally, to a large extent, appropriated by these authorities, who exacted a double vengeance, indeed, upon the offender, by forfeiting his property to themselves instead of to his victim, and then punishing him by the dungeon, the torture, the stake or the gibbet. But the original victim of wrong was practically ignored." Or, as Professor Schafer has summed up: "As the state monopolized the institution of punishment, so the rights of the injured were slowly separated from penal law."[4]

While it is the first consideration in punishment, restitution can hardly serve as the complete and sufficient criterion. For one thing, if one man assaults another, and there is no theft of property, there is obviously no way for the criminal to make restitution. In ancient forms of law, there were often set schedules for monetary recompense that the criminal would have to pay the victim: so much money for an assault, so much more for mutilation, etc. But such schedules are clearly wholly arbitrary, and bear no relation to the nature of the crime itself. We must therefore fall back upon the view that the criterion must be loss of rights by the criminal *to the same extent* as he has taken away.

But how are we to gauge the nature of the extent? Let us return to the theft of the $15,000. Even here, simple restitution of the $15,000 is scarcely sufficient to cover the crime (even if we add damages, costs, interest, etc.). For one thing, mere loss of the money stolen obviously fails to function in any sense as a deterrent to such future crime (although we will see below that deterrence itself is a faulty criterion for gauging punishment). If, then, we are to say that the criminal loses rights *to the extent that he deprives the victim*, then we must say that the criminal should not only have to return the $15,000 but that he must be forced to pay the victim *another* $15,000, so that he, in turn, loses those (to the $15,000 worth of

---

4. William Tallack, *Reparation to the Injured and the Rights of the Victims of Crime to Compensation* (London, 1900), pp. 11–12; Schafer, pp. 7–8.

property) that he had taken from the victim. In the case of theft, then, we may say that the criminal must pay *double* the extent of theft: once for restitution of the amount stolen, and once again for loss of what he had deprived another.[5]

But we are still not finished with elaborating the extent of deprivation of rights involved in a crime. For A had not simply stolen $15,000 from B, which can be restored and an equivalent penalty imposed. He had also put B into a state of fear and uncertainty, of uncertainty as to the extent that B's deprivation would go. But the penalty levied on A is fixed and certain in advance, thus putting A in far better shape than was his original victim. So that for proportionate punishment to be levied we would also have to add *more* than double so as to compensate the victim in some way for the uncertain and fearful aspects of his particular ordeal.[6] What this extra compensation should be it is impossible to say exactly, but that does not absolve *any* rational system of punishment—including the one that would apply in the libertarian society—from the problem of working it out as best one can.

In the question of bodily assault, where restitution does not apply, we can again employ our criterion of proportionate punishment; if A has beaten up B in a certain way, then B has the right to beat up A (or have him beaten up by judicial employees) to a bit more than the same extent. Here allowing the criminal to buy his way out of this punishment could indeed be permitted, but *only* as a voluntary contract with the plaintiff. For example, suppose that A has severely beaten B; B now has the right to beat up A as severely, or a bit more, or to hire someone or some organization to do the beating for him (who in a libertarian society, could be marshals hired by privately competitive courts). But A, of course, is free to try to buy his way out, to pay B for waiving his right to have his aggressor beaten up.

The victim, then, has the right to exact punishment up to the proportional amount as determined by the extent of the crime, but he is also free either to allow the aggressor to buy his way out of punishment, *or* to forgive the aggressor partially or altogether. The proportionate level of punishment sets the *right* of the victim, the permissible *upper bound* of punishment; but how much or whether the victim decides to *exercise* that right is up to him. As Professor Armstrong puts it:

5. This principle of libertarian double punishment has been pithily described by Professor Walter Block as the principle of "two teeth for a tooth."

6. I am indebted to Professor Robert Nozick of Harvard University for pointing out this problem to me.

. . . there should be a proportion between the severity of the crime and the severity of the punishment. It sets an upper limit to the punishment, suggests what is *due*. . . . Justice gives the appropriate authority [in our view, the victim] the *right* to punish offenders up to some limit, but one is not necessarily and invariably *obliged* to punish to the limit of justice. Similarly, if I lend a man money I have a right, in justice, to have it returned, but if I choose not to take it back I have not done anything unjust. I cannot claim more than is owed to me but I am free to claim less, or even to claim nothing.[7]

Or, as Professor McCloskey states: "We do not act unjustly if, moved by benevolence, we impose less than is demanded by justice, but there is a grave injustice if the deserved punishment is exceeded."[8]

Many people, when confronted with the libertarian legal system, are concerned with this problem: would somebody be allowed to "take the law into his own hands"? Would the victim, or a friend of the victim, be allowed to exact justice personally on the criminal? The answer is, of course, yes, since *all* rights of punishment derive from the victim's right of self-defense. In the libertarian, purely free market society, however, the victim will generally find it more convenient to entrust the task to the police and court agencies.[9] Suppose, for example, that Hatfield$_1$ murders McCoy$_1$. McCoy$_2$ then decides to seek out and execute Hatfield$_1$ himself. This is fine, except that McCoy$_2$ may have to face the prospect of being charged with murder in the private courts by Hatfield$_2$. The point is that *if* the courts find that Hatfield$_1$ was indeed the murderer, then nothing happens to McCoy$_2$ in our schema except public approbation for executing justice. But if it turns out that there was not enough evidence to convict Hatfield$_1$ for the original murder, or if indeed some other Hatfield or some stranger committed the crime, then McCoy$_2$ cannot plead any sort of immunity; he then becomes a murderer liable to be executed by the courts at the behest of the irate Hat-

7. K.G. Armstrong, "The Retributivist Hits Back," *Mind* (1961), reprinted in *Theories of Punishment*, ed. Stanley E. Grupp (Bloomington: Indiana University Press, 1971), pp. 35–36.

8. We would add that the "we" here should mean the victim of the particular crime. H.J. McCloskey, "A Non-Utilitarian Approach to Punishment," *Inquiry* (1965), reprinted in *Philosophical Perspectives on Punishment*, ed. Gertrude Ezorsky (Albany: State University of New York Press, 1972), p. 132.

9. In our view, the libertarian system would not be compatible with monopoly state defense agencies, such as police and courts, which would instead be privately competitive. There is no space here to go into the pragmatic question of precisely *how* such an "anarcho-capitalist" police and court system might work in practice. For a discussion of this question, see Murray N. Rothbard, *For a New Liberty* (New York: Macmillan, 1973), pp. 219–52.

field heirs. So that just as, in the libertarian society, the police will be mighty careful to avoid invasion of the rights of any suspect unless they are absolutely convinced of his guilt and willing to put *their* bodies on the line for this belief, so few people will "take the law into their own hands" unless they are similarly convinced. Furthermore, if $Hatfield_1$ merely beat up $McCoy_1$, and then McCoy kills him in return, this too would put McCoy up for punishment as a murderer. So that the almost universal inclination would be to leave the execution of justice to the courts, whose decisions based on rules of evidence, trial procedure, etc., similar to what may apply now, would be accepted by society as honest and as the best that could be achieved.[10]

It should be evident that our theory of proportional punishment— that people may be punished by losing their rights to the extent that they have invaded the rights of others—is frankly a *retributive* theory of punishment, a "tooth (or two teeth) for a tooth" theory.[11] Retribution is in bad repute among philosophers, who usually dismiss the concept quickly as "primitive" or "barbaric" and then race on to

---

10. All this is reminiscent of the brilliant and witty system of punishment for government bureaucrats devised by the great libertarian, H.L. Mencken. Mencken proposed that any citizen,

> having looked into the acts of a jobholder and found him delinquent may punish him instantly and on the spot, and in any manner that seems appropriate and convenient—and that, in case this punishment involves physical damage to the jobholder, the ensuing inquiry by the grand jury or coroner shall confine itself strictly to the question whether the jobholder deserved what he got. In other words, I propose that it shall be no longer *malum in se* for a citizen to pummel, cowhide, kick, gouge, cut, wound, bruise, maim, burn, club, bastinado, flay or even lynch a jobholder, and that it shall be *malum prohibitum* only to the extent that the punishment exceeds the jobholder's deserts. The amount of this excess, if any, may be determined very conveniently by a petit jury, as other questions of guilt are now determined. The flogged judge, or Congressman, or other jobholder, on being discharged from hospital—or his chief heir in case he has perished—goes before a grand jury and makes complaint, and, if a true bill is found, a petit jury is empaneled and all the evidence is put before it. If it decides that the jobholder deserves the punishment inflicted upon him, the citizen who inflicted it is acquitted with honor. If, on the contrary, it decides that this punishment was excessive, then the citizen is adjudged guilty of assault, mayhem, murder, or whatever it is, in a degree apportioned to the difference between what the jobholder deserved and what he got, and punishment for that excess follows in the usual course.

H.L. Mencken, *A Mencken Crestomathy* (New York: Alfred A. Knopf, 1949), pp. 386–87.

11. Retribution has been interestingly termed "spiritual restitution." See Schafer, pp. 120–21. Also see the defense of capital punishment for murder by Robert Gahringer: "An absolute offense requires an absolute negation; and one might well hold that in our present situation capital punishment is the only effective symbol of absolute negation. *What else could express the enormity of*

a discussion of the two other major theories of punishment: deterrence and rehabilitation. But simply to dismiss a concept as "barbaric" can hardly suffice; after all, it is possible that in this case, the "barbarians" hit on a concept that was superior to the more modern creeds.

Professor H.L.A. Hart describes the "crudest form" of proportionality, such as we have advocated here (the *lex talionis*), as "the notion that what the criminal has done should be done to him, and wherever thinking about punishment is primitive, as it often is, this crude idea reasserts itself: the killer should be killed, the violent assailant should be flogged."[12] But "primitive" is scarcely a valid criticism, and Hart himself admits that this "crude" form presents fewer difficulties than the more "refined" versions of the proportionality-retributivist thesis. His only reasoned criticism, which he seems to think dismisses the issue, is a quote from Blackstone: "There are very many crimes, that will in no shape admit of these penalties, without manifest absurdity and wickedness. Theft cannot be punished by theft, defamation by defamation, forgery by forgery, adultery by adultery. . . ."[13] But these are scarcely cogent criticisms. Theft and forgery constitute robbery, and the robber can certainly be made to provide restitution and proportional damages to the victim; there is no conceptual problem there. Adultery, in the libertarian view, is not a crime at all, and neither is "defamation."

Let us then turn to the two major modern theories and see if they provide a criterion for punishment that truly meets our conceptions of justice, as retribution surely does.[14] *Deterrence* was the principle

---

murder in a manner accessible to men for whom murder is a possible act? Surely a less penalty would indicate a less significant crime." Robert E. Gahringer, "Punishment as Language," *Ethics* 71 (October 1960):47–48. (Italics Gahringer's)

On punishment in general as negating an offense against right, cf. also F.H. Bradley: "Why . . . do I merit punishment? It is because I have been guilty. I have done 'wrong' . . . the negation of 'right,' the assertion of not-right. . . . The destruction of guilt . . . is still a good in itself; and this, not because a mere negation is a good, but because the denial of wrong is the assertion of right. . . . Punishment is the denial of wrong by the assertion of right. . . ." F.H. Bradley, *Ethical Studies*, 2nd ed. (Oxford: Oxford University Press, 1927), reprinted in *Philosophical Perspectives on Punishment*, ed. Gertrude Ezorsky (Albany, N.Y.: State University Press of New York, 1972), pp. 109–10.

12. For an attempt to construct a law code imposing proportionate punishments for crime—as well as restitution to the victim—see Thomas Jefferson, "A Bill for Proportioning Crimes and Punishments . . . ," in *The Writings of Thomas Jefferson*, vol. 1, eds. A. Lipscomb and A. Bergh (Washington, D.C.: Thomas Jefferson Memorial Association, 1904), pp. 218–39.

13. H.L.A. Hart, *Punishment and Responsibility* (New York: Oxford University Press, 1968), p. 161.

14. Thus, *Webster's* defines "retribution" as "The dispensing or receiving of reward or punishment according to the deserts of the individual. . . ."

put forth by utilitarianism, as part of its aggressive dismissal of principles of justice and natural law, and the replacement of these allegedly metaphysical principles by hard practicality. The practical goal of punishment was then supposed to be to deter further crime, either by the criminal himself or by other members of society. But this criterion of deterrence implies schemas of punishment that almost everyone would consider grossly unjust. For example, if there were no punishment for crime at all, a great number of people would commit petty theft, such as stealing fruit from a fruitstand. On the other hand, most people have a far greater built-in inner objection to themselves committing murder than they have to petty shoplifting, and would be far less apt to commit the grosser crime. Therefore, if the object of punishment is to deter crime, then a far greater punishment would be required for preventing shoplifting than for preventing murder, a system that goes against most people's ethical standards. As a result, with deterrence as the criterion there would have to be stringent capital punishment for petty thievery—for the theft of bubblegum—while murderers might only incur the penalty of a few months in jail.[15]

Similarly, a classic critique of the deterrence principle is that, if deterrence were our sole criterion, it would be perfectly proper for the police or courts to execute publicly for a crime someone whom *they* know to be innocent, but whom they had convinced the public was guilty. The knowing execution of an innocent man—provided, of course, that the knowledge can be kept secret—would exert a deterrence effect just as fully as the execution of the guilty. And yet, of course, such a policy, too, goes violently against almost everyone's standards of justice.

The fact that nearly everyone would consider such schemes of punishments grotesque, despite their fulfillment of the deterrence criterion, shows that people are interested in something more important than deterrence. What this may be is indicated by the overriding objection that these deterrent scales of punishment, or the killing of

15. In his critique of the deterrence principle of punishment, Professor Armstrong asks: ". . . why stop at the minimum, why not be on the safe side and penalize him [the criminal] in some pretty spectacular way—wouldn't that be more likely to deter others? Let him be whipped to death, publicly of course, for a parking offense; that would certainly deter me from parking on the spot reserved for the Vice-Chancellor!" Armstrong, pp. 32–33. Similarly, D.J.B. Hawkins writes: "If the motive of deterrence were alone taken into account, we should have to punish most heavily those offenses which there is considerable temptation to commit and which, as not carrying with them any great moral guilt, people commit fairly easily. Motoring offenses provide a familiar example." D.J.B. Hawkins, "Punishment and Moral Responsibility," *The Modern Law Review* (November 1944), reprinted in *Theories of Punishment*, ed. Stanley E. Grupp (Bloomington: Indiana University Press, 1971), p. 14.

an innocent man, clearly invert our usual view of justice. Instead of the punishment "fitting the crime," it is now graded in inverse proportion to its severity or is meted out to the innocent rather than the guilty. In short, the deterrence principle implies a gross violation of the intuitive sense that justice connotes some form of fitting and proportionate punishment to the guilty party and to him alone.

The most recent, supposedly highly "humanitarian" criterion for punishment is to "rehabilitate" the criminal. Old-fashioned justice, the argument goes, concentrated on punishing the criminal, either in retribution or to deter future crime; the new criterion humanely attempts to reform and rehabilitate the criminal. But on further consideration, the "humanitarian" rehabilitation principle not only leads to arbitrary and gross injustice, it also places enormous and arbitrary power to decide men's fates in the hands of the dispensers of punishment. Thus, suppose that Smith is a mass murderer, while Jones stole some fruit from a stand. Instead of being sentenced in proportion to their crimes, their sentences are now indeterminate, confinement ending upon their supposedly successful "rehabilitation." But this gives the power to determine the prisoners' lives into the hands of an arbitrary group of supposed rehabilitators. It would mean that instead of equality under the law—an elementary criterion of justice— with equal crimes being punished equally, one man may go to prison for a few weeks. if he is quickly "rehabilitated," while another man remain in prison indefinitely. Thus, in our case of Smith and Jones. suppose that the mass murderer Smith is, according to our board of "experts," rapidly rehabilitated. He is released in three weeks, to the plaudits of the supposedly successful reformers. Meanwhile. Jones, the fruit stealer, persists in being incorrigible and clearly *un*rehabilitated, at least in the eyes of the expert board. According to the logic of the principle, he must stay incarcerated indefinitely, perhaps for the rest of his life; for while the crime was negligible, he continued to remain outside the influence of his "humanitarian" mentors.

Thus, Professor K.G. Armstrong writes of the reform principle:

> The logical pattern of penalties will be for each criminal to be given reformatory treatment until he is sufficiently changed for the experts to certify him as reformed. On this theory, every sentence ought to be indeterminate —"To be determined at the Psychologist's pleasure," perhaps—for there is no longer any basis for the principle of a definite limit to punishment. "You stole a loaf of bread? Well, we'll have to reform you, even if it takes the rest of your life." From the moment he is guilty the criminal loses his rights as a human being. . . . This is not a form of humanitarianism I care for.[16]

16. Armstrong, p. 33.

Never has the tyranny and gross injustice of the "humanitarian" theory of punishment as reform been revealed in more scintillating fashion than by C.S. Lewis. Noting that the "reformers" call their proposed actions "healing" or "therapy,"rather than "punishment," Lewis adds:

> But do not let us be deceived by a name. To be taken without consent from my home and friends; to lose my liberty; to undergo all those assaults on my personality which modern psychotherapy knows how to deliver . . . to know that this process will never end until either my captors have succeeded or I grown wise enough to cheat them with apparent success—who cares whether this is called Punishment or not? That it includes most of the elements for which any punishment is feared—shame, exile, bondage, and years eaten by the locust—is obvious. Only enormous ill-desert could justify it; but ill-desert is the very conception which the Humanitarian theory has thrown overboard.

Lewis goes on to demonstrate the particularly harsh tyranny that is likely to be levied by "humanitarians" out to inflict their "reforms" and "cures" on the populace:

> Of all tyrannies a tyranny exercised for the good of its victims may be the most oppressive. It may be better to live under robber barons than under omnipotent moral busy-bodies. The robber baron's cruelty may sometimes sleep, his cupidity may at some point be satiated; but those who torment us for our own good will torment us without end for they do so with the approval of their own conscience. They may be more likely to go to Heaven yet at the same time likelier to make a Hell of earth. This very kindness stings with intolerable insult. To be "cured" against one's will and cured of states which we may not regard as disease is to be put on a level of those who have not yet reached the age of reason or those who never will; to be classed with infants, imbeciles, and domestic animals. But to be punished, however severely, because we have deserved it, because we "ought to have known better," is to be treated as a human person made in God's image.

Furthermore, Lewis points out, the rulers can use the concept of "disease" as a means for terming any actions that they dislike as "crimes" and then to inflict a totalitarian rule in the name of therapy.

> For if crime and disease are to be regarded as the same thing, it follows that any state of mind which our masters choose to call "disease" can be treated as crime; and compulsorily cured. It will be vain to plead that states of mind which displease government need not always involve moral turpitude and do not therefore always deserve forfeiture of liberty. For our masters

will not be using concepts of Desert and Punishment but those of disease and cure. . . . It will not be persecution. Even if the treatment is painful, even if it is life-long, even if it is fatal, that will be only a regrettable accident; the intention was purely therapeutic. Even in ordinary medicine there were painful operations and fatal operations; so in this. But because they are "treatment," not punishment, they can be criticized only by fellow-experts and on technical grounds, never by men as men and on grounds of justice.[17]

Thus, we see that the fashionable reform approach to punishment can be at least as grotesque, and far more uncertain and arbitrary, than the deterrence principle. Retribution remains as our only just and viable theory of punishment, and equal treatment for equal crime is fundamental to such retributive punishment. The "barbaric" turns out to be the just, while the "modern" and the "humanitarian" turn out to be grotesque parodies of justice.

17. C.S. Lewis, "The Humanitarian Theory of Punishment," *Twentieth Century* (Autumn 1948–49), reprinted in *Theories of Punishment*, ed. Stanley E. Grupp (Bloomington: Indiana University Press, 1971), pp. 304–307; also see Francis A. Allen, "Criminal Justice, Legal Values and the Rehabilitative Ideal," in Grupp, pp. 317–30.

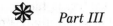

Part III

Responses to Criminal Conduct: Alternative Approaches

The last dimension of criminal justice to be considered here involves the determination of the appropriate penalty to be assessed against the criminal. The papers in this section echo several of the themes presented in the preceding chapters. However, here the task is to formulate a framework from which policy directives might emerge.

Leonard Liggio begins this enterprise by providing a historical examination of the English experience with the transportation of criminals to distant colonies. His analysis explores the origins and impact of such a program and measures its success with an eye toward contemporary application. William McDonald then examines the evolving nature of the victim's role in America, emphasizing the fact that the current exclusion of the victim from any meaningful participation in the criminal process runs counter to the early traditions of American justice. He discerns a need to integrate the victim once again into the justice system.

One such proposal, state compensation to crime victims, is scrutinized by Roger Meiners. In his paper, Meiners considers the enormous costs imposed by such a program as well as the potential for fraudulent abuse inherent in the system. Far more promising is the restitution proposal of Burt Galaway. Galaway surveys the burgeoning field of restitution, analyzing possible difficulties with restitution as well as its many potential benefits. While Galaway advocates the addition of restitution to the range of sentencing options currently employed, Randy Barnett urges consideration of a restitutive paradigm of justice. Building on many of the insights presented by the other contributors, Barnett contends that the crisis facing the criminal justice system calls for nothing less than a complete break with the policies of the recent past and the adoption of a fundamentally new approach to criminal justice—restitution.

Chapter 12

The Transportation of Criminals: A Brief Political-Economic History

Leonard P. Liggio

ANGLO-SAXON ROOTS

The excellence of Anglo-Saxon law concepts and their applicability today is best illustrated by the old system of *frithborh* or frankpledge. Basically, Anglo-Saxon common law was the law applied among neighbors. In the frankpledge system, groups of neighbors, usually ten or twelve, formed a unit that pledged surety for the good behavior of each, including the payment of judicially assigned damages should one of the members of the unit commit an injury to someone within or without the unit. Such units originally must have been based on kinship, for in early forms husbands and wives, having different kindred, had different pledge units. As the protective functions of kinship disappeared with mobility, the protective function was assumed by neighborhood groups that, by the proximity of their members, were able to reduce the cost of protection.

The *frithborh* or frankpledge system was a voluntary, personal association of families in the same neighborhood. In densely populated areas there would be a number of associations. These associations have been described as guilds or *tithings* which agreed, on a periodic basis, to be responsible for the offenses committed by its members against members of other voluntary associations. Every person either had sureties and pledge associates or one would not be able to function beyond one's own land, as no one would deal with one who had no bond or who could not get anyone to pledge their surety with him.

Any dispute or trial or an injury by a pledgeman against a fellow pledgeman, or against one in another surety association, required adjudication in the presence of the neighbors who were members of the voluntary associations, since they were the judges of the law and the facts.[1] Among the punishments for felony crimes were exile or banishment from the jurisdiction and outlawry or declaration of wolfshead, providing for execution on sight if a felon returned to the jurisdiction.

This healthy system tended to reduce or prevent the introduction into any society of anyone who did not have credentials transferred from a previous peaceful participation in a surety association. No one could enter the neighborhood who did not have membership in the local voluntary associations or who did not belong to some recognized equivalent association, such as the association of merchants, with its judicial systems. Thus, social relations were maintained only with people who shared surety protection.

Although suffering serious deformation by the introduction of law systems from the Continent, the benefits of Anglo-Saxon common law concepts continued for most Englishmen, as the continental laws mainly were applied to and benefited the Norman lords and clergy. For example, the rule that an injury could be the subject of inquiry, trial, judgment, and disposition only in the neighborhood in which it occurred—the concept of venue and the jury of twelve judges of law and fact from the neighborhood—continued to be observed.[2]

The maintenance of the jury system and of the nonlegalist lay judicial system of the justices of the peace may have been one of the most important social phenomena in English history, but it has received very little attention compared to the government's activities. The vast majority of the English benefited from the continuation of the concept of the surety system—the view of frankpledge and jury systems. The folk-peace was preserved, and the peace breaker was expelled from the association's neighborhood.

---

1. Thomas P. Taswell-Langmead, *English Constitutional History*, 2nd ed. (London: Stevens and Haynes, 1881), pp. 35–36, 130, 159; J. Laurence Loughlin, "The Anglo-Saxon Legal Procedure," in *Essays in Anglo-Saxon Law* (Boston: Little, Brown, 1876), pp. 270–99; W.S. Holdsworth, *A History of English Law*, 3rd ed. (Boston: Little, Brown, 1923), 2:43–47.

2. Taswell-Langmead, pp. 35–36; William Blackstone, *Commentaries on the Law of England. Of Public Wrongs* (Boston: Beacon Press, 1962), pp.298–303; William Stubbs, *The Constitutional History of England*, 5th ed. (Oxford: Clarendon Press, 1926), 1:93–96; Lysander Spooner, *An essay on the trial by jury* (Boston: John P. Jewett, 1852).

TUDOR LEGISLATION
AND TRANSPORTATION

The drastic changes imposed on English society beginning with the Tudor reigns began to undermine the local systems of crime control, but much of the system persisted into the nineteenth century. Large numbers of agrarian people were dispossessed by the state, and moved about the country. Justices of the peace were required to control this population, but they were reluctant to permit them to settle in the districts because the state made the districts responsible permanently for their upkeep if the migrants did not find employment. The absence of government economic regulation in the rural parts of England encouraged the growth of industry in these areas during the sixteenth and seventeenth centuries, and this in turn contributed to the absorption of at least part of the population that had been dispossessed by the state. On the other hand, the eventual settlement of many of the dispossessed people in London gave rise to a metropolitan area based on government activity—the negation of production— rather than an urban productive area, as described by Jane Jacobs.[3]

The expanded, unproductive population of London produced the metropolitan problem of crime explosion. The courts' options for most felonies were execution or sentencing to prison. The latter had a primary drawback: prisons meant extended costs to the taxpayers to maintain the prison, while after release the criminal returned to society, probably improved only in his criminality by the prison system. The return of felons to society was abhorrent to people who were accustomed to the Anglo-Saxon common law concepts of exclusion of felons by exile or outlawry; there was a preference, where government interfered with those practices, to apply the threat of execution. Transportation of criminals—that is, exiling them to remote prison colonies—served as a substitute for execution, especially for criminals who had already suffered punishment. Transportation of felons was viewed as a more serious punishment than being held in prison and eventually released to society, although it also reduced the cost to taxpayers.

The origins of the system of transportation of felons lies in the Elizabethan era. The act of 39 Eliz. c. 4 (1597) provided that where rogues, vagabonds, and sturdy beggars "shall be dangerous to the inferior sort of people," and shall be incorrigible, justice might ordain that they "be banished out of this Realm, and all other the

3. Jane Jacobs, *The Economy of Cities* (New York: Vintage Books, 1970); id., *The Death and Life of Great American Cities* (New York: Vintage Books, 1961).

Dominions thereof," and "be conveyed into such Parts beyond the Seas as shall be at any Time hereafter for that Purpose assigned by the Privy Council unto her Majesty."[4] Transportation to the Virginia Colony began soon after.

During the seventeenth century, the broadest application of the policy of transportation occurred during the twenty years of Civil War, and the wars with Scotland and Ireland in the mid-seventeenth century. Most of the transportees were Celtic. Scot prisoners of war were transported to the West Indies and to mines in West Africa by Cromwell. Prisoners of the rebellions of 1715 and 1745 who survived the holocaust of English conquest were transported to America. Irish prisoners of war, including women and children, were subjected to transportation as slaves or servants, especially to sugar plantations in the West Indies, where they formed such an incorrigible part of the work force that they were replaced during the latter seventeenth century by more productive African agricultural workers. These slaves were more loyal to English rule than the Irish slaves.[5]

POLITICAL TRANSPORTATION

Basis of Hostility to Criminal Transportation

These origins raise an important issue about transportation. Its history is not a simple one of the transportation of ordinary felons. It is complex because of the intermix of political prisoners, from the Scottish and Irish "rebels" sent to the North American colonies and to the West Indies in the seventeenth and eighteenth centuries, to the Irish and English political prisoners sent to Australia in the later eighteenth and nineteenth centuries.

This association of transportation with political "crimes" dramatically confused the subject, as much of the opposition to transportation of political "criminals" was based on the fact that large numbers of people did not view these individuals as criminals, and viewed transportation—with its hardships, sickness, and chance of death—too severe a punishment for noncriminal offenses. For the same reasons, the government thought that transportation was too good. G.A. Wood wrote in 1927 that "the greatest English criminals remained in England," by which he did not mean those executed, but

---

4. Leon Radzinowicz, *History of English Criminal Law*, (London: Stevens, 1948) 1:109; John Watson, "The Prison System," in *Penal Reform in England*, 2nd ed., eds. L. Radzinowicz and J.W.C. Turner (London: Macmillan, 1946), pp. 164–78.

5. Leonard P. Liggio, "English Origins of Early American Racism," *Radical History Review* (Spring 1976).

"those who plundered their country in habitual political robbery."[6] Similarly, the French use of transportation in the eighteenth century to colonies such as Louisiana was followed by the shipment of political opponents, starting with orthodox clergy and Jacobin radicals in the 1790s, a practice that continued through the nineteenth century.

One of the most outstanding examples of the confusion of transportation of criminals and political "criminals" is Russia's use of Siberia. In 1648 the Russian government introduced exile to Siberia as a punishment, and during the seventeenth century, exile was substituted for the death penalty or other major punishments. Traditionally, the villagers themselves administered justice in Russian villages and they generally exercised their right to include permanent exile as part of the punishment. The government sought to institutionalize this practice by providing that those exiled from their own village were assumed not to be welcomed in another village, thus being required to go to Siberia as settlers. These *Kolodniks* (exiles) formed a large population; between 1823 and 1887 the number of exiles who went to Siberia was 772,979. The tsarist government used large numbers of felons in mines in Siberia; survivors would settle in Siberia at the end of their terms. Less serious criminals were exiled to agricultural settlements.

The most well publicized, however, were the political prisoners, and the use of transportation for political prisoners caused the entire concept to gain a negative reputation. In America this result was due mainly to the role of George Kennan. His book on *Siberia and the Exile System* (1891), and his Society of Friends of Russian Freedom (which included William Lloyd Garrison, Hamilton Holt, Lyman Abbott, Jane Addams, Lillian Wald, Oswald Garrison Villard, Jacob Schiff, and Rabbi Stephen S. Wise) tended to give Americans a bad impression of exile and the transportation system because it was associated with political prisoners. Americans were distressed at any punishment of active Russian disciples of Smith, Buckle, Mill, and Spencer.[7]

The English Transportation System

Transportation of convicts became more regularized in the eighteenth century. The Mutiny Act of 1702 (1 Anne, St. 2, c. 16) pro-

6. Russel Ward, *The Australian Legend* (Melbourne: Oxford University Press, 1958), p. 19; E.J. Hobsbawm and George Rudé, *Captain Swing* (New York: Pantheon Books, 1968), pp. 265–80.

7. George Kennan, *Siberia and the Exile System*, 2 vols. (New York: The Century Co., 1891), 1:78, 80–81, 183–84; Christopher Lasch, *The American Liberals and the Russian Revolution* (New York: Columbia University Press, 1962), pp. 8–9.

vided for conscription into the military instead of transportation. The most important act was that of 1719 (6 Geo. 1, c. 23, s. 9), "An Act for the further preventing Robbery, Burglary, and other Felonies, and for the more effectual transportation of Felons."[8] The American Revolution brought a crisis in English criminal justice, especially in London, as it interrupted the transportation of felons. A solution was found in the late 1780s when transportation to Botany Bay in New South Wales in Australia, and later to Van Diemen's Land (Tasmania) and other parts of Australia, was initiated. This continued until 1867.

Transportation of criminals from London occurred in the context of a unique criminal justice system in England. Outside of London, criminal justice remained in the hands of the neighbors. In a period of severe economic changes precipitated by political intervention, significant problems arose in the agricultural sector. Government intervention uprooted 200,000 yeomen of farmer families during the eighteenth century with severe social consequences. English society was able to handle this social upheaval better than other societies due to the informal and neighborhood-based justice system. English neighborhood justice was founded on the belief that it was preferable to allow some crimes to go unpunished rather than to accept the existence of a police force, since English society had an intense aversion to an army and a police constabulary, as well as to state prosecution of crime. Crime was prosecuted by the victim, who determined the severity of the punishment. This criminal justice system was consistent with the general political philosophy of "salutary neglect" of eighteenth century Whigs, such as Robert Walpole, Henry Pelham, the Duke of Newcastle, and their principal legal advisor for almost half a century, Philip Yorke, Lord Chancellor Hardwicke.[9]

The system of transportation received favorable comment from Enlightenment philosophers such as Voltaire, who said:

> . . . it generally happens that the criminals sent to Siberia in time become honest people. The same is observed in the English colonies. We are astonished at the change, and yet nothing can be more natural. The condemned are forced to continual labour for a livelihood. The opportunities of vice are wanting. They marry and multiply. Oblige men to work, and you certainly make them honest.[10]

8. Radzinowicz, 2:60.

9. Douglas Hay, "Property, Authority and the Criminal Law," in *Albion's Fatal Tree*, eds. D. Hay et. al. (New York: Pantheon, 1975), pp. 17–63, especially pp. 40, 56–60; E.P. Thompson, *Whigs and Hunters* (New York: Pantheon, 1975).

10. James Heath, *Eighteenth Century Penal Theory* (Oxford: Oxford University Press, 1963), p. 146.

Although there were frequent writings about the system of transported convicts in Australia, such as James Murdie's *The Felony of New South Wales* (London, 1837), thorough examination of the transported felons and the colony that they and their descendants established has awaited the attention of modern scholars. Of the more than 160,000 persons transported to Australia as felons, most of them—over 130,000—arrived after 1815. Eighty percent were transported for felony crimes, and a large majority were transported after a previous conviction. Two-thirds were tried in England and were Protestant; one-third were tried in Ireland and were Catholic. A few were Scots. The basis of national differences among the felons was summarized by the saying: "A man is banished from Scotland for a great crime, from England for a small one, and from Ireland, morally speaking, for no crime at all."[11]

Large numbers of Irish convicts were sentenced for the political "crime" of opposition to English rule. The Irish convicts tended to be older than the English, included more married men, had had less trouble with the police, were unskilled workers, and had not moved from their counties of birth, compared to the English convicts. Of women convicts, 43 percent were English, 47 percent Irish, and 9 percent Scots. (Half of the assisted, free immigrants to New South Wales before 1851 were Irish.)

In a letter from the Convict Department in 1850 it was noted that, on the basis of 60,000 convicts still residing in the colony, only 370 were under any kind of punishment. The conduct of the convicts in Australia bears out the view of Voltaire. Governor Macquarie, after nine years in office, wrote in 1819:

You already know that nine-tenths of the population of this colony are or have been Convicts, or the Children of Convicts. You have Yet perhaps to learn that these are the people who have Quietly submitted to the Law and Regulations of the Colony, altho' informed by the Free Settlers and some of the Officers of Government, who have built Houses and Ships,who have made wonderful Efforts, Considering the Disadvantages under which they have Acted, in Agricultural, in Maritime Speculations, and in Manufacturers; these are the Men who, placed in the balance as Character, both

11. L.L. Robson, *The convict settlers of Australia, An enquiry into the Origin and Character of the convicts transported to New South Wales and Van Diemen's Land, 1787–1852* (Melbourne: Melbourne University Press, 1965), pp. 9–10, 74–85, 89–91; Ward, pp. 43–65; Harry Elmer Barnes, *Transportation as a Method of Punishment* (Montclair, New Jersey: Patterson Smith, 1972), pp. 68–92; Harry Elmer Barnes and Hegley K. Teeters, *New Horizons in Criminology* (Englewood Cliffs, New Jersey: Prentice-Hall, 1959), pp. 294–305; Harry Elmer Barnes, *The Repression of Crime: Studies in Historical Penology* (New York: Doran, 1926), pp.86–87; Leon Radzinowicz, *Ideology and Crime* (New York: Columbia University Press, 1966), p. 61.

Moral and political (at least since their Arrival here) in the opposite scale to those Free Settlers.[12]

Charles Darwin, who visited New South Wales in 1836, observed:

The worst feature in the whole case [the transportation system] is, that although there exists what may be called a legal reform, and comparatively little is committed which the law can touch, yet that any moral reform should take place appears to be quite out of the question.... On the whole, as a place of punishment, the object is scarcely gained; as a real system of reform it has failed, as perhaps would every other plan; but as a means of making men outwardly honest—of converting vagabonds most useless in one hemisphere into active citizens of another, and thus giving birth to a new and splendid country—a grand centre of civilisation—it has succeeded to a degree perhaps unparalleled in history.[13]

The emancipated convicts strongly resented the practice of the granting of large estates, mainly to military officers and government officials holding positions in Australia, but also to important immigrants. This system of land grants would become a serious issue in the debate over the penal colony system. Australian-born youth had attitudes that many visitors like Darwin would find unsatisfactory. Australian-born youth scorned entry into government service, preferring any private employment, and labor shortages created very good employment opportunities for youth. Boys of seven and eight became oxen drivers, or craftsmen's aides; teenagers were given responsible assignments. The editor, E.S. Hall, wrote in 1828:

The fact is, Sir, the young men of this Colony have feelings just the reverse of those of the Lower Orders in England and Ireland. The circumstances of the parents of most of them having come to the country in bondage, so far from making them humble, causes them to be the proudest people in the world. They are high-minded even to arrogance. The circumstance of being *free* is felt by them with a strength bordering on a fierce enthusiasm. Nothing can induce them to enter the army, nor take place in the police.[14]

12. Ward, p. 30.
13. Ibid., p. 31.
14. Ibid., pp. 63, 73; Eris O'Brien, *The Foundation of Australia (1786–1800), A Study in English criminal practice and penal Colonisation in the eighteenth century* (London: Sheed & Ward, 1937), pp. 121–91; A.G.L. Shaw, *Convicts and the colonies, a study of penal transportation from Great Britain and Ireland to Australia and other parts of the British Empire* (London: Faber and Faber, 1966), pp. 143, 155, 217, 273, 359; R.M. Hartwell, *Economic development of Van Dieman's Land, 1820–1850* (Melbourne: Melbourne University Press, 1954); James Griffin, ed., *Essays in Economic History of Australia, 1788–1939* (Brisbane: Jacaranda Press, 1967).

Later, when gold was discovered in 1851, it is interesting to note that as part of the tradition of avoiding the police authority, and echoing Anglo-Saxon custom, anyone committing a crime in a goldfield was expelled from that field, and the sanction carried for the other goldfields.[15]

Support and Opposition to Transportation

Many of the eighteenth century writers on crime and punishment who had experience with the transportation system, such as Sir James Fielding and Patrick Colqhohoun, strongly supported it. It was felt to be consistent with the general legal position based upon retribution. Adam Smith, in his *Lectures on Justice, Police, Revenue, and Arms*, favored retributive justice. Lord Kames, in his *History of the Criminal Law*, formulated a legal philosophy rooted in retributive justice. Lord Woodhouslee declared in 1807 that "the foundation of criminal law is retributive justice, that great principle which regulates the redressing of wrongs, and the avenging of injuries." Woodhouslee noted that the severity of criminal law was due to "our departing from the just principle of commensurating the vengeance of the law to the moral guilt of the offender; and from our resorting to the secondary end of punishment, the prevention of crimes, instead of the primary, which is the avenging of them."[16]

Opposition to transportation of felons received its greatest support from the Utilitarians, especially Jeremy Bentham. From the very beginning of the move to Botany Bay as an alternative to transportation to America, Bentham opposed transportation. He advocated the creation of a domestic prison system, the Panopticon, of which he proposed himself as warder. It would have the aim of reforming the criminal and returning him to society as a good citizen. Bentham's utilitarianism was the source of modern prison theory, as well as of criticism of transportation. Bentham and his disciples favored reformation of criminals as a major aim of punishment. They considered the prison—ordered according to their designs—the best method of reformation.

Bentham considered banishment a bad punishment because it had an unequal effect depending on the offender's age, sex, and family ties. The hard labor required to survive in a colony, Bentham be-

15. Ward, p. 111.

16. Adam Smith, *Lectures on Justice, Police, Revenue, and Arms* (Oxford: Clarendon Press, 1896), pp. 126, 142; Lord Kames, "History of the Criminal Law," *Historical Law Tracts* (1761), pp. 1–57; Lord Woodhouslee, *Memoirs of the Life and Writings of the Hon. Henry Home of Kames* (1807), in *History*, ed. Radzinowicz, 1:73, 79, 86; Heath, p. 281.

lieved, had no beneficial attributes in those circumstances. Finally, if the criminal was reformed, he was not readmitted to English society. Bentham objected that transportation lacked an exemplary quality; little impression is made on people at home as a deterrence to their committing crimes. The punishment does not confine and control the convict as an individual; it only removes him from society.

So Bentham viewed transportation as too harsh in that the convict was not protected against the high risk of death, against sickness, or against difficulty in acquiring food in the colonies. He saw it as too easy, because it did not confine and control. Bentham found that it violated certainty, since it could not be predicted which felons would survive and which would not:

> Justice, of which the most sacred attributes are certainty and precision—which ought to weigh with the most scrupulous nicety the evils which it distributes—becomes, under the system in question, a sort of lottery, the pains of which fall into the hands of those that are least deserving of them. Translate this complication of chances, and see what the result will be: "I sentence you," says the judge, "but to what I know not—perhaps to storm and shipwreck, perhaps to infectious disorders, perhaps to famine, perhaps to be massacred by savages, perhaps to be devoured by wild beasts. Away, take your chance, perish or prosper, suffer or enjoy; I rid myself of the sight of you; the ship that bears you away saves me from witnessing your sufferings; I shall give myself no more trouble about you."[17]

Bentham viewed his Panopticon penitentiary as an example to those in the metropolis who might contemplate crime; thus it would be a deterrent. For purposes of deterrence, the actual punishment of the criminals would be less important than the appearance of punishment. The criminals would suffer the punishment of reformation. "By his constant superintendence, the governor would subject the inmates to a new discipline, by his teaching them profitable trades he would impart a new education to them, so that when set free they would be able to take up a useful occupation."[18] Part of Bentham's scheme also involved the belief that by their work, the convicts would be able to pay compensation to the party that was injured.

One of Bentham's leading disciples, Sir Samuel Romilly, was the leading advocate in England of prison and criminal law "reform." While Bentham attacked transportation, Romilly carried forth the

17. Coleman Phillipson, *Three Criminal Law Reformers, Beccaria, Bentham, Romilly* (New York: E.P. Dutton, 1923), pp. 210–13; Jeremy Bentham, *An Introduction to the Principles of Morals and Legislation* (Oxford: Blackwell, 1948), pp. 281–311; Heath, pp. 225–26.

18. Phillipson, pp. 212–13.

campaign in the House of Commons. Based on what he considered the arbitrariness of transportation, Romilly's criticism included the objections that there was no provision for the return of former convicts, and that they were ill-suited to create a well-behaved colony. Concerning the colony of convicts and emancipated convicts in New South Wales, Romilly told Parliament:

> It was, perhaps, the boldest and most unpromising project ever held out to any administration. The colony was to consist entirely of the outcasts of society and the refuse of mankind, of persons who had not ever been left to their own natural profligacy, but who had acquired a matured virility in vice by their education on board the hulks [prison ships in the Thames]. . . . Instead of selecting persons who were acquainted with agriculture and the employments of a country life, the directors of the undertaking chose only those who had been convicted in London and Middlesex, and who, as inhabitants of a large city, might be easily conceived to be the most unfit persons for a new colony.[19]

James Mill, likewise interested in the reformation of the criminal, commented on transportation and convict colonies in his famous essay on colonies for the supplement to the *Encyclopaedia Britannica*, which was reprinted in his *Essays* (1831). Mill's healthy skepticism about the economic benefits of colonization as a government policy contributed to his distaste for the convict and emancipative colonies: "New South Wales of all places on the face of the earth, except, perhaps, a British prison, is the place where there is the least chance for the reformation of an offender, the greatest chance of his being improved and perfected in every species of wickedness."[20]

CONVICT COLONIES AND THE DEBATE OVER ECONOMIC PRINCIPLES

Probably due to the domestic political situation, the classical economists tended not to examine the English social and economic situation, but rather used the overseas areas of Ireland, North America, and Australia as the focus of their empirical work. Donald Winch has noted: "The economic problems raised by colonies and colonization went straight to the root of classical inquiry: free trade, capital accumulation, population pressure, economic growth and the role of the state. Colonial topics furnished a proving ground and a battlefield

19. Ibid., p. 316.
20. Crawford D.W. Goodwin, *The Image of Australia* (Durham, North Carolina: Duke University Press, 1974), p. 12.

for differences of opinion on wider matters of economic analysis and policy."[21] Adam Smith had described how monopoly and imperialism diverted capital, distorted investment, and hindered the rate of economic growth. Bentham in *Emancipate Your Colonies* (1792) had noted the double injustice of imperialism: the subjects of the imperialist state suffered expense and corruption, and the people of the colony were worse governed than under self-government. Among the expenses of colonialism, Bentham noted the general retardation of economic development, and added that "it is the *quality of capital*, not *extent of market*, that determines the quantity of trade."

From the beginning of the nineteenth century, economics began to be influenced by the writings of Thomas Malthus (an influence that eventually served as a source of inspiration for Keynesian economists as well). Malthus' underconsumptionist views particularly influenced the Benthamites. In reply to Malthus' belief that a free market could possibly give rise to a general overaccumulation or overproduction, David Ricardo stated that "all that is produced will be at its fair relative price and will be freely exchanged." This was a formulation of the fundamental economic doctrine derived from Smith by J.B. Say and known as "Say's Law of Markets." Smith held, and J.B. Say stated, that in a free market there are unlimited investment opportunities and that overaccumulation of capital occurs only as a result of government intervention which, in turn, occurs at the behest of special interest groups.

The abandonment of classical economic doctrine in England can be dated from 1830, when a new generation of economists took a different direction. The convict colonies in Australia played a major role in this development. Nassau Senior provided an important continuity in classical economics by his application of Say's contributions and by his interest in utility theory. But the major influences were the "theorists of 1830," especially Edward Gibbon Wakefield and Robert Torrens. For Karl Marx, likewise, 1830 appeared as the termination of classical economics, except as continued by Cobden and Bright; the influence of the theorists of 1830 on Marx was to have immense importance.

The conflict between the anti-imperialist Cobdenite Manchester School and the Benthamite London School of colonial reformers (the theorists of 1830) was irreconcilable. The "liberty" and "liberalism" of the Manchester School was "most mischievous" to Bentham even as late as the 1830s, because "liberty" interfered with

21. Donald Winch, *Classical Political Economy and Colonies* (Cambridge, Massachusetts: Harvard University Press, 1965), p. 2.

security and the government's police functions. For Bentham and his disciples, laissez-faire theory was a mere instrument, while the conservatism of enlightened despotism remained their ideal.

Shortly before his death, Bentham passed the mantle to Edward Gibbon Wakefield and subscribed to the view of Wakefield and the other theorists of 1830 that colonies were the greatest utility, as they would increase the market for England. This return to the language of mercantilism was crucial for nineteenth century economic theory, and was rooted for Wakefield in his abandonment of Say's Law.

Like the mercantilist colonial theorists, Wakefield viewed the economy as glutted with productive facilities; there were insufficient opportunities for the further investment of capital and labor. Wakefield sought to destroy the Ricardian theoretical foundation of capital accumulation in the private sphere and to substitute in its place a "justification for monopoly accumulation through state power." Winch noted: "Wakefield was denying the assumptions of Say's Law by arguing that the demand of 'field of employment' for capital was not coextensive with its supply; that capital accumulation could take place in the absence of profitable investment opportunities and bring about the simultaneous existence of redundant capital and labour."[22]

Wakefield was aware that the controls and institutions of colonialism that had been applied in the seventeenth century had been paralyzed and defeated by the American settlers in the eighteenth century. Wakefield's analysis sought to remedy the failures of control in earlier colonial institutions. Wakefield's interest was to establish "civilized communities" in the colonial societies as an outlet for the overproduction in the mother country. Winch continued: "He wanted colonies to be attractive to all classes of society, to be 'extensions of an old society, . . . with the several parts in the *same relative situation as they occupied before.*'" Security or stability required a status society in order to attract the men who were or should be the governors over their fellow men. The colonies should not be a place where men could escape to freedom from government, status, and domination; rather colonies should involve a re-creation of the parent government, with status and domination for the benefit of the surplus governing class from the old country.

Smith had described a simple combination that provided a market for production, including manufactured goods. Wakefield described another situation—"complex combination" or "concentration"— arising from the relationship of political institutions to property

22. Ibid., p. 79.

and to the market. The attempts of the mercantilists to duplicate this development of "concentration" in the colonies through land grants or commercial privileges had been unsuccessful, especially in America.

Against the classical economists, from Smith to Marx, who considered America as a rather successful free market experiment, Wakefield viewed American history as a constant struggle by the governing class to overcome the freedom resulting from the primary defect in earlier colonial institutions—private property in land. Private property in land, Wakefield indicated, leads to the creation of real wealth and a comfortable existence, but it is the negation of the "complex combinations" upon which a status society is based. Wakefield realized that the export of capital and labor to the colonies did not fundamentally re-create the conditions of the old society, because the land was not monopolized as under feudalism and the people were not debarred from the free acquisition of land, or homesteading.

Feudalism, the expropriation of land through government monopoly, was basic to the "concentration" of capital and labor that Wakefield desired, and his objective was to introduce the effects of feudalism into the new colonies in Australia. Feudalism, he realized, was not merely the monopolization of land but, equally important, the resulting expropriation of the owners created an artificially abundant labor supply. "To achieve combination it was essential to prevent dispersal of the labor force into individual land ownership." Wakefield advocated strong government intervention to prevent the natural tendency toward private ownership of land from undermining complex combinations: "It is in the power, and seems to be within the province of legislation, to interfere with the operation of political economy; in so far, that is, as to prevent or correct the hurtful effects on the production of natural wealth, which arises from a minute sub-division of landed property."[23]

America represented the opposite of Wakefield's theory. Wakefield hated the cheapness of land and the expense of labor that characterized America. Although early nineteenth century American land policy was not formally based on homesteading, Wakefield felt that the low price of land sold by the government had nearly the same effect. Wakefield considered the introduction of black slave labor in

---

23. Ibid., pp. 94, 99, 145; Gertrude Himmelfarb, "The Haunted House of Jeremy Bentham," in *Ideas in History*, eds. Richard Herr and Harold T. Parker (Durham, North Carolina: Duke University Press, 1965), pp. 231–36; A.P. Thornton, *The Imperial Idea and its Enemies* (London: Macmillan and Co., 1959), pp. 8–11; Richard Koebner and Helmut Dana Schmidt, *Imperialism* (Cambridge: Cambridge University Press, 1964), pp. 27–28.

America a crucial event. Since it was not possible to introduce slavery in Australia and New Zealand, either of blacks or of whites ("if for every acre of land that may be appropriated here, there should be a conviction for felony in England, our prosperity would rest on a solid basis"), Wakefield insisted that the government should appropriate all the land and sell it above the market price. The government could then use that income to encourage the immigration of an artificially created labor force that could not easily afford the price of the government-controlled land.

Wakefield's many writings about the Australian convict colonies and their relevance to economic theory had a strong influence on John Stuart Mill, and through Mill on other economists, whether they claimed to be in the classical tradition or in the socialist tradition. Winch notes:

> Mill always treated Wakefield's theoretical ideas with great respect, giving them prominence in his *Principles of Political Economy* (1848). He devoted a chapter to the concept of "combination" because he believed that it was "one of these great practical discoveries, which, once made, appear so obvious that the merit of making them seems less than it is."
>
> Mill's approval of Wakefield's stress on the importance of creating circumstances favourable to the development of markets in new countries led him to abandon the laissez-faire principle in the case of colonization.[24]

Mill was not consistent with reference to Wakefield's "combination" concept; at least Mill became critical of Wakefield's belief in the political necessity of large-scale estates. Mill seemed to have lost a sense of the importance of Say's Law, because he completely overlooked Wakefield's and Torrens' stagnation position. Winch notes:

> Mill acceded to the policy implications of Wakefield's theory while attempting to retain a thin veneer of consistency with his account of the fall of profit in Ricardian terms, and his defence [sic] of Say's Law. In going so far towards Wakefield's point of view Mill "completely undermines the relevance of his theoretical analysis of the impossibility of general glut."[25]

Mill's failure to perceive the loss of a sense of importance of Say's Law in analyzing Wakefield's theory had an important influence on

---

24. Winch, pp. 135–37.

25. Ibid., p. 139; A.W. Coats, "The Classical Economists and the Labourer," in *The Classical Economists and Economic Policy*, ed. A.W. Coats (London: Methuen, 1971), pp. 144–78; Marian Bowley, *Nassau Senior and Classical Economics* (New York: Octagon Books, 1967); Lionel Robbins, *Robert Torrens and the Evolution of Classical Economics* (London: Macmillan, 1958), pp. 247–48.

Marx. Colonel Robert Torrens and Edward Gibbon Wakefield, the so-called theorists of 1830 and founders of the Ricardian socialist tradition, were prominent supporters of government-assisted colonization as a potential outlet for capital goods produced in England. Wakefield wished to limit the opportunity and the extent of property ownership—without reference to the quality of the land and its potential use—by imposing a high purchase price on land. The proceeds from these sales would subsidize immigration to maintain artificially low wage rates.

Wakefield's frequently expressed proposal that the government prevent transported or immigrant labor from owning land for extended periods in order to create artificially a laboring class was strongly criticized by other long-term observers of the Australian economy, such as William Howitt. In 1852 Howitt blasted the Wakefieldian policies the government had adopted:

> Here you have immediately a proof of that ingenuity by which men contrive to defeat the intentions of Providence. Providence has given vast new lands, on which the overflowing population may settle; but selfish and purblind governments immediately lay hold on that which was meant to be a free Gift of God, and dole it out in such modicums that the pressing necessities of arriving immigrants compel them to bid up it auction against each other, till the land of these new countries lying with millions of miles of unoccupied soil becomes far dearer than at the dearest of that which they have left.
>
> The fatal Wakefieldian system of only selling colonial lands at a high price, and only where government pleases, has totally quashed that intermixture of tillage, that diffusion of cheerful villages up the country, which would have converted it from a desert to a place of happy and civilized life. The theory of preventing the too rapid spread of population in new lands, has here prevented it from spreading altogether.[26]

The English statesman Charles Dilke was greatly impressed by the homesteading and immigration policy in America after the Civil War; he was horrified on visiting Australia by the large land monopolies created by the government. American frontier expansion had a great positive impact on Dilke, and he felt that American liberalism was grounded on the Lockean principles of property rights and homesteading.

Dilke's very positive impressions about America contrast with earlier nineteenth century English views of Americans. In the 1820s

---

26. William Howitt, *Land, Labor and Gold* (Boston: Ticknor and Fields, 1885), 1:17, cited in Goodwin, pp. 83, 86.

there were great expectations that Australia would rectify the great mistake in America, where homesteading or Lockean land policies in the colonial period created the conditions and the expectations that led to the American Revolution and the Lockean social system that succeeded the Revolution. This expectation was noted for Van Diemen's Land, "where it is hoped, a better race from the same parent stock is about to spring up, than that of the 'back woodsmen' of North America."[27]

Wakefield argued that the fatal weakness of the convict colonies in Australia was the possibility that emancipatees could gain land easily. A ruling class of feudal landholders and policies negating the Lockean principle of homesteading, he noted, would create a large reserve of wage labor that he considered a necessity for a well-functioning economy. The artificially created labor force would encourage capital investment and create a market for the "overproduction" he believed existed in the English economy. As a student of Wakefield's writings, Karl Marx commented, in the first volume of *Capital*, on Australia's "shameless lavishing of uncultivated colonial land on aristocrats and capitalists" as an illuminating illustration of the artificial creation in new countries of the conditions for exploitation of labor.[28] Wakefield's analysis of the Australian economy shaped Marx's perception of the Australian colonies and profoundly influenced his economic theories. With reference to the Australian colonies, Marx noted:

There the capitalist regime everywhere comes into collision with the resistance of the producer, who, as owner of his own conditions of labor, employs that labor to enrich himself, instead of the capitalist. The contradiction of these two diametrically opposed economic systems, manifests itself here practically in a struggle between them. Where the capitalist has at his back the power of the mother-country, he tries to clear out of his way by force, the modes of production and appropriation, based on the independent labor of the producer. The same interest which compels the sycophant of capital, the political economist, in the mother-country, to proclaim the theoretical identity of the capitalist mode of production with its contrary, that same interest compels him in the colonies to make a clean breast of it, and to proclaim aloud the antagonism of the two modes of production. To this end he proves how the development of the social productive power of labor, cooperation, division of labor, use of machinery on a large scale, etc., are impossible without the expropriation of the laborers, and the corresponding transformation of their means of pro-

27. Goodwin, pp. 7, 84.
28. Ibid., p. 84.

duction into capital. In the interest of the so-called national wealth, he seeks for artificial means to ensure the poverty of the people. Here his apologetic armour crumbles off, bit by bit, like rotten touchwood. It is the great merit of E.G. Wakefield to have discovered, not anything new about the colonies (Wakefield's few glimpses on the subject of Modern Colonisation [sic] are fully anticipated by Mirabeau Pere, the physiocrat, and even much earlier by English economists [the mercantilists]), but to have discovered in the colonies the truth as to the conditions of capitalist production in the mother-country. As the system of protection at its origin attempted to manufacture capitalists artificially in the mother-country, so Wakefield's colonisation [sic] theory, which England tried to enforce by Acts of Parliament, attempted to effect the manufacture of wage-workers in the colonies. This he calls "systematic colonisation [sic]."[29]

Wakefield's analysis of "capitalism's" need for the destruction of the Lockean right of private property by government was the basis of the concluding chapter (XXIII) of the first volume of *Capital*. Marx considered Wakefield's analysis the "purest" theory of capitalism:

> The only thing that interests us is the secret discovered in the new world by the political economy of the old world, and proclaimed on the housetops: that the capitalist mode of production and accumulation, and therefore capitalist private property, have for their fundamental condition the annihilation of self-earned private property; in other words, the expropriation of the laborer.[30]

H.O. Pappé has noted the fundamental role that Wakefield's comments on the Australian convict colonies played in the formulation of Marx's economic theory: "For Marx, his views on colonization were considerably more than a contribution to contemporary controversy; they were to be the crowning confirmation of his economic theory." Bernard Semmel has suggested that the Benthamite pursuit of a new bureaucratic collectivism caused Wakefield to deny Say's Law and to create a "general theory" of imperialism. Marx in turn believed that Wakefield's analysis proved that classical economic theory as well as the existing economy based on government intervention were founded upon exploitation of the laborers and the expropriation of their private property. "One point emerges clearly: much of what has been regarded as characteristically Marxist doctrine was already common Radical belief when Marx came to England in 1849."[31]

29. Karl Marx, *Capital* (New York: Modern Library, 1936), pp. 1:838–39.
30. Ibid., 1:848.
31. H.O. Pappe, "Wakefield and Marx," *Economic History Review*, 2nd ser., 4 (1951):89. Bernard Semmel, "The Philosophical Radicals and Colonialism," *Journal of Economic History* 21 (1961):515.

It would be beyond the scope of this essay to discuss why the above view of the Australian convict colonies gained dominance; certainly it would be part of a general discussion of the motivation and impact of utilitarianism. However, there were economists who were critical of this analysis of the Australian convict colonies. The Scottish economist Sydney Smith noted in 1803 that he feared that the government's policy in Botany Bay was not based on sound economic principles. He opposed the government's attempt to create a subservient and cheap labor force in order to encourage capital investment:

> The high prices of labour which the Governor was so desirous of abating, bid fair, not only to increase the agricultural prosperity, but to effect the moral reformation of the colony . . . the avaricious love of gain, which is so feelingly deplored, appears to us a principle which, in able hands, might be guided to the most salutary purposes. The object is to encourage the love of labour, which is best encouraged by the love of money.[32]

In 1819 Smith criticized the government's interventionism, represented by its control over prices in the Australian convict colonies, its enforced dispersal of population, and its expenditure on public works (upon which Herbert Spencer later commented). By 1828 Sidney Smith was impressed by the development of healthy habits among the children of the convicts: "Instead of treading in the steps of their progenitors, [they] almost invariably render themselves conspicuous by a course of life directly opposite; and are, in a more than ordinary degree, temperate and honest."[33]

Lord Henry George Grey, as colonial secretary, presented a strong critique of the Wakefieldian advocacy of government intervention in colonization:

> There is not (and never has been) any real redundancy of labour in this country; consequently it would be most mistaken policy to seek relief from any temporary difficulties we may experience, by artificially promoting emigration at the public expense, instead of by removing any obstacles to the natural extension of the field of employment at home. It must be borne in mind that active and industrious labourers, by being sent to Australia, cease to become contributors to the wealth and revenue of the mother-country.
>
> To establish the practice of giving relief to those who cannot find work

32. Goodwin, pp. 22−25. Spencer used the example of government intervention in the transportation of Australia to criticize public works, ibid., pp. 55−56. Also see, Herbert Spencer, "Government Colonization," *Social Statics* (New York: Appleton, 1878), pp. 390−405.

33. Goodwin, p. 25.

at home, by sending them to the Colonies where wages are higher than they are here, would therefore be to reverse the position of the good and bad labourers under the wholesome operation of the natural laws of society, and actually to give an advantage over the best labourers to the indifferent ones, on account of their inferiority, by considering their inability to compete with the others in the labour-market at home, a reason for giving them the means of carrying their labour to a higher market in the colonies.... It is clear, that the more the population and wealth of the British Islands increase the lighter will become to their inhabitants the burden of our national debt, and of the taxes to which it compells [sic] us to submit.[34]

Grey's wisdom, however, did not overcome the arguments of the utilitarians in favor of government assistance to immigrants in order to create markets abroad for English goods. The policy of assisted immigration, along with the increase in immigration caused by the discovery of gold in 1851, created a population in the Australian colonies that was divided over the social implications of transportation of criminals. Due to the strength of their connections in England rather than their numbers, and the support of those advocating government assistance of immigration, the utilitarians pressured the English government into ending the system of transportation of convicts and replacing it with a system of penitentiaries for the reformation of prisoners. This was one outgrowth of the movement for the establishment of government police departments and of other continental intrusions into English criminal law.

The criminal law theorist of the late nineteenth century, Sir James Fitzjames Stephen, had opposed the attempts to control crime by endangering the essential liberties of the individual. The growth of a criminal justice bureaucracy to administer the reformation of criminals and infringe on the rights of the citizen was a result of the Benthamite mind set. Stephen was critical of the prison system established to replace transportation, "which provided so effective a method for protecting society at home against criminals by weeding them out and sending them to the colonies."[35] Instead, a great cost was placed on the backs of the law-abiding citizens of England. In contrast to Bentham's deterrence view, he emphasized that punishment must satisfy the "common feeling of hatred" against the criminal:

34. Ibid., pp. 16–17.
35. Leon Radzinowicz, *Sir James Fitzjames Stephen, 1829–1894, and his contribution to the development of criminal law*, Selden Society Lecture (London: Bernard Quaritch, 1957), p. 29; Sir James Fitzjames Stephen, *A history of the criminal law of England* (London: Macmillan, 1883), 1:480–83.

The criminal law thus proceeds upon the principle that it is morally right to hate criminals, and it confirms and justifies that sentiment by inflicting upon criminals punishments which express it.

It is highly desirable that criminals should be hated, that the punishments inflicted upon them should be so contrived as to give expression to that hatred, and to justify it so far as the public provision of means for expressing and gratifying a healthy natural sentiment can justify and encourage it.[36]

If the "direct prevention of crime" was not the proper object of criminal sanctions, Stephen held that reformation had not any position in the criminal law, properly understood. Stephen felt that since inflicting pain was unpleasant to the humane and educated, they had sought to escape the question by looking to education, or reformation, as the solution. Stephen found that the prisons established in place of transportation were founded upon the false concepts of education or reformation. Furthermore, in contrast to expulsion from society, they entailed great expense to citizens. Stephen had an understanding of criminal law rooted in the view that the criminal had by his act excluded himself from society and that his continued presence in the society was an invasion. "There is as much moral cowardice in shrinking from the execution of a murderer as in hesitating to blow out the brains of a foreign invader."[37] The abolition of transportation, which had served as a substitute for executions, made the subject of capital punishment a cause of great controversy.

Given the general recognition that the system of prisons is a form of punishment that has not achieved the goals of citizens, while costing them fantastic sums in taxes to maintain, alternative forms of dealing with criminals are very much in order. At the same time, the operation of the criminal justice system by the government, based upon Benthamite or utilitarian intrusions into the common law customs, has been shown to be totally ineffective. A system of transportation of criminals and their permanent exclusion from established societies would be an effective solution to the necessities of punishment and of finding a modern approach to the criminal justice system left over from the nineteenth century.

The historical examples of transportation provide a strong positive support for that system. That system's excellent record has stood despite the criticisms of the Benthamites and the Ricardian

36. Radzinowicz, *Stephen*, p. 30.

37. Ibid., p. 35. For a recent study of Stephen's criminal law writings, see James Alfred Colaiaco, "Sir James Fitzjames Stephen: the Great Dissenter" (Ph.D. dissertation, Columbia University, 1976), pp. 173–225.

socialists who perceived that the transportation system had not been designed for the purpose of deterrence or reformation or who viewed such a system as an impediment to the government colonization schemes they advocated. Moreover, the record of convict transportation systems has survived despite the public antipathy generated by the subsequent use of such systems to punish political opponents of the government. The system of transportation of criminals deserves a central place in discussions of alternatives to the existing system, which appears to be in an advanced state of collapse.

Chapter 13

The Role of the Victim in America

William F. McDonald

Before the American Revolution, criminals were required to pay back their victims. All defendants convicted of larceny, for example, were required to pay treble damages. If they could not pay, they were given to their victims in servitude for a length of time equal to the amount owed. If the victim preferred, he could sell the defendant. In 1769, a Massachusetts court sentenced defendant Powell to be sold for four years; in 1772, defendant Polydone to be sold for six months; and in 1773, defendant Smith to be sold for fourteen years. Victims who chose to sell their criminals rather than take them as servants were allowed one month in which to find a buyer. After that they had to pay for the criminal's maintenance in jail or the criminal would be released.[1]

The conception of crime in colonial America was very different than it is today. While criminal prosecutions were brought in the name of the state, they were in effect private prosecutions in which the state usually did not play an active role and did not have a vested interest. Crime was conceived of primarily as an injury to the individual victim, not an attack against society.[2] Today, the situation is reversed. Crime is regarded as an offense against the state. The damage to the individual victim is incidental and its redress is no longer regarded as a function of the criminal justice process. The victim is told that if he wants to recover his losses he should hire a lawyer and

1. William F. McDonald, "Towards a Bicentennial Revolution in Criminal Justice," *American Criminal Law Review* 13 (1976):649–73.

2. W. Nelson, "Emerging Notions of Modern Criminal Law in the Revolutionary Era: An Historical Perspective," in *Criminal Justice in America*, ed. Richard Quinney (Boston: Little, Brown and Co., 1974).

sue in civil court. The criminal justice system is not for his benefit but for the community's. Its purposes are to deter crime, rehabilitate criminals, punish criminals, and do justice, but not to restore victims to their wholeness or to vindicate them.

One of the tremendous ironies in the development of the American criminal justice system lies in the changed status of the victim. He once was the central actor in the system and stood to benefit both financially and psychologically from it. Today, he is seen at best as the "forgotten man" of the system and at worst as being twice victimized, the second time by the system itself. The history of concern about criminal justice in this country has reversed. Enormous efforts are made on behalf of criminals. Vast sums have been spent in genuine efforts to humanize punishments, develop rehabilitative techniques, provide indigent persons with legal counsel, and to give all persons ample opportunity to challenge the state's case against them. However, in contrast, there has been little concern for the rights or treatment of victims or the proper role of victims in the administration of justice.

Unlike the criminal, the victim was better off before the Revolution than he is today. In colonial times, police departments and public prosecutors' offices did not exist as they are known today. The victim of crime was on his own. In the cities a victim could call for help from the nightwatchmen, but he was unlikely to do so. The nightwatch was only on duty during certain hours of the night and was composed of decrepit or dishonest old men. The watchmen might be persuaded to chase a fleeing criminal for a few blocks, but once he had gotten away the watchman's duty ended. The victim had to do his own detective work himself or hire someone to do it. If he sought the assistance of the sheriff, he was charged a fee. In Boston, one dollar bought twelve hours of "sheriff's aid in criminal cases." Once the criminal was located, there was an additional fee to the victim of thirty cents for service of criminal warrants.[3] It was not easy to get the sheriff interested in pursuing criminals—even if the victim were wealthy enough to afford these fees. The sheriff's fees for serving civil process were far more lucrative and less dangerous. Thus, the wealthier victims hired private detectives or posted rewards.

When the criminal was finally arrested, the victim's role was not over. He paid an attorney to draw up the indictment, and the victim either prosecuted the case himself or hired an attorney to prosecute it for him. For his efforts the victim reaped certain benefits. There

3. See, generally, Roger Lane, *Policing the City—Boston: 1822–1885* (Cambridge, Mass.: Harvard University Press, 1967).

was the satisfaction of seeing justice being done and tailoring it within the limits of the law to one's own needs. If property had been taken, it would unquestionably be ordered returned. In addition, there were the treble damages that had to be paid.[4]

THE DECLINE

The decline of the victim's importance in the criminal justice system occurred rapidly after the Revolution. The ideas of the Enlightenment, particularly those of the criminal law reformer Caesare Beccaria, were enthusiastically adopted by the young American nation.[5] The principles of his view were as follows: Crime is an offense against society. Punishment must be swift, certain, and equal to the harm done if it is to be effective. If used properly, the criminal justice system can deter crime and reclaim criminals from their fallen state. The Quakers in Pennsylvania had discovered a way to implement these idealistic goals. In contrast to the barbaric penological practices of the heartless British, the new republic would show the world that hardened criminals could be reclaimed by humane and natural methods.[6] Instead of whippings, forced servitude, or the hangman's noose, the Americans would place their criminals in prisons where they could read the Bible, meditate in silence, and come to see the error of their ways. The severity of the punishment could be easily proportioned to the harm done by varying the length of time in prison. The victim had no role to play under this new plan. In fact, his influence over the administration of justice had to be eliminated because it reduced the certainty of punishment. In 1778, the first prison opened in Philadelphia. Within thirty years, eleven states had prisons. In 1805, Massachusetts proudly opened its new prison.[7] Significantly, it was in that same year that a Massachusetts court imposed for the last time the sentence of paying treble damages to the victim of a crime.

During the next century, modern police departments were founded and grew into large bureaucracies; and the offices of public prosecutors assumed responsibility for prosecuting most crimes. The victim was displaced even further. Part of the rationale for the establishment of the police and the expansion of the responsibilities of the

---

4. Nelson, p. 108.

5. McDonald, pp. 654–56.

6. David J. Rothman, *The Discovery of the Asylum* (Boston: Little, Brown and Co., 1971), ch. 4.

7. Harry E. Allen and Clifford E. Simonsen, *Corrections in America: An Introduction* (Riverside, New Jersey: Glencoe Press, 1975), pp. 55–56.

public prosecutor is especially noteworthy. Reformers were concerned about the injustice of a system in which only wealthy victims could afford to buy law enforcement and justice. A publicly supported system would eliminate this inequity.[8]

THE VICTIM TODAY

In contemporary America, the victim's well-being and fair treatment are not the concern of the criminal justice system or any other institution. The victim has to fend for himself every step of the way. When there is a rash of burglaries in his neighborhood, for example, he will have to form a neighborhood vigilante system if he wants any real protection. The "increased police patrols" that the local police will provide amount to nothing more than a few extra passes of a squad car through the general vicinity. The victim might even try to concoct a trap in his house to catch an intruder. He may make a false arrest; or he may be charged with murder if a burglar breaks in and manages to get himself killed by the trap. But, in either case, he runs serious risks of violating the law himself.

When a victim's self-protective measures do lead him to violate the law, it is no defense to say that police protection was inadequate. In Washington, D.C., a retired old gentleman with a lifelong record of lawful behavior had been robbed each of the last two months after he had cashed his social security checks (his sole source of support). By now he was desperate for money. So, when he received his next check he took a pistol with him when he went to cash it. Incredibly, the pistol accidentally fell out of his pocket right in front of a policeman. He was convicted of carrying a dangerous weapon.

After a crime has occurred, the victim continues to be on his own. Some police departments will not even give him a free ride to the hospital.[9] Insurance restrictions permit the transportation of criminals but not of victims. If the victim goes to the hospital in an ambulance and happens to live in one of the few states that have victim compensation laws, the ambulance bill will be one of the items not covered by the law.[10] In cooperating with the prosecution of a criminal case, a victim incurs a variety of financial costs such as trans-

---

8. Christopher Hibbert, *The Roots of Evil* (Boston: Little, Brown, and Co., 1963).

9. M. Baluss, *Integrated Services for Victims of Crime: A County-Based Approach* (Monograph on file with the National Association of Counties, 1975).

10. G. Geis, "Crime Victims and Victim Compensation Programs," in *Criminal Justice and the Victim*, ed. W.F. McDonald (Beverly Hills, California: Sage Publications, 1976), pp. 237–59.

portation and parking, loss of wages, and babysitting expenses. Theoretically, the state helps victims defray the cost of assisting with the prosecution of the case. There are such things as witness fees, but not every jurisdiction has them; where they do exist they are grossly inadequate, mired down in red tape, and taxed, and most victims are not even told about them. Until recently in Philadelphia, Pennsylvania, a victim had to go to eleven different processing steps spread around the courthouse before he could claim his $20 a day witness fee, which was then subject to a city tax. Most victims did not know they were entitled to a fee, and those who had thrown their subpoena away were unable to establish their claim to the fee. In addition to losing a day's wages, the victim may even lose his job. Unlike the arrangement with jury duty, employers are not required to release their employees for witness duty or pay them their normal salaries.

There are also the endless delays and continuances. One trip to the courthouse is never enough. Even under ideal conditions it takes at least three or four trips: first for charging, then grand jury, then motions hearing, then trial, and finally, sentencing. Of course, the system never operates ideally. Thus, one regularly hears about victims who make fifteen or twenty trips to the courthouse. During his many trips the victim becomes very aware of his lowly status in the criminal justice system. The reserved parking is not for him but for the judges, prosecutors, police, clerks, and others. Sumptuous offices have been provided for the judges, but in many courthouses there is no room where the victim can wait comfortably until his case is called. He must either sit in a courtroom or pace the corridors and try to avoid being held in contempt of court for falling asleep in the courtroom or loitering in the hallways. In some jurisdictions he cannot even use the public restrooms. They are closed because of the crimes that have occurred in them.

The victim/witness "lounges" that have been provided in some jurisdictions are a stark contrast to the luxuriousness of the judicial chambers. The lounges are furnished in early American bus station, with rows of stiff plastic chairs lined up monotonously, facing nowhere. Defendants who are on pretrial release or their witnesses may be waiting in the same witness lounge as the victim. Open threats do not have to be made. A constant stare at the victim is adequate to intimidate. The victim arrives at 9:30 A.M. as ordered by the court and tries to keep from sliding out of his plastic seat until late in the afternoon when he is informed by the smiling young prosecutor that his case has been continued again.

The criminal justice system's interest in the victim is only as a means to an end not as an end in himself. The victim is a piece of evidence. The police want to know "just the facts," but the traumatized victim wants to tell the whole frightening story and more. Victims want to be reacted to as human beings and to be treated with care and solicitude. They resent the policeman's professional disinterest and detachment. But it is not just the police. No one in the criminal justice system gives the victim the sympathetic hearing, the opportunity for cathartic release, that victims feel they need. Prosecutors, like the police, only want to hear the relevant facts and to size the victim up regarding his or her articulateness, believability, and deservingness. How will he or she do on the witness stand? Will the typical local jury believe him? If so, will they sympathize with him? Victims who have done something stupid or who have prior criminal records, or who seem in some way to deserve the fate that has befallen them, cannot count on juries—or prosecutors—to vindicate them.

The modern public prosecutor conceives of his job as conservator of limited court resources. There are simply too many cases for the courts to handle. Thus, the prosecutor will keep cases involving unconvincing and unsympathetic victims from clogging the courts. Even if the case has merit, it will be marked for a giveaway type disposition. The prosecutor may refuse to charge the case; or may charge it and later drop it; or charge it and later plea bargain it on terms very favorable to the defendant. The implications here regarding class-biased justice for victims are substantial. Lower income groups are disproportionately represented among victims of crime. They are also more likely to have criminal records and to be less articulate witnesses. Thus, it is more likely that their cases are more frequently given away by the prosecutor than those of higher income victims. The irony of this is that historically the reason for establishing the office of public prosecutor was to ensure that poor victims could get the same kind of justice that the rich victims could afford.

Today's victim will not be told why his case was dropped or plea bargained; nor will he even be notified of the final disposition of the case.[11] For that he will have to call the courthouse and struggle through a labyrinth of referrals to other offices. In the end there is a good chance he will be unable to locate his case. The filing system of the courts and the prosecutors are not cross-referenced by the victim's name. Thus, unless the victim happened to catch the name of the stranger who attacked him, or the police officer who made the

11. R. Lynch, "Improving the Treatment of Victims: Some Guides for Action," in *Criminal Justice and the Victim*, pp. 172–74.

arrest, or the assistant prosecutor who handled the case, he may have to hire a lawyer to find out what happened to his case.

The modern public prosecutor does not have time to coddle victims, to listen to their emotional reactions, or to explain why he is going to take certain actions. Prosecutors claim they do not have the resources to notify victims of the final dispositions of their cases. Every prosecutorial dollar must count and must be used to suppress crime. But it must also be spent in a way that accommodates the realities of the prosecutor's office. Traditionally, that office has been used as a training ground for inexperienced young attorneys fresh out of law school and as launching platforms for careers in higher public offices (Chief Justice Earl Warren and United States Senator Thomas Eagleton are two examples). The high rate of staff turnover among prosecutors (usually two years) means that the prosecutors must use an assembly line organization for their work. Many of the assistant prosecutors will not have sufficient experience to see a case all the way through from beginning to end. For that and other reasons different prosecutors are stationed along the various stages of the process and handle all the cases that reach the processing plant. Typically, the least experienced prosecutors are stationed at the early screening stage end. The most experienced ones handle the trial stages of the most serious crimes. This means that the victim, who may have already explained his case to several different police officers, now has to retell it to each new prosecutor. It also means he experiences no sense of continuity.

When the case finally comes to sentencing, the victim in today's criminal justice system finds that he is not regarded as having a stake in the matter. In stark contrast to Colonial days, he cannot even expect to have restitution ordered, much less treble damages imposed. His views regarding what he believes would be an appropriate sentence are not represented to the judge. Defense counsel will be allowed to appeal to the judge, to beg for mercy, to try to sway the judge's emotions, and to recount in pathetic details his client's tragic childhood. If the defendant is indigent, this patent emotional appeal will be made by counsel paid for by the state. But the victim is not allowed to have his counsel make an appeal. The state does not supply indigent victims with attorneys at sentencing.

Some prosecutors will say that it is the function of the public prosecutor to represent the views of the victim, but this is not and cannot be so. There is a conflict of interests between representing the opinions and wishes of the victim and those of the state. The most frequent example of this is where the victim only wants to get his property back, while the state believes the defendant should be punished. To illustrate the "pro-defendant, anti-victim" mind set in contemporary criminal justice, it is worth mentioning an exquisite double standard. When reformers have urged recently that victims should have an attorney representing them at sentencing, the response has consistently been that that would be improper because the victim would play on the emotions of the judge!

While it is true that the victim's role in the criminal justice system has become less visible and less central since the Revolution, it has not been eliminated. Research in the last decade has shown that the victim's residual role is of critical importance. National surveys of victims have found that an extensive amount of crime is not even reported to the police. The President's Commission on Law Enforcement and Administration of Justice found that 35 percent of the robberies, 35 percent of the aggravated assaults, 40 percent of the larcenies over $50, 90 percent of the consumer fraud, and 74 percent of other frauds were not reported by victims.[12] It has also been found that the vast proportion of the more serious crime, i.e., excluding traffic offenses and disorderly conduct type offenses, that comes to the attention of the criminal justice system comes by way of complaints from victims and other citizens.[13] Very little is the result of on view arrests by police or other police-initiated actions. What is more, contrary to the television model, most detectives do not find new and ingenious sources of evidence. Solving crimes depends heavily upon the information supplied by the victim. It has also been discovered that of those victims who do report their victimizations to the police, many will subsequently refuse to cooperate with the prosecution. In Washington, D.C., the Institute for Law and Social Research found that of 5,042 cases of violent crimes referred for prosecution in the criminal courts in 1973, 52 percent were dropped at screening due to a problem related to the complaining witness.[14]

Once the victim is into the prosecution phase of the criminal justice process the role he plays is usually thought of entirely in terms of his function as a witness, but this is a superficial view that ignores the subrosa but vitally important role of the victim at this stage of the process. To understand this role one must first understand the criminal justice system as a human organization. When it is stripped

12. President's Commission on Law Enforcement and Administration of Justice, *The Challenge of Crime in a Free Society* 22 (New York: Arno Press, 1967).

13. Albert J. Reiss, *The Police and the Public* (New Haven, Connecticut: Yale University Press, 1971).

14. K. Williams, "The Effects of Victim Characteristics on the Disposition of Violent Crimes," in *Criminal Justice and the Victim*, p. 212, n. 15.

of all its mythology, ritual, and noble-sounding purposes, the criminal justice system is just like any other human organization that has been established to perform some function. As such it is subject to a phenomenon known to sociologists as "goal displacement," i.e., the tendency to substitute unofficial goals for the official goals of the organization.[15] One of the criminal justice system's unofficial goals is to minimize strain and maximize rewards for individuals within the organization as well as for the organization itself.[16] A constant potential source of strain is adverse criticism and publicity. Judges and prosecutors prefer to avoid such criticism and are always alert both to the possible sources of criticism and to the ways of deflecting it.

The victim's role can now be understood. He is a potential source of criticism who has to be neutralized. But, he also can be used as a convenient means of deflecting criticism. Prosecutors, judges, and defense counsel understand this and exploit, dupe, and use the unwitting victim accordingly. One widely used tactic for neutralizing the victim is known as "cooling the victim out." Victims are most vengeful, upset, and therefore, likely to be "a problem" immediately after the crime. Therefore, defense counsel will have the cases continued several months until the victim "cools off" and can be "reasonable."[17] Since defense counsel's obligation is to serve his client's interests, his use of this tactic is understandable. But prosecutors also use it. For them it is one of several methods of avoiding the victim's criticism.

If a prosecutor has a case that he believes does not merit prosecution, but he knows the victim will be upset (hence, potentially "a problem") if the case were dismissed or plea bargained, he may delay the case long enough so that either the victim cools down enough to be able to accept a dismissal or the evidence in the case will weaken— i.e., witnesses' memories fade—to the point where the victim can be easily persuaded that the prosecutor "had" to plea bargain the case to a lesser charge. Given the same case, an alternative to cooling the

15. See, generally, James D. Thompson, *Organizations in Action* (New York: McGraw-Hill Book Co., 1967), p. 79.

16. William Chambliss and Robert Seidman, *Law, Order and Power* (Reading, Massachusetts: Addison-Wesley Publishing Co., 1971), p. 266; see also, W.F. McDonald, "Plea Bargaining and the Criminal Justice Process: An Organizational Perspective" (Paper presented at the Annual Meeting of the American Political Science Association, Chicago, 1976, on file with author).

17. See, generally, William F. McDonald, "Notes on the Victim's Role in the American Criminal Justice Process" (Paper presented at the Second International Symposium on Victimology, Boston, 1976. Forthcoming in *Victimology: An International Journal.*)

victim out is to pin the blame for the unpopular decision elsewhere. There are several convenient scapegoats to choose from, including the victim himself.[18]

If the case is a really dangerous one, i.e., high adverse publicity potential, the prosecutor will not dismiss it himself but will take it to the grand jury and have that faceless body do the dirty work. Similarly, if he had a case that he believed was a second degree murder but he knows he would be criticized for being lenient if he did not charge it as first degree murder, he will charge the former and let the trial jury reduce it to the latter. The responsibility for some decisions is passed on to the judge. This is known among prosecutors as "putting the turd in the judge's pocket." It is yet another method of avoiding the appearance of leniency. Instead of recommending the sentence he believes is appropriate in a case, the prosecutor will either make no sentence recommendation or will recommend the maximum. The judge is then forced to go out on a limb and assume sole responsibility for setting the "realistic" sentence. If the case ever "backfires," i.e., the defendant recidivates, the judge will take the rap for having not imposed the maximum. Unfortunately for prosecutors, this ploy does not always work. Judges often recognize it for what it is and counter it by either insisting that the prosecutor commit himself to a realistic sentence recommendation or, if that fails, giving the prosecutor a hard time in other ways.

Sometimes the victim is the fall guy. Take for example the prosecutor who has a case that he would like to dismiss, but the victim is present in the courtroom and could be "a problem." The clever prosecutor waits for the victim to leave the courtroom for a few minutes' break and then quickly has the case called and dismisses it. When the victim returns, the prosecutor profusely apologizes to him, explaining that he should never have left the room. When he did, the case was called and had to be dismissed because he was not present. Sometimes it is the "system" in general that is to blame. For example, when the prosecutor has agreed to a plea bargain that specifies that the prosecutor will keep the victim away from the sentencing hearing, the resourceful prosecutor will notify the victim to come at 1:00 P.M. although the hearing is scheduled for 11:00 A.M. When the victim arrives he will be told that "the system" is to blame for "a last minute change in the schedule."[19]

Many case disposition decisions are contingent upon the assurance of a neutral victim. Defense counsel know that judges are more likely

18. Ibid.
19. Ibid.

to go along with motions to dismiss cases or proposals to reduce charges or impose light sentences if they can be assured that the victim won't complain. Thus, as part of their cooling out strategy, defense counsel will meet with victims, feel them out, see how mad they are and whether they could be satisfied with simple restitution in property offenses or a light sentence in other cases. The feeling out process is done casually and elliptically so as not to tip off the victim to the importance of these off the record remarks.

If it turns out that the victim would be satisfied with restitution or suggests a sentence that he naively believes is severe but in fact is lenient by current standards, counsel will argue to the judge that the victim's wishes should be honored. On the other hand, if the victim "wants blood," different tactics are used. Counsel may pull out his shopworn appeal for mercy and recount to the victim how sorry the defendant is, how he has a wife and kids, and how he grew up in a slum and was neglected by his parents. While this same appeal may get nowhere with judges who have heard it a million times before, its chances of success with victims is much greater.

A major alternative to suckering the victim is simply to keep him out of the matter altogether or at least as much as possible. By plea bargaining, a defendant avoids trial and thereby eliminates the emotional impact of the victim on the judge. In some places this is known as "sneaking the sun past the rooster." As long as the judge does not know and feel the full impact of the crime on the victim, he will be more amenable to a lighter sentence. Sometimes as an extra precaution, defense counsel will ask policemen or prosecutors to tone down their description to the judge of what was done to the victim. Instead of saying "the defendant slashed him with a switchblade big enough and sharp enough to carve up an elephant," say "the defendant inflicted some lacerations."

Victims can be used to help deflect criticism by being given a share in the responsibility for decisionmaking. If the victim agrees to a disposition—i.e., a case dismissal or a plea bargain or particular sentence—it gives prosecutors and judges something to fall back on if the case "backfires." They can always argue that the victim agreed to the disposition. This does not get them completely off the hook, but it helps blunt criticism. It also reduces the probability that the disposition will be criticized. Other than the press, the only likely source of criticism of any particular disposition is the victim. But if the victim has agreed to it, there is less to fear.

Prosecutors do seek the approval of victims for certain decisions. But this is done on a highly selective basis and is not to be regarded as evidence that contemporary prosecutors subscribe to the pre-revolutionary practice of allowing victims to control the prosecution of cases. On the contrary, modern prosecutors vehemently argue that prosecutorial decisions call for the exercise of professional judgment that only they with their learning and experience possess. It is on these grounds that they oppose the suggestion of reformers who lately have suggested that victims should be given more influence over disposition decisions. Yet the importance of professional judgment notwithstanding, prosecutors do seek out the victim's approval in two types of cases: (1) minor crimes that the prosecutor would like to get rid of to lower his caseload, and (2) very serious crimes with a high potential for adverse publicity that the prosecutor wants to or has to plea bargain to avoid losing the case altogether. To illustrate, in many jurisdictions today prosecutors are operating "early diversion" programs. Defendants charged with minor and not too minor crimes and who are first offenders are released pretrial for six months. If they do not recidivate, the charges are dropped. In effect, the prosecutor agrees not to prosecute these suspected criminals. In many of these programs, the prosecutor requires that the victim approve the decision to divert.

As for examples of the prosecutor turning to victims in cases involving serious crimes, there are many. Two will illustrate the point. When the Los Angeles District Attorney decided to plea bargain with Sirhan Sirhan for the assassination of Senator Robert F. Kennedy, he wrote to the Kennedy family to ask for their opinion of what a "suitable sentence" might be.[20] When the state's attorney in Chicago was faced with having to plea bargain in a "cop killer" case, he first held meetings with the relatives of the deceased officer, his fellow officers, and businessmen in the neighborhood where he grew up.[21] No doubt prosecutors can explain how the ends of justice are served by getting the victims' approval in these cases. A more detached observer will also see how the organizational and personal self-interest of the prosecutors also benefit from these practices.

SUMMARY

In the development of criminal justice in America, the victim has gone from central to peripheral actor in the system, from a prime beneficiary to an also-ran. In the name of equal justice for poor victims, bureaucracies were established to apprehend and prosecute

20. Robert G. Kaiser, *RFK Must Die* (New York: E.P. Dutton & Co., 1971), p. 519.

21. Albert Alschuler, "The Prosecutor's Role in Plea Bargaining," *University of Chicago Law Review* 36 (1968):50–112.

criminals. These organizations were supposed to serve the ends of justice better because they would be free of the elements of revenge and self-interest. But, they developed self-interests of their own. Today's victim has not been relieved of major costs in assisting with the prosecution of crimes. What is more, the criminal justice bureaucracies have denied him the satisfaction of participating in the justice process. If anything, the victim is exploited by criminal justice officials and defense attorneys to serve their personal and organizational self-interests.

A movement to improve the treatment of victims has begun in the last few years and has been supported by the Law Enforcement Assistance Administration. Victim-witness lounges are being built. Procedures for claiming witness fees are being streamlined. Special counselors contact victims; assess their social, medical, and financial needs; and refer them to community services. They also provide them with information about the disposition of their cases. Volunteers stay with frightened victims; home repair vans respond to burglarized victims and replace broken locks; and telephone alert systems allow witnesses to stay at home or at work if they can get to the courthouse on an hour's notice. In Sacramento, California, the police have had the courage to do what most bureaucracies would never do: they admit their failures. They write to victims after a period of time has passed and inform them if no arrest has been made in their cases.

The state of Minnesota has been successfully experimenting with a new restitution process. Felons convicted of selected property offenses are given early release from prison and are placed in a halfway house where they can work in the community and pay restitution to their victims on installment plans agreed to by the victims. As of January 1975, sixty-two offenders owed a total of $18,374, of which $5,627 had been paid; $3,505 would not be paid because the offenders had been returned to prison; and the remainder was expected to be paid on schedule. In Peoria, Illinois, an experimental effort is underway to bring the victim into the plea bargaining process. In Suffolk County, Massachusetts, the victim is being involved in shaping the sentencing recommendation to the judge.

These efforts are laudable. They may make the victim's visit to the courthouse more pleasant. But for the most part they are not directed at the fundamental reordering of priorities among criminal justice goals that is needed to achieve a true victim orientation in criminal justice. The interests of the state, the defendant, and the bureaucracy still dominate the criminal justice process in theory and in reality, and they are likely to do so for some time.

❄ *Chapter 14*

Public Compensation of the Victims of Crime: How Much Would It Cost?*

Roger E. Meiners

INTRODUCTION

Former Senator Ralph Yarborough of Texas introduced the first federal "Victims of Crime Act" in the Congress in June 1965.[1] The bill has been reintroduced, with modifications, in every session of Congress since then. A compromise version of the bill, sponsored by Senators Mansfield and McClellan, passed the Senate in September of 1972 by a vote of 60—8, and was passed again by the Senate in 1973. A federal compensation bill appears to have a good chance to become law in the next few years in a form close to its present structure.[2]

Some bills would establish a Violent Crimes Compensation Board as an independent agency within the Justice Department.[3] The board would act as a quasi-judicial body in hearing and granting claims. All

---

*The author would like to thank John Hagel III, Fred McChesney, and Richard Wagner for their assistance.

1. Ralph W. Yarborough, "The Battle for a Federal Violent Crimes Compensation Act: The Genesis of S. 9," *Southern California Law Review* 43 (1970): 93—106.

2. For a review of recent congressional action and to see the various victim compensation bills before the Congress, see U.S. Congress, House, Committee on the Judiciary, *Hearings on Victims of Crime Compensation Legislation*, 94th Cong., 1st and 2nd sess., 1976.

3. The act described here is the one passed by the Senate and is the primary form the bill has maintained over the years. Different bills contain variations. For instance, H.R. 3686, co-sponsored by seventeen House members in 1977, essentially provides for subsidies to the states, but would not establish victim compensation in federal jurisdictions.

attorneys who appear before the board in connection with any case could file for and be paid for their work by the board.

After deducting any private insurance payments received, the board would be authorized to make payments of not less than $100 to the victims of crime, to be paid in lump sum or on a periodic basis. Victims in federal jurisdictions are entitled to be compensated for medical expenses, loss of earnings, and other pecuniary losses up to $50,000. "Intervenors" in the commission of a crime, individuals injured in an attempt to prevent a crime or stop an assailant, also are entitled to collect for property losses, though there is no maximum limit in these cases. These payments would apply to injuries sustained as a result of any proven criminal act.

A Criminal Victim Indemnity Fund would be established to help pay for the awards. With this program, all federal courts would take into consideration the financial condition of convicted felons, who have caused personal injury, property loss, or death, and order the felon to pay a fine of not more than $10,000, in addition to any other penalty. All other funds would come from the budget of the Department of Justice.

The Violent Crimes Compensation Board would sit on all cases that occur in federal jurisdictions, such as the District of Columbia and Puerto Rico, and would be authorized to pay 75 percent of the costs of state-operated programs that meet the standards set by the board. Funds would be administered by the Law Enforcement Assistance Administration.

The proposed federal program to assist victims of crimes presents an interesting opportunity for the application of some aspects of the theory of public choice that have been developed in recent years. In particular, there is an opportunity for application of the emerging theory of bureaucracy. This chapter explores why the victim compensation bill has emerged, why it is likely to pass Congress, how much it is apt to cost in operation, who the major beneficiaries would be, and how the government officials running the programs could be expected to behave in pressing for expansion.

POTENTIAL COSTS OF A
COMPENSATION PROGRAM

In a crude calculation of the possible cost of national victim compensation, Duane G. Harris estimated that in 1970 public victim compensation would have cost over $1 billion.[4] Harris based his esti-

---

4. Duane G. Harris, "Compensating Victims of Crime: Blunting the Blow," *Business Review* (Federal Reserve Board, Philadelphia, June 1972), p. 19.

mate on the assumption that 700,000 victims of violent crimes (the estimated number in 1970) would all receive compensation payments averaging about $1,500 each, which was comparable to workmen's compensation payments in New York and Pennsylvania. Extrapolating this figure to 1974, Harris' method of estimation would yield annual payments of about $3.2 billion.[5]

A 1972 staff study by the Program and Management Evaluation Division of the Office of Operations Support of the Law Enforcement Assistance Administration (LEAA) estimated that, if compensation programs were implemented in every state by fiscal 1974, and the federal program provided 75 percent subsidization of the state programs, by fiscal 1979, when the program would be operational nationwide, it would cost $26,845,000. Of this, $21,084,793 would be the share of the federal government. This estimate took cost figures of the New York and Maryland state compensation programs for the early 1970s and extrapolated the numbers to the rest of the country. It accounted for the lower crime rates in other states and the higher maximum payment allowed by the federal plan. The LEAA believed this estimate was superior to another projection that simply extrapolated the New York and Maryland programs nationally, yielding a total cost estimate of $34,200,000 for fiscal 1976.[6] H.R. 3686 (95th Cong., 1st sess., 1977), a victim compensation bill, provides $40 million for the fiscal year ending in 1978, $50 million for 1979, and $60 million for 1980.

The Harris estimate is crude and may be rejected on the basis that some of its assumptions are inappropriate. In particular, the condition that all victims would receive compensation is incorrect, at least for the near future, as most victims of crime are now protected by private insurance. On the other hand, the LEAA estimate seems designed primarily to stimulate support for a program that would benefit the LEAA. Bureaus often understate the estimated cost of new programs so that they are more appealing to legislators. In any case,

5. Harris' estimate of 700,000 victims was based on figures from the FBI's *Uniform Crime Reports*, which are replaced here by the superior LEAA data. As Table 14–1 shows, there were approximately 1.7 million victims of violent crimes in 1974. These crime victims would have received average payments of about $1,900 each, assuming that the cost of victimization increased at the same rate as the general price index since 1970. Price index from *National Economic Trends*, Federal Reserve Bank of St. Louis.

6. U.S. Congress, Senate, Committee on the Judiciary, *Hearings on S. 16, S. 33, S. 750, S. 1946, S. 2087, S. 2426, S. 2748, S. 2856, S. 2994, and S. 2995, Victims of Crime*, 92nd Cong., 1st sess., 1971 and 1972, citing: U.S. Department of Justice, Law Enforcement Assistance Administration, "Victims of Crime Act of 1972," Staff Study, Program and Management Evaluation Division (Washington, D.C.: U.S. Government Printing Office), pp. 719–47.

that estimate is based on assumptions of dubious validity, as will be discussed below.

It is true that an accurate estimate is difficult. One based on conservative assumptions is made below, utilizing some limitations assumed by bureaucrats involved with compensation programs. Since government officials have incentives to understate the likely costs of new programs, this estimate may be suspected to be on the low side.

An analysis prepared for the state senate of Washington of the victim compensation bill that was passed and implemented there in 1973 contains estimates of the future cost of the program. The estimates were based primarily on the experience of the state of Maryland, which has had a compensation program for a relatively long time, and, as a state, is similar to Washington in size and in amount of crime. The Maryland program is also the closest to the federal proposal in coverage. Based on previous program performance in Maryland, both states estimated that 5.8 percent of all victims of violent crimes would receive compensation in fiscal 1975.[7]

An estimate of the number of victims of violent crimes resulting in injury is given in Table 14−1, using statistics provided by the comprehensive victimization survey taken by the LEAA for 1974. The estimates of criminal victimization provided by the LEAA surveys are used here rather than the FBI's *Uniform Crime Reports,* which

Table 14−1.   Victimization Rate per 1,000 Population Age Twelve and Over for Incidents Resulting in Injury[a]

Crime	1974 Rate	Total Number
Rape and attempted rape	1.0	164,562
Robbery with injury	2.3	378,493
Aggravated assault with injury	3.3	543,055
Simple assault with injury	3.5	575,967
Total		1,662,077

[a]Population age twelve and over was 164.6 million. Injury is defined as "serious injury (e.g., broken bones, loss of teeth, internal injuries, loss of consciousness) or an undetermined injury requiring two or more days of hospitalization."

Source: National Criminal Justice Information and Statistics Service, *Criminal Victimization in the United States: A Comparison of the 1973 and 1974 Findings,* National Crime Panel Survey Report, No. SD−NCP−N3 (Washington, D.C.: U.S. Government Printing Office, 1976).

7. The figure in Maryland was expected to rise from 4.5 percent in 1974 to 7.1 percent in 1976. The 5.8 percent estimate for 1975 will be used for this estimate. Figures provided by the administrator of the Crime Victims Act of the state of Washington in correspondence with the author.

have been the traditional source of estimates of victimization. The LEAA surveys have revealed that most crimes are not reported to the police. Victim compensation would provide an added incentive for victims to report their victimization. This estimate excludes some crimes that potentially would also be compensated, such as murder, arson, and crimes inflicted on persons under twelve years of age. It also excludes millions of crimes "when the extent of the injury was minor (e.g., bruises, black eyes, cuts, scratches, swelling) or is undetermined but requiring less than 2 days of hospitalization."[8]

Assuming that only 5.8 percent of the crimes with injury were compensated, there would have been almost 100,000 awards nationally in 1974. Bringing the estimate forward to 1975, one could assume the same number of compensations.[9] The mean compensation award for 1975 in the state of Washington, using past experience in Maryland, was estimated at $4,061. This is close to the $4,000 figure used here, and is near the mean award of $4,725 given in Massachusetts in fiscal 1974.[10]

Multiplying the figures above would yield a total compensation bill of $400 million nationally for 1975. This amount ignores administrative costs that would probably add at least another 10 percent to this total. Considering that both the crime rate and hospitalization costs are increasing, an estimate of a one-half billion dollar annual outlay for the late 1970s would not seem out of order, based on the assumptions made here. This estimate does not account for the impact of federal subsidization, which will be discussed later.[11]

POLITICAL PRESSURES

A victim compensation program of the size just discussed would be large enough to make some difference in the financial position of numerous crime victims. The LEAA Staff Report, on the other hand,

8. *Criminal Victimization in the United States: A Comparison of 1973 and 1974 Findings*, p. 70.

9. These figures are sufficiently rough that only the general magnitude of the numbers is important. LEAA surveys indicate that the number of victimizations was not rapidly increasing during that time period, in contrast to the FBI's report of large annual increases in reported crime.

10. Figures provided by the administrators of Washington and Massachusetts compensation programs in correspondence with the author.

11. This estimate assumed that every state adopted victim compensation along the lines of the federal program, which is like the Maryland plan. It does not assume aggressive pushing for expansion of the program, nor does it assume that more than 5.8 percent of violent crime victims would be compensated. This figure probably would increase over time. The Maryland and Washington compensation directors forecasted rapid growth.

envisioned annual compensation of about $25 million. If awards averaged $1,000, which is below what is given currently in any state with a compensation program, only 25,000 victims, less than 2 percent of the victims of crime with injury, would be assisted annually. A program of this magnitude would be insignificant and would stir little interest in any sector. In fact, numerous groups have actively supported the measure, presumably because there are incentives to do so. One can consider some of the possible motives of the supporters, noting which groups perceive benefits from passage, and why there is no organized opposition to the bill.

The American Bar Association has enthusiastically endorsed a governmental compensation program.[12] The rationale for this support is easy to discover. As proposed, most federal bills allow all individuals who wish to file a claim for compensation to do so with or without the assistance of a lawyer. However, if one secures the services of a lawyer in pressing a claim, whether that claim is successful or not, the compensation board would pay the fees of the lawyer.

In several states' victim compensation programs, lawyers receive 15 percent of the award given the victim, out of the victim's payments. Applying this percentage to the estimated one-half billion dollars to be given in awards, lawyers might collect $75 million annually for successful claims alone. Assuming that a lawyer can operate an office for about $75,000 a year, including his salary, office help, office rental, and other expenses, the pursuit of successful claims could provide full time employment for 1,000 lawyers.[13] In a rapidly growing profession such subsidies are welcomed; this program would not support a massive number of lawyers, but a number large enough to make action by the lobbying arm of the profession worthwhile. Since a large number of congressmen are lawyers, they undoubtedly see as reasonable this provision of the proposed program.

The International Association of Chiefs of Police was an early supporter of compensation for crime victims, unanimously passing a resolution in favor of adoption at the 1966 annual conference.[14] Although there is no direct assistance for policemen in the compensation legislation, it usually was joined with legislation providing fed-

---

12. Senate Committee on the Judiciary, *Victims of Crime*, pp. 489–91; and House Committee on the Judiciary, *Victims of Crime Compensation Legislation*, pp. 89–108.

13. This estimate was based on past information gathered on lawyers' income and expenses. U.S. Bureau of the Census, Census of Selected Service Industries, *1972 Subject Series–Legal Services*, SC72–5–4 (Washington, D.C.: U.S. Government Printing Office, 1975).

14. Senate Committee on the Judiciary, *Victims of Crime*, pp. 491–92.

eral payments for policemen and firemen killed in the line of duty. By supporting both pieces of legislation some logrolling is accomplished, although it is possible that victim compensation would be supported on its own merits.

The continual growth of crime has placed the efficiency and quality of public police services under question.[15] Most citizens who are victimized have little incentive to call the police because usually there is little the police can do for them.[16] The odds that the police will capture criminals are low, so that without some monetary reward victims will simply incur time costs by cooperating with the police.[17] A compensation program would have a potential twofold beneficial effect for police bureaus. First, because some victims would be compensated, the public might be mollified that something is "being done" for the innocent victims, for whom there is general sympathy. This would relieve some of the pressure on the police to "do something" about the criminals. Second, because one must report a crime to the police to be able to apply for compensation, there would be an increase in the number of crimes reported. This added workload and perceived increase in crime would provide justification for an increase in police budgets.

The Department of Justice would benefit from the adoption of the compensation program. Because the federal commission and the program funds would be administered through the Justice Department, the department could be expanded in size, budget, and sphere

15. According to a 1970 survey of Louis Harris and Associates, 33 percent of the individuals interviewed in a nationwide survey rated the job done by local law enforcement officials unfavorably. National Criminal Justice Information and Statistics Service, *Sourcebook of Criminal Justice Statistics—1973*, Michael J. Hineland et al., ed. (Washington, D.C.: U.S. Government Printing Office, 1974), p. 134.

16. Surveys taken in thirteen large American cities on victimization in 1972 showed that between 40 and 51 percent of all crimes of violence were reported to the police. For all personal crimes the figures were even lower, ranging from 31 to 41 percent. National Criminal Justice Information and Statistics Service, *Crime in the Nation's Five Largest Cities*, A National Crime Panel Survey Report (Washington, D.C.: U.S. Government Printing Office, 1974), p. 28; National Criminal Justice Information and Statistics Service, *Crime in Eight American Cities*, A National Crime Panel Survey Report (Washington, D.C.: U.S. Government Printing Office, 1974), p. 38.

17. In 1971 there were 5.4 million offenses known by the police in 4,500 cities with a population of 105 million. Only 20.9 percent of the known offenses were cleared by the police (by arrest). Forty-six and a half percent of the known violent crimes were cleared by the police. Since the LEAA studies indicate that less than one-half of all crimes are reported to the police, it is likely that only about 10 percent of all offenses are cleared by arrest and that only about 20 percent of all violent crimes are cleared by arrest. *Sourcebook of Criminal Justice Statistics—1973*, p. 290; *supra* note 16.

of influence. This would account for the LEAA study, which pushed for adoption of the program, claiming that the cost would be trivial. The message to the politicians is that a visible and probably popular program can be instituted at little cost. Even if the estimate is wrong, it is doubtful that any punitive action would be taken against the agency responsible for the estimate, especially years after the fact. The LEAA study employed highly suspect assumptions that severely lowered the estimated cost. Once implemented, however, the federal government would be bound by the law to pay for whatever costs the program incurred. Congressmen would be hard pressed to vote for a reduction of benefits to innocent victims of crime.

The political popularity of compensation programs is evidenced by its rapid adoption in most Anglo-Saxon jurisdictions, including over a dozen American states since 1965 (not including "Good Samaritan" statutes). Because the states would benefit significantly from the federal subsidy, and the officials running the state programs would benefit the most, there has been much lobbying by the states for enactment of the federal program.[18] Some states have passed victim compensation legislation, but have been waiting to fund the program until the federal subsidy becomes available. The compensation bill easily passed the Senate in September 1972 and again in March 1973. The bill has since sat in the House Judiciary Committee, supposedly held in a backlog by the Watergate business and since then by the massive bill (S. 1) that would have rewritten a large portion of federal crime statutes. It is uncertain when the legislation might be adopted, but it has been endorsed by most major national leaders, including ex-President Ford.[19]

Although there are relatively few specific pressure groups that would benefit from the legislation, it may be viewed by legislators as a program that would be generally popular and apparently would not hurt anyone. The public popularity of such a program was tested in 1966 before victim compensation became an issue of which many people were aware. A poll taken on behalf of the President's Commission on Law Enforcement and Administration of Justice revealed that about 60 percent of the responses were favorable to public compensation and about 30 percent were opposed.[20] Given the increased concern about the extent of crime in the last decade, the results of a

18. See, for example, the large number of witnesses from state programs, House Committee on the Judiciary, *Victims of Crime Compensation Legislation.*

19. *Miami Herald*, 20 June 1975, p. 1 (President Ford endorses victim compensation along with other crime-related measures); *New York Times*, 1 December 1971, p. 52 (support by Democrats).

20. *Sourcebook of Criminal Justice Statistics—1973*, p. 156.

similar survey today might be even more favorable. There is general sympathy for victims of crime, and legislators perceive this emotion. The compensation program would indeed do something for some innocent victims of crime. The inefficient aspects of the program are of such a subtle nature that they probably would not be linked to the program by many individuals, so there does not appear to be any group that is likely to oppose the bill.[21]

Two groups that would appear to benefit from compensation, but are likely to have little political input, are judges and criminals. Over time, judges have seemed less willing to send criminals to prison, as evidenced by the general trend of a falling prison population in relation to the nation's population.[22] This may partly be due to the extensive use of plea bargaining, the actions of parole boards, and expanded use of probation. If crime victims receive payments, the deeds of criminals may seem less grievous and may politically justify the sentences given to criminals. Such sentences are viewed as too lenient by some, and are an important political issue.[23] Criminals would, of course, directly benefit from any general reduction in prison sentences. Another manner in which criminals would benefit, although it would make little difference in practice, is that the incentive of a victim to sue a criminal for civil damages to recover the costs of a crime would be reduced, simply because it would be cheaper and easier for a victim to collect from the state. Also, to the extent that moral scruples deter crime and the extent of damages inflicted on victims, the consciences of criminals may be eased by the knowledge that victims may be partially compensated for the damage inflicted in the commission of crimes.

21. The only organized opposition to the proposal that may be expected would be from private insurance companies. These companies have made no public sign of awareness or concern. Correspondence with six major insurance companies and numerous professional insurance organizations and lobbying arms has revealed no interest in the issue. It is possible that interest would emerge if the program were to become nationwide. However, as currently proposed, the legislation may not appear to be a threat to insurance interests.

22. The rate of court commitments as a rate per 100,000 civilian population fell by half between 1954 and 1970. Actual prison population, state and federal, fell from 212,953 in 1960 to 196,429 in 1970. The number of prisoners received from courts fell from 88,575 in 1960 to 79,351 in 1970. *Sourcebook of Criminal Justice Statistics—1973*, pp. 346–47.

23. For one explanation of the phenomenon of the lack of will to punish, see James M. Buchanan, "The Samaritan's Dilemma," in *Altruism, Morality, and Economic Theory*, ed. Edmund S. Phelps (New York: Russell Sage Foundation, 1975).

INCENTIVES OF POLITICIANS
IMPLEMENTING COMPENSATION
PROGRAMS

The public choice theory of bureaucracy provides guidance for predicting how the participants in a public program can be expected to act.[24] The primary prediction that can be made about the compensation plan is that it will grow rapidly after initiation. The bill that passed the Senate in 1973 would have appropriated $5 million for the implementation of the program. That amount was based on the recommendation of the LEAA study. Clearly the budget would increase rapidly in subsequent years, as the federal government would be obligated to pay for the expenses of the federal bureau, claims in federal jurisdictions, and up to 75 percent of expenses incurred by states giving compensation that meets the guidelines set down by the federal agency. For example, the state of Washington budgeted $1.1 million for compensation awards for fiscal 1975, the first full year of operation there.[25] On a nationwide basis, assuming that crime in Washington is comparable to the rest of the nation, this would imply $65 million in compensation payments, in a start-up year apart from administrative costs. The federal government's share of this expense would be about $50 million.

In the last few years, many states have implemented and funded compensation programs. Some, possibly most, of these programs were implemented in anticipation of the federal subsidy that would be received when the compensation bill passed Congress. This was definitely the case in Rhode Island and in Illinois, which ". . . enacted a victim compensation statute in 1973, but the legislature failed to appropriate funds to support the program, thus, presumably, keeping it in limbo, perhaps until federal funds are forthcoming."[26] The states that currently do not have compensation programs could be expected to adopt them in response to the heavy federal subsidy. Presumably they would receive assistance in establishing programs from the LEAA, which would directly benefit from the

24. Gordon Tullock, *The Politics of Bureaucracy* (Washington, D.C.: Public Affairs Press, 1965); Anthony Downs, *Inside Bureaucracy* (Boston: Little, Brown & Co., 1967); and William Niskanen, *Bureaucracy and Representative Government* (Chicago: Aldine, 1971).

25. Amount from budget presentation to 1975 legislature, Office of the Administrator, Crime Victims Act, Olympia, Washington, in correspondence with author.

26. Herbert Edelhertz and Gilbert Geis, *Public Compensation to Victims of Crime* (New York: Praeger Publications, Inc., 1974), p. 174.

number of states with programs as well as from the scope of the program nationally.

The incentives for state legislators to support victim compensation are easy to discern. If they do not support compensation, they allow federal tax dollars paid by their state residents to be shifted to states that have the program. The federal subsidy reduces the price to a state of providing a compensation program.[27] Once the federal program is implemented, if the federal government pays 75 percent of the outlays of the state programs, the cost of compensation falls to one-fourth of its actual level from the perspective of the state legislators.[28] Many states have not implemented compensation programs on their own volition because the expenditures outweigh the benefits perceived by the legislators. With federal subsidization, the price of providing awards to victims as seen by legislators falls. This then increases the incentive to begin such a program. The legislators are faced with the choice of financing compensation to get the federal subsidy or allowing their constituents to pay federal taxes for the programs in other states.[29]

A budget estimate of over one-half billion dollars for a nationwide compensation system was derived previously. This estimate was based on the assumption that compensation was instituted in every state and at the federal level, and that each state reached a level of awards projected by the Washington and Maryland experiences. This estimate did not reflect the subsidy effect on the size of the program. Once the impact of, say, a 75 percent subsidy is taken into account, the states would be found to engage in more compensation than they would have without federal assistance.[30] Assuming a constant level of demand on the part of the legislators for compensation, the program would quadruple in size in each state, which would mean a national compensation budget of over $2 billion annually.

This would be achieved by increasing the size of the average compensation payment as well as by increasing the number of compen-

27. Richard E. Wagner, *The Public Economy* (Chicago: Markham Publishing Co., 1973), pp. 66–67; Wallace E. Oates, *Fiscal Federalism* (New York: Harcourt, Brace, Jovanovich, Inc., 1972), pp. 75–78.

28. Different versions of the victim compensation proposal have offered different levels of federal subsidization for state programs. Most would pay 75 percent of the states' costs, but H.R. 3686, a 1977 compensation bill, would have the federal government pay the states 100 percent of the current cost of paying compensation for crimes subject to federal jurisdiction, and 50 percent of the cost of compensation for crimes in state jurisdiction.

29. Wagner, pp. 66–67.

30. See Albert Breton and Ronald Wintrobe, "The Equilibrium Size of a Budget-Maximizing Bureau," *Journal of Political Economy* 83 (February 1975): 195–207.

sation awards granted in each state. Without federal subsidies, the states of Maryland and Washington expect to pay an average of $4,000 per compensation, as has Massachusetts with payment guidelines lower than the proposed federal standards. With a 75 percent federal subsidy, if a state grants $16,000 per award, the cost to the state remains at $4,000. A state could also continue to make awards averaging $4,000, but make four times the number of payments, and the federal subsidy would leave the cost to the state constant. What would emerge in practice is uncertain, probably some combination of the two extremes. The important point is the potential for growth of the compensation programs that could occur due to the impact of the federal subsidy.

INCENTIVES OF GOVERNMENT OFFICIALS OPERATING COMPENSATION PROGRAMS

Once public compensation became nationwide, those in charge of operating the programs would have incentives to expand the programs, so as to enhance the power of their bureaus, and the prestige and pay of their own positions. The federal bureau operating the subsidy program would have no incentive to reduce the growth of the state bureaus since they have concurrent incentives.[31] These motives are not inconsistent with the motives of the victims and their lawyers, who will want to receive the largest awards possible as often as possible.

The size of the bureau that would operate the federal program is difficult to estimate. There would be two parts to the program. One would be the LEAA, which would administer funds to be distributed to the state programs. The other would be the independent compensation board within the Justice Department, which would handle all compensation claims in the District of Columbia and all other federal jurisdictions.

Because the federal board would have jurisdiction over a population comparable to that of a small state, one can extrapolate the estimates for the federal board to the states to derive the size of the bureaucracies that might emerge to direct the programs. The 1972 LEAA Staff Report proposed the staff requirements for the Violent Crimes Compensation Board, which are duplicated in Table 14-2. This staff was projected to go into effect the first year of operation and remain constant in size over the years as the volume of compensation cases increased.

31. Wagner, p. 123.

Table 14−2. **Violent Crimes Commission Board Staffing**

Number of Positions	Position Title	Grades	Total Pay
1	Board Chairman	Level III	$ 40,000
1	Member	Level IV	38,000
1	Member	Level IV	38,000
1	Executive Secretary	Level V	36,000
5	Staff Personnel	GS−13−15	109,000
1	General Counsel	Level V	36,000
5	Staff Personnel	GS−13−15	109,000
1	Director, Hearings, Review, and Appeals	GS−15	25,583
10	Staff Personnel	GS−11−13	158,660
10	Expert and Consultant Services (man years)	5 MY	110,000
36	Total Staffing Costs		$701,043
	Administrative Costs (estimate) (salaries and expenses)		250,000
		Total	$951,043

Source: U.S. Congress, Senate, Committee on the Judiciary, *Victims of Crime*, p. 742, citing Staff Study, "Victims of Crime Act of 1972."

Since civil service salaries increased after 1972, a rounded figure of $1.1 million can be used for 1975 administrative costs. Although federal jurisdiction includes less than 1 percent of the nation's population (District of Columbia and other federal jurisdictions), while an average state would have 2 percent, for simplicity it will be assumed that this commission represents the average size of the commissions that would exist in every state with a compensation program.[32] This would result in a total administration bill of about $55 million, as was assumed previously when the size of the entire program was estimated.[33]

Although the authors of the LEAA study assumed that the staff would begin and remain at this size, that assumption is difficult to accept, considering the motives of government officials and the history of other bureaus. The growth of other independent commissions

32. The federal board would also cover compensation cases that arise via cases through federal district courts, which would give the board a larger workload than if it dealt only with the portion of the population in federal districts.

33. An administrative cost that is excluded here, as it is in most governmental cost estimates, is the annual value of the office space occupied by the bureau. In prime locations in major cities this cost is not negligible.

that handle various types of claims may provide some evidence as to the possible growth rate of the Violent Crimes Compensation Board.

The Occupational Safety and Health Review Commission was established by a December 1970 act of Congress. In fiscal 1972, the first full year of operation, the commission had twenty-three employees, and a $400,000 budget.[34] By fiscal 1975, the appropriation had grown to $5.5 million for a staff of 175, which was used to review about 3,000 cases in that year. On a somewhat smaller scale, the Indian Claims Commission, which hears and adjudicates the claims of Indians, grew from twenty-two employees in 1965 to forty-four in 1975. The budget increased from $313,000 to $1.3 million in the same period. It was estimated that the commission completed review of 438 claims during fiscal 1975. For both of these commissions, the total average cost per claim examined was about $2,000. The National Labor Relations Board, which has had a nearly constant number of employees over the past decade, has had its budget more than double in that time to $62.7 million in fiscal 1975. This was allocated to cover about 45,000 unfair labor practices and representation cases, for an average administrative cost of $1,400 per case examined during the year.

The average claim cost figures of these commissions are not necessarily comparable to the costs that would be incurred by compensation commissions, but the general administrative expense appears to be higher for other quasi-judicial bodies than one might guess based on the LEAA Staff Report, which concerned itself only with the administration of victim compensation. If the administrative expense per case were only $400, far below the expenses incurred by some existing bureaus, then 100,000 cases would cost $40 million to administer nationally, as estimated previously. Although this figure may not be very accurate, it does not seem unreasonably high, based on the performance of other bureaus charged with investigating and settling claims cases. Adding these administrative costs to the estimate made earlier of $400 million in compensation would yield a total expense of $440 million.

State victim compensation programs are relatively new and few in number. The incentives that bureaus have to expand have been amply demonstrated by the theoretical models of bureaucracy and the empirical evidence that exists.[35] Most have been able to expand rapidly in their first few years of operation, so that they have not

34. All figures from *The Budget of the U.S. Government*, various fiscal years (Washington, D.C.: U.S. Government Printing Office).

35. For example, see Thomas Borcherding, ed., *Budgets and Bureaucrats: The Origins of Government Growth* (Durham: Duke University Press, 1977).

had to resort to arguing for an expansion of functions to justify budget increases. The California program has increased in budget approximately by the amount of the original budget every year since inception in 1967. If federal subsidies are forthcoming, the growth of such state bureaus would be likely to accelerate.

After the programs are well established, the desire for continued growth may induce the bureaus to fight for expansion of responsibilities. If the crime rate continues to increase as it has in the past two decades, the bureaus will experience a continued natural expansion. There are three other aspects of normal operation that will enable the bureaus to take full advantage of their positions, given existing conditions. First, unlike private insurance companies, the compensation boards have little reason to prevent all but the most blatant fraud. Second, given the positions of lawyers in the operation of these programs, there will be incentives to bring more and more cases to the boards for consideration and to work for the maximum compensation. Third, the public would require a certain amount of time to become aware of the compensation program, so that information dissemination would yield increased claims.

Numerous articles by legal scholars have expressed concern that fraud would be a problem, the prevention of which would require vigilance by the compensation boards. Actually, fraud would not be a significant problem if it were made a felony and treated harshly when uncovered. However, the boards will experience better budgetary growth if they assume a passive role with respect to inflated claims. Moreover, since it is unpleasant and possibly politically dangerous to reject claims, administrators will be more likely to accept inflated claims than would be the case in private insurance. In a public bureau a one dollar cut in compensation leads to a one dollar cut in the budget. In a private enterprise the administrators who prevent fraud and padding are more likely to benefit from such efforts.[36]

It is possible that compensation boards may intentionally be blind to problems of fraud. As of the sixth full year of operation of compensation in England, the executive secretary of the British board reported: "No case has yet come to the board's notice in which compensation was obtained by fraud, and the safeguards therefore appear to be effective."[37] This is similar to the experience of the several

36. See Armen Alchian and Harold Demsetz, "Production, Information Costs, and Economic Organization," *American Economic Review* 62 (December 1972); and Ludwig von Mises, *Bureaucracy* (New Rochelle, New York: Arlington House, 1969).

37. David H. Harrison, "Criminal Injuries Compensation in Britain," *American Bar Association Journal* 57 (May 1971):479.

American states' programs, which claim to have experienced little problem with fraud. In Massachusetts:

> No action has been taken against claimants because of the subsequent discovery that they recovered payments from the offenders or from some other source that duplicated compensation received earlier under the compensation statute. There is no machinery in the attorney general's office that could be adapted to monitoring or policing such abuse.
>
> Fraud does not appear to have been a problem in administering the Massachusetts crime victim compensation program. There have been no referrals for criminal investigation or prosecution.[38]

The state of New York uses investigators in its compensation program to establish the validity of claims, and some fraudulent cases have been rejected on the basis of the investigation. But, as the chief investigator noted, "as long as someone is actually the innocent victim of a crime and his claim is bona fide, padding is not looked at particularly harshly, but we must naturally eliminate all padding. . . ." Similarly:

> The Board appears to adopt an attitude of benevolent skepticism in such matters, based on the idea that the victims are after all the "good guys" and that they ought to be treated with kindness and compassion and not badgered about minor discrepancies in their claims.
>
> The Board also takes pride in the fact that it has on occasion taken the initiative to develop a factual basis for a claim where the claimant was unable to do so.

In general the attitude is, as expressed by the chief investigator, "If we can make an award under the law, we make it."[39]

Although it is impossible and inefficient to ferret out all fraud and padded claims, the attitude of the compensation boards may be such as to encourage fraud and padding to some politically acceptable level. It may be comparable to welfare and food stamp fraud, which are significant, but are generally not prevented until they become so large as to irritate voters and lead politicians to call for some action— which, on occasion, has been taken.[40]

38. Edelhertz and Geis, p. 127.

39. Ibid., pp. 49–51.

40. One of the most noted instances was the welfare reform program in California led by Governor Reagan, which removed 176,000 recipients from the relief rolls and saved an estimated $300 million annually. *The New York Times,* 2 February 1972, p. 34; 12 August 1972, p. 24. More recently there has been considerable discussion about reducing fraud in food stamp procurement, see Kenneth W. Clarkson, *Food Stamps and Nutrition* (Washington, D.C.: American Enterprise Institute, 1975), pp. 31–32.

The second feature of standard operating procedures that would help the boards to grow is the incentive presented to lawyers to bring numerous cases for compensation. One issue that has not been fully settled is whether the lawyers would receive some portion of their claimants' awards for their fees, or whether the lawyers would be granted fees separately. The 1973 version of the Victims of Crime Act stated:

> The Board shall publish regulations providing that an attorney may, at the conclusion of the proceedings under this part, file with the Board an appropriate statement for a fee in connection with services rendered in such proceedings.
>
> ... the Board shall award a fee to such attorney on substantially similar terms and conditions as is provided for the payment of representation under Section 3006A of title 18 of the United States Code.[41]

Section 3006A of Title 18 of the United States Code states, concerning the amount to be awarded attorneys, that the "... court determined that reasonable attorneys' fees for successful plaintiff was $30 per in-court hour and $20 per out-of-court hour, plus miscellaneous expenses reasonably incurred."[42] It will be at the discretion of the states whether lawyers will be paid fees by the board for bringing cases that do not result in compensation. If they are to receive fees only for successful cases, lawyers would serve as a screening service for many cases and prevent some bad cases from going to the boards for consideration.

If fees are set as a percent of the award, lawyers will be less willing to help process small claims. There would be some minimum expected level at which lawyers would be willing to assist victims, but the decision in each case would depend upon the time involved in the particular case, the value of the lawyer's time, and the expected value of the award. There would be an incentive to make the claim as large as would be reasonable in the eyes of the boards, so as to maximize the fee and to serve as an incentive for potential claimants to engage the services of a lawyer.

If fees are awarded by the board on the basis of the work performed in the case, lawyers would be willing to bring any size case for compensation, given the expected chance of success. They would have an incentive to induce victims to bring forward all potential claims that appear compensable. If attorneys are to receive fees from

41. U.S. Congress, Senate, *Victims of Crime Act of 1973*, 93rd Cong., 1st sess., S. 300, p. 19.

42. *United States Code Annotated*, Title 18, Sec. 3006A, in Pamphlet No. 2, pt. 1 (St. Paul, Minnesota: West Publishing Co., 1975), p. 586.

the boards for all cases, successful or not, they would encourage all victims to become award claimants, yielding a staggering volume of claims. If states operate under different guidelines for fees, there will be an interesting comparison available in the future for examining the effects of the different fee methods.

A third factor that will help the compensation programs to expand naturally, although the boards can assist in this area, is that information about many compensation programs is not widespread. Hence, potential claimants could be ignorant of the possibilities of compensation, as they have been in states that currently have programs.[43]

New York is overcoming this information problem by asking other agencies, such as hospitals and police departments, to refer victims to the compensation board. Lawyers can also be expected to serve as an information source for potential claimants. Furthermore, one would expect some lawyers to specialize in compensation proceedings once the program becomes large enough to encourage full-time devotion to that activity. Indeed, "there are indications in Massachusetts and New Jersey that the advent of no-fault automobile insurance may induce the bar to increase its attention to victim compensation practice."[44]

As such natural inducements to expansion begin to diminish in impact on budgetary growth, the administrators of compensation programs can be expected to attempt to expand the functions of the boards in order to maintain the growth of their bureaus. If not already allowed in the enacting legislation or in all states with programs, one obvious manner to encourage a larger volume of claims is to allow attorneys fees to be paid by the boards, independent of the size of the claim and independent of the success of the claim. This is argued as logical by many legal scholars, as one would expect, because "claimants truly need them [lawyers], and [otherwise] the public will be deprived of monitors to help keep boards responsive and fair."[45] Since many legislators and most judges are lawyers, the logic and equity of this argument may be obvious to them, so that it would not be surprising to see it emerge.

Another change, which could emerge legislatively or judicially, is the removal of the lower and upper limits on payments to victims.

43. This has frequently been noted by administrators of existing state compensation programs. See, for example, the testimony of the attorney general of New Jersey, House Committee on the Judiciary, *Victims of Crime Compensation Legislation*, p. 277.

44. Edelhertz and Geis, p. 278. The gradual expansion of advertising by lawyers would hasten this process.

45. Edelhertz and Geis, p. 278.

Federal legislation would set the limits at $100 and $50,000, as written currently. However, in New York and Maryland there are no limits on the level of payments that may be made for medical purposes, and, given the tragic nature of some victims' injuries and the staggering medical costs these entail, it is easy to see that the $50,000 limit will appear inadequate in a number of cases. Legislative or judicial sympathy may lead to a removal of the upper payment limit.[46] Removal of the $100 lower claim limit, which is standard in all states' compensation programs, has been called for by a former commissioner in Maryland and by others sympathetic to the plight of those victims whose losses are less than $100.[47] Such a move would expand the volume of claims received, which would increase the needed administrative staffs.

Since compensation programs are *ex gratia*, to the state they have the same status as a welfare payment. Individuals are not allowed to sue the state for compensation should the board reject a claim or be unable to accept it under existing guidelines. However, in most states with programs, as well as in the proposed federal program, judicial review of awards would be allowed. Such review will cause the boards to spend a certain amount of time in the courts defending their decisions, which would expand the range of required functions. Boards would have to weigh the relative merits of granting larger claims versus contesting the claims in courts. More important, though, is the possibility that by judicial decree the courts may expand the range of compensation payments for victims, even if the legislature will not. By judicial interpretation judges rewrite the law. This area has no reason to be exempt from such actions. It is certain that lawyers will attempt to expand the programs by this method.

An obvious and logical possibility for long-range expansion of compensation programs is in the area of nonpecuniary damages. Most rape victims incur small pecuniary damages, but may incur large pain and suffering costs. Only in the state of Hawaii can victims currently receive compensation for such psychic losses, even though they are a true cost of victimization. The proposed federal legislation does not include such awards and presumably would not reimburse the states for any such awards. It is likely that some program administrators,

46. The current medical malpractice problem may encourage upper limits on payments. States are unlikely to allow multimillion dollar awards, but may be willing to allow the costs incurred to be compensated. A type of medical no-fault insurance similar in coverage to victim compensation has been proposed by Senators Kennedy and Inouye. See "The Doctors' New Dilemma," *Newsweek*, 10 February 1975, p. 41.

47. Edelhertz and Geis, p. 278.

lawyers, and victims would push for expansion of compensation payments into this area. Whether it happens by legislative action or by judicial fiat, potentially it would add huge sums to compensation awards, as these costs are common and sizeable.

The expansion of victim compensation into noncriminal areas is a possibility for the future. If national medical care is instituted, much of the function of existing compensation programs could be eliminated. Administrators would have to find other victims to assist to keep their bureaus functioning. New Zealand absorbed its victim compensation program into a universal accident compensation system that "covers everyone in the country . . . for any kind of accident—no matter how or when it happens or who is at fault."[48] Traditional systems of civil liability were seen as capricious and inequitable, so the common law right of action against tort-feasors was abolished.[49] Further expansion of compensation to cover all property losses is also under consideration in New Zealand, and was once proposed in a bill before the New York legislature. This would be a possible extension of powers for a state compensation board, so further advocacy may be expected.

If such a program was expanded in scope of operation, it would significantly reduce the scope of coverage by private insurance. Existing legislation, which appears to be little more than a slight expansion of the small compensation programs that exist in several states, probably poses little threat to areas now covered by private insurance. In the short run there may be some changes in the coverage of private insurance policies. Companies could offer lower rates on medical and income insurance by excluding losses that would be covered by public compensation. Much like the insurance policies that have arisen to cover losses not covered by Medicare, supplemental crime loss policies could be offered. This would, of course, place many people under the public compensation program who would not qualify currently because they have private coverage for crime losses.

CONCLUSION

Public compensation is structured to have the taxpayers provide a balm for the suffering of innocent victims of crime. Once enacted, it may reduce the chances for institution of a restitution program, by

48. "To Accident Victims, New Zealand Offers the Balm of Money," *Wall Street Journal*, 16 September 1975, p. 1.

49. J.L. Fahy, "The Administration of the Accident Compensation Act of 1972," *Economic Bulletin* 592 (1975), Canterbury Chamber of Commerce, Christchurch, New Zealand.

which criminals would make payments to their victims. If victims are compensated by the state, the demand for satisfaction from the criminals may be reduced, so that the basic problem, crime, will not be addressed.

Like many governmental programs, victim compensation is designed with the best of intentions, and appears to cost relatively little to achieve a desirable goal. In reality, victim compensation threatens to emerge as another tentacle of leviathan, encompassing far more in territory and dollars than ever envisioned. Numerous similar stories have unfolded in recent years, and victim compensation would seem likely to offer one additional instance of such bureaucratic growth.

✳ *Chapter 15*

Restitution as an Integrative Punishment

Burt Galaway

The process of imposing criminal justice sanctions in this country lacks both an appropriate rationale and form.

Without a clear, widely accepted sanctioning rationale, the criminal justice system becomes susceptible to faddism. The history of correctional programming might well be characterized as the coming and going of a series of sanctioning fads for either "rehabilitating" or "punishing" the convicted offender. Will restitution simply become one of this series? The current increasing popularity of restitution programming, coupled with the considerable disillusionment with other criminal justice sanctions,[1] creates a reasonable likelihood that restitution may turn out to be a criminal justice fad.

Restitution refers to a sanction imposed by an authorized official of the criminal justice system that requires the offender to make a money or service payment either to the direct victims of the crime or to substitute victims. The definition is broad enough to include the use of restitution in pretrial diversion programs and in programs directed toward securing a negotiated settlement for criminal matters when this process has the support and approval of an appropriate official of the criminal justice system. Earlier work has suggested that a useful restitution typology can be developed by focusing on the form of restitution (monetary or service) and on whether the victim is a direct or substitute victim.[2]

1. Gilbert Geis, "Restitution by Criminal Offenders: A Summary and Overview," in *Restitution in Criminal Justice*, eds. Joe Hudson and Burt Galaway (Lexington, Massachusetts: Lexington Books, 1977), p. 147. (Hereafter cited as *Restitution in Criminal Justice*.)

2. Joe Hudson and Burt Galaway, "Issues in the Correctional Implementation of Restitution to Victims of Crime," in *Considering the Victim: Readings*

Type I restitution involves monetary payments by the offender to the direct or actual victims of the crime. Restitution may be made directly by the offender to the victim or made through the offices of an intermediary. This appears to be the most prevalent type of restitution and as a condition of probation is the typical form of restitution found in the Minnesota Restitution Center,[3] the Georgia Restitution Shelters,[4] and in the nineteen restitution programs surveyed by Chesney, Hudson, and Galaway.[5]

Type II restitution refers to monetary payments made by the offender to some community agency. Restitution of this type differs from a fine in that the recipient of the restitution is a charitable organization. Type II restitution is used when the victim requests that payment be made to some charity, when the victim cannot be located or does not wish to participate in a restitution scheme directly, or when the victim has not experienced any loss. West German juvenile courts may order that juvenile and youthful offenders make payment to a worthwhile community charity as a corrective sanction.[6] The Minnesota Restitution Center has made use of Type II restitution in instances where the victims could not be located or did not wish to participate in a restitution plan.[7]

Type III restitution requires that the offender make restitution in the form of personal service to the victim. While this may be rather infrequently used, examples of Type III restitution are found in the reports of restitution projects. The Pilot Alberta Restitution Center (PARC) reports a case in which a sixteen year old youth from a welfare family burglarized the home of an elderly woman; the woman, a pensioner, had out of pocket losses of about $70. The youth and woman met with PARC staff to develop a restitution agreement that obligated the youth to a cash payment of $60 and also required the shoveling of snow from the victim's sidewalks through the winter

in *Restitution and Victim Compensation*, eds. Joe Hudson and Burt Galaway (Springfield, Illinois: Charles C. Thomas Publisher, 1975), pp. 351–59. (Hereafter cited as *Considering the Victim.*) Also Burt Galaway, "Toward the Rational Development of Restitution Programming," in *Restitution in Criminal Justice*, pp. 77–89.

3. Robert Mowatt, "The Minnesota Restitution Center: Paying Off the Ripped Off," in *Restitution in Criminal Justice*, pp. 190–215.

4. Bill Read, "The Georgia Restitution Program," in *Restitution in Criminal Justice*, pp. 216–27.

5. *Restitution in Criminal Justice*, pp. 3–4.

6. Federal Republic of Germany, Ministry of Justice, "The Treatment of Young Offenders in the Federal Republic of Germany." (Mimeographed in English, n.d.)

7. Mowatt.

season.[8] The Victim-Offender Reconciliation Project (VORP) in Kitchener, Ontario, offers several illustrations of Type III restitution, including a case in which fifteen and sixteen year old offenders worked for a church and several small businesses they had burglarized until the value of the work (at $2 per hour) equaled the value of the losses. In another case, three young men (average age of twenty-one) worked seven hours each in the store from which they had stolen goods.[9] A juvenile probation officer in Minnesota and one in South Dakota have said that they occasionally require juvenile offenders to clean up the damage resulting from their vandalism of vacation cabins.

Type IV restitution occurs when the offender is required to provide service for the community. The Community Service Orders Program in Great Britain established as a result of the Wootten Committee report of 1970[10] is the best example of Type IV restitution. In Great Britain, offenders are ordered to spend from 40 to 240 hours of volunteer labor in community organizations in lieu of jail sentences or fines.[11] Similar organized programs exist for offenders in Portland, Oregon,[12] Oakland, California,[13] and Annapolis, Maryland.[14] The use of community service as a probation condition apparently is widespread, and was reported in use in eleven of nineteen restitution programs surveyed in 1976.[15]

In the past one hundred years, restitution has probably been frequently imposed as a condition of probation.[16] Restitution has never, however, been a central component in probation theory

8. Pilot Alberta Restitution Center, *Progress Report: The Pilot Alberta Restitution Center: September 1, 1976—February 29, 1976* (Unpublished report, 1976).

9. Mennonite Central Committee, "A Proposal for Victim-Offender Reconciliation," and "Victim/Offender Reconciliation Project—Progress Report." (Materials from the Mennonite Central Committee, Kitchener, Ontario, November 13, 1975.)

10. Advisory Council on the Penal System, *Non-Custodial and Semi-Custodial Penalties* (London: Her Majesty's Stationery Office, 1970).

11. K. Pease, et. al., *Community Service Orders* (London: Her Majesty's Stationery Office, 1975); and John Harding, "Community Service Restitution by Offenders," in *Restitution in Criminal Justice*, pp. 101–30.

12. Donald E. Clark, "Community Service: A Realistic Alternative for Sentencing," *F.B.I. Law Enforcement Bulletin* (March 1976):3–6.

13. Sylvia Sullivan, "Convicted Offenders Become Community Helpers," *Judicature* 56 (March 1973):333–35.

14. Maryland Department of Juvenile Services, "Community Arbitration Program" (Unpublished, n.d.).

15. *Restitution in Criminal Justice*, pp. 8–9.

16. Edwin H. Sutherland and Donald R. Cressey, *Principles of Criminology*, 5th ed. (New York: J.B. Lippincott Company, 1955).

or practice. Despite the arguments of Irving Cohen[17] and Albert Eglash,[18] probation officers have not generally perceived restitution as a useful correctional tool. In the 1970s, however, restitution has been losing its obscurity. The Minnesota Restitution Center was established in 1972 to test the use of restitution in a community corrections setting,[19] and this program has served as a model for a number of additional programs in the United States and Canada. At the same time, yet independently, restitution was playing a more central role in juvenile court dispositions in victim assistance projects in St. Louis, Missouri,[20] and Rapid City, South Dakota.[21] An international restitution symposium was held in Minnesota in 1975 to examine operational issues arising from the use of restitution as a criminal justice sanction and to stimulate additional interest in restitution programming. In 1976 the Law Enforcement Assistance Administration funded seven additional pilot restitution programs for adult offenders. The National Institute of Juvenile Justice and Delinquency Prevention anticipates funding an additional series of pilot restitution programs for juvenile offenders in 1977. Both of these efforts are being subjected to a national evaluation that should help determine future directions for restitution programming. In 1976, Chesney, Hudson, and Galaway identified, from their own files, nineteen operational restitution programs in the United States and Canada in which restitution was a central programming component.[22]

Additionally, restitution appears to be gaining more acceptance as a condition of probation. In 1972, the National Advisory Commission on Criminal Justice Standards and Goals recognized the willing-

17. Irving E. Cohen, "The Integration of Restitution in the Probation Services," *Journal of Criminal Law, Criminology and Police Science* 34 (1944): 315–21, reprinted in *Considering the Victim*, pp. 332–39.

18. Albert Eglash, "Creative Restitution: Some Suggestions for Prison Rehabilitation Programs," *American Journal of Corrections* 20 (November–December 1958):20–22, 34; also ibid., "Creative Restitution—A Broader Meaning for An Old Term," *Journal of Criminal Law, Criminology and Police Science* 48 (1958):619–22, reprinted in *Considering the Victim*, pp. 284–90; Paul Keve and Albert Eglash, "Payments on a 'Debt to Society,' " *NPAA News* 36 (September 1957):1–2.

19. Joe Hudson and Burt Galaway, "Undoing the Wrong: The Minnesota Restitution Center," *Social Work* 19 (May 1974):313–18; *Considering the Victim*, pp. 351–59; Michael Serrill, "Repaying the Victim: Minnesota's Restitution Center," *Corrections Magazine* 1 (January–February 1975):14–20; Mowatt, pp. 190–215.

20. Wilbert Long, Chief Juvenile Officer for the Twenty-Second Judicial Circuit of Missouri, personal correspondence, October 10, 1974.

21. Herbert Edelhertz, *Restitutive Justice: A General Survey and Analysis* (Seattle: Battelle Human Affairs Centers, 1975).

22. *Restitution in Criminal Justice*, pp. 3–4.

ness to make restitution as one of the factors that would favor a nonprison sentence for the "nondangerous offender"[23] and recommended that fines not be imposed when they would interfere with the offender's ability to make restitution.[24] At least two states have adopted policies establishing restitution as a condition of probation or deferred sentence (Iowa and Colorado). A recent Minnesota survey indicates that the judges and probation officers have reasonably positive attitudes toward the use of restitution.[25] A survey is currently being conducted by the Institute of Policy Analysis in Eugene, Oregon, to determine the extent to which restitution is employed in the nation's juvenile courts. This research should provide additional data with which to evaluate the use of restitution as a probation condition.

The increasing acceptance and expansion of restitution programming during the 1970s has been consistent with statements of a number of standard setting bodies including the National Council on Crime and Delinquency, Council of Judges,[26] the American Bar Association,[27] the American Law Institute,[28] Chief Justice Earl Warren's Conference on Advocacy in the United States,[29] and the Law Reform Commission of Canada.[30] In contrast, the 1967 United States President's Commission on Law Enforcement and the Administration of Justice made no mention of restitution in the final report and only a brief reference in one of the task force reports.[31]

Shortly after the establishment of the Minnesota Restitution Center, an editorial writer for the *Minneapolis Star* noted[32] that the

23. National Advisory Commission on Criminal Justice Standards and Goals, *Corrections* (Washington, D.C.: U.S. Government Printing Office, 1973), p. 151.

24. Ibid., p. 162.

25. Steven Chesney, "The Assessment of Restitution in the Minnesota Probation Services," in *Restitution in Criminal Justice*.

26. "Model Sentencing Act, 2nd Ed.," *Crime and Delinquency* 18 (October 1972):1–14.

27. *Standards Relating to Sentencing Alternatives and Procedures* (New York: Office of Criminal Justice Project, Institute of Judicial Administration, 1968), 2.7(c)(iii); and *Standards Relating to Probation* (New York: Office of Criminal Justice Project, Institute of Judicial Administration, 1970), 3.2(c)(viii).

28. "Article on Suspended Sentences, Probation, and Parole," *Model Penal Code* (1962):301.1(2)(h)

29. *A Program for Prison Reform* (Cambridge, Massachusetts: Roscoe Pound-American Trial Lawyers Foundation, 1972).

30. *Working Paper No. 3: The Principles of Sentencing and Dispositions* (Ottawa: Information Center, 1974); and *Working Papers Nos. 5 and 6: Restitution and Compensation; Fines* (Ottawa: Information Center, 1974).

31. *Task Force Report: Corrections* (Washington: United States Government Printing Office, 1967).

32. "Editorial," *Minneapolis Star*, 1 August 1972.

attractiveness of restitution could be found in its appeal both to liberals (let's do something to treat offenders more humanely) and to conservatives (let's make them pay for their crime and do something about the victims). A participant in the First International Restitution Symposium suggested, however, that one ought to be skeptical of any phenomenon that appears acceptable to both the right and left wings of the political spectrum.[33] A healthy skepticism is necessary to avoid faddism by stimulating a sharper analysis of the role that restitution might play within the criminal justice system.

Stephen Schafer has served as one of the most consistent modern advocates of the use of restitution.[34] Consistent with his view, restitution is being advocated here as a form of punishment rather than an alternative to punishment. Schafer suggested that restitution provides a mechanism for integrating the multiple purposes for imposing sanctions.[35]

Four reasons to support assigning restitution a definite role in the criminal justice sanctioning system will be examined: (1) restitution should have a larger role in the criminal justice system because the practice provides an additional punishment that can be used either in addition to or instead of the sanctions currently available; (2) the restitution sanction has the potential for reconciling victims and offenders; (3) restitution will provide a vehicle for the inclusion of the victim into the criminal justice process; and (4) restitution procedures can be integrated into the current organizational structures without the need for additional programs or bureaucracies requiring substantial public expenditures.

RESTITUTION WILL INCREASE
SANCTIONING OPTIONS

The American criminal justice system is caught in a sanctioning dilemma. The system vacillates between failing to impose any meaningful sanction on large numbers of offenders (probation) and, alternatively, overpunishing a comparative few (imprisonment). The large majority of convictions lead to probation, which, in practice, is a fairly meaningless sanction.[36] Usually, offenders report infrequently

33. Geis, p. 145.

34. Stephen Schafer, "The Proper Role of a Victim-Compensation System," *Crime and Delinquency* 21 (January 1975):45–49; Schafer, *Compensation and Restitution to Victims of Crime*, 2nd ed. (Montclair, New Jersey: Smith, Patterson, Publishing Corp., 1970); and Schafer, *The Victim and His Criminal* (New York: Random House, 1968).

35. Schafer, *Compensation and Restitution to Victims of Crime*, pp. 117–29.

to an overworked, allegedly harrassed probation officer who dutifully notes the reporting date in a case record and offers little in the way of supervision, limitation on freedom, or other requirements that might be effectively enforced against the offender. At the other extreme, a comparatively small number of convicted persons are sent to prison, but those imprisoned tend to be sentenced for substantial lengths of time. Restitution is one option that would bridge the gap between these two extremes. When used as the sole penalty or added to already existing sanctions, it would in some cases increase the harshness of penalties, while in others restitution would avoid over-punishment, thus providing a just result.

A largely unexplored area is identifying which types of offenses (or offenders) might appropriately call for restitution as the only penalty imposed. Karl Menninger, in *The Crime of Punishment*,[37] suggested, for example, that those convicted for writing bad checks were offenders for whom the only necessary action would be an order of restitution that should also include a payment to the state to partially compensate for the cost of apprehending and processing the offender. The British Community Service Orders Program involves the sole use of Type IV restitution with adult offenders as an alternative to custodial sentences, fines, and probation. After being tested in six pilot areas, the program was found to be sufficiently successful that it has now been expanded throughout Great Britain, Wales, and Scotland and is being used for some offenders with substantial records of prior conviction.[38] In three of the pilot areas, the median number of previous convictions for persons entering the program during the pilot phase was three, and in the remaining three areas the median number was four. Forty-three percent of the persons entering the program had previously served one or more custodial sentences, while 6 percent had served five or more custodial sentences.[39] Jurisdictions within the United States appear reluctant to test the use of restitution as the sole sanction though a recently funded LEAA restitution project in Georgia moves in this direction. A population of property offenders will make restitution as they are able and will be free from further obligations to the criminal justice system once the restitution requirement is fulfilled.[40]

36. James Q. Wilson, *Thinking About Crime* (New York: Basic Books, 1975).

37. Karl Menninger, *The Crime of Punishment* (New York: Viking Press, 1968), pp. 67–68, 251.

38. Pease, et. al.

39. Ibid., p. 40.

40. Bill Read, "How Restitution Works in Georgia," *Judicature* 60 (February 1977): 323–31.

Restitution can, of course, be combined with other sanctions, as exemplified by its wide application as a condition of probation. It would require, however, a more systematic enforcement of a restitution requirement to make the probation sanction a more severe, and perhaps appropriate, punishment. The state of Georgia is currently managing four restitution shelters in which residents, most of whom are probationers, are required to reside while working in the community and completing court-ordered restitution.[41] Kathleen Smith has developed a proposal by which offenders would pay restitution plus a discretionary fine, both to be set by the sentencing judge. They would serve a custodial sentence but would receive the prevailing labor rates and upon completing payment of the restitution amount and the fine, they would be released from custody.[42]

Restitution might also be used to reduce the severity of penalties imposed against some offenders. The Minnesota Restitution Center was developed to see whether a group of property offenders could be managed in a residential community corrections center from which they would make restitution as an alternative to prison. While the persons coming into the center did serve significantly less time in prison than a control group (both groups having been randomly selected from a defined population), a preliminary follow up of the two groups indicates that the restitution group, by serving four months imprisonment, residence in a community corrections center, and then parole supervision, was subjected to a longer period of state supervision than the control group, which experienced imprisonment and parole.[43] Members of the restitution group were also somewhat more likely to have their parole revoked because of a technical violation.[44] Whether a shorter period of time in prison and a longer period of time on parole is less harsh than a longer period of time in prison and a shorter period of time on parole is an open question, yet nevertheless, for this group of property offenders, restitution made from a community corrections center was successfully substituted for imprisonment. Recently this sort of role for restitution was endorsed by Minnesota's leading legislative advocate of determinate

41. Read, "The Georgia Restitution Program," pp. 216–27.

42. Kathleen Smith, *A Cure for Crime: The Case for the Self-Determinate Prison* (London: Duckworth, 1965); Id., "Implementing Restitution Within A Penal Setting: The Case for the Self-Determinate Sentence," in *Restitution in Criminal Justice*, pp. 131–146.

43. Minnesota Department of Corrections, *Interim Evaluation Results: Minnesota Restitution Center* (St. Paul: Minnesota Department of Corrections, 1976), p. 50.

44. Ibid., p. 39.

sentencing.[45] The potentially positive impact of the determinate sentence on the prison population, coupled with the increasing need for new, costly prison construction, has led to the suggested use of restitution shelters for property offenders as an alternative to imprisonment in order to provide sufficient prison space for offenders who commit crimes of violence without the need to invest substantial capital in prison construction.

If restitution were employed more explicitly as a criminal justice sanction, to what extent would the practice be perceived as fair to both victim and offender? This question assumes that the sanctions that are imposed must generally be perceived as fair sanctions if the cohesiveness of the society and the respect of its institutions are to be maintained. If victims do not perceive the sanction as fair, they are likely to withdraw their support from such a system, and, conceivably, to seek other private alternatives. Ernest van den Haag[46] and John Stookey[47] point out that this may become an increasingly serious problem as a higher proportion of the population experiences criminal victimization. Similarly, if offenders do not perceive that they are being handled fairly, they may well be bitter at the perceived injustice, and this attitude may manifest itself as future criminal behavior.

Requiring an offender to take steps to redress the wrongs committed would seem, *prima facie*, to be a fair requirement, and though the evidence is not overwhelming, research results point in this direction. A metro poll conducted in 1972 indicated that 87 percent of a random sample of the residents of the metropolitan Minneapolis-St. Paul area favored ". . . letting the criminal work to repay the victim directly while living at a halfway house"; two-thirds of the sample would not object to having a halfway house located in their neighborhood.[48] Steve Chesney's research concerning restitution in the Minnesota probation services indicates that judges, probation officers, offenders, and victims all tended to perceive that restitution was a fair requirement.[49] Gandy, in research conducted in Colorado, found strong support and acceptance of restitution among populations of police officers, probation and parole officers, members of a

45. "Restitution for Victims, Inmate Separation Urged," *Minneapolis Star*, 14 January 1977.

46. Ernest van den Haag, *Punishing Criminals* (New York: Basic Books, 1975).

47. John Stookey, "The Victim's Perspective on American Criminal Justice," in Hudson and Galaway, eds., *Restitution in Criminal Justice*, pp. 19–25.

48. "Metro Poll," *Minneapolis Star*, 11 January 1972.

49. Chesney, pp. 160, 162, 165–66.

large women's community service club, and social work students, and he concluded that restitution may be viewed as an added form of punishment.[50] Marsella and Galaway, in research conducted in 1976 in Duluth, Minnesota, explored how juvenile offenders, their victims, their parents, police officers investigating the victimization, and the probation officer assigned to the youth perceived restitution when imposed on specific youths in relation to specific victimizations. While the sample was quite small, these subjects overwhelmingly perceived restitution as a fair requirement.[51]

While the evidence does suggest that restitution will be perceived as fair by offenders, victims, and the general population, there may be reluctance to accept restitution as the sole requirement. Chesney's study found that victims felt that punishments in addition to restitution should be imposed, and probation officers and judges concurred in this view.[52] Similar findings resulted from the Marsella and Galaway research.[53] Victims, probation officers, and police officers tended to recommend supervised probation when asked to select a single sanctioning choice. When offered the choice of combining possible sanctions, however, the overwhelming favorite of these respondents was supervised probation linked with restitution. Youths and parents tended to be somewhat more likely to select restitution as the sole sanction and tended to be somewhat more imaginative in their combinations. Parents, for example, showed considerable interest in combining restitution to the victim with the requirement that the young person participate in community service, apparently reflecting the parents' concern that activities be structured to absorb some of the young person's spare time.

In summary, restitution offers an additional sanction alternative for the criminal justice system. Restitution can be used alone; in combination with other sanctions such as probation, making probation a more meaningful punishment; and, under some circumstances, might be used as an alternative to such harsher sanctions as imprisonment. The evidence to date suggests that restitution would be perceived as a fair sanction by both offenders and victims, though there may be some reluctance to accepting restitution as the only

50. John Gandy, "Community Attitudes Toward Creative Restitution and Punishment" (Doctoral dissertation, University of Denver, 1975).

51. William Marsella and Burt Galaway, "An Exploratory Study of the Perceived Fairness of Restitution As A Sanction for Juvenile Offenders" (Unpublished research, University of Minnesota, School of Social Development, Duluth, Minnesota, 1976).

52. Chesney, pp. 160–63, 165.

53. Marsella and Galaway.

sanction. Considerable work is required to define those circumstances under which restitution might be used as a sole sanction and how it might be appropriately combined with other punishments.

RESTITUTION MAY LEAD TO
VICTIM-OFFENDER RECONCILIATION

Restitution, as a punishment, holds considerable potential for the reconciliation of offender and victim. In this sense, restitutional sanctions will contribute to a more cohesive, integrative society by reducing the sense of alienation that the offender may feel and by engaging the offender in socially acceptable behavior that is likely to result in offenders' receiving a higher degree of acceptance from victims and other members of the community.

Dockar-Drysdale has commented on the importance of restitution in assisting disturbed children and making amends for their wrongdoing.[54] Albert Eglash offers "creative restitution" as a rehabilitative procedure for offenders by providing them with an opportunity to enhance their self-esteem as they engage in restitutive acts.[55] August Aichhorn, in his psychoanalytic treatise on the treatment of delinquents, suggests rectification as a displinary technique,[56] while, more recently, R.M. Foxx and N.H. Azrin have developed restitutive procedures based on learning theory for the reduction of aggressive and disruptive behavior on the part of retarded and brain-damaged patients.[57] The use and importance of restitution in self-help organizations such as Alcoholics Anonymous is well known and has been suggested as a useful psychological treatment tool by O.W. Mowrer.[58]

Brickman has analyzed procedures for handling rules violators in sporting events for possible application to rules violators in criminal

54. B. Dachar-Drysdale, "Damage and Restitution," *British Journal of Delinquency* (July 1953):4—13.

55. Eglash, "Creative Restitution: Some Suggestions for Prison Rehabilitation Programs," pp. 20—22, 34; Id., "Creative Restitution: A Broader Meaning for an Old Term," pp. 619—22; Id., "Beyond Restitution—Creative Restitution," in *Restitution in Criminal Justice*, pp. 91—99.

56. August Aichhorn, *Wayward Youth* (New York: Viking Press, 1935).

57. R.M. Foxx and N.H. Azrin, "Restitution: A Method of Eliminating Aggressive-Disruptive Behavior of Retarded and Brain Damaged Patients," *Behavior Research and Therapy* 10 (1972):15—27.

58. O.H. Mowrer, *The Crisis in Psychiatry and Religion* (Princeton: Van Nostrand, 1961); Id., *The New Group Therapy* (Princeton: Van Nostrand, 1964); Id., "Loss and Recovery on Community," in *Innovations in Group Psychotherapy*, ed. George M. Gazada (Springfield, Illinois: Charles C. Thomas Publisher, 1968), pp. 130—48.

proceedings. He suggests the greater use of restitution as a means of placing greater emphasis upon fairness and minimizing the disruption of relationships between law violators and the rest of society.[59] Brickman's work draws from what is called "equity theory," a social-psychological orientation of particular relevance to understanding restitution's effects on criminal offenders.[60] Equity theorists postulate that a sense of social equity existing between offender and victim is upset as a result of wrongdoing. The resulting conditon of inequity creates distress on the part of both victim and offender. Two types of strategies are available to the offender for reduction of distress. The wrongdoer can reduce distress through the use of *justification strategies* including derogation of the victim, minimization of the victims suffering, and denial of responsibility for the act. The justification strategies are similar to the neutralization techniques that, as Sykes and Matza theorized, are used by delinquent youth to neutralize guilt and shame that follow the delinquent act and to protect the youth from condemnation of others. Techniques of neutralization include denial of responsibility, denial of injury, and denial of the victims.[61] On the other hand, wrongdoers may restore equity by *compensating the victim* for harm done, i.e., restitution, thereby reducing the offender's need to make use of justification strategies, and, hopefully, reducing the sense of psychological alienation between victim and offender.

Additionally, the "just world theory"[62] leads to a prediction that the unrestored victim may experience derogation from the rest of society. This theory is based on the proposition that people need to believe in a just world, so, consequently, when some apparent injustice is not restored, the theory postulates that this will lead to the conclusion that the victims were deserving of what they experienced.

59. Philip Brickman, "Crime and Punishment in Sports and Society," *Journal of Social Issues* (Forthcoming 1977).

60. Elaine Walster, Ellen Berscheid, and G. William Walster, "New Directions in Equity Research," *Journal of Personality and Social Psychology* 25 (1973): 151–76; Leonard Berkowitz and Elaine Walster, eds., *Equity Theory: Toward A General Theory of Social Interaction, Advances in Experimental Social Psychology*, vol. 9 (New York: Academic Press, 1976).

61. David Matza and Gresham Sykes, "Techniques of Neutralization: A Theory of Delinquency," *American Sociological Review* 22 (1957):664–69.

62. M.J. Lerner, "Observed Evaluation of a Victim: Justice, Guilt and Veridical Perception," *Journal of Personality and Social Psychology* 20 (1971):127–35; Id., "All the World Loathes a Loser," *Psychology Today* (June 1971):51–54, 66; M.J. Lerner and G. Matthews, "Reactions to Suffering of Others Under Conditions of Indirect Responsibility," *Journal of Personality and Social Psychology* 5 (1967):319–25; and M.J. Lerner and C.H. Simmons, "Observers' Reaction to the 'Innocent Victim': Compassion or Rejection," *Journal of Personality and Social Psychology* 4 (1966):203–10.

The phenomenon of blaming the victim has, in other contexts, of course, been noted by others[63] and may well apply to attitudes toward crime victims as well.

The idea that the restitution sanction may have these ameliorative results rests largely on clinical and laboratory evidence that still awaits field testing in the criminal justice system. The theoretical literature is sufficiently well developed, however, to suggest that restitution as a sanction may lead to increased integration of victim and offender, victim and community, and offender and community.

RESTITUTION WILL PROVIDE AN OPPORTUNITY FOR THE INVOLVEMENT OF THE VICTIM IN THE CRIMINAL JUSTICE PROCESS

The crime victim's role in the criminal justice system is largely limited to the decision of whether or not to put the process in motion by reporting the crime to the police. Apparently large numbers of victims (well over half in many types of crimes) choose not to involve themselves at all.[64] The role of those victims who do decide to precipitate the system is usually limited to the occasional giving of evidence. They also are manipulated by defense and/or prosecuting attorneys who attempt to get the victims in or out of the courtroom, as when such a maneuver is in the best interests of their case.[65]

Proposals have been suggested to give the victim a more meaningful role in the criminal process. Marvin Wolfgang has recommended a system in which information regarding disposition of a case would be routinely reported back to the victim, and LeRoy Schultz advocates the inclusion of information secured from the victim in the pre-sentencing investigation report prepared by probation officers.[66] More

63. William Ryan, *Blaming the Victim* (New York: Pantheon Books, 1971).

64. Philip Ennis, *Criminal Victimization in the United States: A Report of A National Survey* (Washington, D.C.: U.S. Government Printing Office, 1967); United States Department of Justice, *Criminal Victimization in the United States: A Comparison of 1973 and 1975 Findings* (Washington, D.C.: U.S. Government Printing Office, 1976).

65. For a discussion of the victim's role, see William McDonald, "Criminal Justice and the Victim: An Introduction," in *Criminal Justice and the Victim*, ed. William McDonald (Beverly Hills: Sage Publications, 1976), pp. 17–55; Id., "Notes on the Victim's Role in the Prosecutorial and Dispositional Stages of the American Criminal Justice Process" (Paper presented at the Second International Symposium on Victimology, Boston, Massachusetts, September 1976, forthcoming in *Victimology: An International Journal*).

66. LeRoy Schultz, "The Pre-Sentence Investigation and Victimology," *University of Missouri at Kansas City Law Review* 35 (Summer 1967): 247–60.

recently, a number of victim assistance programs have been endorsed by the National District Attorneys Association and some have been funded by the Law Enforcement Assistance Administration. The goals of these programs are, however, quite varied. Some are directed at providing remedial services to victims, and these seem to be much more acceptable than programs aimed at providing the victim with an opportunity for input into criminal justice decisionmaking. The few abortive attempts in the latter direction have been largely unsuccessful, though recently the city fathers of Jersey City advanced a proposal that would involve busing groups of elderly persons to be present in the courtroom when offenders who committed crimes against the elderly are sentenced.[67]

The closed nature in which many criminal justice decisions are made, the lack of opportunity for the victim to have any input, and the failure to provide the victim with even the most sketchy information about the outcome of the proceedings may inevitably lead to a sense of frustration and dissatisfaction with the criminal justice system. Public support for the criminal justice system would be enhanced and extreme proposals such as the Jersey City example less likely, if victims had more systematic opportunity for involvement in the criminal process. Restitution programming provides such a mechanism for victim involvement in the criminal justice process. Laura Nader notes that in small-scale societies the victim is a key part of the reparation process, and she suggests that if a society does nothing to compensate innocent crime victims, the social control system is unlikely to be respected.[68] Restitution provides a way for victims to be made aware of the actual disposition of the case and to express their points of view as to the proper disposition.

In determining the amount of payment, present restitution programming illustrates both an arbitration and negotiation approach to decisionmaking. Some programs have an arbitrator collect evidence as to losses and then arrive at a decision of the restitution amount, while other programs, such as the Minnesota Restitution Center[69] and the Restitution in Probation Experiment in Iowa,[70] involve the

67. "Program Would Enlist Elderly in War on Crime," *Minneapolis Star*, 24 January 1977.

68. Laura Nader and Elaine Combs-Schilling "Restitution in Cross-Cultural Perspective," in *Restitution in Criminal Justice*, pp. 27–44.

69. Hudson and Galaway, "Undoing the Wrong: The Minnesota Restitution Center"; Mowatt, "The Minnesota Restitution Center."

70. Bernard Vogelgesang, "The Iowa Restitution Probation Experiment," in *Restitution in Criminal Justice*, pp. 134–45.

offender and victim in a process of negotiation to arrive at an agreement as to the restitution amount.

Will involvement of victims in the dispositional phase of the criminal justice process create injustices? This seems unlikely for a number of reasons. First, victim *input* to the process is considerably different than victim *control* of the decisionmaking. An official of the criminal justice system would still be making the final decision and would be in a position to correct unreasonable victim demands. Second, the likelihood that victims may inflate claims and thereby victimize offenders is also controllable. Procedures, such as those used by insurance companies or other types of negotiation procedures, could be useful to correct overstated claims by victims. Also, differences between victim's and offender's assessments of damages may result as much from underestimation of the part of offenders as from overestimation on the part of victims. The Marsella and Galaway research indicated, for example, a substantial difference in the loss estimates by juvenile offenders compared with estimates of *their own parents*, as well as of probation officers, police, and victims. Adults tended to place the loss at a much higher figure than the young person.[71] This underestimating could result from lack of knowledge as to the costs of repairing damages, or the use of the justification strategy of minimizing damages. Third, there isn't any particular reason to believe that victims' desired sanctions will be any more severe than are those of present sentencing officials. By and large, victims involved with the Minnesota Restitution Center did not object to the offenders who had victimized them leaving prison to make restitution after having served only four months.

Restitution is one method for involving victims in the criminal justice system. This involvement seems most appropriate at the dispositional stage, which, of course, can occur in a negotiation between defense and prosecuting attorneys or on the basis of a judge's careful consideration of presentence reports and other information. Involvement of the victim can be structured in different ways—present projects offer examples of both arbitration and mediation in the area of assessing the amount of restitution. Increased victim involvement will likely create more support for the criminal justice system and there is little reason to believe that the victim's participation would work an injustice to the offender.

71. Marsella and Galaway.

RESTITUTION CAN BE INCORPORATED IN THE PRESENT ORGANIZATIONAL STRUCTURES FOR THE DELIVERY OF CRIMINAL JUSTICE SANCTIONS

The final argument in support of restitution is a practical one. Since restitution can be integrated into the present system of criminal justice sanctions, there is no need for additional organizations and bureaucracies. The survey of nineteen operational restitution programs revealed programs operating at all stages of the criminal justice process.[72] They include diversion programs operating out of the office of prosecutors, within the context of probation, in conjunction with residential community corrections projects, and coupled with work release. Restitution is a central component in the Adult Diversion Project administered by the Pima County Attorney's Office in Arizona.[73] Restitution has been incorporated into probation in the programs of the Georgia Restitution Shelters,[74] Pilot Alberta Restitution Center,[75] and the Victim Assistance Programs in St. Louis, Missouri,[76] and Rapid City, South Dakota.[77] Restitution is incorporated in institutional programs in Ottawa, Ontario,[78] and in Massachusetts.[79] The Minnesota Restitution Center is illustrative of the use of restitution in a community corrections center. Recently, however, the state of Minnesota Department of Corrections closed the center to utilize these resources to further develop restitution programming in probation and parole services to secure wider application of the restitution approach.

Restitution programming can also be found outside the criminal justice system. The Financial and Debt Counselling Services in Milwaukee works closely with court officials to monitor restitution

72. *Restitution in Criminal Justice*, pp. 3−4.

73. Edelhertz, pp. 57−59.

74. Read, "The Georgia Restitution Program"; Id., "How Restitution Works in Georgia."

75. Pilot Alberta Restitution Center, *Progress Report: September 1975−February 1976*.

76. Long, personal correspondence, October 10, 1974.

77. Edelhertz, pp. 55−57.

78. Paul Sonnichsen, personal correspondence from restitution coordinator, Ottawa Community Resource Centre, Ontario Ministry of Correctional Services, May 17, 1976.

79. Stephen Blesofsky, "Victim Restitution/Mutual Agreement Programming" (Paper presented at the Second International Symposium on Victimology, Boston, Massachusetts, September 1976).

payments as a condition of probation;[80] the Victim/Offender Reconciliation Project in Ontario is administered by a private organization but works closely with probation officials to bring about a reconciliation of victims and probationers through the use of restitution.[81] Restitution can also play an important role in dispute settlement procedures such as those currently being piloted by the American Arbitration Association[82] and the Night Prosecutor's Program in Columbus, Ohio.[83] These programs involve victims and offenders in an attempt to resolve criminal violations in a noncriminal procedure. While initially established to handle private criminal complaints, the Columbus program has expanded to other areas such as resolving bad check disputes. The Law Reform Commission of Canada has recommended securing negotiated settlements of most property crimes as an alternative to criminal justice processing with restitution playing an important role in these procedures.[84]

CONCLUSIONS

The use of restitution as a criminal justice sanction has been gaining considerable support. Restitution expands the sanctioning options available to courts, deters development of justification strategies on the part of the offender, and integrates the victim into the criminal justice process. Restitution programming can be incorporated into present organizational structures for the delivery of sanctioning programs. In addition, restitution can be incorporated into pretrial diversion projects and might also play a central role in programs to involve victims and offenders in negotiating settlements for criminal matters. The continued, cautious development of restitution programming with an eye to maximizing its integrative potentials is one of the most hopeful and potentially constructive approaches to criminal justice reform.

80. William Allen, personal correspondence from executive director, Financial and Debt Counselling Services, Inc., Milwaukee, Wisconsin, July 1975.

81. Mennonite Central Committee, "A Proposal for Victim-Offender Reconciliation," and "Victim/Offender Reconciliation Project—Progress Report."

82. Janet Kole, "Arbitration as an Alternative to the Criminal Warrant," *Judicature* (February 1973):295–97; Philip Eklund, "The Problem of Over-criminalizing Human Conflict: A Civil Alternative" (Paper presented to the American Society of Criminology, Annual Meeting, Chicago, November 1974).

83. United States Department of Justice, *An Exemplary Project: Citizen Dispute Settlement* (Washington, D.C.:U.S. Government Printing Office, 1974); John Palmer, "Prearrest Diversion: Victim Confrontation," *Federal Probation* 38 (1974):12–18.

84. Law Reform Commission of Canada, *Working Paper No. 3: The Principles of Sentencing and Dispositions*, (Ottawa: Information Canada, 1974).

✳ *Chapter 16*

Restitution: A New Paradigm of Criminal Justice*

Randy E. Barnett

This paper will analyze the breakdown of our system of criminal justice in terms of what Thomas Kuhn would describe as a crisis of an old paradigm—punishment. I propose that this crisis could be solved by the adoption of a new paradigm of criminal justice—restitution. The approach will be mainly theoretical, though at various points in the discussion the practical implications of the rival paradigms will also be considered. A fundamental contention will be that many, if not most, of our system's ills stem from errors in the underlying paradigm. Any attempt to correct these symptomatic debilities without a reexamination of the theoretical underpinnings is doomed to frustration and failure. Kuhn's theories deal with the problems of science. What made his proposal so startling was its attempt to analogize scientific development to social and political development. Here, I will simply reverse the process by applying Kuhn's framework of scientific change to social, or in this case, legal development.[1]

*This is an expanded version of an article that originally appeared in *Ethics* 87 (1977):279–301. The paper was made possible by a research fellowship from the Law and Liberty Project of the Institute for Humane Studies, Menlo Park, California. Also, I wish to extend my appreciation to John V. Cody, Davis E. Keeler, Murray N. Rothbard, and Lloyd L. Weinreb for their invaluable criticism and comments. I am greatly in their debt and hope to be able at some future time to make suitable restitution.

1. What immediately follows is a brief outline of Thomas Kuhn's theory. Those interested in the *defense* of that theory should refer to his book, *The Structure of Scientific Revolutions*, 2nd ed., enl. (Chicago: University of Chicago Press, 1970). A paradigm is an achievement in a particular discipline that defines the legitimate problems and methods of research within that discipline.

In the criminal justice system we are witnessing the death throes of an old and cumbersome paradigm, one that has dominated Western thought for more than 900 years. While this chapter presents what is hoped to be a viable, though radical alternative, much would be accomplished by simply prompting the reader to reexamine the assumptions underlying the present system. Only if we are willing to look at our old problems in a new light do we stand a chance of solving them. This is our only hope, and our greatest challenge.

THE ROOTS OF WESTERN CRIMINAL JUSTICE

For nearly a millenium, the focus of Western criminal justice has been on one thing—the punishment of the criminal. This is not to say that the rationale for punishment has always been the same—far from it. Reasons and justifications have been many and varied. Whatever the end may be, however, punishment remains the means. It was not always thus.

While it is true that punishment for offensive behavior is as old as man himself, it only came to dominate Western European society, as we shall see, in the eleventh and twelfth centuries. What is most interesting is the nature of the system that preceded the rise of punishment. An examination of the "primitive" Germanic (Frankish and Anglo-Saxon) and Irish tribal folk law yields surprising conclusions.[2]

This achievement is sufficiently unprecedented to attract new adherents away from rival approaches while providing many unsolved questions for these new practitioners to solve. As the paradigm develops and matures, it reveals occasional inabilities to solve new problems and explain new data. As attempts are made to make the facts fit the paradigm, the theoretical apparatus gradually becomes bulky and awkward, like Ptolemaic astronomy. Dissatisfaction with the paradigm begins to grow. Why not simply discard the paradigm and find another that better fits the facts? Unfortunately, this is an arduous process. All the great authorities and teachers were raised with the current paradigm and see the world through it. All the texts and institutions are committed to it. Radical alternatives hold promise but are so untested as to make wary all but the bold. The establishment is loath to abandon its broad and intricate theory in favor of a new and largely unknown hypothesis. Gradually, however, as the authorities die off and the problems with the old paradigm increase, the "young turks" get a better hearing in both the journals and the classroom. In a remarkably rapid fashion, the old paradigm is discarded for the new. Anyone who still clings to it is now considered to be antiquated or eccentric and is simply read out of the profession. All research centers on the application of the new paradigm. Kuhn characterizes this overthrow of one paradigm by another as a revolution.

2. What follows is a brief summary of an extremely rich and interesting historical period. Those interested in a more expanded outline should see Stephen Schafer, *Compensation and Restitution to Victims of Crime*, 2nd ed. cnl. (Montclair, New Jersey: Patterson Smith Publishing Corp., 1970); Richard E. Laster, "Criminal Restitution: A Survey of its Past History and an Analysis of its

In the absence of any developed central political authority, monetary sanctions were substituted for unrestricted violence, the "blood feud," to resolve interclan conflicts.[3] While every tribe had its own law, the content of these laws was markedly similar from tribe to tribe:[4]

> The first written collection of tribal laws, such as the Salic Law of the Franks (about 500 A.D.) and the Law of Ethelbert of Kent (about 600 A.D.) were concerned chiefly with controlling the blood-feud by establishing monetary rates of payment. These could serve as a basis of negotiations between the household of a victim and that of his assailant, or as the basis of adjudication by the tribal assembly. . . . There was an extremely elaborate system of accounting: under the Laws of Ethelbert, for example, the four front teeth were worth 6 shillings each, the teeth next to them four, the others one; thumbs, thumbnails, forefingers, middle fingers, ringfingers, little fingers and their respective fingernails were all distinguished and a separate *bot* (price) was set for each. . . .[5]

The Germanic system of composition[6] had its analogue in medieval Ireland as well: "The honor-price (*dire* or *enclann*) was the payment due to any free man if his honor or rights were injured or impugned in any fashion by another person."[7] Penalties were fixed for specific crimes according to the seriousness of the offense and the social rank of the victim.[8]

Even in Iceland the normal penalty for murder was the giving of: ". . . blood money varying in amount according to the social status of the deceased. . . . Murder was a purely civil wrong, a matter for

Present Usefulness," *University of Richmond Law Review* 5 (1970):71–80; L.T. Hobhouse, *Morals in Evolution* (London: Chapman & Hall, 1951); Bruce Jacobs, "The Concept of Restitution: An Historical Overview," in *Restitution in Criminal Justice*, eds. Joe Hudson and Burt Galaway (Lexington, Massachusetts: Lexington Books, 1977), pp. 45–62; those interested in a cross-cultural historical analysis should see Laura Nader and Elaine Combs-Schilling, "Restitution in Cross-Cultural Perspective," in *Restitution in Criminal Justice*, pp. 27–44.

    3. Harold Berman, "The Western Legal Tradition" (Unpublished, Harvard Law School, 1975), p. 99; Schafer, p. 5.

    4. Berman, p. 99.

    5. Ibid.; See also Schafer, p. 6; Frederick Pollock and Frederic William Maitland, *The History of English Law* (Cambridge: Cambridge University Press, 1898), 2:460.

    6. "Among the Franks, Goths, Burgundians, and other barbarous peoples, this was the name given to a sum of money paid, as satisfaction for a wrong or personal injury, to the person harmed." *Black's Law Dictionary*, 4th ed., rev. (St. Paul, Minnesota: West Publishing Co., 1968), p. 358.

    7. Joseph R. Peden, "Property Rights in Medieval Ireland: Celtic Law versus Church and State," *Journal of Libertarian Studies* 1 (1977):86.

    8. Ibid.

the individuals or families affected to avenge or compromise as they thought fit. In fact, they always or almost always compromised by the giving and acceptance of an agreed sum of money."[9]

A.S. Diamond's research on the sanctions imposed for homicide confirms the fact that fines were the accepted sanction throughout the Western World. He summarizes his findings as follows. Of the fifty to one hundred scattered tribal communities "as to which the information available is of undoubted reliability," 73 percent called for a pecuniary sanction versus 14 percent that demanded death— better than five to one. The remaining 13 percent called for a certain number of persons to be handed over to the family of the victim as a sanction. This too is actually a fine, though not a monetary one. One hundred percent of the Early and Early Middle codes, as Diamond labels them, beginning with the Salic code mentioned above (500– 600 A.D.) and lasting through the Anglo-Saxon laws (900–1100 A.D.), called for pecuniary sanctions for homicide. It was not until the Late Middle and Late codes (including England, 1150 A.D. and onwards) that death was established as the exclusive (100 percent) sanction for intentional homicide.[10]

To understand why this sudden and rapid shift occurred, it is necessary to take note of certain historical events: "Two closely interconnected factors . . . made for conscious overt change: one was the influence of Christianity on legal concepts; the other was the development of the kingship as a trans-local and trans-tribal institution, uniting large areas containing various peoples."[11] The Norman conquest of Europe marked the beginning of a radical change in societal structure. The anarchical, communitarian tribal society was soon to be supplanted by the hierarchical feudal system and the rise of the nation state.

With the conquest of England, ownership of all land reverted to the king, William the Conqueror, who then granted large tracts to his favorites and to the church. These grants were then "sub-infeuded" to men of less influence. Legal and political authority was vested in the king as chief lord. The king was no longer a tribal chief (*dux*), but truly a king (*rex*).[12]

The rise of Christianity begat a rise in power and influence of ecclesiastical law: "Jurists all over Europe . . .began to organize and synthesize the tribal, local and feudal customs of the various Euro-

9. A.S. Diamond, *Primitive Law* (London: Longmans, Green and Co., 1935), p. 148.

10. Ibid., p. 316, n. 5.

11. Berman, p. 107.

12. Ibid., p. 108.

pean peoples . . . and various earlier collections and interpretations of those ecclesiastical writings, decisions and decrees."[13] This was the canon law. With this system as their model and rival, the kings created their own new secular legal system.[14]

Prior to this, the nascent state concerned itself only with its own affairs and disputes: "It did not include among its functions the repression of wrongs between individual and individual, between family and family, between clan and clan."[15] As the king came to be considered a ruler with divine authority, this policy of noninterference in private disputes rapidly changed. The crown began to claim a share of the composition payment as:

> . . . a commission for its trouble in bringing about a reconciliation between the parties, or, perhaps as the price payable to the malefactor either for the opportunity which the community secures for him of redeeming his wrong by a money payment, or for the protection which it affords him after he has satisfied the award, against further retaliation on the part of the man whom he has injured.[16]

As the kings monopolized the institutions of dispute settlement, their share of the payments increased as well, eventually to absorb the whole amount.[17] The issues of injury and damages to the victim became divorced from the criminal law and became a separate field in civil law.[18] The criminal law now concerned itself entirely with offenses against the king—so-called "breaches of the king's peace." As Oppenheimer puts it:

> Clothed with divine honors the king enters the area of primitive justice. Disobedience to his command is sacrilege. At first but one god among many, he becomes before long the only one that has to be reckoned with in the sphere of criminal law. The law now flows exclusively from his will, and every act of transgression is an act of revolt against his omnipotence . . . the monarch thus becomes the main channel through which notions primarily belonging to private law find their way into criminal jurisprudence.[19]

13. Ibid., p. 114.
14. Ibid.
15. Heinrich Oppenheimer, *The Rationale of Punishment* (London: University of London Press, 1913), p. 162.
16. Ibid., pp. 162–63.
17. Stephen Schafer, "Restitution to Victims of Crime—An Old Correctional Aim Modernized," *Minnesota Law Review* 50 (1965): 246, n. 6.
18. Schafer, *Compensation and Restitution*, p. 7.
19. Oppenheimer, pp. 173–74.

Once this new attitude was established in England, it was not long before the English kings and church authorities sought to extend their influence to other parts of Europe. Thus, the Anglo-Norman invasion and partial conquest of Ireland in the late twelfth century brought with it a concerted effort to do away with the Irish legal system.[20] It took the English five centuries to finally accomplish this goal.[21]

The system of composition throughout Europe only surrendered after a struggle.[22] Far from being abandoned by the people voluntarily, it was deliberately and forcibly co-opted by the crown and then discarded. The image of state criminal punishment arising from a bloody Hobbesian jungle is pure myth. Monetary payments had replaced violence as the means of dispute settlement and functioned well for over 600 years. It was only through the violent conquest of England, Ireland, and other parts of Europe that state criminal punishment was reluctantly accepted.

THE CRISIS IN THE PARADIGM OF PUNISHMENT

> Political revolutions are inaugurated by a growing sense, often restricted to a segment of the political community, that existing institutions have ceased adequately to meet the problems posed by an environment they have in part created. . . . In both political and scientific development the sense of malfunction that can lead to crisis is prerequisite to revolution.[23]

Kuhn's description of the preconditions for scientific and political revolutions could accurately describe the current state of the criminal law. However, simply to recognize the existence of a crisis is not enough. We must look for its causes. The Kuhnian methodology suggests that we critically examine the paradigm of punishment itself.

The problems that the paradigm of punishment is supposed to solve are many and varied. A whole literature on the philosophy of punishment has arisen in an effort to justify or reject the institution of punishment. For our purposes the following definition from the *Encyclopedia of Philosophy* should suffice: "Characteristically punishment is unpleasant. It is inflicted on an offender because of an offense he has committed; it is deliberately imposed, not just the natural consequence of a person's action (like a hangover), and the

20. Peden, p. 88.
21. Ibid., p. 94.
22. Schafer, *Compensation and Restitution*, p. 9.
23. Kuhn, p. 92.

unpleasantness is *essential* to it, not an accompaniment to some other treatment (like the pain of the dentist's drill)."[24]

Two types of arguments are commonly made in defense of punishment. The first is that punishment is an appropriate means to some justifiable end such as, for example, deterrence of crime. The second type of argument is that punishment is justified as an end in itself. On this view, whatever ill effects it might engender, punishment for its own sake is good.

The first type of argument might be called the *political* justification of punishment, for the end that justifies its use is one that a political order is presumably dedicated to serve: the maintenance of peaceful interactions between individuals and groups in a society. There are at least three ways that deliberate infliction of harm on an offender is said to be politically justified.

1. One motive for punishment, especially capital punishment and imprisonment, is the "intention to deprive offenders of the power of doing future mischief."[25] Although it is true that an offender cannot continue to harm society while incarcerated, a strategy of punishment based on disablement has several drawbacks.

Imprisonment is enormously expensive. This means that a double burden is placed on the innocent, who must suffer the crime and, in addition, pay through taxation for the support of the offender and of his family if they are forced onto welfare. Also, any benefit of imprisonment is temporary; eventually, most offenders will be released. If their outlook has not improved—and especially if it has worsened—the benefits of incarceration are obviously limited. Finally, when disablement is permanent, as with capital punishment or psychosurgery, it is this very permanence, in light of the possibility of error, which is frightening. For these reasons, "where disablement enters as an element into penal theories, it occupies, as a rule, a subordinate place and is looked upon as an object subsidiary to some other end which is regarded as punishment. . . ."[26]

2. Rehabilitation of a criminal means a change in his mental *habitus* so that he will not offend again. It is unclear whether the so-called treatment model that views criminals as a doctor would view a patient is truly a "retributive" concept. Certainly it does not con-

---

24. Stanley I. Benn, "Punishment," in *The Encyclopedia of Philosophy*, ed. Paul Edwards (New York: Macmillan Publishing Co., 1967), 7:29 (emphasis added).

25. Oppenheimer, p. 255.

26. Ibid.

form to the above definition characterizing punishment as deliberately and essentially unpleasant. It is an open question whether any end justifies the intentional, forceful manipulation of an individual's thought processes by anyone, much less the state. To say that an otherwise just system has incidentally rehabilitative effects that may be desirable is one thing, but it is quite another to argue that these effects themselves justify the system. The horrors to which such reasoning can lead are obvious from abundant examples in history and contemporary society.[27]

Rehabilitation as a reaction against the punishment paradigm will be considered below, but one aspect is particularly relevant to punishment as defined here. On this view, the visiting of unpleasantness itself will cause the offender to see the error of his ways; by having "justice" done him, the criminal will come to appreciate his error and will change his moral outlook. This end, best labeled "reformation," is speculative at best and counterfactual at worst. On the contrary, "it has been observed that, as a rule . . . ruthless punishments, far from mollifying men's ways, corrupt them and stir them to violence."[28]

3. The final justification to be treated here—deterrence—actually has two aspects. The first is the deterrent effect that past demonstrations of punishment have on the future conduct of others; the second is the effect that threats of future punishment have on the conduct of others. The distinction assumes importance when some advocates argue that future threats lose their deterrent effect when there is a lack of past demonstrations. Past punishment, then, serves as an educational tool. It is a substitute for or reinforcement of threats of future punishment.

As with the goals mentioned above, the empirical question of whether punishment has this effect is a disputed one.[29] I shall not attempt to resolve this question here, but will assume *arguendo* that punishment even as presently administered has some deterrent effect. It is the moral question that is disturbing. Can an argument from deterrence alone "justify" in any sense the infliction of pain on a

27. See Thomas Szasz, *Law, Liberty, and Punishment* (New York: Macmillan Publishing Co., 1963).

28. Giorgio del Vecchio, "The Struggle against Crime," in *The Philosophy of Punishment*, ed. H.B. Acton (London: Macmillan Co., 1969), p. 199.

29. See, e.g., Samuel Yochelson and Stanton E. Samenow, *The Criminal Personality. Vol. I: A Profile for Change* (New York: Jason Aronson, Inc., 1976), pp. 411–16.

criminal? It is particularly disquieting that the actual levying of punishment is done not for the criminal himself, but for the educational impact it will have on the community. The criminal act becomes the occasion of, but not the reason for, the punishment. In this way, the actual crime becomes little more than an excuse for punishing.

Surely this distorts the proper functioning of the judicial process. For if deterrence is the end, it is unimportant whether the individual actually committed the crime. Since the public's perception of guilt is the prerequisite of the deterrent effect, all that is required for deterrence is that the individual is "proved" to have committed the crime. The actual occurrence would have no relevance except insofar as a truly guilty person is easier to prove guilty. The judicial process becomes, not a truth-seeking device, but solely a means to legitimate the use of force. To treat criminals as means to the ends of others in this way raises serious moral problems. This is not to argue that men may never use others as means, but rather to question the use of force against the individual because of the effect such use will have on others. It was this that concerned del Vecchio when he stated that "the human person always bears in himself something sacred, and it is therefore not permissible to treat him merely as a means towards an end outside of himself."[30]

Finally, deterrence as the ultimate justification of punishment cannot rationally limit its use. It "provides *no* guidance until we're told *how much* commission of it is to be deterred."[31] Since there are always some who commit crimes, one can always argue for more punishment. Robert Nozick points out that there must be criteria by which one decides how much deterrence may be inflicted.[32] One is forced therefore to employ "higher" principles to evaluate the legitimacy of punishment.

It is not my thesis that deterrence, reformation, and disablement are undesirable goals. On the contrary, any criminal justice system should be critically examined to see if it is having these and other beneficial effects. The view advanced here is simply that these utilitarian benefits must be incidental to a just system; they cannot, alone or in combination, justify a criminal justice system. Something more is needed. There is another more antiquated strain of punishment theory that seeks to address this problem. The *moral* justifications of punishment view punishment as an end in itself. This

30. Del Vecchio, p. 199.

31. Robert Nozick, *Anarchy, State, and Utopia* (New York: Basic Books, 1974), p. 61 (emphasis in original).

32. Ibid., pp. 59–63.

approach has taken many forms.[33] On this view, whatever ill or beneficial results it might have, punishment of lawbreakers is good for its own sake. This proposition can be analyzed on several levels.

The most basic question is the truth of the claim itself. Some have argued that "the alleged absolute justice of repaying evil with evil (maintained by Kant and many other writers) is really an empty sophism. If we go back to the Christian moralists, we find that an evil is to be put right only by doing good."[34] This question is beyond the scope of this treatment. The subject has been extensively dealt with by those more knowledgeable than I.[35] The more relevant question is what such a view of punishment as a good can be said to imply for a system of criminal justice. Even assuming that it would be good if, in the nature of things, the wicked got their "come-uppance," what behavior does this moral fact justify? Does it justify the victim authoring the punishment of his offender? Does it justify the same action by the victim's family, his friends, his neighbors, the state? If so, what punishment should be imposed and who should decide?

It might be argued that the natural punishment for the violation of natural rights is the deserved hatred and scorn of the community, the resultant ostracism, and the existential hell of *being* an evil person. The question then is not whether we have the right to inflict some "harm" or unpleasantness on a morally contemptible person—surely, we do; the question is not whether such a punishment is "good"— arguably, it is. The issue is whether the "virtue of some punishment" justifies the *forceful* imposition of unpleasantness on a *rights violator* as distinguished from the morally imperfect. Any *moral* theory of punishment must recognize and deal with this distinction. Finally, it must be established that the state is the legitimate author of punishment, a proposition that further assumes the moral and legal legitimacy of the state. To raise these issues is not to resolve them, but it would seem that the burden of proof is on those seeking to justify the use of force against the individual. Suffice it to say that I am skeptical of finding any theory that justifies the deliberate, forceful imposition of punishment within or without a system of criminal justice.

The final consideration in dealing with punishment as an end in itself is the possibility that the current crisis in the criminal justice system is in fact a crisis of the paradigm of punishment. While this,

33. For a concise summary, see Oppenheimer, p. 31.

34. Del Vecchio, p. 198.

35. See, e.g., Walter Kaufmann, *Without Guilt and Justice* (New York: Peter H. Wyden, Inc., 1973), esp. ch. 2.

if true, does not resolve the philosophical issues, it does cast doubt on the punishment paradigm's vitality as the motive force behind a system of criminal justice. Many advocates of punishment argue that its apparent practical failings exist because we are not punishing enough. All that is needed, they say, is a crackdown on criminals and those victims and witnesses who shun participation in the criminal justice system; the only problem with the paradigm of punishment is that we are not following it.[36] This response fails to consider *why* the system doggedly refuses to punish to the degree required to yield beneficial results and instead punishes in such a way as to yield harmful results. The answer may be that the paradigm of punishment is in eclipse, that the public lacks the requisite will to apply it in anything but the prevailing way.

Punishment, particularly state punishment, is the descendant of the tradition that imparts religious and moral authority to the sovereign and, through him, the community. Such an authority is increasingly less credible in a secular world such as ours. Today there is an increasing desire to allow each individual to govern his own life as he sees fit provided he does not violate the rights of others. This desire is exemplified by current attitudes toward drug use, abortion, and pornography. Few argue that these things are good. It is only said that where there is no victim the state or community has no business meddling in the peaceful behavior of its citizens, however morally suspect it may be.[37]

Furthermore, if the paradigm of punishment is in a "crisis period," it is as much because of its practical drawbacks as the uncertainty of its moral status. The infliction of suffering on a criminal tends to cause a general feeling of sympathy for him. There is no rational connection between a term of imprisonment and the harm caused the victim. Since the prison term is supposed to be unpleasant, at least a part of the public comes to see the criminal as a victim, and the lack of rationality also causes the offender to feel victimized. This reaction is magnified by the knowledge that most crimes go unpunished and that even if the offender is caught, the judicial process is long, arduous, and far removed from the criminal act. While this is obvious to most, it is perhaps less obvious that the punishment paradigm is largely at fault. The slow, ponderous nature of our system of justice

36. See, e.g., "Crime: A Case for More Punishment," *Business Week*, 15 September 1975, pp. 92–97.

37. This problem is examined, though not ultimately resolved, by Edwin M. Schur in *Crimes Without Victims—Deviant Behavior and Public Policy, Abortion, Homosexuality, and Drug Addiction* (Englewood Cliffs, New Jersey: Prentice-Hall, Inc., 1965).

is largely due to a fear of an unjust infliction of punishment on the innocent (or even the guilty). The more awful the sanction, the more elaborate need be the safeguards. The more the system is perceived as arbitrary and unfair, the more incentive there is for defendants and their counsel to thwart the truth-finding process. Acquittal becomes desirable at all costs. As the punitive aspect of a sanction is diminished, so too would be the perceived need for procedural protections.

A system of punishment, furthermore, offers no incentive for the victim to involve himself in the criminal justice process other than to satisfy his feelings of duty or revenge. The victim stands to gain little if at all by the conviction and punishment of the person who caused his loss. This is true even of those systems discussed below that dispense state compensation based on the victim's need. The system of justice itself imposes uncompensated costs by requiring a further loss of time and money by the victim and witnesses and by increasing the perceived risk of retaliation.

Finally, punishment that seeks to change an offender's moral outlook, or at least to scare him, can do nothing to provide him with the skills needed to survive in the outside world. In prison, he learns the advanced state of the criminal arts and vows not to repeat the mistake that led to his capture. The convict emerges better trained and highly motivated to continue a criminal career.

The crisis of the paradigm of punishment has at its roots the collapse of its twin pillars of support: its moral legitimacy and its practical efficacy. As Kaufmann concludes, "the faith in retributive justice is all but dead."[38]

ATTEMPTS TO SALVAGE THE PARADIGM OF PUNISHMENT

"All crises begin with the blurring of a paradigm and the consequent loosening of the rules for normal research."[39] And yet until a new paradigm is presented, authorities will cling to the old one, either ignoring the problem or salvaging the paradigm with ad hoc explanations and solutions. Why are paradigms never rejected outright? Why must there always be a new paradigm before the old one is abandoned? Kuhn does not explicitly discuss this, but R.A. Childs hypothesizes "that, as such, paradigms may serve the function of increasing man's sense of control over some aspect of reality, or

38. Kaufmann, p. 46.
39. Kuhn, p. 82.

some aspect of his own life. If this is so, then we would expect that a straightforward abandonment of a paradigm would threaten that sense of control."[40]

This psychological need for an explanation may in turn explain the many efforts to shore up the paradigm of punishment. The three attempts to be examined next have at their roots a perception of its fundamental errors, and at the same time they highlight three goals of any new paradigm of criminal justice.

Proportionate Punishment

The king abandoned the composition system for the system of punishment because punishment struck terror in the hearts of the people, and this served to inspire awe for the power of the king and state. But there was no rational connection between the seriousness of the crime and the gravity of the punishment and, therefore, no limit to the severity of punishment. Hideous tortures came to be employed: "But some of the men of the Enlightenment sought to counter the inhumanity of their Christian predecessors with appeals to reason. They thought that retributive justice had a mathematical quality and that murder called for capital punishment in much the same way in which two plus two equals four."[41]

The appeal to proportionality was one of the early attempts to come to grips with deficiencies in the paradigm of punishment. It was doomed to failure, for there is no objective standard by which punishments can be proportioned to fit the crime. Punishment is incommensurate with crime. This solution is purely ad hoc and intuitive. We shall, however, find the *goal* of proportionate sentencing useful in the formation of a new paradigm.

Rehabilitation

It was noted earlier that the infliction of punishment tends to focus attention on the plight of the criminal. Possibly for this reason, the next humanitarian trend was to explore the proper treatment of criminals. Punishment failed to reform the criminal, and this led observers to inquire how the situation might be improved. Some felt that the sole end of the penal system was rehabilitation, so attention was turned to modifying the criminal's behavior (an obviously manipulative end). Emphasis was placed on education, job training, and discipline.

Unfortunately, the paradigm of punishment and the political reali-

40. R.A. Childs, "Liberty and the Paradigm of Statism," in *The Libertarian Alternative*, ed. Tibor Machan (Chicago: Nelson-Hall Co., 1974), p. 505.

41. Kaufmann, p. 45.

ties of penal administration have all but won out. There is simply no incentive for prison authorities to educate and train. Their job is essentially political. They are judged by their ability to keep the prisoners within the walls and to keep incidents of violence within the prison to a minimum; as a result, discipline is the main concern. Furthermore, since he is sentenced to a fixed number of years (less time off for good behavior—so-called good time), there is no institutional incentive for the prisoner to improve himself apart from sheer boredom. Productive labor in prison is virtually nonexistent, with only obsolete equipment, if any, available. Except perhaps for license plates and other state needs, the prisoners produce nothing of value; the prisons make no profit and the workers are paid, if at all, far below market wages. They are unable to support themselves or their families. The state, meaning the innocent taxpayer, supports the prisoner, and frequently the families as well via welfare.

Rehabilitation has been a long-time goal of the penal system, but the political nature of government-run prisons and the dominance of the paradigm of punishment has inevitably prevented its achievement. Prisons remain detention centers, all too temporarily preventing crime by physically confining the criminals.

Victim Compensation

It is natural that the brutalities resulting from the paradigm of punishment would get first attention from humanitarians and that the persons subjected to those practices would be next. Until recently, the victim of crime was the forgotten party. Within the last few years a whole new field has opened up, called victimology.[42] With it has come a variety of proposals, justifications, and statutes.[43]

Certain features are common to virtually every compensation proposal: (1) compensation for crimes would be dispensed by the state from tax revenue; (2) compensation is "a matter of grace" rather than an assumption by the state of legal responsibility for the criminal loss suffered by the victim; (3) most proposals allow for aid only on a "need" or "hardship" basis; (4) most are limited to some sort of crime of violence or the threat of force or violence; and (5) none questions the paradigm of punishment.

42. For a brief definition of "victimology," see Emilo C. Viano, "Victimology: The Study of the Victim," *Victimology* 1 (1976): 1–7. For an extensive collection of papers on various aspects of victimology, see Emilo C. Viano, ed., *Victims and Society* (Washington, D.C.: Visage Press, 1976).

43. For a discussion and list of symposiums, journal articles, and statutes concerning victim compensation, see Steven Schafer, *Compensation and Restitution*, pp. 139–57, and appendix; see also Joe Hudson and Burt Galaway, eds., *Considering the Victim: Readings in Restitution and Victim Compensation* (Springfield, Illinois: Charles C. Thomas, 1975), esp. pp. 361–436.

The goal of these proposals and statutes is laudable. The victim *is* the forgotten man of crime. But the means proposed is the same tired formula: welfare to those in "need." In short, the innocent tax-payer repays the innocent victim (if the victim can prove he "needs" help), while the guilty offender is subjected to the sanction of pun-ishment with all its failings. Like proportionate punishment and re-habilitation, the goal of victim compensation is a recognition of very real problems in our criminal justice system, and at the same time it ignores the source of these problems: our conception of crime as an offense against the state whose proper sanction is punishment. Until a viable, new paradigm is presented, ad hoc solutions like the ones discussed here are all that can be hoped for. And it is a vain hope indeed, for they attack the symptoms while neglecting the causes of the problem. What is needed is a new paradigm.

OUTLINE OF A NEW PARADIGM

The idea of restitution is actually quite simple. It views crime as an offense by one individual against the rights of another. The victim has suffered a loss. Justice consists of the culpable offender making good the loss he has caused. It calls for a complete refocusing of our image of crime. Kuhn would call it a "shift of world-view." Where we once saw an offense against society, we now see an offense against an individual victim. In a way, it is a common sense view of crime. The armed robber did not rob society; he robbed the victim. His debt, therefore, is not to society; it is to the victim. There are really two types of restitution proposals: a system of "punitive" restitution and a "pure" restitutional system.

Punitive Restitution
"Since rehabilitation was admitted to the aims of penal law two centuries ago, the number of penological aims has remained virtually constant. Restitution is waiting to come in."[44] Given this view, res-titution should merely be added to the paradigm of punishment. Stephen Schafer outlines the proposal: "[Punitive] restitution, like punishment, must always be the subject of judicial consideration. Without exception it must be carried out by personal performance by the wrong-doer, and should even then be equally burdensome and just for all criminals, irrespective of their means, whether they be millionaires or labourers."[45]

44. Gerhard O.W. Mueller, "Compensation for Victims of Crime: Thought Before Action," *Minnesota Law Review* 50 (1965):221.
45. Schafer, *Compensation and Restitution*, p. 127.

There are many ways by which such a goal might be reached. The offender might be forced to compensate the victim by his own work, either in prison or out. If it came out of his pocket or from the sale of his property this would compensate the victim, but it would not be sufficiently unpleasant for the offender. Another proposal would be that the fines be proportionate to the earning power of the criminal. Thus, "A poor man would pay in days of work, a rich man by an equal numbers of days' income or salary."[46] Herbert Spencer made a proposal along similar lines in his excellent "Prison-Ethics," which is well worth examining.[47] Murray N. Rothbard and others have proposed a system of "double payments" in cases of criminal behavior.[48] While closer to pure restitution than other proposals, the "double damages" concept preserves a punitive aspect.

Punitive restitution is an attempt to gain the benefits of pure restitution, which will be considered shortly, while retaining the perceived advantages of the paradigm of punishment. Thus, the prisoner is still "sentenced" to some unpleasantness—prison labor or loss of X number of days income. That the intention is to preserve the "hurt" is indicated by the hesitation to accept an out-of-pocket payment or sale of assets. This is considered too "easy" for the criminal and takes none of his time. The amount of payment is determined not by the *actual harm* but by the *ability of the offender to pay*. Of course, by retaining the paradigm of punishment this proposal involves many of the problems we raised earlier. In this sense it can be considered another attempt to salvage the old paradigm.

Pure Restitution

"Recompense or restitution is scarcely a punishment as long as it is merely a matter of returning . . . stolen goods or money. . . . The point is not that the offender deserves to suffer; it is rather that the offended party desires compensation."[49] This represents the complete overthrow of the paradigm of punishment. No longer would the deterrence, reformation, disablement, or rehabilitation of the criminal be the guiding principle of the judicial system. The attainment of these goals would be incidental to, and as a result of, reparations paid to the victim. No longer would the criminal deliberately be made to suffer for his mistake. Making good that mistake is all that would be required. What follows is a possible scenario of such a system.

46. Ibid.

47. Herbert Spencer, "Prison-Ethics," in *Essays: Scientific, Political and Speculative* (New York: D. Appleton & Co., 1907), 3:152–91.

48. Chapter 11.

49. Kaufmann, p. 55.

When a crime occurred and a suspect was apprehended, a trial court would attempt to determine his guilt or innocence. If found guilty, the criminal would be sentenced to make restitution to the victim.[50] If a criminal is able to make restitution immediately, he may do so. This would discharge his liability. If he were unable to make restitution, but were found by the court to be trustworthy, he would be permitted to remain at his job (or find a new one) while paying restitution out of his future wages. This would entail a legal claim against future wages. Failure to pay could result in garnishment or a new type of confinement.

If it is found that the criminal is not trustworthy, or that he is unable to gain employment, he would be confined to an employment project.[51] This would be an industrial enterprise, preferably run by a private concern, which would produce actual goods or services. The level of security at each employment project would vary according to the behavior of the offenders. Since the costs would be lower, inmates at a lower security project would receive higher wages. There is no reason why many workers could not be permitted to live with their families inside or outside the facility, depending, again, on the trustworthiness of the offender. Room and board would be deducted from the wages first, then a certain amount for restitution. Anything over that amount the worker could keep or apply toward further restitution, thus hastening his release. If a worker refused to work, he would be unable to pay for his maintenance, and therefore would not in principle be entitled to it. If he did not make restitution, he could not be released. The exact arrangement that would best provide for high productivity, minimal security, and maximum incentive to work and repay the victim cannot be determined in advance. Experience is bound to yield some plans superior to others. In fact, the experimentation has already begun.[52]

While this might be the basic system, all sorts of refinements are

50. The nature of judicial procedure best designed to carry out this task must be determined. For a brief discussion of some relevant considerations, see Laster, pp. 80–98; Burt Galaway and Joe Hudson, "Issues in the Correctional Implementation of Restitution to Victims of Crime," in *Considering the Victim*, pp. 351–60. Also to be dealt with is the proper standard of compensation. At least initially, the problem of how much payment constitutes restitution would be no different than similar considerations in tort law. This will be considered at greater length below.

51. Such a plan (with some significant differences) has been suggested by Kathleen J. Smith in *A Cure for Crime: The Case for the Self-Determinate Prison Sentence* (London: Gerald, Duckworth & Co., 1965), pp. 13–29; see also Morris and Linda Tannehill, *The Market for Liberty* (Lansing, Michigan: Privately printed, 1970), pp. 44–108.

52. For a recent summary report, see Chapter 15.

conceivable, and certainly many more will be invented as needs arise. A few examples might be illuminating. With such a system of repayment, victim *crime insurance* would be more economically feasible than at present and highly desirable. The cost of awards would be offset by the insurance company's right to restitution in place of the victim (right of subrogation). The insurance company would be better suited to supervise the offender and mark his progress than would the victim. To obtain an earlier recovery, it could be expected to innovate so as to enable the workers to repay more quickly (and, as a result, be released that much sooner). The insurance companies might even underwrite the employment projects themselves as well as related industries that would employ the skilled worker after his release. Any successful effort on their part to reduce crime and recidivism would result in fewer claims and lower premiums. The benefit of this insurance scheme for the victim is immediate compensation, conditional on the victim's continued cooperation with the authorities for the arrest and conviction of the suspect. In addition, the centralization of victim claims would, arguably, lead to efficiencies which would permit the pooling of small claims against a common offender.

Another highly useful refinement would be *direct arbitration* between victim and criminal. This would serve as a sort of healthy substitute for plea bargaining. By allowing the guilty criminal to negotiate a reduced payment in return for a guilty plea, the victim (or his insurance company) would be saved the risk of an adverse finding at trial and any possible additional expense that might result. This would also allow an indigent criminal to substitute personal services for monetary payments if all parties agreed.

Arbitration is argued for by John M. Greacen, deputy director of the National Institute for Law Enforcement and Criminal Justice. He sees the possible advantages of such reform as the

> ... development of more creative dispositions for most criminal cases; for criminal victims the increased use of restitution, the knowledge that their interests were considered in the criminal process; and an increased satisfaction with the outcome; increased awareness in the part of the offender that his crime was committed against another human being, and not against society in general; increased possibility that the criminal process will cause the offender to acknowledge responsibility for his acts.[53]

53. John M. Greacen, "Arbitration: A Tool for Criminal Cases?" *Barrister* (Winter 1975):53; see also Galaway and Hudson, *Considering the Victim*, pp. 352–55; "Conclusions and Recommendations, International Study Institute on Victimology, Bellagio, Italy, July 1–12, 1975," *Victimology* 1 (1976):150–51; Ronald Goldfarb, *Jails: The Ultimate Ghetto* (Garden City, New York: Anchor Press/Doubleday, 1976), p. 480.

Greacen notes several places where such a system has been tried with great success, most notably Tucson, Arizona, and Columbus, Ohio.[54]

Something analogous to the medieval Irish system of *sureties* might be employed as well.[55] Such a system would allow a concerned person, group, or company to make restitution (provided the offender agrees to this). The worker might then be released in the custody of the surety. If the surety had made restitution, the offender would owe restitution to the surety, who might enforce the whole claim or show mercy. Of course, the more violent and unreliable the offender, the more serious and costly the offense, the less likely it would be that anyone would take the risk. But for first offenders, good workers, or others that charitable interests found deserving (or perhaps unjustly convicted) this would provide an avenue of respite.

RESTITUTION AND RIGHTS

These three possible refinements clearly illustrate the flexibility of a restitutional system. It may be less apparent that this flexibility is *inherent* to the restitutional paradigm. Restitution recognizes rights in the victim, and this is a principal source of its strength. The nature and limit of the victim's right to restitution at the same time defines the nature and limit of the criminal liability. In this way, the aggressive action of the criminal creates a *debt* to the victim. The recognition of rights and obligations makes possible many innovative arrangements. Subrogation, arbitration, and suretyship are three examples mentioned above. They are possible because this right to compensation[56] is considered the property of the victim and can therefore be delegated, assigned, inherited, or bestowed. One could determine in advance who would acquire the right to any restitution that he himself might be unable to collect.

The natural owner of an unenforced death claim would be an insurance company that had insured the deceased. The suggestion has been made that a person might thus increase his personal safety by insuring with a company well known for tracking down those who injure its policyholders. In fact, the partial purpose of some insurance schemes might be to provide the funds with which to track down the malefactor. The insurance company, having paid the beneficiaries, would "stand in their shoes." It would remain possible, of course, to simply assign or devise the right directly to the benefi-

---

54. Greacen, p. 53.

55. For a description of the Irish system, see Peden; for a theoretical discussion of a similar proposal, see Spencer, pp. 182–86.

56. Or, perhaps more accurately, the compensation itself.

ciaries, but this would put the burden of enforcement on persons likely to be unsuited to the task.

If one accepts the Lockean trichotomy of property ownership,[57] that is, acquiring property via exchange, gifts, and *homesteading* (mixing one's labor with previously unowned land or objects), the possibility arises that upon a person's wrongful death, in the absence of any heirs or assignees, his right to compensation becomes unowned property. The right could then be claimed (homesteaded) by anyone willing to go to the trouble of catching and prosecuting the criminal. Firms might specialize in this sort of activity, or large insurance companies might make the effort as a kind of "loss leader" for public relations purposes.

This does, however, lead to a potentially serious problem with the restitutional paradigm: what exactly constitutes "restitution"? What is the *standard* by which compensation is to be made? Earlier we asserted that any such problem facing the restitutional paradigm faces civil damage suits as well. The method by which this problem is dealt with in civil cases could be applied to restitution cases. But while this is certainly true, it may be that this problem has not been adequately handled in civil damage suits either.

Restitution in cases of crimes against property is a manageable problem. Modern contract and tort doctrines of restitution are adequate. The difficulty lies in cases of personal injury or death. How can you put a price on life or limb, pain or suffering? Is not any attempt to do so of necessity arbitrary? It must be admitted that a fully satisfactory solution to this problem is lacking, but it should also be stressed that this dilemma, though serious, has little impact on the bulk of our case in favor of a restitutional paradigm. It is possible that no paradigm of criminal justice can solve every problem, yet the restitutional approach remains far superior to the paradigm of punishment or any other conceivable rival.

This difficulty arises because certain property is unique and irreplaceable. As a result, it is impossible to approximate a "market" or "exchange" value expressed in monetary terms. Just as there is no rational relationship between a wrongfully taken life and ten years in prison, there is little relationship between that same life and $20,000. Still, the nature of this possibly insoluble puzzle reveals a restitutional approach theoretically superior to punishment. For it must be acknowledged that a real, tangible loss *has* occurred. The problem is

57. For a brief explanation of this concept and several of its possible applications, see Murray N. Rothbard, "Justice and Property Rights," in *Property in a Humane Economy*, ed. Samuel L. Blumenfeld (La Salle, Illinois: Open Court Publishing Co., 1974), pp. 101–22.

only one of incommensurability. Restitution provides *some* tangible, albeit inadequate, compensation for personal injury. Punishment provides none at all.[58]

It might be objected that to establish some "pay scale" for personal injury is not only somewhat arbitrary but also a disguised reimplementation of punishment. Unable to accept the inevitable consequences of restitutional punishment, the argument continues, I have retreated to a pseudorestitutional award. Such a criticism is unfair. The true test in this instance is one of primacy of intentions. Is the purpose of a system to compensate victims for their losses (and perhaps, as a consequence, to punish the criminals), or is its purpose to punish the criminals (and perhaps, as a consequence, to compensate the victims for their losses)? The true ends of a criminal justice system will determine its nature. In short, arbitrariness *alone* does not imply a retributive motive. And while arbitrariness remains to some extent a problem for the restitutional paradigm, it is less of a problem for restitution than for punishment, since compensation has *some* rational relationship to damages and costs.

ADVANTAGES OF A RESTITUTIONAL SYSTEM

Assistance to Victims

The first and most obvious advantage is the assistance provided to victims of crime. They may have suffered an emotional, physical, or financial loss. Restitution would not change the fact that a possibly traumatic crime has occurred (just as the award of damages does not undo tortious conduct). Restitution, however, would make the resulting loss easier to bear for both victims and their families. At the same time, restitution would avoid a major pitfall of victim compensation-welfare plans: since it is the criminal who must pay, the possibility of collusion between victim and criminal to collect "damages" from the state would be all but eliminated.

The Reporting of Crime

The possibility of receiving compensation would encourage victims to report crimes and to appear at trial. This is particularly true if there were a crime insurance scheme that contractually committed the policyholder to testify as a condition for payment, thus rendering unnecessary oppressive and potentially tyrannical subpoenas and

58. That the "spiritual" satisfaction that punishment may or may not provide is to be recognized as a legitimate form of "compensation" is a claim retributionists must defend.

contempt citations. Even the actual reporting of the crime to police is likely to be a prerequisite for compensation. Such a requirement in auto theft insurance policies has made car thefts the most fully reported crime in the United States. Furthermore, insurance companies that paid the claim would have a strong incentive to see that the criminal was apprehended and convicted. Their pressure and assistance would make the proper functioning of law enforcement officials all the more likely.

Restitution: A Rehabilitation Aid

Psychologist Albert Eglash has long argued that restitution would aid in the rehabilitation of criminals. "Restitution is something an inmate does, not something done for or to him. . . . Being reparative, restitution can alleviate guilt and anxiety, which can otherwise precipitate further offenses."[59] Restitution, says Eglash, is an active effortful role on the part of the offender. It is socially constructive, thereby contributing to the offender's self-esteem. It is related to the offense and may thereby redirect the thoughts that motivated the offense. It is reparative, restorative, and may actually leave the situation better than it was before the crime, both for the criminal and victim.[60]

Restitution: A Self-Determinative Sentence

This is a genuinely "self-determinative" sentence.[61] The worker would know that the length of his confinement was in his own hands. The harder he worked, the faster he would make restitution. He would be the master of his fate and would have to face that responsibility. This would encourage useful, productive activity and instill a conception of reward for good behavior and hard work. Compare this with the current probationary system and "indeterminate sentencing" where the decision for release is made by the prison bureaucracy, based only (if fairly administered) on "good behavior"; that is, passive acquiescence to prison discipline. Also, the fact that the worker would be acquiring *marketable* skills rather than more skillful methods of crime should help to reduce the shocking rate of recidivism.

---

59. Albert Eglash, "Creative Restitution: Some Suggestions for Prison Rehabilitation Programs," *American Journal of Correction* 40 (November-December 1958):20.

60. Ibid.; see also Eglash's "Creative Restitution: A Broader Meaning for an Old Term," *Journal of Criminal Law and Criminology* 48 (1958):619–22; Burt Galaway and Joe Hudson," Restitution and Rehabilitation—Some Central Issues," *Crime and Delinquency* 18 (1972):403–10.

61. Smith, pp. 13–29.

Taxpayers' Savings

The savings to taxpayers would be enormous. No longer would the innocent taxpayer pay for the apprehension and internment of the guilty. The cost of arrest, trial, and internment would be borne by the criminal himself. In addition, since now-idle inmates would become productive workers (able, perhaps, to support their families), the entire economy would benefit from the increase in overall production.[62]

Crime Would No Longer Pay

Criminals, particularly shrewd white collar criminals, would know that they could not dispose of the proceeds of their crime, and, if caught, simply serve time. They would have to make full restitution, plus enforcement and legal costs, thereby greatly increasing the incentive to prosecute. While this would not eliminate such crime, it would make it rougher on certain types of criminals, like bank and corporation officials, who harm many by their acts with a virtual assurance of lenient legal sanctions.[63] It might also encourage such criminals to keep the money around for a while so that, if caught, they could repay more easily. This would make a full recovery more likely.

A restitutional system of justice would benefit the victim, the criminal, and the taxpayer. The humanitarian goals of proportionate punishment, rehabilitation, and victim compensation are dealt with on a *fundamental* level, making their achievement more likely. In short, the paradigm of restitution would benefit all but the entrenched penal bureaucracy and enhance justice at the same time. What then is there to stop us from overthrowing the paradigm of punishment and its penal system and putting in its place this more efficient, more humane, and more just system? The proponents of punishment and others have a few powerful counterarguments. It is to these that we now turn.

OBJECTIONS TO RESTITUTION

Practical Criticism of Restitution

It might be objected that "crimes disturb and offend not only those who are directly their victim, but also the whole social

62. An economist who favors restitution on efficiency grounds is Gary S. Becker, although he does not break with the paradigm of punishment. Those interested in a mathematical "cost-benefit" analysis should see his "Crime and Punishment," *Journal of Political Economy* 76 (1968):168–217.

63. This point is also made by Minocher Jehangirji Sethna, "Treatment and Atonement for Crime," in *Victims and Society*, p. 538.

order."[64] Because of this, society—that is, individuals other than the victim—deserves some satisfaction from the offender. Restitution, it is argued, will not satisfy the lust for revenge felt by the victim or the "community's sense of justice." This criticism appears to be overdrawn. Today most members of the community are mere spectators of the criminal justice system, and this is largely true even of the victim.[65] One major reform being urged presently is more victim involvement in the criminal justice process.[66] The restitution proposal would necessitate this involvement. And while the public generally takes the view that officials should be tougher on criminals, with "tougher" taken by nearly everyone to mean more severe in punishing, one must view this "social fact" in light of the lack of a known alternative. The real test of public sympathies would be to see which sanction people would choose: incarceration of the criminal for a given number of years, or the criminal's being compelled to make restitution to the victim. While the public's choice is not clearly predictable, neither can it be assumed that it would reject restitution. There is some evidence to the contrary.[67]

64.. Del Vecchio, p. 198.

65. William F. McDonald, "Towards a Bicentennial Revolution in Criminal Justice: The Return of the Victim," *American Criminal Law Review* 13 (1976): 659; see also his paper "Notes on the Victim's Role in the Prosecutional and Dispositional Stages of the Criminal Justice Process" (Paper presented at the second International Symposium on Victimology, Boston, September 1976); Jack M. Kress, "The Role of the Victim at Sentencing" (Paper presented at the Second International Symposium on Victimology, Boston, September 1976).

66. McDonald, "Towards a Bicentennial Revolution," pp. 669–73; Kress, pp. 11–15. Kress specifically analyzes restitution as a means for achieving victim involvement.

67. In two types of studies conducted for the Ventura County Board of Supervisors, Ventura, California, support for a restitutional program was indicated:

> Both the citizen attitude survey and the Delphi goal-seeking exercise revealed a strong concern for the *victim* as the 'forgotten man' of criminal justice. The Delphi panelists, in particular, emphasized the need for new kinds of criminal penalties in which the offender would be required to make restitution to his victim(s).

Development of a Model Criminal Justice System (Santa Barbara, California: Public Safety Systems, 1973), p. 85. The report recommends the implementing of a system of restitution. In the two cities mentioned earlier (Columbus and Tucson), support, at least by the parties involved, appeared strong. In the thousands of cases arbitrated by trained law students in Columbus, only 4 percent proceeded further up in the criminal system. In Tucson after one year the program has been successful in all but nine of 204 cases (with the cost of handling each case at $304 compared with $1,566 required to process the average felony case). General approval of restitution in lieu of punishment was indirectly referred to in the *Columbia Law Review*'s oft-cited study, "Restitution and the Criminal Law":

This brings us to a second practical objection: that monetary sanctions are insufficient deterrents to crime. Again, this is something to be discovered, not something to be assumed. There are a number of reasons to believe that our current system of punishment does not adequately deter, and for the reasons discussed earlier, an increase in the level of punishment is unlikely. In fact, many have argued that the deterrent value of sanctions has less to do with *severity* than with *certainty*,[68] and the preceding considerations indicate that law enforcement would be more certain under a restitutional system. In the final analysis, however, it is irrelevant to argue that more crimes may be committed if our proposal leaves the victim better off. It must be remembered that our goal is not the suppression of crime; it is doing justice to victims.

A practical consideration that merits considerable future attention is the feasibility of the employment project proposal. A number of questions can be raised. At first blush, it seems naively optimistic to suppose that offenders will be able or willing to work at all, much less earn their keep and pay reparations as well. On the contrary, this argument continues, individuals turn to crime precisely because they lack the skills that the restitutional plan assumes they have. And if these workers have the skills, but refuse to work, what could be done? Would not the use of force to compel compliance be tantamount to slavery? This criticism results in part from my attempt to sketch an "ideal" restitution system; that is, I have attempted to outline the type toward which every criminal justice system governed by the restitution paradigm should strive. This is not to say that every aspect of the hypothetical system would, upon implementation, function smoothly. Rather, such a system could only operate ideally once the paradigm had been fully accepted and substantially articulated.

With this in mind, one can advance several responses. First, the

---

[E]ven where the complainant can be persuaded to continue the criminal case, after having received private satisfaction, his apathy is often so pronounced and his demeanor so listless that he becomes an extremely weak witness. . . . Also the knowledge of actual restitution seems to greatly assuage the jury. Even the knowledge of the existence of a civil suit can lead the jury to recommend leniency or acquittal.

CLR 39 (1939):1189; see also n. 31. Restitution, it seems, is accepted and preferred by the average person. Early studies indicate that, when properly administered, even offenders perceive a restitutionary sanction as fair (William Marsella and Burt Galaway, "Study of the Perceived Fairness of Restitution as a Sanction for Juvenile Offenders" [Paper presented to the Second International Symposium on Victimology, Boston, September 1976]); see Chapter 15.

68. Yochelson and Samenow, pp. 453–57.

problem as usually posed assumes the offender to be highly irrational and possibly mentally unbalanced. There is no denying that some segment of the criminal population fits the former description.[69] What this approach neglects, however, is the possibility that many criminals are making rational choices within an irrational and unjust political system. Specifically I refer to the myriad laws and regulations that make it difficult for the unskilled or persons of transitory outlook[70] to find legal employment.[71] I refer also to the laws that deny legality to the types of services that are in particular demand in economically impoverished communities.[72] Is it "irrational" to choose to steal or rob when one is virtually foreclosed from the legal opportunity to do otherwise? Another possibility is that the criminal chooses crime not because of foreclosure, but because he enjoys and obtains satisfaction from a criminal way of life.[73] Though morally repugnant, this is hardly irrational.

Furthermore, it no longer can be denied that contact with the current criminal justice system is itself especially damaging among juveniles.[74] The offenders who are hopelessly committed to criminal behavior are not usually the newcomers to crime but those who have repeated exposure to the penal system. In Kuhn's words, "Existing institutions have ceased to meet the problems posed by an environment *they have in part created.*"[75] While a restitutionary system

---

69. For a discussion rejecting the usefulness of the latter description, see Szasz, pp. 91–146; for a recent study verifying Szasz's thesis, see Yochelson and Samenow, esp. pp. 227–35.

70. Edward C. Banfield put forth his controversial theory of time horizon in his book *The Unheavenly City* (Boston: Little, Brown & Co., 1970) and amplified it in *The Unheavenly City Revisited* (Boston: Little, Brown & Co., 1974), and, most recently, in Chapter 5. See also Chapter 1. A contrary, but ultimately compatible view, is presented by Yochelson and Samenow, pp. 369–72.

71. For example, minimum wage laws, and so-called closed shop union protectionist legislation.

72. For example, laws prohibiting gambling, prostitution, sale of drugs, "jitney" cab services, etc.

73. Yochelson and Samenow, *The Criminal Personality*, pp. 247, 249: "It is not the environment that turns a man into a criminal. Rather it is a series of choices that he makes at a very early age. . . . [T]he criminal is not a victim of circumstances." This is in essence the main conclusion of their research. (For a concise summary of their provocative book, see Joseph Boorkin, "The Criminal Personality," *Federal Bar Journal* 35 [1976] : 237–41.) In *The Criminal Personality. Volume 2: The Process of Change* (New York: Jason Aronson, Inc., 1977) they relate and examine the methods they have employed to change the criminal thought pattern. Of course, such an approach can itself be subject to abuse. See Chapter 4.

74. See, e.g., Edwin M. Schur, *Radical Noninterventionism, Rethinking the Delinquency Problem* (Englewood Cliffs, New Jersey: Prentice-Hall, Inc., 1973).

75. Kuhn, p. 92 (emphasis added).

might not change these hard core offenders, it could, by the early implementation of sanctions perceived by the criminal to be just, break the vicious circle which in large part accounts for their existence.

Finally, if offenders could not or would not make restitution, then the logical and just result of their refusal would be confinement until they could or would. Such an outcome would be entirely in their hands. While this "solution" does not suggest who should justly pay for this confinement, the problem is not unique to a restitutionary system. In this and other areas of possible difficulty we must seek guidance from existing pilot programs as well as from the burgeoning research in this area and in victimology in general.

Theoretical Criticisms of Restitution

Richard Epstein has attempted to rationalize the historic distinction between criminal law and tort law.[76] He concludes, quite correctly, that the traditional division can only be explained by the notion of *mens rea* or criminal intent. Tort law involves compensating wrongfully injured victims. The criminal law, on the other hand, is concerned with punishing persons for their bad intentions as manifested by their bad acts.

The proof of this distinction for Epstein is the law of attempts. This category of crime specifies that: "When a person attempts to commit a crime such as murder, but fails for some reason to achieve his intended result, he may be guilty of an attempt."[77] Since an attempt may or may not result in an actual harm to an identifiable victim, those that do not may not, under a restitutive theory of justice, be subject to a sanction. Epstein views this as a fundamental flaw in a restitutionary approach, for he feels that those persons with bad intentions deserve punishment. Such a position is supported by John Hospers' paper[78] on the deserts theory of retribution.

It is interesting to note that the history of criminal justice that I sketched earlier bears out this characterization. Pollock and Maitland observe that: "Ancient law has as a general rule no punishment for those who have tried to do harm but have not done it. The idea of punishment is but slowly severed from that of reparation, and where no harm is done there is none to be repaired."[79] And: "[English law] started from the principle that an attempt to do harm was no

76. See Chapter 10.
77. Note, "Why Do Criminal Attempts Fail? A New Defense," *The Yale Law Journal* 70 (1960):160.
78. Chapter 8.
79. Pollock and Maitland, p. 507.

offence [sic]."[80] As Jerome Hall put it: "Criminal attempt is conspicuous for its absence in early English law. There is not the slightest suggestion of theory or general doctrine. . . . [T]here seem to have been no specific findings of liability for wrong-doing that fell short of the major crimes."[81]

What then of the criticism? Under a pure restitutionary approach there can be no compensation without a harm having occurred, and without compensation, there is no liability. Without a real victim, in short, there can be no crime. Unless one can justify a retreat to some sort of "symbolic" payment, which is doubtful, it seems that we are forced to the conclusion that a *bare* criminal attempt, even with an "overt act," is, without more, not a crime. It is important to note that though not itself a crime, the concept of an attempt is not irrelevant to a proper theory of justice. Rather, as we will see, it will assume a role of no small importance.

While such a suggestion to abolish attempts as a separate category of crime might seem absurd at first, a closer analysis reveals a basic plausibility. The most important observation to be made is that most unsuccessful attempts worthy of sanction are still crimes in a restitutionary system. For example, attempted murder is usually an aggravated assault and battery, attempted armed robbery is usually an assault, attempted car theft or burglary is usually a trespass. In this way the law of attempt is actually a form of double counting whose principle function is to enable the police and prosecutor to overcharge a crime for purposes of a later plea negotiation. Furthermore, some categories of attempt, such as conspiracy laws and possessory laws—e.g., possession of burglarious instruments—are shortcuts for prosecutors unable or unwilling to prove the actual crime and are a constant source of selective, repressive prosecutions.

In fact and in theory, any attempt to violate individual rights that resulted in an actual harm, such as the creation of fear on the part of the intended victim or bystanders (an assault), would be a crime in a restitutionary system and sanctionable as such. The only type of unsuccessful attempt that would escape liability would be the case of someone who unsuccessfully tried to commit a crime without otherwise violating anyone's rights and *without anyone knowing about it.* It surely is not absurd to ask whether anyone's rights have really been violated, and if not, whether a crime has actually occurred. It may, in fact, be both a practical as well as a theoretical virtue that

80. Ibid., p. 507, n. 4.

81. Jerome Hall, "Criminal Attempts—A Study of the Foundations of Criminal Liability," *The Yale Law Journal* 49 (1940):789, 791.

badly motivated but harmless acts are not labeled as criminal. In any case, no system governed by any principle can prosecute acts that no one knows about.

Does this mean that an attempt to commit a crime has no relevance to crime? As I indicated earlier, I think it does.[82] Most objections to the abolition of attempt are not really intent-motivated at all, but instead revolve around the fear that we would be legally powerless to prevent or deter crimes if we had to wait for damages to be incurred before we could rightly act. But it does not follow from the proposition that one cannot prosecute an unsuccessful or abandoned attempt that harmed no one, that one can do nothing about an attempt in progress. Rather, if someone is truly attempting to commit a crime, then the victim and anyone who is willing to help him can engage in self-defense. Once this is recognized, the question is not *whether* you can act to protect yourself, but *when*.

The proper answer to this question is not the quantitative one that Robert Nozick, for one, seems to favor of asking how high a probability of harm must exist before you can defend yourself.[83] Such an approach would all but abolish the concept of individual rights, upon which, presumably, his theory is or should be grounded. The correct response is a qualitative one, and it is precisely the approach taken by the traditional theory of attempt. In a case less than a certainty, the only justifiable use of force is that used to repel an overt act that is something more than mere preparation, remote from time and place of the intended crime. It must be more than "risky," it must be done with the specific intent to commit a crime and directly tend in some substantial degree to accomplish it. He who uses force in any other circumstance is himself an aggressor.

Let's say, for example, that you are minding your own business when someone gets it into his head that you are about to attack him. He then jumps on you in the mistaken belief that you are attempting to attack him. You bring an action for restitution for assault and battery on Professor Epstein's theory of strict causal liability. He justifies his action as self-defense. To sustain his burden of proof and avoid liability, he must prove that you were in fact attempting to

82. I agree with Professor Epstein that the crime of attempt includes both intention and an "overt act." This is the definition I will use here. An overt act ". . . must . . . be something more than mere preparation, remote from time and place of the intended crime; [It must be] . . . done with the specific intent to commit the [crime], and directly tend in some substantial degree to accomplish it. . . ." (*State v. Dumas*, 118 Minn. 77, 84, 136 N.W. 311, 314 [1912] quoted in Lloyd L. Weinreb, *Criminal Law* [Mineola, New York: Foundation Press, 1969], p. 375).

83. See Nozick.

attack him. If he cannot sustain his burden then, regardless of his good faith belief, the principle of comparative justice between the parties dictates that he is liable. This is, in fact, how Professor Epstein decides what, in essence, is the same set of facts in the case of *Courvoiser v. Raymond*.[84]

This is not to say that such a qualitative judgment is an easy one; on the contrary, matters of proof in this area are quite difficult. To ascribe a particular quality to an act, it is critical to determine the attacker's state of mind, and in this way evidence of the total circumstances and especially motive becomes probative. Motive is not a part of the *prima facie* case, and a good prosecutor is quick to point this out to a jury. Motive is merely evidence of intent that itself is only a necessary, but insufficient, indicia of the quality of the act. In this way it is probably more accurate to say that you need the intent to prove the nature of the act than to say (as Epstein seems to) that you need the act to prove the nature of the intent.

Though attempts that have caused no harm are not crimes in a restitutionary scheme, it can now be seen that while the attempt is in progress, its qualitative nature justifies the use of self-defense by the victim or, as his agent, by law enforcement authorities. Attempt is therefore an important, though sometimes misunderstood, concept in criminal law. And before finishing this discussion it should be pointed out that Epstein's principle of comparative justice (not to mention simple restitutionary justice) dictates that the cost of a justified self-defense effort must be born by the attempting party, in which case the act would no longer be a pure attempt, but, since a loss has been wrongfully inflicted, this would be a completed crime and compensable on pure restitutionary principles.

In the last analysis, I do not conclude that Professor Epstein is fundamentally wrong in his explication of the current criminal justice paradigm. Rather, I conclude that he accurately perceives the dominant assumptions of the current paradigm and shows that unless the restitutionist is prepared to reject those assumptions, restitution can only be integrated in a compromised manner. But Professor Epstein merely restates the assumptions, he does not defend them. If a pure restitutional paradigm is correct, then the assumptions are false and there remains no theoretical obstacle to an admittedly radical departure from the current criminal justice paradigm: the complete and total implementation of a restitutionary theory of justice.

84. 23 Colo. 113, 47 Pac. 284 (1896), discussed in his article "A Theory of Strict Liability," *Journal of Legal Studies* 2 (1973):173.

Distributionary Criticisms of Restitution

There remains one criticism of restitution that is the most obvious and the most difficult with which to deal. Simply stated, it takes the following form: "Doesn't this mean that rich people will be able to commit crimes with impunity if they can afford it? Isn't this unfair?" The *practical* aspect of this objection is that whatever deterrent effect restitution payments may have, they will be less for those most able to pay. The *moral* aspect is that whatever retributive or penal effect restitution payments may have they will be less for those who are well off. Some concept of equality of justice underlies both considerations.

Critics of restitution fail to realize that the "cost" of crime will be quite high. In addition to compensation for pain and suffering, the criminal must pay for the cost of his apprehension, the cost of the trial, and the legal expenditures for *both* sides. This should make even an unscrupulous wealthy person think twice about committing a crime. The response to this is that we cannot have it both ways. If the fines would be high enough to bother the rich, then they would be so high that a project worker would have no chance of earning that much and would, therefore, have no incentive to work at all. If, on the other hand, you lower the price of crime by ignoring all its costs, you fail to deter the rich or fully compensate the victim.

This is where the option of arbitration and victim crime insurance becomes of practical importance. If the victim is uninsured, he is unlikely to recover for all costs of a very severe crime from a poor, unskilled criminal, since even in an employment project, the criminal might be unable to earn enough. If he had no hope of earning his release, he would have little incentive to work very hard beyond paying for his own maintenance. The victim would end up with less than if he had "settled" the case for the lesser amount that a project worker could reasonably be expected to earn. If, however, the victim had full coverage criminal insurance, he would recover his damages in full, and the insurance company would absorb any disparity between full compensation and maximal employment project worker's output. This cost would be reflected in premium prices, enabling the insurance company that settled cases at an amount that increased the recovery from the criminal to offer the lowest rates. Eventually a "maximum" feasible fine for project workers would be determined based on these considerations. The "rich," on the other hand, would naturally have to pay in full. This arrangement would solve the practical problem, but it should not be thought of as an imperative of the restitutional paradigm.

The same procedure of varying the payments according to ability to pay would answer the moral considerations as well (that the rich are not hurt enough) and this is the prime motive behind *punitive* restitution proposals. However, we reject the moral consideration outright. The paradigm of restitution calls not for the (equal) hurting of criminals, but for restitution to victims. Any appeal to "inadequate suffering" is a reversion to the paradigm of punishment, and by varying the sanction for crimes of the same magnitude according to the economic status of the offender, it reveals its own inequity. *Equality of justice means equal treatment of victims.* It should not matter to the victim if his attacker was rich or poor. His plight is the same regardless. Any reduction of criminal liability because of reduced earning power would be for practical, not moral, reasons.

Equality of justice derives from the fact that the rights of men should be equally enforced and respected. Restitution recognizes a victim's right to compensation for damages from the party responsible. Equality of justice, therefore, calls for equal enforcement of each victim's right to restitution. Even if necessary or expedient, any lessening of payment to the victim because of the qualities of the criminal is a violation of that victim's rights and an inequality of justice. Any such expedient settlement is only a recognition that an imperfect world may make possible only imperfect justice. As a practical matter, a restitutional standard gives victims an enormous incentive to pursue wealthy criminals, since they can afford quick, full compensation. Contrast this with the present system, where the preference given the wealthy is so prevalent that most victims simply assume that nothing will be done.

The paradigm of restitution, to reiterate, is neither a panacea for crime nor a blueprint for utopia. Panaceas and utopias are not for humankind. We must live in a less than perfect world with less than perfect people. Restitution opens the possibility of an improved and more just society. The old paradigm of punishment, even reformed, simply cannot offer this promise.

OTHER CONSIDERATIONS

Space does not permit a full examination of other less fundamental implications of such a system. I shall briefly consider five.

Civil Versus Criminal Liability

If one accepts a restitutionary standard of justice, what sense does it make to distinguish between crime and tort, since both call for payment of damages? For most purposes I think the distinction collapses. Richard Epstein, in a series of brilliant articles, has articulated a theory of strict liability in tort.[85] His view is that since one party has caused another some harm and one of the parties must bear the loss, justice demands that it falls on the party who caused the harm. He argues that intention is only relevant as a "third stage" argument; that notwithstanding some fault on the part of the plaintiff (a second stage argument), the defendant intended the harm and is therefore liable.[86] With a restitutional system I see no reason why Epstein's theory of tort liability could not incorporate criminal liability into a single "system of corrective justice that looks to the conduct, broadly defined, of the parties to the case with a view toward the protection of individual liberty and private property."[87]

There would, at least initially, be some differences, however. The calculation of damages under the restitutionary paradigm that includes cost of apprehension, cost of trial, and legal costs of both parties would be higher than tort law allows. A further distinction would be the power of enforcers to confine unreliable offenders to employment projects.[88]

85. Epstein, pp. 151–204.

86. Richard A. Epstein, "Intentional Harms," *Journal of Legal Studies* 3 (1975):402–408; see also his article "Defenses and Subsequent Pleas in a System of Strict Liability," *Jour. of Legal Stud.* 3 (1974):174–85.

87. Epstein, "Intentional Harms," p. 441. As indicated above, Epstein himself would disagree based on his emphatic distinction between tort and criminal law. He rests this distinction on two characteristics of the criminal law: (1) that its function is to punish (and therefore *mens rea* is required and more stringent procedural safeguards are appropriate); and (2) that since the defendant is prosecuted by the state, fairness as between the parties is not relevant. From these assumptions, Epstein reasons quite correctly that the two systems are inherently different. It should be obvious that a restitutionary paradigm undermines both assumptions. Gilbert M. Cantor, in "An End to Crime and Punishment" (*Shingle* 39 [May 1976]:99–114), takes precisely this view, arguing that

the time has come to abolish the game of crime and punishment and to substitute a paradigm of restitution and responsibility. I urge that we assign (reassign, actually) to the civil law our societal response to the acts or behaviors we now label and treat as criminal. The goal is the *civilization* of our treatment of offenders. I use the word, "civilization" here in its specific meaning: to bring offenders under the civil, rather than the criminal law; and in its larger meaning: to move in this area of endeavor from barbarism toward greater enlightenment and humanity. (p. 107; emphasis in original.)

88. It would seem that the only way to account for these differences would be an appeal to the *mens rea* or badness of the criminal as opposed to the unintentional tortfeasor. Yet such an approach, it might be argued, is not available to a restitutionary system that considers the moral outlook of an offender to be irrelevant to the determination of the proper criminal sanction. A possible response is that this overstates the restitutionist claim. That a criminal's mental state does not justify punishment does not imply that it is not relevant to *any* aspect of the criminal justice process. It may well be that it is relevant to the consideration of methods by which one is justified in extracting what, on other grounds, is shown to be a proper sanction, that is, restitution.

Criminal Responsibility and Competency

Once a criminal sanction is based not on the offender's badness but on the nature and consequences of his acts, Thomas Szasz's proposal that the insanity plea be abolished makes a great deal of sense,[89] as does his argument that "all persons charged with offenses —except those grossly disabled—[are fit to stand trial and] should be tried.[90] On this view, Epstein's concept of fairness *as between the parties* is relevant. A restitution proceeding like a

> lawsuit is always a comparative affair. The defendant's victory ensures the plaintiff's [or victim's] defeat. . . . Why should we prefer the injurer to his victim in a case where one may win and the other lose? . . . As a matter of fairness between the parties, the defendant should be required to treat the harms which he has inflicted upon another as though they were inflicted upon himself.[91]

Victimless Crimes

The effect of restitutional standards on the legality of such crimes as prostitution, gambling, high interest loans, pornography, and drug use is intriguing. There has been no violation of individual rights, and consequently no damages and, therefore, no liability. While some may see this as a drawback, I believe it is a striking advantage of the restitutional standard of justice. So-called victimless crimes would in principle cease to be crimes. As a consequence, criminal elements would be denied a lucrative monopoly, and the price of these services would be drastically reduced. Without this enormous income, organized crime would be far less able to afford the "cost" of its nefarious activities than it is today.

Legal Positivism

What is true for victimless crimes is true for the philosophy of legal positivism. On the positivist view, whatever the state (following all the correct political procedures) says is law, is law; hence, whatever the state makes a crime is a crime. A restitutional standard would hold the state to enforcing individual rights through the recovery of individual damages.

89. Szasz, pp. 228–30.

90. Ibid., pp. 228–29. "The emphasis here is on gross disability: it should be readily apparent or easily explicable to a group of lay persons, like a jury" (p. 229). But even the qualification of gross disablement might be unjustified (see Yochelson and Samenow, pp. 227–35).

91. Epstein, "Strict Liability," p. 398. In Chapter 10, p. 253, he takes exactly this approach with the insanity defense in tort law.

Legal Process

Because the sanction of crime would no longer be punitive, the criminal process could explore less formal procedures for dispute settlement. Also, the voice of the victim would be added to the deliberations. One possible reform might be a three-tiered verdict: guilty, not proven, and not guilty. If found "guilty," the offender would pay all the costs mentioned above. If the charges are "not proven," then neither party would pay the other. If found "not guilty," the defendant would be reimbursed by the enforcement agency for his costs and inconvenience. This new interpretation of "not guilty" would reward those defendants who, after putting on a defense, convinced the trier of fact that they were innocent.[92]

These and many other fascinating implications of restitution deserve a more thorough examination. As any new paradigm becomes accepted, it experiences what Kuhn calls a period of "normal research," a period characterized by continuous expansion and perfection of the new paradigm as well as a testing of its limits. The experimentation with restitutionary justice will, however, differ from the trial and error of the recent past, since we will be guided by the principle that the purpose of our legal system is not to harm the guilty but to help the innocent—a principle that will above all restore our belief that our overriding commitment is to do justice.

92. For other intriguing criminal process reforms see Lloyd L. Weinreb, *Denial of Justice* (New York: The Free Press, 1977).

Index

About the Contributors

Professor Edward C. Banfield is the George D. Markham Professor of Government at Harvard University. Professor Banfield is the author or co-author of eleven books, including *The Moral Basis of a Backward Society* and *The Unheavenly City*.

Professor Richard Epstein teaches at the University of Chicago Law School. His published work, including "Intentional Harms" in the *Journal of Legal Studies* and "A Theory of Strict Liability" in the *Journal of Legal Studies*, cover such diverse areas of legal theory as medical malpractice, constitutional law and tax law.

Professor Burt Galaway teaches at the University of Minnesota. He has written numerous articles on the use of restitution in the criminal justice system and he has co-edited several books, including *Considering the Victim: Selected Readings in Victim Compensation and Restitution* and *Restitution in Criminal Justice*.

Professor Ronald Hamowy is Associate Professor of Intellectual History at the University of Alberta and was a visiting Associate Professor at Simon Fraser University. He is the author of articles in the history of legal and social theory.

Professor John Hospers teaches at the University of Southern California. He is the author of two textbooks on philosophy, *Human Conduct* and *Introduction to Philosophical Analysis*, and he edits *The Personalist*, an international philosophical quarterly.

Professor Walter Kaufmann teaches at Princeton University. He is a prolific author and translator, and among his most recent works are *The Future of the Humanities*; *Existentialism, Religion and Death*; *Without Guilt and Justice*, and *Tragedy and Philosophy*.

Professor Leonard Liggio teaches in the American Studies Program at the State University of New York at Old Westbury. He is director of the Center for Cultural Diversity, and in addition to having written numerous articles and papers, Professor Liggio is co-editor of the recently published *Watershed of Empire: Essays on New Deal Foreign Policy*.

Professor William F. McDonald is Research Director of the Institute of Criminal Law and Procedure and teaches in both the Sociology Department and the Law School of Georgetown University. In addition to having published numerous articles, Professor McDonald is also editor of *Criminal Justice and the Victim*, and he is presently pursuing research on plea bargaining and other dimensions of the criminal justice system.

Dr. Roger E. Meiners is pursuing a J.D. degree as a John M. Ohlin Fellow at the Law and Economics Center of the University of Miami Law School. He will begin teaching in the Department of Management at Texas A & M University in 1978. Dr. Meiners' Ph.D. dissertation, "The Economics of Victim Compensation," is forthcoming as a book. In addition to pursuing research on this subject, Dr. Meiners is working on various research projects integrating the disciplines of law and economics.

Professor Gerald P. O'Driscoll teaches at Iowa State University. He has written extensively on the economic theory of Friedrich A. Hayek and is the author of the forthcoming *Economics as a Coordination Problem: The Contributions of Friedrich A. Hayek*. Professor O'Driscoll's current research interests include law and economics, property rights and resource allocation, and the history of economic thought.

Dr. Mario J. Rizzo is a Post Doctoral Fellow in Law and Economics at New York University where is he pursuing research on the economic rationale of tort law and the concept of economic efficiency. Dr. Rizzo's doctoral thesis examined "Rents, Property Values and the Cost of Crime to Victims."

Professor Murray N. Rothbard teaches in the economics department of the Polytechnic Institute of New York. Professor Rothbard is the author of numerous books in the fields of history and Austrian economic theory, including *Man, Economy and State*; *Power and Market*; *America's Great Depression*; and a multivolume study of the American revolution, *Conceived in Liberty*. Professor Rothbard is also editor of the *Journal of Libertarian Studies* published by the Center for Libertarian Studies.

Dr. Stanton E. Samenow is a clinical research psychologist in the "Program for the Investigation of Criminal Behavior" at St. Elizabeth's Hospital in Washington, D.C. In addition to several articles, Dr. Samenow has co-authored with Dr. Samuel Yochelson a three volume study on *The Criminal Personality*, the first volume of which has already been published.

Professor Thomas Szasz teaches psychiatry at the Upstate Medical Center of the State University of New York at Syracuse. He is a prolific author, having published more than ten books, including such recent works as *Pain and Pleasure: A Study of Bodily Feelings*; *The Myth of Mental Illness*; *Law, Liberty and Psychiatry*; and *The Manufacture of Madness*.

Professor James Q. Wilson is the Henry Lee Shattuck Professor of Government at Harvard University. He has also served as chairman of the White House Task Force on Crime (1967) and as director of the Joint Center for Urban Studies at MIT and Harvard. In addition to many articles, Professor Wilson is the author of six books, including *Varieties of Police Behavior, Political Organizations*, and *Thinking About Crime*.

✳

About the Editors

Randy E. Barnett is a graduate of Northwestern University and received his J.D. from Harvard Law School. Mr. Barnett has prosecuted numerous criminal cases in Cook County, Illinois and in Middlesex County, Massachusetts. He co-directed with John Hagel III the Symposium on Crime and Punishment at Harvard Law School from which many of the papers in this collection are taken. His published articles include "Restitution: A New Paradigm of Criminal Justice" and a critique of Robert Nozick's *Anarchy, State, and Utopia*. Mr. Barnett will be an Assistant State's Attorney in Cook County, Illinois.

John Hagel III graduated from Wesleyan University and received a B. Phil. from Oxford University. He is enrolled in the joint MBA–JD program at Harvard Business School and Harvard Law School. He is the author of numerous published articles as well as a book on *Alternative Energy Strategies: Opportunities and Constraints*. Mr. Hagel is the President of the Center for Libertarian Studies.

HV
8675
A74   Assessing the
           criminal